Economics of the Pandemic

The year 2020 marked the time when China expected to attain its goal of building a moderately prosperous society in all respects. Yet it has witnessed the emergence of COVID-19 as a global pandemic that has spread to almost all countries and regions throughout the world. This serious public health disaster has brought with it severe economic shock, resulting in unexpected challenges to the completion of economic and social development goals.

This title compiles the latest research, from a variety of perspectives, into the impact of COVID-19 on the Chinese economy. Economic experts and scholars from the Chinese Academy of Social Sciences analyze the current trends as well as short-term and long-term countermeasures in the agricultural, industrial, employment, and public health sectors and focus on supply and demand. They argue that China's actions toward and promotion of economic recovery need to adapt to variability and uncertainty, and policy choices should be made in the light of the dialectical relationship between variance and invariance.

The book will appeal to students and scholars of economics, political science, and social development.

Cai Fang, Professor, PhD in Economics, is Chief Expert of the National High-end Think Tank at the Chinese Academy of Social Sciences, where he is an Academician. His recent publications include *Demographic Perspective of China's Economic Development* (2020) and *Perceiving Truth and Ceasing Doubts* (2020).

China Perspectives

The *China Perspectives* series focuses on translating and publishing works by leading Chinese scholars, writing about both global topics and China-related themes. It covers Humanities & Social Sciences, Education, Media and Psychology, as well as many interdisciplinary themes.

This is the first time any of these books have been published in English for international readers. The series aims to put forward a Chinese perspective, give insights into cutting-edge academic thinking in China, and inspire researchers globally.

To submit a book proposal, please contact the Taylor & Francis Publisher for the China Publishing Programme, Lian Sun (Lian.Sun@informa.com)

Titles in economics include:

The Economics of Government Regulation
Fundamentals and Application in China
Wang Junhao

Macroeconomic Policy and Steady Growth in China
2020 Dancing with Black Swan
Edited by Zhang Xiaojing

Political and Economic Analysis of State-Owned Enterprise Reform
Huiming Zhang

Political Economy in the Evolution of China's Urban-Rural Economic Relations
Fan Gao

China's New Normal, Supply-side, and Structural Reform
Cai Fang

For more information, please visit www.routledge.com/China-Perspectives/book-series/CPH

Economics of the Pandemic

Weathering the Storm and
Restoring Growth

**Edited by
Cai Fang**

Translated by Li Yanqing

Routledge
Taylor & Francis Group

LONDON AND NEW YORK

中国社会科学出版社
CHINA SOCIAL SCIENCES PRESS

This book is published with financial support from the Innovation Project of the Chinese Academy of Social Sciences (CASS).

First published 2021
by Routledge
2 Park Square, Milton Park, Abingdon, Oxon OX14 4RN

and by Routledge
605 Third Avenue, New York, NY 10158

Routledge is an imprint of the Taylor & Francis Group, an informa business

English version by permission of China Social Sciences Press.

British Library Cataloguing-in-Publication Data
A catalogue record for this book is available from the British Library

Library of Congress Cataloging-in-Publication Data
A catalog record has been requested for this book

ISBN: 978-1-032-02648-0 (hbk)
ISBN: 978-1-032-02649-7 (pbk)
ISBN: 978-1-003-18444-7 (ebk)

DOI: 10.4324/9781003184447

Typeset in Times New Roman
by Newgen Publishing UK

Contents

Figures

Tables

Contributors

Cai Fang is Professor at the Chinese Academy of Social Sciences. His research interest is economic development and population economics in China.

Deng Zhou is Associate Professor at the Institute of Industrial Economics, Chinese Academy of Social Sciences. His research interests are industrial structure and technological innovation.

Du Yang is Professor at the Institute of Population and Labor Economics, Chinese Academy of Social Sciences. His research interest is labor economics.

Feng Ming is Associate Professor at the National Academy of Economic Strategy, Chinese Academy of Social Sciences. His research interest is macroeconomics and international finance.

He Dexu is Professor at the National Academy of Economic Strategy, Chinese Academy of Social Sciences. His research interest is finance.

He Jun is Professor at the Institute of Industrial Economics, Chinese Academy of Social Sciences. His research interest is technological innovation and industry policy.

Huang Qunhui is Researcher at the Institute of Economics, Chinese Academy of Social Sciences. His research interest is industrial economics.

Huang Yana is Assistant Professor at the Institute of Industrial Economics, Chinese Academy of Social Sciences. Her research interests are industrial development and labor economy.

Li Shuangshuang is Assistant Professor at the National Academy of Economic Strategy, Chinese Academy of Social Sciences. Her research interest is open-economy macroeconomics and international trade.

Li Xuesong is Professor in the Institute of Industrial Economics, Chinese Academy of Social Sciences. His research interest is China's economy and economic policy evaluation.

Lu Qianwen is Assistant Research Fellow in the Rural Development Institute, Chinese Academy of Social Sciences. His research interest is rural development.

Pan Yuqing is a PhD candidate in the Department of Economics at the University of Chinese Academy of Social Sciences. Her research interest is public economics and public finance.

Peng Wensheng is Chief Economist at the China International Capital Corporation Limited. His research interests include macroeconomy and financial markets.

Shi Dan is Professor at the Institute of Industrial Economics of the Chinese Academy of Social Sciences. Her research interests are energy economy and economic growth.

Wang Hongju is Professor at the National Academy of Economic Strategy, Chinese Academy of Social Sciences. His research interest is macroeconomics and monetary policy.

Wei Houkai is Director and Professor at the Rural Development Institute, Chinese Academy of Social Sciences. His research interest is regional economics and rural development.

Xia Jiechang is Professor at the National Academy of Economic Strategy, Chinese Academy of Social Sciences. His research interest is service economy and industry development.

Xu Xiujun is Senior Fellow at the Institute of World Economics and Politics, Chinese Academy of Social Sciences, and a Professor at the School of International Relations of the University of Chinese Academy of Social Sciences. His research interests include global economic governance and international political economy.

Yu Chang is a postdoctoral researcher at the Institute of Industrial Economics, Chinese Academy of Social Sciences. His research interests are industrial development and economic growth.

Zhang Binbin is Assistant Professor at the National Academy of Economic Strategy, Chinese Academy of Social Sciences. His research interest is labor and development.

Zhang Xiaojing, is Professor of Economics and Director of the Institute of Finance & Banking, Chinese Academy of Social Sciences. His research interests are open economy macroeconomics, macro finance, and development economics.

Zhang Yuyan is a member of the Chinese Academy of Social Sciences, where he is also Senior Fellow and Director of the Institute of World Economics and Politics. He is Professor and Head of the School of International

Relations at the University of Chinese Academy of Social Sciences. His research interests are world economy and international political economy.

Zhao Jin is Senior Research Fellow at the National Academy of Economic Strategy, Chinese Academy of Social Sciences, and a Professor and doctoral supervisor at the University of Chinese Academy of Social Sciences. Her research focus is on international trade, China's opening to the outside world, and economic friction between major powers.

Zhu Hengpeng is Deputy Secretary of the Party Committee and Professor in the Institute of Economics, Chinese Academy of Social Sciences, and Deputy Dean and Professor in the Department of Economics at the University of Chinese Academy of Social Sciences. His research interest is public economics, finance, and social security.

Preface

The novel coronavirus, named COVID-19 by the World Health Organization, has evolved into a global pandemic, spreading to almost all countries and regions throughout the world. With millions of cases, COVID-19 is the sort of public health crisis that only occurs once in a blue moon. This crisis has not only taken the lives of many people and harmed the health of many others, but also endangered people's livelihoods, especially those in low-income groups, and even threatened the survival of mankind due to its devastating effects on economic activities. The pandemic has not yet reached its peak, and the impact on life and the economic shocks it has caused have not been fully estimated. However, more and more evidence and analysis shows that in terms of impact on the economy and society, this pandemic is likely to exceed any similar crisis in the past century, whether caused by natural disasters or financial turmoil.

A pandemic will always bring huge economic shocks, deflect the normal development of a single country and the world as a whole from the established track, and cause serious damage to the economy and society. Correspondingly, the greatest challenge during the pandemic is how to secure people's basic livelihoods, and the most urgent task after the pandemic is how to resume normal economic activities. Therefore, to a certain extent, economists—like epidemiologists, public health experts, and medical workers—shoulder an unshakable professional responsibility as part of the joint efforts of mankind to counter the pandemic. In other words, even if only 1% of economists make an affirmative contribution, or even if only 1% of policy tools are applicable, it is now the time for economists to exert their role.

The economic researchers of the Chinese Academy of Social Sciences have been keeping a close watch on relevant economic impacts throughout the outbreak, spread, and prevention and control of the pandemic. They have conducted timely investigations, analyses, and studies from their respective disciplines and put forward corresponding policy suggestions. We once thought that the novel coronavirus in China would have only a short-term impact. Therefore, many studies were short term, and policy recommendations also focused on short-term responses. We previously thought that once the epidemic was brought under control, work and production could be resumed gradually and prudently and that China's economy would be able to return to its normal track. With the spread of the coronavirus on a global scale, it has quickly plunged the global economy into a deep recession, which will inevitably have a huge negative impact on China's economic recovery. Most economic researchers came to realize that we must be prepared for a protracted battle and adopt corresponding strategies and measures to counter the pandemic itself and achieve recovery of China's economy.

This book is intended to provide the longer-term considerations and analyses of economic researchers at the Chinese Academy of Social Sciences based on the current situation and near-term countermeasures. The authors have examined the impact of the global spread of the pandemic on different aspects of the Chinese economy and have analyzed, from both demand and supply sides, issues such as the work related to agriculture, rural areas and farmers, industrial and supply chains, employment and people's livelihoods, interaction between China's economy and the world economy, and implications for public health and risk prevention and control. In order to identify the uncertain characteristics of the pandemic and its impact on the economy and to explore the corresponding policy choices, we also invited Mr. Peng Wensheng to write a chapter for this book.

Like a wayward devil, COVID-19 is still raging on around the world, and its impact on the economy and people's livelihoods is also expanding and deepening. Correspondingly, we need to update our analysis to keep pace with the evolution of the COVID-19 spread. Timely recording of analyses and understanding of the impacts of the pandemic will undoubtedly provide the basis for further studies on the development of the pandemic and its impact on China and the world economy. Therefore, we hereby devote the preliminary results in this book to our peers and friends who are concerned about related issues, and we sincerely welcome any criticisms and suggestions from readers.

Introduction

Cai Fang

The year 2020 was an extremely important year for China. According to the arrangements of the 19th National Congress of the Communist Party of China, this year was expected to complete a series of important economic and social development indicators and attain the goal of completing the building of a moderately prosperous society in all respects. Particularly, China was expected to double its 2010 gross domestic product (GDP) and per capita income for both urban and rural residents by the year 2020 and ensure that poverty was eliminated in all poor counties and regions based on the current standards. This year was also the final year of the period covered by the 13th Five-Year Plan. However, the outbreak and large-scale spread of COVID-19 around the Spring Festival unexpectedly and severely disrupted normal social and economic activities and brought severe challenges in achieving the annual economic and social development goals.

After implementing a series of strict and effective measures such as testing and screening, admission of patients, prevention and control, isolation, and lockdown, the novel coronavirus, named COVID-19 by the World Health Organization (WHO), has gradually been effectively controlled in China. But the coronavirus has further evolved into a global pandemic (the highest level of disease transmission defined by the WHO), spreading to almost all countries and regions throughout the world. The world's major economies have been severely affected by the pandemic, and the shrinkage of economic activities caused by active isolation or the abnormal volatility of the stock market due to active adjustment or panic has pushed the world economy quickly into a state of recession. Meanwhile, for fear of "backflow" of COVID-19 from outside the country and its resurgence in China, the country is facing many difficulties in resuming work and production. In other words, the global pandemic and the world economy's accelerating downward trend have in turn created serious obstacles to China's economic recovery. Obviously, in such a context, China is unlikely to remain completely unaffected, and great efforts are needed to achieve the expected economic recovery.

DOI: 10.4324/9781003184447-1

The "gray rhino" event, the "black swan" event, or the frog event?

In the realm of economic studies, it is a common practice to compare the impact of COVID-19 with the economic impacts caused by previous epidemics, or with the impacts of previous economic crises and financial crises. However, the evolution of this pandemic and its impact on the economy are very different from previous events. The greatest difference between this pandemic and an economic recession or financial crisis is that the evolution of the pandemic itself as well as the measures, and the timing of those measures, that various countries will adopt to counter it, and the resulting economic impacts and effects of the response measures, are also extremely uncertain.

The outbreak of COVID-19 and its evolution into a global pandemic show variability and multiplicity. The factors causing economic impacts are not only fraught with predictable risks, but also have many uncertain characteristics beyond risks. In addition to the impact on economic activities and capital markets during its spread, COVID-19 has also brought special difficulties to the post-pandemic economic recovery. Therefore, for China, which has effectively controlled the spread of COVID-19 and started to resume work and production, we would rather slightly overestimate the difficulties of economic recovery after the pandemic. Only by taking precautions in understanding can we respond effectively from a policy perspective.

First, the outbreak of the pandemic is to some extent in line with the characteristics of a gray rhino event – a metaphor for highly probable but neglected threats that have an enormous impact. Even neglecting the history of the 20th century and earlier, many similar epidemics have occurred since the beginning of the 21st century, including severe acute respiratory syndrome (SARS) in 2003, which had a total of 8,096 cases and claimed the lives of 774 people throughout the world from November 2002 to July 2003; the N1H1 influenza in 2009, which caused an estimated death toll between 151,700 and 575,400; the Middle East Respiratory Syndrome, which spread widely in 2012 and had a mortality rate as high as 35%; the Ebola virus, with an extremely high mortality rate, which still breaks out from time to time.[1]

As early as in 2018, Bill Gates, a world-renowned entrepreneur and philanthropist, wrote an article warning that the world, especially the United States, was not ready for the next pandemic. Gates predicted that a possible pandemic would cause the deaths of more than 30 million people worldwide. He believed that the world should attach great importance to this possibility and urged countries to better understand how a disease would spread, using scenario simulation, combat exercises, and prevention exercises, and how to respond through isolation measures and information notification to avoid panic and missteps.[2] Regrettably, almost all countries were ill-prepared for the COVID-19 pandemic, and many countries have responded very inappropriately. What Bill Gates predicted has unfortunately come true.

Economists have also showed much concern about this potential risk. The reports and academic research papers of the World Bank show that the neglect of such risk is mainly manifested in the lack of related invest-ment. On the one hand, from the perspective of preventive expenditure and assistance for epidemic diseases in developing countries, there have long been insufficient expenditures and assistance; on the other hand, the governments of developed countries have responded with only temporary measures when serious epidemics have occurred, greatly increasing the level of assistance during an outbreak and reducing the scale of expenditure afterwards.[3] Thus, the governments of many countries were ill-prepared for this pandemic. Government and society tend to perceive a highly probable gray rhino event in the same way as a black swan event – an extremely rare event that is unfore-seen and has an enormous impact.

Second, in some ways, this pandemic also has characteristics of a black swan event. After all, the outbreak of a global pandemic is not a *common* event. The SARS epidemic that happened 18 years ago is still fresh in the memory of Chinese people. None of the other infectious diseases that have spread globally have dramatically affected China. Therefore, in terms of time and space, as the outbreak of a pandemic is expected to be a rare event, this has restrained people's thinking and actions, so all countries were ill-prepared for the outbreak of this pandemic and its ultimate severity.

Moreover, COVID-19 is unique in that it continues to present unexpected evolutionary processes, so experts in epidemiology and public health have to update their knowledge about it. Even the information and experience provided by the countries where COVID-19 broke out early on was repeatedly ignored by policymakers in those countries where it broke out some time later. Correspondingly, the disruptive nature of the pandemic on economic activ-ities and its impact on economic recovery are also characterized by numerous variables and strong uncertainties, resulting in a series of recurring effects. In this sense, gray rhinos and black swans are not enough to fully characterize the pandemic. Perhaps "frogs" can better illustrate such variability.

During the growth and development of frogs and some other amphibians, very significant changes, called metamorphosis in biology, occur in their morphology and living habits. For example, from fertilized eggs in water to tadpoles in water to young frogs in water to amphibious adult frogs, they undergo significant changes, including in the development of their morph-ology, physiological characteristics, behavior and activity patterns, and eco-logical performance. In addition, like chameleons, many frogs have the ability to change color, which can produce amazing effects.

The natural mechanism of coronavirus has high mutation probability and rapid mutation speed, and its evolution track cannot yet be fully explained epidemiologically. As a result, in the process of its spread, it has shown vari-ability in many aspects, such as mode of infection, infectivity, mortality rate, effectiveness of therapies, and group characteristics of affected subjects. Such variability results in huge unpredictability in terms of its impact on economic and social activities. Economists, who are accustomed to using past data to predict future trends, are often left without options in such cases.

For example, at a certain point in time previously, based on the evolution of COVID-19 at that time, economists had concluded that this epidemic was different from any of the other pandemics after World War II because it had hit the most important economy in the world.[4] Who would have expected that this epidemic would evolve into a global pandemic so quickly, with almost no country in the world remaining unaffected? The forward-looking judgment made previously soon turned into an afterthought. In this sense, treating the global spread of this pandemic and its economic consequences as a kind of frog event can make us more accustomed to unexpected changes in understanding and more forward-looking and adept at making contingent decisions when dealing with the reality of COVID-19.

Economic recovery: V-shaped, U-shaped, or W-shaped?

After the outbreak of economic recessions or various types of economic crises in the past, people usually hope to see a V-shaped recovery; that is, a quick and sustained recovery from the bottom until the economy returns to the state it was in before the recession or crisis. During the endemic period of COVID-19 in China, we had envisaged that the epidemic would be mainly confined to China. As the spread of an epidemic follows an epidemiological inverted V-shaped curve symbolizing a rapid increase in number of infections, a peak, and a rapid decline until it disappears, its impact on the economy and subsequent economic recovery can be expected to show a V-shaped track immediately following the inverted V-shaped curve.

It was not unrealistic to make such an estimation at that time. China had experienced a similar situation when SARS broke out in 2003, and at that time there was indeed an inverted V-shaped epidemiological curve (Figure 0.1) followed by a V-shaped economic recovery curve. The SARS epidemic in 2003 lasted only a relatively short period of time. Of the total infections throughout the world, the mainland of China and the Hong Kong Special Administrative Region accounted for 87.5%, and the rest were scattered in different countries and regions. SARS did not have a significant impact on the global economy since most of the economies affected by the epidemic, other than Canada, were relatively small, with China's economic aggregate at that time accounting for only 4.3% of global GDP.

The SARS peak occurred in March 2003, and the negative impact of the epidemic on China's economy only became apparent after that and was limited to the second quarter. Factors such as limiting people's outdoor activities caused the suppression of household consumption in the second quarter. However, in the second half of the year and even in the following year, residents' compensatory consumption has made up for the losses of demand to a large extent.

For example, the total retail sales of social consumer goods in May 2003 alone increased by 4.5% compared with the same period of the previous year. However, this growth rate gradually rose to nearly 10% in the second half

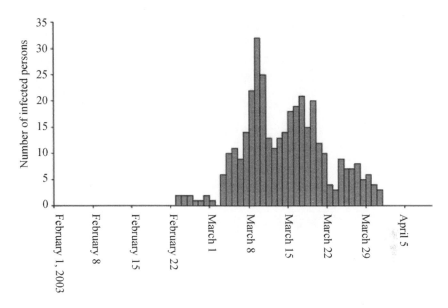

Figure 0.1 Global epidemiological curve of SARS infections.
Source: www.who.int/csr/sarsepicurve/2003_04_08/en/index1.html

of the year, and it was much higher than 10% in 2004. The GDP growth rate, which was 11.1% in the first quarter of 2003, dropped to 9.1% in the second quarter, and rose to 10% in the third and fourth quarters, achieving an annual growth rate of 10%. That is to say, corresponding to the rapid outbreak and disappearance of the epidemic and its corresponding epidemiological inverted V-shaped curve, a perfect V-shaped economic recovery curve was formed subsequently.

COVID-19, characterized by great variability, strong infectivity, and wide spread, was declared a "pandemic" by the WHO. While China has effectively controlled the epidemic and it has entered the second half or even the end of the inverted V-shaped curve, the number of overseas infections begun to rise sharply, and as early as on February 26, 2020, the number of new confirmed cases in other parts of the world surpasses the mainland of China. Globally, the epidemiological curve of COVID-19 has started to extend outside China, and its first half was rapidly climbing upward. As for when and to what extent it will reach its peak, so far this cannot be predicted. In other words, if it is connected with China's inverted V-shaped curve, the global epidemiological curve is following an inverted W-shaped trend (Figure 0.2 and Figure 0.3).

From December 31, 2019, to July 1, 2020, a total of 10.446 million COVID-19 cases were confirmed in 209 countries and regions around the world, and 511,000 died from the virus. The number of infections occurring in the past

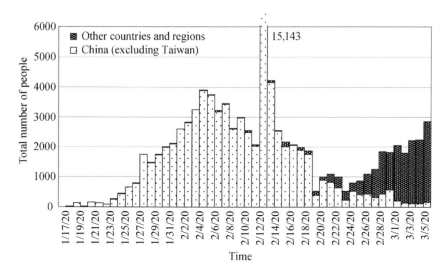

Figure 0.2 Global epidemiological curve of COVID-19, January 17–March 5, 2020.
Source: www.ecdc.europa.eu/en/geographical-distribution-2019-ncov-cases

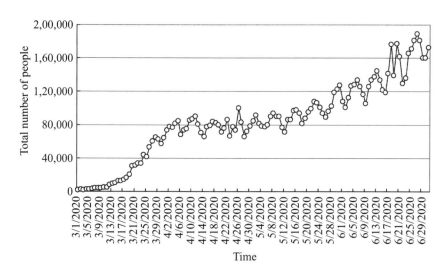

Figure 0.3 Global epidemiological curve of COVID-19, March 1–July 1, 2020.
Source: www.ecdc.europa.eu/en/geographical-distribution-2019-ncov-cases

14 days accounted for 22.0%, which means that the pandemic is still raging on. China has formed successive relations with other countries and regions in the world. We can observe the sequence and development trend of COVID-19 based on the proportion of the number of confirmed cases in the total

number of confirmed cases in the last 14 days. Taking July 1, 2020, as the base time, the proportion was 0.4% in China, 18.9% in the United States, 9.2% in Europe, 36.1% in Africa, 25.1% in the Americas, and 26.2% in Asia.[5] On the one hand, globally, the growth of new infections has been slowing down. On the other hand, comparing China with other countries and regions, China has practically controlled the spread of the pandemic, while the infections other countries and regions are still on the rise.

People generally believe that whether the global pandemic is finally controlled will not depend on the country and region where the pandemic broke out first, but on the country or region that is the last one to successfully control the pandemic. Similarly, even if the ultimate recovery of China's economy will not depend on the country or region that is the last one to successfully control the pandemic, at the least, China will be constrained by the major economies and the world economy as a whole.

The impact of the worldwide spread of the pandemic on the global economy is bound to be serious. It will push the global economy into recession based on various aspects such as the global economic aggregate, manufacturing value added, total exports of goods and services, and foreign direct investment. Even when the pandemic is brought under global control and economic activities restart, the disruption of the manufacturing supply chain, increased poverty, and reduced consumption power due to large-scale unemployment and loss of income, as well as unilateralism, nationalism, rise of trade protectionism, and even the obvious regression of economic globalization, will make it difficult for various countries and the global economy to recover, and it will take a long time.

When the inverted V-shaped epidemiological curve that has been fully demonstrated in China is observed alongside the inverted V-shaped epidemiological curve for the rest of the world as a whole, it is easy to conclude that the trajectory of China's economic recovery will not be the expected V shape. Before the change in this global pandemic trend, we only needed to keep a close eye on our goal of resuming work and production. Now, we need to keep one eye on China's economic recovery and the other eye on the economic performance of other countries and the world.

In other words, in the context of economic globalization, given that China is an open economy, other major economies and the global economy will inevitably affect China's economic recovery to a large extent. If the global economy is plunged into deep recession, this will inevitably interfere greatly with China's economic recovery process and policy implementation options after the pandemic is under control.

Based on the trend, the International Monetary Fund substantially revised down its previous forecast for 2020. According to its April 2020 forecast, the world economy was expected to have negative growth (−3.0%), with an average growth rate of −6.1% for advanced economies and −1.0% for emerging market economies and developing countries.[6] Although China was still performing well among major economies, its forecast GDP growth rate was only 1.2%.[7] The World Bank made the more optimistic forecast that the global economy would shrink by 5.2% in 2020, and apart from China, which was expected to achieve a 1% growth rate, all major economies were expected to experience negative growth.[8] Meanwhile, based on the World Trade Organization's forecast, global trade in goods was expected to shrink by 13% (optimistic) to 32% (pessimistic).[9] The National Bureau of Statistics of China announced a GDP growth rate of −6.8% in the first quarter of 2020. This is undoubtedly the lowest growth rate since the reform and opening up.

Without doubt, it is too early to make any definite predictions about the extent to which the world economy will decline under the global pandemic. However, considering the uncertainty of COVID-19 and its economic impact, we may use analysis by Dr. Roubini to provide a reference scenario. He believed that the global economy is facing triple risks, and there are three possible scenarios: the pandemic cannot be controlled, the economic policy tools to respond to the event are insufficient, or a geopolitical white swan event occurs.[10] Keeping worst-case scenarios in mind, we can now make a judgment that the Chinese economy will not achieve the V-shaped recovery trajectory as originally anticipated. More specifically, anticipating China's economic recovery, we should consider the following possibilities to strive for the best possible results.

The first possibility is that affected by the significant deterioration of other countries' economic conditions and the severe recession of the global economy, China's economy will recover at a pace significantly slower than originally expected. Even with a relatively good recovery, there will be a delay in the V-shaped trajectory benchmark; that is, it will linger for longer at the bottom or on the way up, forming a U-shaped recovery trajectory. A less optimistic scenario is that a "bathtub-like" recovery may take place; that is, affected by the disruption of the global supply chain and under the assumption that it will be more difficult to resume work and production, the economy will stay at the bottom for longer and it will take longer to return to economic growth.

The second possibility is that corresponding to the epidemiological inverted W-shaped curve of the global spread of COVID-19, China's economic recovery will be dragged down to a greater extent by the global economic recession, forming a larger-span W-shaped economic recovery trajectory. That is, the recovery process will be unstable with substantial danger of relapses. Even under less optimistic scenarios, especially when China's economy is repeatedly disturbed by the contradiction between the supply side and the demand side, it will take longer for economic activities to recover, and cyclical relapses may occur even more frequently. However, this W-shaped trajectory is not horizontal, but upward, which means that the Chinese economy will eventually return to the track of potential growth rates.

The third possibility is that if the coronavirus continues to mutate and surge from time to time, becoming a long-term cyclical epidemic, a corresponding type of economic cycle may appear, and economic growth will also fluctuate along a horizontal S-shaped curve. There is some possibility that herd immunity will be achieved in various countries or that the successful development of specific drugs and effective vaccines will benefit everyone in every part of the world. Still, economic activities in the world and every region will be locked down from time to time, and the Chinese economy will be affected accordingly.

Of course, a reliable forecast is that the Chinese economy will follow a recovery trajectory resembling the shape of the check mark of Nike's logo: on the one hand, due to the impact of its domestic spread, the economic downturn occurred very quickly; on the other hand, affected by the changes in the global spread curve, the economic recovery process will be steady and slow and last for a longer time. To a certain extent, this shape can indeed describe the trajectory of China's economic recovery after the pandemic, but the difference in the recovery effect can alter the slope of the second half of this tick.

Similarities and differences

Economists tend to say, "Never let an economic crisis go to waste!" It means that various economic recessions and economic crises of varying degrees of severity due to different causes will eventually cause harm to a country's economy and people's livelihoods that people don't want to see, and if people fail to draw lessons from those painful experiences, the price would be paid in vain.

In addition, economists are also arguing about whether this crisis is the same or different from the last one. In fact, historical experience has repeatedly shown that every economic crisis has its own unique characteristics. Meanwhile, every crisis also bears some similarities with other crises. Countries, societies, and individuals that have been harmed by crises will undoubtedly feel the pain, and each has its own misfortunes.

Economic history was fraught with economic disasters caused by economic recessions, financial crises, and pandemics. These events are usually long-term hot topics in discussions about economic theories and economic policies. To some extent, the conclusions of these painful lessons and coping experiences have incubated and given birth to many theoretical innovations in economics. Globally, the COVID-19 pandemic is far from over. Therefore, our current task is not to summarize or reflect on it. Based on the experience and lessons of past events and related theoretical discussions, we should focus on the matters related to the response to the impact of the pandemic. We may raise questions from several important perspectives for comparison and reflection, and we can explore the common grounds (similarities) found in different events and the differences between them.

First, in the face of major shock factors, it is important for macroeconomic policies to respond in a timely manner, and based on historical experience, policy responses have been conservative in most cases and passive because they failed to meet actual needs. Therefore, in retrospect, every step of the policy response was not an "overreaction." Especially in the face of a highly volatile and unpredictable pandemic, timely and effective policy response is very important to eliminate the effect of uncertainty of the evolution of the event and the uncertainty of policy orientations, thereby avoiding double market panic.

In Keynes's view, economic decisions often come from the impulsivity of the actors themselves, not always from estimation of the average. Therefore, there is instability due to the characteristics of human nature. This is what economists call "animal spirits."[11] Such impulsivity will inevitably lead to irrational characteristics in individual economic decision-making. We can also understand irrationality of economic activity from another perspective; that is, the situation in which economic activity is disrupted by shocks can be manifested as a decrease in the expected mean value, or as an increase in the variance of the value.[12]

A fall in the expected mean is usually manifested in withdrawal of investors and decreased investment, then decline in output, which is mainly a response to risk; a rise in variance is manifested in fluctuation of investment activities and output as well as sharp fluctuation of the capital market and commodity trade caused by uncertain factors. As investment activities are driven by animal spirits, as far as its normal state is concerned, there are naturally overvaluation factors or bubbles. When encountering sudden increases in risk and uncertainty, people will naturally interpret them based on the information they can obtain, leading to so-called circulated narration, and react accordingly.[13]

In such cases, even if you do not want to figure out whether such a response is a rational market adjustment, an irrational psychological panic, an inappropriate response to distorted information, or a misinterpretation of uncertain information, it will eventually push the market and the economy into unbearable chaos. Risk and uncertainty are differentiated in the following way: the former can be reflected by specific information, so the market's reaction to it is predictable, at least theoretically; the essence of the latter lies in the insufficiency, unavailability, and even distortion of information, so the market's response to it is unpredictable.

The stock market's response to the unpredictability of the COVID-19 pandemic was generated by four "circuit breakers" that occurred on March 9, 12, 16, and 18, 2020, respectively, in the United States. The circuit breaker mechanism was first used in response to Black Monday, on October 19, 1987 – the worst stock market crash experienced by the United States; the first circuit breaker was applied on October 27, 1997. For this reason, US macroeconomic policies underwent large-scale adjustments just to avoid a possible panic and violent fluctuations in the stock market, despite policymakers' intention to win votes or knowing that the policy of cutting interest rates might not work.

It is of course necessary to make adjustments in economic policy in order to prevent a panic and the resultant sharp decline in the real economy that would be detrimental to people's livelihoods, even if they are not fully appropriate for the symptoms. It is also clear that this kind of policy is to a certain extent only symbolic and will never rival more targeted and substantive policy measures to relieve economic pressures.

Second, the coronavirus has imposed impacts on the real economy simultaneously or successively from both demand and supply sides, which is also reflected in the production factor market and commodities market. Market conditions are determined by interweaving demand and supply factors; however, generally speaking, under the market economy, short-term impacts mostly come from the demand side, while supply-side factors mainly affect longer-term economic performance.

As the theoretical and policy source of countercyclical adjustment, macroeconomics, especially the economic cycle theory, was born to address demand-side impacts. Accordingly, all instruments in the macroeconomic policy toolbox were also designed for this purpose. Although the economic histories of all countries have seen shocks from the supply side, such as the petroleum shock and various natural disasters in the 1970s, there is a general lack of experience of applying macroeconomic policies to deal with supply-side shocks, and the means to do so are often not available.

The impacts of COVID-19 on the Chinese economy have been manifested from the very beginning in a combination of demand-side and supply-side factors. In order to strictly implement social distancing, lockdown, and quarantine measures, consumer activities related to personal mobility and aggregate consumer activities, such as accommodation, catering, tourism, entertainment, passenger transport, and other consumer demands, had been totally suppressed, and production and operating activities had also been banned. As China experienced the first wave of the epidemic, the supply-side arrangement to stop work and production led to delays or even interruptions in producers' supply in many other countries.

When the domestic pandemic situation improves, the gradual progress of resuming work and production is expected to change the supply condition, but it will be difficult to repair the damage caused to the supply chain during the shutdown. Moreover, the manufacturing halt and contraction caused by the global pandemic and protectionist measures have exerted a new round of demand-side impacts on Chinese producers.

This kind of impact is superimposed and its consequences are very serious. Therefore, greater efforts are required to implement policy that deals with dilemmas. Take the labor market as an example. While many workers could not find jobs, enterprises still found it hard to recruit workers. This is reflected in the labor market indicators. On one hand, the unemployment rate was expected to rise, and on the other hand, the recruitment rate remained at a high level. Therefore, we need to make good use of instruments in the traditional policy toolbox and try to change our way of thinking so as to choose appropriate policies.

Third, the coronavirus did much harm to human life and health. However, there is a wide gap in basic health status between rich countries and poor ones and between groups with different income levels, as the availability of immunization, medical treatment, and rehabilitation opportunities as well as the degree of, and tolerance to, the economic impact of the pandemic are all different. Nobel laureate in economics Angus Deaton pointed out in reviewing the pandemic and the history of human resistance that technologies for preventing and treating epidemic infectious diseases are usually transmitted step by step from top to bottom according to the social hierarchy. Therefore, for the economist who revealed the phenomenon of the United States "dying of despair," not all people are created equal in the face of the virus.[14]

In modern society, it is true that the universality and availability of medical technologies have been greatly improved. Moreover, in the face of the coronavirus, both billionaires and political elites with high standing in developed countries and informal employees struggling on the poverty line in developing countries can become infected and will pay the price in terms of their health and life afterwards. However, there is no doubt that there are great differences between countries and social groups as to whether there is a choice to avoid infection, what kind of treatment can be obtained after testing positive, and whether vaccines are offered in a fair manner once they are available. Many data in the United States have shown that the death rate of African Americans and Hispanic Americans infected with the COVID-19 virus is several times higher than that of Caucasians. These data provide evidence for the hypothesis that not everyone is equal before the coronavirus.

No matter the cause of economic crisis, its impact on people should not be evaluated by its magnitude, but by its nature. For example, a financial crisis may lead to losses of trillions of dollars to the financial industry; also, it may cause a large number of workers earning minimum wage to lose their jobs. Specifically, the impact of losses suffered by individuals, bankers, and workers is not the same. Bankers just lose capital owners' money and investors just lose high capital gains; but workers and their families lose the basic incomes needed for their survival.

Therefore, during the coronavirus pandemic, low-income countries and groups have faced greater probability of bearing the shocks, because they lacked perfect medical security conditions, and as a result, their lives and health were subject to greater threats and injuries. Furthermore, when the pandemic reached its peak, measures such as city lockdowns and quarantine halted all economic activities. Vulnerable countries were short of sufficient resources and financial resources to maintain necessary testing, treatment, care, and protection of residents' basic livelihoods. Ordinary workers were also more likely to lose their jobs and sources of income and became exposed to life and health risks. When the economy started to recover, just as economic growth did not produce the trickle effect of income distribution, the life of ordinary workers could not naturally return to normal with the overall economic recovery. At this point, the capital letter "K" illustrates the polarized economic recovery during the pandemic.

Fourth, in the face of COVID-19 impacts, monetary policy and fiscal policy need to work together. Fiscal policy should play a more important role because of its more targeted and effective implementation mechanisms. In macroeconomics, the division of labor and coordination between the two macroeconomic policy toolboxes has been a long-standing topic of debate. In recent years, it has generated a new set of discussions. The development of some research fields and the policy implementation suggestions obtained have gained more and more recognition, even appearing in the election platforms of US presidential candidates.

In the debate on whether the reason for long-term economic stagnation lies in supply-side or demand-side factors, many fundamental understandings are yet to be agreed, but some consensus has been reached unconsciously; for example, that monetary policy alone cannot bear the important task of stimulating economic growth. Due to long-term low interest rates or even negative rates in developed countries and the implementation of quantitative easing policies, monetary policy instruments are certainly insufficient to withstand the economic shocks caused by the coronavirus, and there is narrow space for macroeconomic regulation. It is therefore believed that more fiscal policy measures should be used. However, there has been no agreement on the choice of policy instruments.

In view of the special impacts of the pandemic, differences in viewpoints may be put aside while a higher level of policy consensus is reached. In emergencies, including wars and disasters, necessary expenditures for safeguarding national security, economy, and people's livelihoods, such as subsidies for residents' income, relief for small and medium-sized enterprises, and payment of basic social insurance, are the government's responsibility and are not bearable by citizens and the private sector. At the same time, in this particularly difficult period, normal public finance revenue cannot meet the needs of large-scale additional expenditures. This needs to be solved by the government increasing the general public finance deficit ratio or increasing the government debt according to the characteristics of its own financial structure and the nature of various expenditure items.[15]

It is thus clear that in the balance between monetary policy and fiscal policy, fiscal policy now occupies a leading position while monetary policy focuses on the implementation of the former. During the pandemic, people had to stop work and production, which led first to open unemployment and underemployment and then to loss or even complete loss of income, seriously threatening the basic livelihoods of low-income families. Even if there were conditions for complete resumption of work and production, the interrupted supply chain still needs time to repair, and the global pandemic may further damage the supply chain. Therefore, large-scale financial expenditure to ensure full payment of social insurance and social assistance is far more important than ensuring sufficient liquidity in the financial sector.

Economists and even central bankers are increasingly willing to admit that in the face of the epidemic, the role of monetary policy is relatively auxiliary, its duty being to ensure that the implementation of government relief policies are supported financially and not restricted by insufficient liquidity in the market.

For example, former Federal Reserve chairmen Bernanke and Yellen pointed out in a co-authored article that the role of monetary policy at this time is to meet the following needs: first, additional demand for liquidity is needed under the conditions of home quarantine and electronic trading; second, under such special circumstances, lenders need additional confidence in lending money; third, whether it is the economic recovery after short-term or long-term pandemic that has caused businesses and families to suffer losses, credit should be available whenever needed.[16] In addition, monetary policy also needs to mention monetary financing.

Fifth, the time, method, path, and effect of economic recovery is determined by the characteristics and direction of national and global development. Therefore, all measures should be taken by the government at the proper time according to the process and sequence of events and the types and characteristics of macro policies. In the early stage of the outbreak, the epidemiological inverted V-shaped curve was in the rising stage, before reaching peak value. In order to control the fast spread of the pandemic, the most important task was to implement strict prevention and control measures, including city lockdowns, quarantine, cancellation of gatherings, etc. At this time, it was inevitable that economic activities would be reduced or even stopped. However, after the pandemic reached its peak, the inverted V-shaped curve entered the downward phase, and the resumption of work and production was on the agenda. Further, economic recovery was given a higher priority when the spread of the pandemic was reliably contained.

Accordingly, macroeconomic policies and other policy measures are also affected by the characteristics of the pandemic. It is necessary to choose the right time to issue them, or the expected results cannot be achieved. For example, policies aiming to stimulate citizen consumption, especially encouraging compensatory consumption, cannot produce the expected results when society is still under lockdown, and monetary policies aiming to maintain necessary and sufficient liquidity may be needed at different stages, but they should be adapted to main policy objectives at each point in time and should not become an independent objective. Macroeconomic policies aiming to restore and stimulate investment cannot be implemented during a period of general quarantine of the whole society and before economic activities begin to resume. Social support policy aiming to ensure people's basic livelihoods should be present from the beginning and should run through the development of the pandemic and its economic impact in various forms.

As for the trend of the pandemic globally, there will be a dilemma when the epidemiological curve ascends for a long time and it is difficult to predict when it will decline: on one hand, resuming economic activities before the pandemic is contained may cause more people to be infected, and the pandemic curve is difficult to stabilize, particularly in the stage of decline; on the other hand, due to long-term inability to resume work and production, a considerable number of people will have lost their jobs and sources of income, and their basic livelihoods may be increasingly threatened. Under such circumstances, it is certainly more important for the government to implement relief policy than to allow the market to fluctuate according to its own impulses.

Finally, control of the pandemic and resumption of economic activities are difficult aims that must be achieved, and the trade-offs and dilemmas between the two must be rigorously handled. Despite the initial low death rate in China, the coronavirus is spreading fast and will eventually cause losses of life and health when a great number of people are infected. Therefore, the implementation of strict prevention and control measures through mobilization is inevitable. China's successful experience in this regard reflects an absolute, or universally applicable, principle. Under conditions where the pandemic is under control, it will also be a top priority to resume work and production as soon as possible, which is also an absolute principle that applies around the globe. However, there is indeed a dilemma between these two absolute principles.

China has been successful in its lockdown of key areas such as Wuhan and its implementation of quarantine measures nationwide. China was the first to contain the pandemic and restore economic activities, because it used the phased development of the pandemic to apply spatial separation of prevention and control measures, adopted a two-track transition mode, and distinguished the priorities of virus containment and resumption of work and production according to the phased development of COVID-19 between regions. It was precisely because prevention and control were carried out at all costs in the early stage that the process of economic recovery could be accelerated in the latter stage on the premise that the number of infected people would not rebound. This successful approach also provides a benchmark model to deal with the relationship between coronavirus containment and resumption of work and production.

In view of the fact that the rest of the world is still in the rising stage of the inverted V-shaped curve of the coronavirus epidemiology, countries, including China, may also experience a W-shaped track in their economic recovery, and they need to carry out smart and scientific policy design rather than relying on traditional macroeconomic policies, combine government responsibilities with epidemiological curve laws, and solve the dilemma of virus containment and recovery of economic activities. According to China's successful experience in containing the pandemic and the dilemma encountered, this two-track transition model that separates space from time can be further expanded to an updated version that sees time and space in parallel, which can be implemented as appropriate under the conditions of necessary testing and treatment of those affected by the virus.

This model involves the following key steps. First, when basic conditions are met, those vulnerable to coronavirus should be fully tested, and those tested should be divided into two groups: a safety group and a risk group. Second, when the two groups are fully isolated, the safety group is asked to return to work, while the risk group continues to be quarantined and tested. Third, when more and more people are tested and treated, the proportion of safety groups should be expanded and the risk groups downsized so as to accelerate transition of the double-track system to the safe single track. With this transitional approach, we will minimize the time between coronavirus quarantine and resumption of work and production.

The coronavirus pandemic and its impact on the global economy have many similarities with the experience of other pandemics and economic recessions in history. For example, familiar scenes in economic history include uncertainties around the pandemic itself, inadequacy of information, government's untimely judgment of the situation that resulted in inappropriate decisions, parties' "passing the buck" to shirk their responsibilities, market shocks, lingering economic recovery, etc.

The COVID-19 pandemic also shows many unique features. Aside from the evolution of the coronavirus being extremely "cunning" and its transmission mode being unique, a distinctive feature of the current situation is that China's economy already makes up a huge proportion in the world economy and makes a unique contribution to the growth of the world economy. China's manufacturing industry has occupied a central position in the global supply chain. China's economic growth is undergoing energetic transformation. While the world is at a higher stage of globalization, the undercurrent of anti-globalization has also reached a climax. All of the above have posed unprecedented challenges to China and the world in coping with economic recession in 2020.

In addition, the occurrence and evolution of the pandemic and its impacts on economic activities have also exposed a series of problems that have been neglected under normal conditions. For example, public health emergency response systems, coordination and cooperation between countries under the condition of globalization, storage and allocation of emergency materials, and maintenance and repair of manufacturing supply chains have all met with severe challenges during the pandemic. For this reason, economists need to think more deeply in order to put forward countermeasures and suggestions to address various difficulties and foresee the future.

Recovering China's economy while adapting to variability

Variability and unpredictability are the main characteristics of the coronavirus pandemic itself and its impacts on a country's economy. In view of this, in the process of economic recovery, China's economy needs to keep abreast of the global pandemic situation, respond to accurate information in a timely manner, and maintain sufficient patience and concentration to keep to its own bottom line. That is to say, while seeking progress in stability, China's deployment and promotion of economic recovery need to adapt to variability and uncertainty, and policy choices should be made to deal with the dialectical relationship between variance and invariance. For this reason, we have made a preliminary analysis of some important aspects of China's taking the lead in economic recovery policy, and we put forward corresponding policy suggestions.

First, amid uncertainties around the global trend of the coronavirus and its economic impact, we unswervingly promote the recovery of the Chinese economy. As the world's second-largest economy and one of the fastest-growing countries, China contributed more than 28% to global economic growth in 2009–2019. Therefore, with other economies and even the world economy in recession, recovery of China's economy is China's own top priority but by no means represents a zero-sum game for the world economy and inevitably has a positive spillover effect on other economies. More importantly, the significance to the world of China's rapid return to normal economic growth is not just based on an abstract concept of economic aggregate; rather, it contributes to many important aspects of the economies of other countries and the world economy.

When the coronavirus became a global pandemic and China took the lead in controlling the virus and resuming work and production, China provided other countries with much-needed medical equipment, protective equipment, and drugs, drawing on its own strong production capacity, as well as medical staff and rich experience in coping with an epidemic. For example, with countries entering the peak of the outbreak one after another, provision of various articles made in China, including ventilators and medical masks, and dispatches of expert medical teams have already played an important role in the global fight against the pandemic. In addition, China will continue to provide humanitarian assistance when some poor countries, especially those along the the Belt and Road Initiative route, are hit by the pandemic and fall into extreme difficulties.

Up to now, China still maintains its position as a global manufacturing center with strong manufacturing capabilities. It is also the only country in the world that has all the categories in the United Nations standard industrial classification, with 41 at the two-digit level, 207 at the three-digit level, and 666 at the four-digit level. In 2018, China's export of goods accounted for 12.7% of the world's total. With the proportion of manufacturing in China's total exports of goods as high as 93.4%, China's manufacturing exports rank first in the world, accounting for 17.2% of the world's manufacturing exports; this is 74.0% higher than Germany, which ranks second.

Before the outbreak of the pandemic, economic globalization was hit by various policy tendencies, such as unilateralism, populism, nationalism, and trade protectionism. The United States also launched trade wars against many important economies, including China, and pushed for decoupling from China's economy and supply chain. After the outbreak in various countries, there appeared protectionist tendencies among neighboring countries, and the trend of anti-globalization seemed to be further on the rise. However, challenges facing the world economy under the impact of the pandemic have proven the irreversibility of globalization. During and after the recovery of the Chinese economy, China will play an irreplaceable role in maintaining and repairing the global supply chain with its own production and supply, thus preventing retrogression of economic globalization.

China has the largest population and the second-largest economy in the world, but it also has the largest number of people with mid-level income. The resulting ultra-large market and its potential will provide huge demand pull for subsequent recovery of the world economy. On the one hand, after the return to normal life in Chinese society, household consumption has rebounded in both alternative and compensatory aspects, which also leads to consumption related to public health and other areas, thus generating large-scale new growth points of demand. On the other hand, in the process of restoring economic growth and stabilizing employment, larger-scale investment activities will also be formed. There will also be investment growth points as part of construction of new infrastructure for 5G networks, big data centers, and artificial intelligence. All these demand factors will inevitably produce significant spillover effects under the condition of economic globalization and provide opportunities for investors from other countries.

Also, the highest priority should be given to stabilizing employment, ensuring people's livelihoods, and achieving the goal of poverty alleviation so as to fulfill the goals and tasks of economic and social development. The fundamentals of China's long-term economic and social development have not changed, nor will they be changed by the coronavirus; that is, the supply of production factors and productivity will not be affected for a long time. Therefore, the overall achievement of the predetermined economic and social development goals, especially the landmark goal of building a well-off society in an all-round way, is still a task that must be strived for with great efforts.

However, the global pandemic has, after all, resulted in the worst crisis in a century, as it has directly or indirectly caused a huge negative impact on China's economy and society, and inevitably caused a certain degree of interference in realizing specific indicators of economic and social development throughout 2020. It was also realistic to reduce some specific quantitative indicators; for example the annual expected target for GDP growth rate was not preset. In fact, with a growth rate of −6.8% in the first quarter, if the growth rate reaches 5% to 6% throughout the year, it will mean an overheating in the rest of the year.

At the same time, we should adhere to the concept of people-centered development and reasonably determine the policy priorities for economic recovery and the efforts needed to achieve the goals. China has stepped out of the most severe moment of pandemic spread, but the adverse impact on macroeconomy is already very serious. In addition, the supply chain has been damaged due to the global pandemic, and the impact on the real economy has far exceeded that of the 2003 SARS epidemic and the 2008–2009 global financial crisis. Accordingly, employment is bound to encounter unprecedented impact, which will further affect the actual income growth of urban and rural residents and cause great difficulties for ordinary families trying to maintain their basic livelihoods.

Referring to the Sahm rule,[17] an empirical method used by an American economist to judge whether the economy is in recession – that is, to observe whether the smooth level of unemployment rate in the last three months is 0.5 percentage points or more higher than the lowest point in the past 11 months – it can be seen that the smooth value of the urban unemployment rate in first three months of 2020 was 5.8%, 0.8 percentage points higher than the 5.0% (the lowest point in the past 11 months) witnessed in April and May 2019 (Figure 0.4), and the high unemployment rate has continued since then. Looking at this indicator from the perspective of macroeconomic prosperity, it is clear that economic prosperity has entered a low point, while from the perspective of residents' basic security, it means that necessary policy measures are urgently needed to ensure people's livelihoods.

In response to the sustained impact of the coronavirus on employment, a more active employment policy should include more unconventional measures so as to ensure people's livelihoods through stable employment. First, all macroeconomic policies aimed at resuming economic activities and thus stimulating economic growth have the effect of promoting employment at the same time. They should be mobilized and implemented to the greatest extent possible, and the employment policy should be incorporated into macro policy. Second, as for the structural, frictional, and cyclical factors in

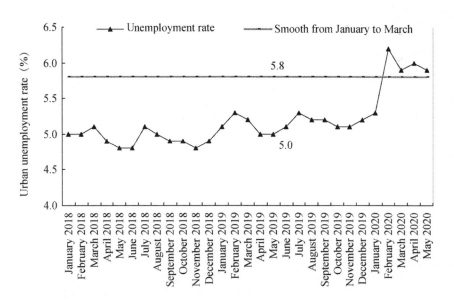

Figure 0.4 Urban unemployment rate and the Sahm rule.

Source: calculated by the author using online data from the National Bureau of Statistics: www.stats.gov.cn/

unemployment, various relevant policy measures should be used to reduce the overall unemployment rate. Third, surplus unemployment insurance benefits should be returned to help stabilize jobs, and these should also be used to expand the scope of payments, especially to cover unemployed migrant workers who are returning to urban areas and are not covered by unemployment insurance. In addition, cash needs to be paid directly to families affected by the pandemic by designing more inclusive, direct, and rapid projects.

An important requirement to ensure and improve people's livelihoods is that the goal of lifting all the poor in rural areas out of poverty should be unshakeable. It is also important for achieving annual objectives and tasks. No effort should be spared in fulfillment of this goal. Since the 18th National Congress of the Communist Party of China, the number of poor people in rural areas has decreased by 93.48 million; that is to say, in each year of the period 2012–2019, more than 10 million people were lifted out of poverty. The task for the year of 2020 was to lift the remaining 5.51 million rural poor out of poverty. According to the rate of poverty alleviation in recent years, even considering that the phenomenon of partial return to poverty may make the work more difficult, and combined with in-depth implementation of a rural revitalization strategy to consolidate the achievements of poverty alleviation, fulfillment of the goal can be expected.

However, the unexpected coronavirus pandemic itself and the measures taken to contain it have inevitably hindered migrant workers ability to go out to work, and the income of migrant workers in poor areas and poor families has been greatly reduced. Migrant workers' income accounts for a high proportion of the income of rural families and migrant work is an important way out of poverty, so this has not only hindered the removal from poverty of the remaining group of people, but also caused some families that have just got out of poverty to fall into poverty once again. At a time when the battle against poverty coexists with special challenges, it is necessary in the last mile to step up efforts towards poverty alleviation by unconventional means. For the government, the most effective way is to unconditionally include all members of the rural population failing to meet the poverty alleviation standard in the scope of the minimum income guarantee.

Also, in the process of recovering the economy by taking advantage of the ultra-large market advantage, it is necessary to properly handle the relationship between promoting household consumption and expanding construction investment. Before the outbreak of the pandemic, tertiary industry and household consumption had become the main contributing factors to China's economic growth. For example, among three major demand factors (net export, investment, and consumption) driving China's economic growth, the contribution of final consumption to GDP growth reached 57.8% in 2019. In the final consumption, urban and rural residents accounted for 70.0%. Meanwhile, tertiary industry and household consumption were also the areas hit most directly and severely by the pandemic. Therefore, promoting resumption of work and production in the tertiary industry and stimulating household consumption after the pandemic should be the entry points for resuming economic activities, stabilizing employment, and ensuring people's livelihoods.

According to World Bank statistics, total global final consumption in 2018 was 62.6 trillion US dollars, of which China contributed 11.6%, which was 46.9% of the contribution from upper-middle-income countries. While there is still a big gap between China and developed countries in terms of per capita income and per capita consumption, China's total final consumption is equivalent to 71.8% of the total consumption of eurozone countries due to China's huge population and economic scale. Judging from the economic rationality of consumption behavior and past experience, there will be some special consumption tendencies among residents in the process of economic recovery after the pandemic. Consumption behavior should be stimulated through policies to ensure basic income, and the availability and convenience of products and services should be improved through business model innovation and market segmentation so as to fully tap their expansion potential.

The first one is compensatory consumption. Generally speaking, once the inhibition of normal consumption caused by coronavirus impacts is lifted, consumers will be driven by both actual needs and psychological needs to purchase goods and services that have large demand elasticity and are most inhibited. As a result, unconventional purchase demand will be generated. In the process of pandemic prevention and control, these goods include some household goods for which consumer spending has been greatly reduced, especially branded goods that are relatively high-end and not suitable for online purchase, such as advanced cosmetics.

The second is alternative consumption. Under the condition that the demand for certain goods or services cannot be met, other goods or services with similar utility or the same consumption preference can become the object of alternative consumption. For example, aggregated and experiential consumption, such as in tourism, theaters, and group consumption, which were most affected by the pandemic and difficult to recover, can be turned to other consumption items that are more private and have similar effects, or they will be realized by different consumption modes.

The third is guidable consumption. This refers to the consumption content in which consumer preferences can be cultivated within a certain period of time with the change of consumption concept. Public health events such as the coronavirus, which has lasted for a long time and has led to huge lifestyle and health costs, will induce new consumption behaviors related to healthy living. Home quarantine will also induce some consumption habits to form new hot spots of consumption. This includes demands for healthcare products, sports and fitness activities, domestic items to improve home hygiene and environment, psychological counseling activities, and more private means of transportation.

Under normal situations of economic development, the fundamental way to promote household consumption is to expand employment and increase income, enhance consumption power, and improve the level and coverage of social security so as to reduce consumers' worries. However, the most effective approach to stabilizing and recovering household consumption relates to public expenditure functions of governments at all levels, with implementation of effective basic living security policies being important under such abnormal circumstances as huge disasters and during subsequent periods of recovery.

Judging from the difference between per capita disposable income and household consumption expenditure, as households move from lower to higher position of per capita income, their savings tend to increase. That is to say, as the savings rate of low-income households is very low, they are least able to resist impacts on employment and income. The conventional relief systems such as the minimum income guarantee are deficient in terms of identification of the target population and speed of response, which makes it difficult to fully cover the entire population affected by the coronavirus. Therefore, an inclusive relief policy such as universal cash distribution is needed to achieve the goal of stimulating household consumption while safeguarding people's livelihoods.

The advantage of the ultra-large market is also reflected in China's huge potential to expand investment. Under special circumstances, this is also a necessary driving force for China's economic recovery. At this special moment, there is particular need for infrastructure investments aiming to improve points of weakness and optimize structures, construction projects highly dependent on domestic supply chains and aiming to improve domestic supporting capabilities, construction of public health and strategic emergency material reserve facilities, and new infrastructure construction represented by 5G base stations, the industrial Internet, and artificial intelligence, as well as construction projects with great employment flexibility and obvious multiplier effects.

However, when using investment to implement economic stimulus, we need to fully draw lessons from past experiences and hold on to several bottom lines. We must persist in giving full rein to the decisive role of the market in allocating resources, avoid accumulation of non-performing debts and an unreasonable increase in leverage ratios, prevent new inefficient production capacity and excess production capacity, curb accumulation of systemic risks and hidden dangers, inhibit retrogression in the effectiveness of pollution prevention, and control and the effectiveness of supply-side structural reforms.

It is also necessary to prevent economic growth from becoming dependent on investment demand and returning to the traditional development mode. In the past, when the macroeconomy was hit by demand-side shocks, the contribution of capital formation to economic growth would increase significantly. Once the dependence on investment was formed, the demand structure would be unbalanced, thus damaging the sustainability of economic growth. For a long time, investment has dominated the demand-driven economic growth in China, and rapid economic growth is always accompanied by a high investment rate. Moreover, expanding investment has been used as an alternative demand factor in the event of economic shocks (such as declining exports).

For example, from 1998 to 2019, capital formation contributed more than 50% to GDP growth, and the GDP growth rate was highly positively correlated with the capital formation contribution rate. In the same period of GDP growth, the contribution of capital formation and the contribution of net exports showed a significant negative correlation. In order to increase investment-driven stimulus policies, we must think about these kinds of lessons from the past and avoid repeating the same mistakes.

Finally, the urgent tasks of resuming economic activities, stabilizing the growth rate, and safeguarding people's livelihoods should be closely combined with the goals of long-term reform and development. Economic history has indicated that crises are often times when weak points and structural contradictions are fully exposed. Accordingly, coping with crises and getting out of difficulties can produce long-term sustainable results while also achieving immediate results by accelerating the established long-term reform and development tasks. The coronavirus pandemic has exposed huge economic and social shortcomings and risks, the most prominent of which is incomplete or atypical urbanization. Urbanization is also expected to make important contributions to China's long-term economic and social development. This combination of urgent tasks with long-term goals has given urgency to the task of speeding up new urbanization with migrant workers settling in cities and towns.

In 2019, when China's rate of urbanization among the permanent population reached 60.6%, the urbanization rate of the registered population was only 44.4%. In other words, 22.7 million people dwelling in cities and towns in China were not regarded as permitted urban households. The majority of this group (76.7%) was composed of 174 million migrant workers who had left the villages and towns where their households were registered. Some significant impacts caused by this situation, such as cutting the effective supply of labor force, reducing the efficiency of resource reallocation, and weakening the comparative advantage of the manufacturing industry, have attracted the attention of economists. However, the pandemic has exposed obvious drawbacks of large-scale quarantining of people and households and isolation of family members in different places.

If 70% of migrant workers return home during the Spring Festival every year, the pressure on transportation formed in a very short period of time can generate a nationwide super-normal flow of up to 120 million people. The coronavirus pandemic has exposed the drawbacks of this atypical urbanization. That is, in addition to the difficulties in spring transportation caused by big crowds returning to their rural homes or returning to the city under normal circumstances, there are additional risks caused by the epidemic and the dense flow of people, including serious difficulties for the operation of enterprises caused by migrant workers' failure to return to the city in time to resume work, substantial reduction in migrant workers' and rural residents' incomes, and risk of disruption or even damage to the manufacturing supply chain.

Therefore, accelerating new urbanization and efforts to reform the household registration system so that migrant workers and their family members can settle in cities and towns where they work will reduce the future economic and social risks and promote the long-term sustainable development of China's economy and society by means of increasing labor supply, reducing manufacturing costs, improving labor productivity, improving the equalization of basic public services, improving income distribution, and expanding household consumption.

Notes

1 Richard Baldwin and Beatrice Weder di Mauro, Introduction, in Richard Baldwin and Beatrice Weder di Mauro (eds) *Economics in the Time of COVID-19*, London: CEPR Press, 2020, pp. 6–7.
2 Bill Gates, Innovation for Pandemics, *The New England Journal of Medicine*, 2018, Vol. 378, No. 22, pp. 2057–2060.
3 Olga Jonas, Pandemic Risk, *Finance & Development*, December 2014, pp. 16–18.
4 Richard Baldwin and Eiichi Tomiura, Thinking Ahead about the Trade Impact of COVID-19, in Richard Baldwin and Beatrice Weder di Mauro (eds) *Economics in the Time of COVID-19*, London: CEPR Press, 2020, pp. 59–72.
5 See European Centre for Disease Prevention and Control, COVID-19 situation update worldwide, as of week 18, updated May 12, 2021: www.ecdc.europa.eu/en/geographical-distribution-2019-ncov-cases
6 International Monetary Fund, *World Economic Outlook, Chapter One: the Great Lockdown*, Washington, DC: International Monetary Fund, April 2020, pp. ix, 7.
7 International Monetary Fund, *World Economic Outlook, Chapter One: the Great Lockdown*.
8 World Bank, *Global Economic Prospects, June 2020*, Washington, DC: World Bank Group, 2020, p. 4.
9 World Trade Organization, *Annual Report 2020*, Geneva: World Trade Organization: www.wto.org/english/res_e/booksp_e/anrep_e/anrep20_e.pdf
10 Nouriel Roubini, A Greater Depression? *Project Syndicate*, March 24, 2020: www.project-syndicate.org/commentary/coronavirus-greater-great-depression-by-nouriel-roubini-2020-03?barrier=accesspaylog
11 John Maynard Keynes, *The General Theory of Employment, Interest and Money*, Beijing: Huaxia Publishing House, 2004, p. 124.
12 When Krugman talked about the uncertainty of Trump's trade policy, he thought it was a fall in the mean, not a rise in the variance. See Paul Krugman, Tariff Tantrums and Recession Risks: Why Trade War Scares the Market So Much, *The New York Times*, August 7, 2019. However, if we distinguish between "risk" and "uncertainty," a fall in the expected mean mentioned by Krugman refers to the consequences of increased risk, while the uncertainty caused by unpredictability and insufficient information is more likely to be manifested as a rise in variance.
13 It is noteworthy that Robert J. Shiller had foreseen the bursting of the Internet bubble in 2000 and the fall in housing prices in 2007; and based on the principles of narrative economics, he also warned in advance of the huge market turbulence

caused by a novel coronavirus epidemic. For his narrative economics, see Robert J. Shiller, *Narrative Economics*, *Cowles Foundation Discussion* Paper, No. 2069, New Haven, CT: Cowles Foundation for Research in Economics, January 2017.

14 Angus Deaton, We May Not All Be Equal in the Eyes of Coronavirus, *Financial Times*, April 6, 2020.

15 Mario Draghi, We Must Mobilise as if for War, *Financial Times*, March 27, 2020.

16 Ben Bernanke and Janet Yellen, How the Fed Can Lesson Lasting Damage from the Pandemic, *Financial Times*, March 19, 2020.

17 Claudia Sahm, Direct Stimulus Payments to Individuals, in Heather Boushey, Ryan Nunn, and Jay Shambaugh (eds.), *Recession Ready: Fiscal Policies to Stabilize the American Economy*, Washington, DC: The Hamilton Project and the Washington Center on Equitable Growth, 2019, pp. 67–92.

1 Economic impact of the COVID-19 pandemic

*Li Xuesong, Wang Hongju, Feng Ming,
Li Shuangshuang, and Zhang Binbin*

As the worst global crisis since World War II, the COVID-19 global pandemic is having an unprecedented impact on the global and Chinese economies, leading to a sharp global economic recession and presenting a unique set of challenges for China's economic development. The impact of this epidemic has led to global crisis, which is essentially the crisis of people's livelihoods, and tremendous uncertainty still exists about the future development of the global pandemic—more time is needed for the economy to return to normal.

The mechanism of pandemic spread and the mechanism of economic impact

Mechanism of pandemic spread

The wide spread of the COVID-19 pandemic across the world has made the persistently sluggish world economy even worse, and lack of adequate understanding of emerging viral infectious diseases has made it especially difficult to accurately predict the trend the pandemic will take in the short term. Thus the uncertainties around economic activities and the pandemic itself increase.

Baker et al. (2020) have pointed out that these uncertainties include the power of the virus itself, the availability of antigen and antibody detection, the affordability of the medical system, the development period for an effective vaccine, the final death toll, the social isolation period, the near- and short-term economic impacts of the pandemic, the pace of economic recovery after the pandemic subsides, the continuity of government intervention policy, the extent to which consumption patterns have changed, and medium- and long-term impacts on enterprise survival, innovation, and investment in human capital. The impact of infectious diseases on economic operation is equivalent to adding a quasi-exogenous variable into the economic system, while how this variable itself changes requires sufficient understanding. Therefore, research on the scale of output variables affected by the pandemic requires basic knowledge of pandemic spread.

DOI: 10.4324/9781003184447-2

An epidemic model is used to analyze the spread of infectious diseases. The fundamental work of Kermack and McKendrick (1927) provided a blueprint for the development of the epidemic model. They thought that depending on the circumstances of infection, people can be divided into three major groups: Susceptible, Infected, and Removal. The way out of Removal is either recovery or death, and this will affect the size of the total population. Severity of the disease varies, determining the probability of patients facing death or recovery; the core issue of the epidemic model is to understand dynamic changes in the numbers of people in the three major groups and the main factors influencing the changes.

In their generic, simplified mathematical model, Kermack and McKendrick (1927) assumed that during the outbreak, the difference between birth rate and non-epidemic deaths may not be considered; rather, total population may be regarded as three groups, and in different time intervals, probability of transition among the three conditions is given exogenously. Considering the end of the pandemic, the point at which the continuous transition finally stabilizes needs to be made clear—does the end of pandemic mean there are no uninfected people any more, or that there is a combination of infection, recovery, death, and other factors while many people remain uninfected? If, in the initial population, all uninfected people have the same opportunity of infection, the way to get complete immunity is to experience the illness-recovery process, but the end of pandemic does not necessarily require everyone to be infected: at the given infection, recovery, and mortality rates, the number of infected people will stop increasing at a threshold of population density. Kermack and McKendrick's research focused on the potential threshold leading to the rapid spread of infectious diseases or subsiding from the viewpoint of population density; they did not make straightforward social policy suggestions. Since their analysis of the evolution of the relative number of three groups of people and the influencing factors provided a fundamental perspective for the development of the epidemic model, their model was called the Kermack–McKendrick model or the SIR model.

Due to the generality of the classic SIR model, relaxing its prerequisites or including more factors that might influence pandemic spread or continuity may achieve a richer meaning. For example, in a concise epidemic model that only contains an "uninfected-infected" process, Kremer (1996) relaxed the homogeneity assumption of the initial population when he analyzed the impact of the AIDS epidemic on the behaviors of different groups based on the endogenous setting of spread parameters in the model.

Tassier (2013) introduced special forms of the SIR model, including the SI form, in which only Susceptible-Infected was considered, the SIS form, in which only Susceptible-Infected-Removal was considered, and the addition of population dynamics into the SIR model. He analyzed decision-making and the economic quantitative methods of the private sector and the public sector from the viewpoint of externality caused by infectious diseases.

Wang and Hennessy (2015) took the SIS model as reference when investigating the general optimal policy of government when facing infectious diseases in animals. Since the COVID-19 outbreak, extensions based on the SIR model have been used widely by public health researchers and economists (Atkeson, 2020).

Mechanism of economic impact caused by pandemic spread

Infectious viruses may be spread extensively through human social activities, and this may generate huge negative externality. Government decisions will also inevitably become trapped in the dilemma of saving lives and stabilizing the economy. According to the sequence of the SIR model, if the severity of the pandemic is widely known among the public, the rational Susceptible group will consciously limit chances of interacting with people and reduce economic activities to lessen the possibility of moving from Susceptible to Infected. The Infected will also voluntarily restrict the intensity of their economic activities, even if these are not restricted by government; because of their health conditions and their intention to avoid moving from Infected to Removal, the balanced result is a shrinking of the entire economic activity. Which economic activities are affected in the process of the pandemic's spread and to what extent they will be hit by unforeseen shocks are the concerns of most economists (e.g. Barro et al., 2020; Keogh-Brown et al., 2010; Lee and McKibbin, 2004; Ludvigson et al., 2020).

Besides the sudden shutdown of the personnel-intensive economy during the epidemic, which poses direct short- to medium-term impacts on the economy, if the virus hazard goes beyond what is expected, large areas affected by the pandemic might also suffer medium- and long-term adverse consequences.

From the perspective of the health of human capital, Almond (2006) found that the population that were in gestation during the Spanish flu outbreak had a higher proportion of disability, less educational attainment and income, and lower socioeconomic status in adulthood.

McKibbin and Sidorenko (2013) have pointed out the following effects of a pandemic: since death reduces life span and diseases decrease labor efficiency, labor supply is reduced; investment in human capital decreases alongside lower life expectancy; with the increase of business costs, government financial pressure increases; and a persistent epidemic will influence national savings and investment.

Bell and Gersbach (2013) have warned that if there is a lack of adequate protection, a long-term continuous high mortality rate caused by an epidemic will destroy human capital formation and lead to economic paralysis.

However, Young (2005) thought that it is best not to be too pessimistic after a pandemic. Although AIDS and other infectious diseases have a severe impact on the workforce, this mainly affects workers with relatively low levels of education; also such events encourage people to restrict unhealthy behaviors and learn lessons from the crises.

With respect to the COVID-19 global pandemic, although the precise end point was still unclear as of April 2020, the economics community generally believed that the pandemic spread would add a heavy burden to economic society.

According to Barro et al. (2020), with respect to the impact of the COVID-19 pandemic on economic society, it is helpful to take a glimpse at the destructive power of 1918–1920 Spanish flu pandemic. If applying the mortality rate of the Spanish flu pandemic indiscriminately to the current world population, the most pessimistic scenario corresponds to a shocking death toll.[1] Barro et al. (2020) also showed that the gross domestic product (GDP) of a typical country would drop 6 percent, private consumption would decrease by 8 percent, and economic downturn would be comparable to the 2008–2009 global financial crisis. Although the transnational flow frequency of the current population is far higher than in the 1920s, this does not lead to faster recession due to a pandemic. Modern public health technology, quarantine conditions, etc. are far better now than they were during the Spanish flu pandemic.

However, a questionnaire survey carried out by Bartik et al. (2020) with American small businesses shows that if the results are extrapolated, the damage caused by the COVID-19 pandemic to the economy is far greater than the effects of the Spanish flu pandemic.

Eichenbaum et al. (2020), in a study of the United States, included individual behavior, adequacy of health facilities, government control of the epidemic, expectations for vaccines and specific medicines, and other factors in the extended SIR model. Considering that channels of pandemic spread consist mainly of contact between people at places of consumption, contact at work, and contact during social activities, and considering that the rate of spread of the pandemic will be affected by the scale of infected populations, it is necessary to implement controls for different spread scenarios and different groups at different stages of pandemic development. According to a simulation of the ideal scenario, in the case of accurate implementation of optimal control measures, peak infection rate of COVID-19 will be 0.9 percent of the total population, mortality rate will be 0.2 percent of the total population, and consumption will decrease by 16.8 percent in the first year after pandemic outbreak. If controls are not implemented, although consumption will only decrease by 7 percent at competitive balance, the peak infection rate and the mortality rate will be up to 4.7 percent and 0.4 percent, respectively. Thus, planning how to save more lives and simultaneously stabilize consumption and other economic activities is a challenge for policymakers.

With the wide spread of the COVID-19 pandemic, personnel-intensive economic sectors have been suffering from the shock of emergency shutdown, and most monetary authorities of developed economies rapidly started implementing monetary policy instruments similar to those used to cope with the 2008–2009 global financial crisis.

Using a "Keynesian supply shock" model, Guerrieri et al. (2020) pointed out that a negative impact on the supply side might lead to an excessive reaction on the demand side. Loss of output and unemployment caused by lack of demand will be far greater than the loss of output and employment caused by the shock to the supply side itself—the economic impact brought by COVID-19 in terms of business, employee turnover, and exit of enterprises has such features. Therefore, Guerrieri thought that conventional fiscal policy does not work as well as easy monetary policy and that the optimal strategy is to close the personnel-intensive sector and provide a large payment guarantee to the affected workers.

Faria-e-Castro (2020) thought that the economic shock brought about by the COVID-19 pandemic would be especially negative, leading to a 20 percent unemployment rate in the United States, and that residents who rely on labor income and bank credit would be affected most severely. Considering the externality of aggregate demand, a sudden shutdown of the personnel-intensive service sector would inevitably transfer the decline in economic activity to the non-service sector and financial sector under the action of general equilibrium logic; increased unemployment would lead to a wave of defaults; and damage to the financial system would aggravate the recession. He simulated the effect of fiscal policies in the US non-service sector based on a nonlinear dynamic random general equilibrium model that included increased government purchase, reduced income tax, increased unemployment insurance, implementation of unconditional transfer payments, and wage payments to service enterprise workers by the government. Faria-e-Castro thought that for residential borrowers experiencing the biggest impact on income, increasing unemployment insurance is the most effective instrument, although savers prefer unconditional transfer payments; if the aim is to stabilize employment in the affected sector, then a financial solution that helps increase also works.

Global economic recession and potential series of secondary risks

The COVID-19 pandemic broke out at the beginning of 2020 and developed into a global pandemic rapidly, becoming the most serious global public health crisis in this century and having a major unexpected negative impact on the global economy. Under the influence of the pandemic, the global economy inevitably falls into severe recession. Wide and continuous spread of the epidemic will also trigger a chain reaction, resulting in a series of secondary risks.

Global economic recession under the impact of the pandemic

Before the outbreak of the COVID-19 pandemic, international organizations predicted about 2 percent global economic growth in 2020—this reflects no economic fundamentals leading to global economic recession. However, the sudden outbreak and rapid spread of COVID-19 caused unprecedented quarantine worldwide, and the global economy changed rapidly from being basically stable to being in a rapid recession, evolving into the Great Lockdown crisis, next only to the Great Depression.

The pandemic has had a huge impact on the global economy both on the demand side and the supply side; the real economy in hard-hit countries and regions encountered "shock" impact, which locked down normal economic activities severely; and the global economy fell into recession rapidly. The International Monetary Fund (IMF) predicted that the global economy would fall into a great recession beyond that experienced in the financial crisis in 2008–2009, that it would shrink significantly in the first half of 2020, and that the annual economic growth rate would also change to −4.9 percent, resulting in a great recession with the most extensive scope since the twentieth century and of the deepest severity since World War II.

Because countries took border blockade measures to control the pandemic, the global pandemic has affected international trade activities severely, causing disruption of global staff turnover and goods trading; the global supply chain has been broken, and the already sluggish global trade has become worse. The volume of global trade in 2020 dropped most notably since the global financial crisis in 2008–2009.

With global supply chain disruption and extensive shutdowns worldwide, the COVID-19 pandemic will cause a more serious negative impact on global foreign direct investment (FDI). The United Nations Conference on Trade and Development predicted that global FDI in 2020 would drop 40 percent to below USD 1 trillion for the first time, marking a 15-year low.

The United States, Europe, Japan, and other developed economies sank into a deep recession collectively. As the United States entered the pandemic outbreak, industrial production and services were disrupted, and the economy suffered a severe decline. A recession greater than the Great Depression appeared in the second quarter. The United States launched a massive USD 2.2 trillion fiscal stimulus program and an unlimited quantitative easing program, hoping to ensure the survival of small- and medium-sized enterprises severely affected by the pandemic and to support the unemployed through difficult times. However, in the case of widespread disruption of production and operation activities during the pandemic, these measures could not prevent a sharp economic contraction, and it was thought that the US GDP might decrease even more in the second quarter of 2020, and go into a deep recession. In addition to GDP being in steep decline, surging unemployment is also a challenge for American policymakers. Due to protests by the unemployed, the US government has been eager to restart the economy even though the pandemic itself has not yet been controlled effectively. Undoubtedly, this will place additional difficulty on measures to contain the coronavirus, increasing the risk of an uncontrolled pandemic—the economy might be even harder hit by strict control of the outbreak again. As the epidemic spreads across Europe, coupled with fragile economic fundamentals, the European economy will also suffer significant negative growth. Decline in economic growth will be particularly evident in Italy and Spain where the pandemic has been most severe. The IMF predicted a decline in economic growth of more than 9 percentage points in both countries in 2020 compared to 2019. Japan's economy was originally in the relatively low growth category and will go into a deep recession under the impact of the pandemic.

Sharp decline in the economic growth of emerging and developing economies brings more uncertainties. Although economic contraction of emerging and developing economies will be 2.8 percent in 2020, as predicted by the IMF in the World Economic Outlook in June 2020, premature relaxation of COVID-19 control measures will lead to rapid rebound of pandemic. Brazil's economy will slip back into significant negative growth as the impact of the epidemic continues and merchandise exports drop; economic growth of both Russia and South Africa will decrease greatly, with these countries entering negative growth. India's economic growth has been relatively high in recent years, yet quick spread of pandemic has restricted economic activities, and economic growth will also inevitably enter a large downward phase.

Global pandemic might trigger secondary risks

If the global pandemic continues over a long period, prominent contradictions will aggravate the impact on the global economy and might cause secondary risks and even economic and financial crisis in some countries.

Longer duration of the pandemic will lead to a longer and deeper impact on the economy

Whereas the spread of the pandemic will bring about a larger diffusion effect and a crowding out effect of medical supplies, difficulty of control will increase significantly. In particular, as the pandemic enters a period of rapid spread, even in developing countries with relatively low medical resources, global prevention and control pressure increases greatly. As the vaccine is administered unevenly across the world, the risk of repeated pandemic waves cannot be excluded. Under the background of global pandemic spread and asynchronous periods of pandemic evolution in different countries, economic growth of countries that first experienced the outbreak will also go into passive decrease due to slack demand of other countries, and such passive decrease will last longer if the pandemic continues.

Severe impact on the global supply chain aggravates the periodical ebb of globalization

The evolution of the pandemic varies in different countries. Although the pandemic was inhibited in China, as other countries entered the outbreak period, the broken supply chain could not be repaired in the short term. Individual developed countries are using the pandemic to speed up contraction of their global layout of the industry chain. The pandemic triggers the risk of reconstruction of the global supply chain, as some transnational corporations tend to localize and regionalize production based on risk control and the governments of some developed countries intentionally encourage overseas enterprise backflow with support policies, accelerating localization of the supply chain—this will aggravate the periodical ebb of globalization. In addition, as the global epidemic continues to spread, some countries tighten export trade controls successively on grain, vegetables, and fruits, and raise trade barriers.

Competition between countries impedes global cooperation against COVID-19 and economic recovery

In recent years, significant changes have taken place in the relations among great powers, China–US relations have shifted from cooperation to competition, the opposition of the United States to other allies has become more apparent in the G7, disagreement in the European Union grows with each passing day, and nationalism and splittism are rising extensively worldwide. This has led to a different approach to fighting the epidemic and stabilizing the economy from the active international joint response to challenges during the 2008–2009 global financial crisis—there is now more blame and competition than cooperation among great powers. On the one hand, in international diplomacy involving the great powers, the source of the pandemic has become an object of blame. On the other hand, great powers scramble for epidemic-resistant materials in the international market, benefiting themselves at the expense of their neighbors. Distrust between great powers is rising unprecedentedly at a time when global solidarity is needed most for a joint response to challenges; this is leading to the extremely unfavorable dilemma between epidemic prevention and control and economic stabilization.

Effect of stimulus policies is reduced greatly due to supply chain disruption

On the one hand, interest rate levels in developed countries are already very low, and the global debt level has risen to a record high, so monetary and fiscal policy space for stimulating the economy is limited. On the other hand, fiscal and monetary easing is effective in boosting the economy against traditional economic depression by expanding demand, but the effect of boosting the economy is reduced greatly when normal production and consumption activities are disrupted by the pandemic. In addition, different from the fund flow that was disrupted in the 2008–2009 global financial crisis, which could be solved by capital injection, it is the supply chain that is disrupted in the pandemic, and this could not be solved only by capital injection.

*Continuous spread of the pandemic will trigger financial crisis
and other systematic risks*

The steep decline in enterprise operating revenue and household income restricts solvency significantly, and the financial industry will face great pressure due to debt default. As previously mentioned, the IMF warned that the impact of the pandemic on the financial industry would be comparable to the 2008–2009 global financial crisis. The global financial market has been turbulent since February 2020, massive capital flight has occurred in emerging economies, nearly half of the world's countries have solicited emergency asset support from the IMF, and continuing pandemic spread might lead to financial crisis in some economically and financially fragile emerging economies. Sharp economic recession caused by the COVID-19 pandemic might lead to debt default risk in western European countries due to lack of monetary sovereignty. With significant contraction in demand for crude oil in international markets, oil prices remain low, and petroleum-exporting countries in the Middle East face risk of government financial crisis and sovereign debt crisis. In addition, the United Nations Food and Agricultural Organization sends a warning as more and more countries intend to initiate partial restrictions on grain exports: the world could face a food shortage crisis, and soaring food prices might appear in some countries.

Negative impact of the pandemic on China's economy

A significant drop in economic growth due to the pandemic

After the pandemic outbreak in China, its economy encountered impacts both on the supply side and the demand side; then the global pandemic led to China's economy being impacted by both overseas market demand and domestic demand. China's GDP growth rate was −6.8 percent, an unprecedented drop in economic growth, in the first quarter of 2020. China has successively strengthened grid-based pandemic prevention and control and centralized quarantine measures, shut down some cities, and restricted entry from some countries. Industrial added value decreased greatly due to delayed opening up of factories and reduced production. Hit by the pandemic, entrepreneurs' pessimistic expectations deepened, and demand for investment in fixed assets fell significantly. Consumer demand also decreased greatly, with tourism, transport, entertainment, and sports consumption falling significantly during the Spring Festival. The medical industry ran at full capacity and e-commerce demand increased, but as a whole, consumption and tertiary industries were hit hard.

The negative impact of the COVID-19 pandemic on household consumption was extremely evident in the early stage of epidemic prevention and control. To reduce travel and public gatherings, most consumption activities that take place during the Spring Festival, such as dinners with friends or family and leisure shopping, were cancelled, and were hard to make up for later. At the same time, closure of scenic spots and places of public consumption basically put tourism, movies, karaoke entertainment, and other recreation and entertainment consumption, for which it should have been high season, into stagnation.

Residential and consumer services have also been affected by decreased consumer demand. A large number of catering enterprises whose food orders for Spring Festival were cancelled had already purchased raw materials in advance; this, along with the plus the cost burden of retaining staff, meant that these enterprises have suffered huge losses. Meanwhile, the income from travel agencies, scenic spots, accommodation, and other tourism-related enterprises has fallen sharply; the film industry lost the "golden Spring Festival season," which has repeatedly resulted in new box office records; and in the education sector, the income from winter vacation training has also decreased. In addition, the life service industry, including bathing, beauty treatments, and hairdressing, in which small and micro businesses are dominant, was mostly out of service. In retail, although sales volumes increased for respirators, disinfectants, and other protective articles as well as certain drugs, the cost of "guaranteed supply" of agricultural products, daily necessities, and other consumer goods was high; moreover, there was a drop in sales of clothing, household appliances, and luxuries that are usually in high demand. The overall impact on retail has been very negative. In addition, affected by inconvenient travel between regions and other factors, transport and other producer services have also suffered large negative impacts.

Under normalized pandemic prevention and control in the second quarter, resumption of work and production was quickened in China, and recovery continued on the supply side. However, as control measures remained to some extent, there was a large impact on low-income groups, medium, small, and micro enterprises, and consumption and manufacturing investment. Other demand-side indicators recovered slowly. Thus, economic recovery was unbalanced. From the supply side, industrial production in the second quarter—especially equipment manufacturing and high-tech manufacturing—maintained stable recovery: service production changed from fall to rise, the modern service industry recovered quickly, consumer services recovered slowly, and the digital economy was increasingly developed. From the demand side, consumption continued to decrease in the second quarter, although more narrowly: consumption upgrades and online retail kept strong, but total retail sales of consumer goods did not restore positive growth. Considering that the indicator of total retail sales of consumer goods does not cover household consumption of services, the latter is more affected by epidemic prevention and control measures and may recover more slowly; thus, true recovery of consumer demand is weaker than the statistical data suggests. Affected by the deterioration of the enterprise balance sheet after the outbreak, manufacturing investment in the second quarter has further decreased, though less significantly on a year-on-year basis. The growth rate of investment in high-tech industry and social field changed from fall to rise.

Employment encounters a sudden impact and urban unemployment increases

Since the pandemic exerts a direct impact on consumption, micro, small and medium enterprises are affected, while in the service industry, micro, small and medium enterprises are dominant in terms of employment, closely related to consumption. If rural migrant workers are unable to return to cities after visiting their hometowns, the labor force participation rate decreases, and unemployment becomes a more serious issue.

Urban unemployment reached its highest ever value in February 2020, and since then has remained high, showing prominent contradictions in aggregate employment. Enterprise employment tends to be tight in outlook; entrepreneurship activities have been sluggish, post-stabilizing pressure has increased, and overall labor demand has become weak. Research using focus groups has shown that employment is an important issue for rural migrant workers and fresh college graduates. Re-employment difficulty of rural migrant workers back to cities and unemployed personnel is high, and employment and contract signing of college and university graduates are lagged. Overall progress of rural migrant workers back to cities is tardy, especially migrant workers from non-poor families who are not covered by policies of labor service output and promotion of employment. The proportion not returning to cities is high—nearly half of rural migrant workers in some counties and cities of the western region do not come back to cities from their hometowns. Among rural migrant workers in China, about 135 million lived in urban areas at the end of 2019. Relevant statistics show that nearly 10 percent of rural migrant workers did not return to work at the end of May. This means that nearly 13.50 million rural migrant workers did not come back to cities for work. The scale of graduates of colleges and universities is about 8.74 million in 2020, and the employment signing rate dropped significantly at the end of June on a year-on-year basis, although job selection contract signing activities might be postponed due to epidemic prevention and control, yet the main reason is still insufficient supply of jobs. With respect to industries, work resumption of enterprises was still insufficient in the first quarter. Enterprises and institutions postponed personnel recruitment, restricting the demand for labor force. Innovation and entrepreneurship activities were affected by the pandemic, the quality of many existing innovation and entrepreneurship platform projects was poor, and extinction of some "greenhouse type" innovation and entrepreneurship platforms was accelerated by the impact of the pandemic. Meanwhile, some new positive factors also appeared on the labor market, such as online recruitment, online interviews, and other personnel recruitment methods. Faster person-job fit, online education, financial, science and technology, and high-end services and network retail and other zero contact economies were less affected by the pandemic.

Since the second quarter, emerging manufacturing industries such as 3D printing, smart devices, and charging pile have recovered quickly, but direct employment-driven effect is not strong; clothing, shoes and hats, culture and education, arts and crafts, and other traditional labor-intensive manufacturing industries have recovered unsteadily; artificial substitution technique has been popularized quickly. Overall employment of cloud economy, platform economy and other new business forms as well as high-tech service industry are stable, but demand for labor in service sector of high employment such as catering, entertainment and household management is insufficient. In addition, the pandemic quickens the transformation of employment type and operation mode; competitive advantage of highly skilled workforce becomes more prominent in market.

Food prices rise evidently, structural inflation and deflation coexist

After the outbreak of the COVID-19 pandemic, supply of respirators, disinfectants, and other epidemic prevention articles fell short of demand, and prices rose quickly. Conduction blocks between supply and demand also appeared in some districts for commodities with higher dependence on logistics, such as vegetables, fruits, and meat. Consumers faced a rise in the price of vegetables and meat, and it became difficult to buy these products, yet producers faced inventory overstock and it was difficult to sell these products. Affected by the pandemic, demand for most services, such as catering, accommodation, tourism, transport, and movies, dropped dramatically, and equilibrium price fell sharply, having a price but no sales.

After the global pandemic, price trends become more complicated. After lockdown of cities and countries in some European and American developed countries, the international aviation industry suffered a great toll, international demand for crude oil reduced greatly, and negotiation between Saudi Arabia and Russia for production curtailment broke down, so the price of crude oil slumped. China's external dependency on crude oil imports is above 70 percent; the drop in price of international crude oil drove a drop in the price of crude oil and downstream chemical products in China. The pandemic has intensified countries' risk awareness and economic sovereignty awareness, and agricultural exporters including Russia and Vietnam restricted grain exports and stepped up the pressure of grain price rise in China.

In the first quarter of 2020, general prices in China had typical structural characteristics. On the one hand, affected by the rise in food prices, such as pork, in the first quarter, Consumer Price Index (CPI) was still at a high level; on the other hand, core CPI, Producer Price Index (PPI), and GDP deflator that may characterize the state of macroeconomy in a better way were sluggish. Core CPI in February and March 2020 was only 1.0 percent and

1.2 percent, respectively, more than that in the same period of last year; PPI decreased by 0.4 percent and 1.5 percent, respectively.

As epidemic prevention and control has been stable in China, general price increase fell back after March 2020. Increase of the core CPI on a year-on-year basis was kept at a low level. The main reasons for the fallback of the rise in CPI are as follows. First, the pandemic impact on production and intermediate links declined sharply and production and logistics recovered quickly, while recovery of consumption was slow due to social risk aversion and oversupply appeared on many products—recovery of consumption in relation to dining out, tourism, accommodation, transport, offline entertainment, and other services was especially lagging. Second, the price of pork passed over its cyclical peak in February 2020, and changed from a rise to a fall. It was predicted that the carry-over effect of the fall in pork price would continue to exert downward pressure on CPI in the second half of the year. Third, supply of epidemic prevention articles such as respirators and disinfectant increased, while demand decreased; the short supply at early stages of pandemic no longer existed, so price returned to normal. Although the decrease in PPI on a month-on-month basis narrowed, the decrease on a year-on-year basis was significant. While price decreases grew in major industries, industrial fields faced obvious structural deflation risks.

Trade declines sharply, international market share rises by stages

With the global pandemic, many countries took entry restriction measures—international economic and personnel exchanges decreased significantly, overseas demand decreased noticeably, export decreased, import of intermediate goods faced risk of supply chain disruption. According to customs statistics, in the first quarter of 2020, China's total volume of trade in goods decreased by 8.4 percent on a year-on-year basis: exports decreased by 13.3 percent; and imports decreased by 2.8 percent. Trade surplus was USD 13.2 billion, based on import and export offsetting, a marked decrease of 81.9 percent compared with the same period in 2019. According to the statistics of the State Administration of Foreign Exchange, China's trade deficit in services from January to February 2020 was USD 32.6 billion, 24.8% lower than the same period last year. Since cross-border movement of people was restricted by the pandemic, some countries took restrictive measures like stopping visas, suspending air or shipping services, cancelling exhibitions, and keeping personnel exchanges with China in a suspended state. Outbound travel makes up the highest proportion of China's services trade deficit, with international travel disruption and outbound travel deficit decreasing significantly. The scale of productive services trade also decreased with the decrease in goods trade.

In the second quarter of 2020, China's total imports and exports decreased significantly. With respect to quarterly changes, China's export growth in the second quarter decreased less significantly than in the first quarter, import growth decreased more significantly than in the first quarter, and recessionary trade surplus expanded. Main reasons include, first, that some exports of China to developed countries in the first quarter were postponed, to be delivered in the second quarter, and that accelerated restart of the economy in developed countries also temporarily increased some demands. Second, China's pandemic control and its resumption of work and production were better than the international community in the second quarter of 2020, and this was helpful for some Chinese products as they could substitute some products normally provided by countries hard hit by the pandemic during the shutdown in the international market. Third, the pandemic temporarily increased demand from foreign countries for Chinese medical supplies and equipment. In the second quarter of 2020, export of Chinese plastic products, textiles, and medical devices relating to epidemic prevention increased by more than 50 percent on a year-on-year basis; total stimulation of export growth was about 5 percentage points. Fourth, normalized epidemic prevention and control in China in the second quarter reduced the import demand for means of production and means of livelihood. The United States intensified the technical examination and blockade of China, and imports of equipment and technologies urgently needed for Chinese high-tech industry showed negative growth continuously. It is noteworthy that in the context of significant decrease in global trade in the second quarter, the decrease in China's exports was lower than the global decrease, and thus China's share in the global export market increased by stages—while dependency of China on the external world decreased, the dependency of the external world on China increased.

Duration of the pandemic is still a dominant influence on future impacts

The economic depression caused by the pandemic is different from traditional economic depression. Government bailouts may relieve people's livelihood difficulties, but normal monetary stimulus do not work well. After the outbreak, loan growth slowed, new household loans decreased, growth of money supply and savings deposits increased, reflecting a slow velocity of money, insufficient demand for household loans, and pessimistic expectations for future income under epidemic prevention and control.

In March 2020, the epidemic prevention and control improved continuously in China, resumption of work and production sped up, and decreases in main economic indexes noticeably improved. Compared with January and February, China's negative economic growth was better than expected in the first quarter; overall economic and social development was stable. Rural areas and agricultural production were less affected by the pandemic, and the cybereconomy, emerging service industries relating to the digital economy, and the financial industry kept growth. In the first quarter of 2020 for China, added value of primary industry decreased by 3.2 percent, added value of secondary industry decreased by 9.6 percent, and added value of tertiary industry decreased by 5.2 percent. The decrease in scale of primary industry and tertiary industry was lower than for secondary industry. With the added value of information transmission, the software and IT service industry and the financial industry increased by 13.2 percent and 6.0 percent, respectively. But a considerable gap existed between the data on the production side and the expenditure side, and problems caused by epidemic prevention and control, such as poor circulation of production, income and expenditure, and insufficient effective demand, were still very prominent. Future economic development still depends on the effect of domestic and foreign pandemic duration and control.

At the end of June 2020, the international pandemic was not well controlled internationally, and the spread accelerated: the world was in a new dangerous phase. From April to May 2020, the number of newly confirmed cases in the world per day fluctuated within the range of 70,000 to 110,000. The global pandemic accelerated again in June: the number of newly confirmed cases per day rose rapidly, up to about 170,000 to 190,000 per day; at the end of June, the total confirmed COVID-19 cases in the world exceeded 10 million. There were several reasons for this. First, anxious deblocking and resumption of work and production in some districts of the United States, plus rallies in some districts, led to explosive growth of new cases. Second, fast growth occurred in the number of newly confirmed cases in South American countries, such as Brazil and Mexico, and in developing countries, such as India. Further accelerated spread of the pandemic in foreign countries meant that the epidemic curve of new cases had not yet reached its apex and was rising far beyond the original expectation.

In the second quarter of 2020, China's economic growth was better than growth of developed countries, but development of the pandemic internationally and the global economic depression in the second half of the year would bring severe challenges to China's economy. First, the global pandemic continued to worsen quickly; in the medium term, China's merchandise exports were affected by international economic depression and international blockade, and demand from developed countries and emerging markets for China's traditional labor-intensive products slackened. Short-term growth of medical supplies exports relating to epidemic prevention and control could not make up for the medium- and long-term downward pressure of general merchandise exports. In the second quarter, China's merchandise exports relating to interpersonal interaction, including Coke and cigarettes, and labor-intensive products, such as shoes and hats, clothing, bags and cases, as well as steel, containers, and washing machines, decreased greatly, which reflected the negative impact of international slack in demand for China's exports. Second, due to the large population in developing countries and a relative shortage of medical resources, accelerated pandemic spread might lead to humanitarian disaster and consequences that are hard to predict in these countries, and these factors might lead to COVID-19 becoming a long-term worldwide epidemic disease. This could compel China's normalized epidemic prevention and control to evolve in the long term, beyond the initial expectations. Production and lifestyles will change. Third, the global pandemic could exacerbate the staged reversal of globalization and de-sinicization.

The pandemic presents a unique set of challenges for China's economic development

While the global economy fell into a deep recession, China's economy could not detach itself from the interconnected world, and the global pandemic has presented a unique set of challenges for China's economic development.

Real economy suffers from external demand shock, uncertainties in economic growth increase

The outbreak epidemic curve for pandemic spread in developed and developing countries has wave characteristics; testing technology, medicines for prevention and treatment, and vaccine development are changing quickly. These factors bring high uncertainty to the future development of the pandemic internationally. As a highly contagious virus, the global pandemic triggered by COVID-19 might exist for a long time, evolving into a seasonal epidemic disease. We should remain on high alert for wave development of the pandemic, as well as subsequent global economic depression, and prepare a long-term plan. Against this background, uncertainties increase in China's economic growth significantly in the second half of 2020 and year round.

Higher risk of disruption to the import supply chain, prominent problems of enterprise supply chain security

In China's foreign trade structure, intermediate goods trade has accounted for 60–70 percent of imports for a long time, and above 40 percent of exports. Due to the outbreak of the pandemic in the United States and Europe, quite a few enterprises stopped production and shut down, leading to a severe impact on China's import supply chain from those areas.

The United States, Germany, and France, among other countries, are at the upstream of China's industry chain in mechanical equipment, automobile-building and shipbuilding, power-generating equipment, aviation space flight, precision instruments, medical devices, pharmaceutical chemicals, and other fields that supply some important raw materials and parts. If the pandemic lasts long, China's import supply chain will face risk of disruption.

Quick adjustment of global industry chain layout, increasing relocation pressure for enterprises

With the combined impact of a new round of industry revolution and techno-logical change, there has been an adjustment of industrial strategic layout in developed countries and various "anti-globalization" forces: developed countries are using the pandemic to shrink their degree of participation in the global value chain, return mid to high end manufacturing links to their home country, and transfer mid to low end links to Southeast Asia, Africa, Eastern Europe, and elsewhere. The important position of China in the global industry chain is being weakened gradually, and the pressure for enterprises to relocate too rapidly has increased. The global pandemic further exacerbates this trend. Following the pandemic impact, the United States now attaches more importance to phrases like "Made in the USA" and "Buy American." In accordance with the National Emergencies Act and the Defense Production Act, backflow of some industry chains, especially the medical industry chain, is set to go ahead.

With the impact of the pandemic, some industry chains, once broken, might not recover. For a long-term consideration of business stability, some transnational corporations might adjust their China-oriented production chains so as to reduce their dependence on a single supplier and source of supply. Under the dual influence of the pandemic and Sino–US economic and trade frictions, some influential multinational enterprises, including BMW and Apple, are considering adjusting or planning to adjust their spatial layout of global purchase, production, assembly, and sales.

Poverty alleviation becomes more arduous, the issue of re-poverty is more prominent

The main task at the latter stage of poverty alleviation in 2020 was to address poverty of the approximately 5.5 million people who make up the remaining poor population—this is the group for which it is most difficult to end poverty. The global pandemic has become another major risk factor on top of existing poverty factors, and it might push some groups already out of poverty back into poverty again, and possibly generate an amplification effect. Mopping up and consolidation of achievements in poverty alleviation face more challenges simultaneously.

First, global recession will compress investment in social poverty alleviation, and it will be more difficult to achieve this aim. Second, poor populations will have fewer opportunities to participate in the market and increase income. The existing income increase mechanism cannot be consolidated, and the channel for the poor to get out of poverty through employment is squeezed. Contraction of overseas market demand reduces work opportunities for the rural labor force. Some poverty alleviation projects and workshops might be postponed and even aborted. Third, household consumption becomes more prudent, cultural consumption such as rural tourism is suppressed, and employment income of poor families decreases correspondingly. Demand for characteristic poverty alleviation products shrinks and restricted exports compels capacity compression, which influences the cash flow of poor households directly.

Significantly fewer employment opportunities, noticeably higher employment pressure on specific groups

Export enterprises face large-scale chargeback and denial of orders due to the pandemic. Due to loss of exports in the manufacturing industry and related industries, employment challenges will change from "no person to work" at the early stage of the pandemic to "nothing to do" at a later stage. The impact of global recession on exports might lead to a tide of unemployment in Chinese foreign trade enterprises; ordinary manufacturing workers and rural migrant workers will face very high employment pressure. Local blocking or breaking of the supply chain might lead to risk of an employment landslide for the whole industry chain.

Even the recovery of service and construction industries in China to a large extent cannot quickly offset the loss of employment in foreign trade enterprises. The pandemic will also weaken the capability of the service industry to provide new employment and industrial transfer employment. After the outbreak of the pandemic, quite a few enterprises have cancelled annual recruitment plans, and the employment problem—especially the pressure for employment of fresh college graduates—has increased. External environmental deterioration has led to sluggish jobs growth, and this will also increase the complexity of labor disputes, employment discrimination, and other problems.

Drastic shock in global financial market, sudden change in external financial environment

Due to the global pandemic, global stocks, bonds, foreign exchange, and commodity markets are in a turbulent period. The historical four "fuses" occurred in the American stock market. A 20–40 percent drop occurred in stock markets in the United States, Europe, and Japan as well as in emerging market countries. International oil prices dropped from 55 dollars/barrel to below 25 dollars/barrel. Funds gathering in safe assets accelerated, an emblematic yield on the 10-year treasury note dropped to below 1 percent, and the scale of global negative interest rate bonds further expanded.

In contrast, China's financial market is relatively stable: at the end of March 2020, the Shanghai Composite Index dropped only 12 percent compared to before the outbreak. On the one hand, the negative impact on China's capital market caused by the spread of panic in global markets could hardly be avoided. Asset prices of some industries and enterprises affected seriously by the pandemic have plummeted, and a high level of attention is needed to prevent financial risks. On the other hand, due to staggered domestic and foreign epidemic prevention and control, RMB assets might show staged risk off, plus a lot of liquidity released in quantitative easing by central banks in the United States and Europe. Overseas funds might speed up their flow into the market within a period, presenting new challenges to cross-border capital management and the RMB exchange rate policy.

Note

1 In the most severe cases, a mortality rate of 2 percent of the population in 2020 represents the death of 150 million persons globally (see Barro et al., 2020).

References

Almond, D. (2006). Is the 1918 Influenza Pandemic Over? Long-Term Effects of in Utero Influenza Exposure in the Post-1940 US Population. *Journal of Political Economy*, 114(4), 672–712.

Atkeson, A. (2020). *What Will be the Economic Impact of Covid-19 in the US? Rough Estimates of Disease Scenarios.* National Bureau of Economic Research Working Paper Series, No. 26867.

Baker, S. R., Bloom, N., Davis, S. J., and Terry, S. J. (2020). *Covid-Induced Economic Uncertainty*. National Bureau of Economic Research Working Paper Series, No. 26983.

Barro, R. J., Ursúa, J. F., and Weng, J. (2020) *The Coronavirus and the Great Influenza Pandemic: Lessons From the "Spanish Flu" for the Coronavirus's Potential Effects On Mortality and Economic Activity.* National Bureau of Economic Research Working Paper Series, No. 26866.

Bartik, A. W., Bertrand, M., Cullen, Z. B., Glaeser, E. L., Luca, M., and Stanton, C. T. (2020). *How are Small Businesses Adjusting to Covid-19? Early Evidence from a Survey*. National Bureau of Economic Research Working Paper Series, No. 26989.

Bell, C. and Gersbach, H. (2013). Growth and Enduring Epidemic Diseases. *Journal of Economic Dynamics and Control*, 37(10), 2083–2103.

Eichenbaum, M. S., Rebelo, S., and Trabandt, M. (2020). *The Macroeconomics of Epidemics.* National Bureau of Economic Research Working Paper Series, No. 26882.

Faria-E-Castro, M. (2020). *Fiscal Policy During a Pandemic*. Federal Reserve Bank of St. Louis Working Paper Series, No.2020-006D.

Guerrieri, V., Lorenzoni, G., Straub, L., and Werning, I. (2020). *Macroeconomic Implications of Covid-19: Can Negative Supply Shocks Cause Demand Shortages?* National Bureau of Economic Research Working Paper Series, No. 26918.

Keogh-Brown, M. R., Smith, R. D., Edmunds, J. W., and Beutels, P. (2010). The Macroeconomic Impact of Pandemic Influenza: Estimates From Models of the United Kingdom, France, Belgium and the Netherlands. *The European Journal of Health Economics*, 11(6), 543–554.

Kermack, W. O. and McKendrick, A. G. (1927). A Contribution to the Mathematical Theory of Epidemics. *Proceedings of the Royal Society A*, 115(772), 700–721.

Kremer, M. (1996). Integrating Behavioral Choice Into Epidemiological Models of Aids. *The Quarterly Journal of Economics*, 111(2), 549–573.

Lee, J. and McKibbin, W. J. (2004). Globalization and Disease: The Case of SARS. *Asian Economic Papers*, 3(1), 113–131.

Ludvigson, S. C., Ma, S., and Ng, S. (2020). *Covid-19 and the Macroeconomic Effects of Costly Disasters*. National Bureau of Economic Research Working Paper Series, No. 26987.

McKibbin, W. and Sidorenko, A. (2013). Global Consequences of Pandemic Influenza. In M. Fullilove and A. Bubalo (eds.), *Reports from a Turbulent Decade,*

10th Anniversary Collections, The Lowy Institute for International Policy, Penguin, 244–246.

Tassier, T. (2013). *The Economics of Epidemiology*, SpringerBriefs in Public Health, Springer.

Wang, T. and Hennessy, D. A. (2015). Strategic Interactions Among Private and Public Efforts When Preventing and Stamping Out a Highly Infectious Animal Disease. *American Journal of Agricultural Economics*, 97(2), 435–451.

Young, A. (2005). The Gift of the Dying: The Tragedy of Aids and the Welfare of Future African Generations. *The Quarterly Journal of Economics*, 120(2), 423–466.

2 COVID-19's impact on agriculture, rural areas and farmers and countermeasures

Wei Houkai and Lu Qianwen

Since the outbreak of novel coronavirus ("COVID-19" for short), through tireless efforts, epidemic prevention and control of the situation has become better and better in China. The first pandemic peak has passed in China, but the epidemic has been spreading fast outside the country. China faces an increasing risk of infectious disease outbreaks from imported cases; normalized epidemic prevention and control measures will have to remain in place for a long time. The COVID-19 pandemic and its prevention and control measures have made a big impact on normal economic and social functioning and the stability of global industry and supply chains. They have also influenced agricultural and rural development, peasant work, and social order, and they have increased difficulty of achieving the goals of poverty alleviation and building a moderately prosperous society in all respects in rural areas. As a whole, the impact of the COVID-19 pandemic on agriculture and rural areas is less pronounced than that on other industries and cities. In the first quarter of 2020, the added value of primary industry in China decreased by 3.2 percent. Its decline was the lower than that in secondary and tertiary industries.[1] However, due to the weak foundation of agricultural and rural development, and the quality of rural businesses, and more potential risks to farmers' income, the COVID-19 pandemic has exerted greater influence on rural tourism, sales of agricultural products, supply of agricultural materials and other rural service industries as well as rural employment, rural infrastructure, and public service construction. Therefore, in the precondition of scientific and accurate rural epidemic prevention and control, we should restore agricultural and rural economic order, stabilize employment of rural migrant workers, make efforts to increase farmers' income, speed up poverty alleviation and construction of infrastructure and public services, ensure completion of building of a moderately prosperous society in all respects, and guarantee overall poverty alleviation.

The impact of the pandemic on agriculture, rural areas, and farmers

The spread of the COVID-19 pandemic has caused fear and panic, and prevention and control measures, such as strict control of traffic, village and road

DOI: 10.4324/9781003184447-3

closures, shutdown of production, and prohibition of group gatherings, have also significantly influenced ongoing production and operation, employment, way of life, and entertainment. Under the COVID-19 pandemic, activities that are more labor-intensive and which rely more on mobility of the population and gatherings or have higher material circulation were affected more severely, and the duration of the effect will not diminish with suspension of control measures, but will emerge gradually. Although epidemic prevention and control are improving all the time in China and economic and social order recovered quickly, worldwide spread of the pandemic continues, and normalized epidemic prevention and control measures are required to prevent importation of pandemic cases to China. In this context, the impact of the COVID-19 pandemic on agriculture, rural areas, and farmers will be comprehensive, deep, and continuous. In agriculture, new types of agricultural businesses, agricultural production services, agricultural factors, and supply of fresh and live agricultural products will be affected significantly, leading to the rise of agricultural production costs and higher operating risks. For farmers, migrant work will be hindered, unemployment risk will increase, the slowdown of income growth is inevitable, and the income of some groups will decrease. In rural areas, industrial development will be impacted heavily, the implementation of poverty alleviation projects and the progress of infrastructure construction will be postponed, and a shortage of public service capacity to protect against public safety events will be exposed by the outbreak. During the outbreak, local governments and some rural businesses actively took measures against the impact of the pandemic, such as promoting accelerated development of new industry, new business forms, and new modes, thereby alleviating the impact to some degree.

Agricultural production keeps stable as a whole, but operating risk increases

When strict epidemic prevention and control measures have been taken in different places, field agricultural production has usually been in "off-season." The agricultural production affected has been the relatively active plantation of "shopping basket" products or aquaculture and poultry in season, as well as in production and operation activities of new types of agricultural businesses. With respect to the impact of the pandemic on agricultural production, China has taken measures to restore production in a timely manner, ensuring the normal supply of agricultural products. These measures include strict implementation of the "green channel" system, provincial governors' responsibility for the "rice bag" (i.e. grain supply), and mayors' responsibility for the shopping basket system; printing and distribution of guidelines for spring farming; and quickening resumption of production in enterprises upstream and downstream of the aquaculture and poultry industries, solving overstock of poultry and aquatic products and "marketing difficulties." These measures have stabilized agricultural production, facilitated spring farming, spring seeding, and spring management, provided abundant supply in the agricultural product market, and guaranteed national grain security. In 2020, the sown area of summer grain crops was stable, the per unit area yield increased somewhat, and the total summer grain output continued to grow.[2] However, epidemic prevention and control measures have had a big impact on the input and marketability of agricultural production factors; worldwide continuous spread of the pandemic has led to higher risks to the world economy, more instability and uncertainties in the domestic supply of agricultural factors, the price of agricultural products, and the operation of the agricultural chain. As a whole, agricultural production costs will increase and income will decrease in the short term, and the agricultural production order and agricultural product supply will maintain overall stability in the long term; however, agricultural businesses will face greater risk.

Investment in agriculture, forestry, animal husbandry, and fishery decreases significantly

During epidemic prevention and control, some agriculture infrastructure and operation construction projects were stopped; factor mobility, material supply, and product sales were negatively affected; and investment in agriculture, forestry, animal husbandry, and fishery decreased significantly. According to data from the National Bureau of Statistics of China, from January to March 2020, investment in the fixed assets of agriculture, forestry, animal husbandry, and fishery (excluding rural households) decreased by 16.1 percent year-on-year (YoY) in China.[3] The main decline occurred in January and February, when investment in the fixed assets of agriculture, forestry, animal husbandry, and fishery decreased by 24.7 percent YoY: investment in agriculture decreased by 31.9 percent, investment in forestry decreased by 17.4 percent, investment in animal husbandry decreased by 7.7 percent, investment in fishery decreased by 41.9 percent, and investment in professional and auxiliary activities of agriculture, forestry, animal husbandry, and fishery decreased by 18.5 percent. The decrease in investment has hit fishery and agriculture more than other industries, with decreases of 17.4 percent and 7.4 percent more than the average decline of investment in fixed assets in the same period, respectively. This shows that the impact of the COVID-19 pandemic on investment in fishery and agriculture is especially serious. In January and February, private investment in the fixed assets of agriculture, forestry, animal husbandry, and fishery decreased by 26.3 percent in China; the decline was 1.6 percent higher than that of total investment in the fixed assets of agriculture, forestry, animal husbandry, and fishery.[4] With effective control of the pandemic, investment in agriculture, forestry, animal husbandry, and fishery has been restored gradually in different places: the decline has narrowed rapidly, and growth has become evident. From January to May 2020, investment in fixed assets of agriculture, forestry, animal husbandry, and fishery (excluding rural households) showed an increase of 1.8 percent YoY in China; within this figure, investment in fixed assets of animal husbandry increased by 35.3 percent, but investment in agriculture and forestry fishery decreased to different degrees.[5]

New types of agricultural businesses face operation difficulties

Compared with small rural households, family farms, farmers' cooperatives, and other new types of agricultural businesses have large scale and great strength, surpassing traditional agricultural production cycles. Factor products are traded frequently and so are affected by epidemic prevention and control measures more easily. Rural village and road closures prohibited workers from gathering and stopped entry of non-villagers, directly restricting the trading of factors and products of new types of agricultural businesses.

The proportion of small rural households in slack season is 51.74 percent, and the proportion of new types of agricultural businesses in slack season is 18.8 percent. Correspondingly, daily production and operation activities of 81.2 percent of new types of agricultural businesses have been affected by the pandemic,[6] as have the daily production and operation activities of 68.6 percent of family farms,[7] mainly in the form of restrictions for employees but also restricted supply of agricultural materials and affected product sales. As a result, new types of agricultural businesses have faced cash flow difficulties, and many normal business activities have become hard to sustain, trapped in business distress. Aided by the resumption of work and production, new types of agricultural businesses have recovered production activities gradually. New types of agricultural businesses are facing a long period of operation difficulties.

Greater impact on sales and price of fresh and live agricultural products

During the rapid spread of the pandemic in China, some fresh and live agricultural products were unsaleable, and businesses suffered heavy losses. Most agricultural products in the shopping basket, including vegetables, meat, eggs, milk, fish, and fruit, are sold as soon as they are produced. During closures of rural villages and roads, production shut down; most urban and rural livestock, poultry slaughtering, live poultry trading, catering places and trade markets were shut down. In turn, supply and demand of fresh and live agricultural products that would normally be in shopping season were disrupted—sales were severely affected. As farmers could not sell products in the short term, they had to bear losses and even kill livestock and dump animal products to prevent losses. According to a survey, 6.3 percent and 27.3 percent of livestock farms encountered rejection and limited purchase of raw milk, respectively, and 86.7 percent of farms saw price reductions for raw milk. Due to rejection and limited purchase or difficulty of transport, 12.5 percent of livestock farms had to dump milk. At the end of February

2020, average loss per head in the surveyed farms reached 476 Yuan.[8] Under normalized epidemic prevention and control, although all-around measures have been taken, comprehensive recovery to normalcy still needs time.

Though affected by the COVID-19 pandemic and the African swine fever as well as other factors, the price of agricultural products did rise significantly at one point during the outbreak. According to data from the National Bureau of Statistics of China, from January to March 2020, there was a price rise in food, tobacco, and alcohol of 14.9 percent YoY, of which the price rise in fresh vegetables was 9.0 percent and the price rise in livestock meat was 80.8 percent; within the latter, the price rise in pork was 122.5 percent, the price rise in beef was 21.0 percent, and the price rise in mutton was 11.2 percent. However, from a monthly perspective, the price of main agricultural products decreased in March on a month-on-month basis, although the YoY price index still increased continually. Yet price of fresh fruit decreased by 5.6 percent YoY from January to March.[9] Price of eggs was also falling, now hitting the bottom, facing dull sales and marketing difficulties. With the recovery of production operation, transport, logistics and distribution, etc., transportation and marketing of agricultural products has recovered gradually. Especially when driven by livestream e-commerce, online retail rose rapidly, connecting production and marketing of agricultural products.

Agricultural production costs increase due to restricted service provision

Both small rural households and new types of agricultural businesses outsource their uneconomical links, such as agricultural machinery operation, agricultural material transport and distribution, agricultural product marketing and transport, and agricultural technical service, to agricultural service providers. During village and road closures, agricultural productive services were affected severely because service could not be provided normally in villages or across regions. Most agricultural shops, agricultural product and material carriers, and agricultural machinery service providers stopped their services. According to a survey, about three quarters (75.65 percent) of agricultural service providers were affected by the pandemic and could not provide normal services, 30.22 percent of whom stopped services due to worry about the pandemic and 27.11 percent of whom stopped cross-region services due to restricted transport.[10] During the spread of the pandemic, service costs increased due to inability to hire workers and purchase agricultural materials normally, and inability to provide services normally. Just over three quarters (76.3 percent) of service organizations stated there was an increase of total costs to different degrees.[11] The increased costs of agricultural service providers were transferred to agricultural businesses along with the additional cost of epidemic prevention measures; agricultural production costs in season would increase. According to a survey, during the outbreaks the average increase of total production costs of family farms was 22.9 percent, and the total costs of more than 70 percent of the farms increased by 20 to 40 percent.[12] At present, agricultural production order is recovering quickly, but under normalized epidemic prevention and control, the impact of the pandemic on provision of agricultural services and on agricultural production and operation always exists to a greater or lesser degree—this made the increase in agricultural production costs in 2020 inevitable.

Emergence of new business forms and models with a proactive response to the pandemic accelerates

Facing the impact of the epidemic, many agricultural businesses and service providers took active measures to reduce operating loss. In order to relieve the impact of the pandemic on agriculture, local governments encouraged agricultural businesses and service providers to innovate production operation models, maintain agricultural production and operation order, and quicken the generation of new business forms and models. First, businesses needed to speed up popularization of the direct selling model for new agricultural products. Agricultural product transportation and marketing enterprises in many places adopted online order placement and offline contactless delivery, established a direct link between urban residents or communities and agricultural businesses, and solved the marketability problem of fresh and live agricultural products. Second, businesses needed to accelerate the development of e-commerce models for new agricultural products. During the spread of the pandemic, logistics interruption and the closing of online shops led to dull sales for some local agricultural products. After logistics were restored, people actively adopted new e-commerce models, such as live video selling, to speed up the sales of unsaleable agricultural products, so as to support farmers. Third, businesses needed to promote the trustee model for agricultural production. Many local agricultural service providers signed service agreements with rural households online, provided uniform agricultural services, and utilized video platforms for live broadcasts of work processes, so as to avoid direct contact with rural households and to ensure work quality and increase yield and efficiency. Fourth, they had to show the advantages of agricultural service networks or systems. Local service providers with a complete network or system, such as a supply and marketing cooperative system, play a prominent role in the supply of agricultural materials as well as the transportation and marketing of agricultural products and maintenance of agricultural production order. These new changes show new trends of modern agricultural development. The impact of the pandemic forms a reverse pressure and promotes penetration and integration of modern agricultural production models and traditional agriculture.

Increasing farmers' income and social order are affected to different degrees

In different parts of China, there were closures of cities, villages, roads, etc. during the lunar Spring Festival. Most rural migrant workers, traders, and students returned to their hometowns. With sustainable epidemic prevention and control measures, normal social order, production and operation activities and employment behaviors of rural residents were impacted to different degrees. Under normalized epidemic prevention and control, these impacts will last for varied periods, so rural residents face uncertainty in terms of income increases and even notable risk of income decrease.

Rural migrant workers are hindered from returning to work, unemployment pressure increases

To prevent and control the epidemic, the Spring Festival holiday was extended, and resumption of work and production was postponed. Resumption of production was postponed for 10 days in over 20 districts of China, and the normal production time of most enterprises was compressed significantly.[13] At the same time, malls, stores, catering facilities, entertainment venues, and factories not essential for everyday life were required to close down, transregional traffic and population movement was restricted, and home quarantine measures were implemented strictly for the floating population. Thus, quite a few migrant workers could not return to work as scheduled; there was a long period of waiting for jobs and joblessness, and unemployment was inevitable. Rural migrant workers are mainly employed in small and micro businesses and individual businesses in which resumption of work and production was more difficult and happened more slowly; plus there was a low employment stability of rural migrant workers and a high proportion of flexible employment. Thus, the degree of impact of the pandemic was significantly higher for this group than other employment groups. According to monitoring data from the Ministry of Industry and Information Technology, as of February 26, 2020, the work resumption rate of small and medium-sized enterprises was just 32.8 percent,[14] while the work resumption rate of large and medium-sized enterprises at that time approached 80 percent. As of March 29, the work resumption rate of small and medium-sized enterprises reached 76.8 percent.[15] Compared with large and medium-sized enterprises, resumption of work and production in small and micro businesses clearly lagged. As of March 7, 2020, 78 million rural migrant workers returned to work in China, accounting for only 60 percent of the rural migrant workers who returned to their hometowns during the Spring Festival.[16] As of May 24, nearly 10 percent of rural migrant workers had not returned to work in China.[17] Considering the progress of resumption of work and production and the quarantine time required for rural migrant workers before returning to work in different places, rural migrant workers generally lost 30 to 60 days of work in 2020 compared to normal years; if unemployment risk is taken into account, the job-waiting time of some rural migrant workers might have been longer. More importantly, with impact of the pandemic on the macroeconomy becoming more and more evident, as well as the disturbance caused by the global pandemic on the normal order of the global industry chain and supply chain, labor-intensive industries at the low end of the global industry chain and supply chain will be affected first. These are the industrial fields in which most rural migrant workers are hired, so rural migrant workers will face greater employment pressure, and their unemployment risk will also increase significantly. At present, some export-oriented industrial parks and machining towns and enterprises have encountered cancellation of orders or a substantial drop in new orders. From January to March 2020, China's total exports decreased by 11.4 percent YoY.[18] In April and May, although total exports increased by 8.2 percent and 1.4 percent YoY, respectively,[19] amplitude was obviously less than that in the same period in 2019.

Growth of farmers' income declines, risk of decreased income intensifies

Finally, the impact of the pandemic on agricultural production operation and rural employment is reflected in income changes among rural residents. Under the impact of the pandemic, a decrease in income of rural residents will be inevitable, income in individual industries of different sources will decrease, and the risk of income decrease will be unavoidable for some groups. In the first quarter of 2020, per capita disposable income of rural residents actually decreased by 4.7 percent; the average monthly income of migrant workers from rural areas decreased by 7.9 percent.[20] According to Ye Xingqing et al. (2020), at the beginning of the outbreak, a substantial number of farmer households faced income decline. They estimated that the nominal growth rate of year round per capita wage income of rural migrant workers might decrease by 1.45 to 2.46 percent, and the nominal growth rate of per capita disposable income of rural residents might decrease by 2.59 to 3.59 percent.[21] In another survey,[22] rural households estimated the impact of the pandemic on annual income in mid-February 2020; only 1.38 percent of the households thought annual income could keep up with previous growth, and over three quarters (76.8 percent) thought annual income would decrease by more than 5 percent (see Figure 2.1). Specifically, the more severe the outbreak is, the more deeply the households are affected—new types of agricultural businesses and non-agricultural businesses would be affected more deeply, as would agricultural cash crop cultivation and livestock and poultry and non-agricultural consumer services. From late February 2020, local governments promulgated measures to promote resumption of work and production, and the impact of the pandemic on farmers' income was lessened gradually. However, resumption of work and production needs to be a process, taking into account changes in epidemic development. The basis for the sustainable increase in farmers' income is weakened; we should be on high alert to the

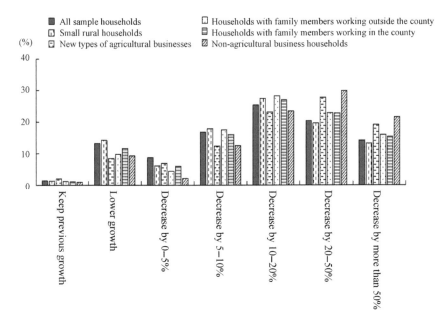

Figure 2.1 Estimated impact on annual income of different types of rural households.

Source: Online survey by the Rural Organization and System Research Team at the Rural Development Institute, Chinese Academy of Social Sciences, February 11–14, 2020

risk of decreased income for this group. Under normalized epidemic prevention and control, affected by uncertain factors in the macroeconomy and foreign trade, the risk of decreased income of rural migrant workers evidently surpasses those who work locally.

Farmers' temporary consumption declines sharply, and daily consumption is suppressed

During the Spring Festival, most outgoing personnel return to their hometowns and visit relatives and friends and dine together—traditional activities are intensive, and it's the shopping season for rural residents. After epidemic prevention and control measures were taken, rural festival activities were halted and most farmers stayed at home, reducing temporary consumption significantly during the festival. Affected by the risk of decreased income, daily consumption might be suppressed for a long time. First, short supply and price rises occurred for meat and vegetables. In recent years, rural traffic and food retail have developed rapidly. Spring Festival shopping[23] custom fades away, and fresh and live agricultural products that cannot be stored easily are bought for immediate use. Therefore, due to short supply, price rises occurred on some fresh and live agricultural products after village and road closures and restriction of transport. According to data released by the National Bureau of Statistics of China, from January to February 2020, rural consumer prices rose by 6.3 percent YoY, 1.3 percent higher than in urban areas; the price rise was mainly driven by price rises of livestock meat and fresh vegetables and other foods: the price rise of rural livestock meat was 90.0 percent YoY, and the price rise of rural fresh vegetables was 13.3 percent YoY.[24] But things changed in March: on a month-on-month basis, rural consumer prices decreased by 1.3 percent, 1.0 percent, and 0.9 percent in March, April, and May, respectively: the price of livestock meat, eggs, fresh vegetables, fresh fruits and other foods decreased a on month-on-month basis, and the price in May of aquatic products rose by 1.3 percent on month-on-month basis.[25]

Second, temporary consumer demand during the festival fell sharply. With the restrictions on mobility of rural personnel and gatherings, and due to the interruption of transport logistics and production shutdown, temporary consumption triggered by festival activities declined sharply. This was due specifically to three conditions: the hindrance of cross-village, cross-region supply of processed food, live poultry, fresh eggs, live fish, fresh milk, and fruits that require immediate processing, transportation, and distribution, leading to passive reduction of rural residents' consumption; for epidemic prevention and control, visiting relatives and friends was generally prohibited in rural areas, so consumption of drinks, fresh flowers, toys, eggs and milk, snacks, and other gifts decreased; party banquets, recreation, and entertainment activities were suspended, thus consumption of corresponding catering and accommodation dropped dramatically. According to data released by the National Bureau of Statistics of China, due to the pandemic, retail sales of consumer goods in rural areas decreased by 17.7 percent YoY from January to March 2020, then decreased by 7.7 percent YoY in April, and by 3.2 percent YoY in May; there was an overall decrease of 13.0 percent YoY from January to May.[26] From January to March 2020, the per capita consumption expenditure of rural residents was 3,334 Yuan, a decrease of 5.4 percent YoY (a decrease of 10.7 percent after deducting the price factor).[27]

Third, daily consumption might be suppressed for a long time. Compared with income and consumption levels of urban residents, overall income and consumption levels of farmers are a bit low, and during the risk period for income decrease caused by the pandemic, daily consumption will be suppressed. Mainly lifestyle and entertainment consumption, as opposed to consumption of necessities, will decrease significantly—this will affect, for example, high-quality meat, eggs and milk, fresh vegetables, organic agricultural products, and leisure travel. Rural low-income groups will be vulnerable, and they might struggle and face food shortages when their income is affected.

It is more difficult to remedy the "shortcomings" of rural areas in the building of a moderately prosperous society in all respects

It's emphasized in the China No. 1 Central Document of 2020 that the last bastion of poverty alleviation must be conquered, and outstanding shortcomings in the key areas of agriculture, rural areas, and farmers must be remedied in order to build a moderately prosperous society in all respects. The outbreak of the pandemic and sustained strict control measures delayed the progress in some areas and affected works to realize the target tasks, and it also exposed weak links in infrastructure and public services in the rural governance system and showed that governing capacity needs to be modernized. Thus it is more difficult to achieve the building of a moderately prosperous society in all respects and overall poverty alleviation in rural areas.

Rural industrial development suffers a big hit

Rural industry revitalization is critical to overall rural revitalization and the basis for sustainable and stable income growth for farmers. To promote rural industry revitalization, we should acknowledge the leading role of new types of businesses and service providers and fully promote deep integration of modern high-efficiency agriculture with secondary and tertiary industries. While prevention and control measures affect new types of businesses and non-agricultural industry development most evidently, time is needed for recovery, consolidation, and enhancement. First, the development of new types of businesses and service providers will be affected. Under the impact of the pandemic, new types of agricultural businesses and service providers will go through a rough patch; non-agricultural businesses will not be spared either, and they might even suffer a greater loss due to missing the most important business season in the year (see Figure 2.2).

Second, rural non-agricultural industries will recover slowly. Rural non-agricultural industries have developed rapidly in recent years. In particular, the leisure travel industry, healthcare for the elderly, and other consumer services of new business forms and new models have emerged as new drivers of rural industry revitalization. Due to the pandemic, rural catering facilities, accommodation, leisure, sight-seeing, and entertainment venues have been suspended, and work resumption in processing and transportation businesses has been postponed. Since most rural businesses are small and micro businesses and individual businesses, and with the difficulty of recovering consumption of urban and rural residents—such as dining out, tourism, and leisure—in a short time, the resumption progress of work and production in rural non-agricultural industries will be slower than the overall progress in urban and rural areas, and the rough period will last longer.

Third, channels for bringing industry sinking and factors the countryside will be impeded. Integration of urban and rural industries and bringing urban high-quality factors to the countryside rely on organic connection of

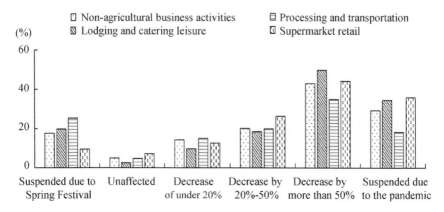

Figure 2.2 Affected non-agricultural business activities of households and their operating income in February 2020.

Source: Online survey by the Rural Organization and System Research Team at the Rural Development Institute, Chinese Academy of Social Sciences, February 11–14, 2020

urban and rural industry chains. Epidemic prevention and control measures lead to interruption of urban and rural transport, factor mobility, and productive services, influence normal operation of urban and rural industry chains, and interrupt the already connected urban and rural industry integration and factor sinking channels. Meanwhile, under the impact of the pandemic and with a background of short supply of factors in the overall macroeconomy, rural industry development will face greater constraints of funds, talent, services, technologies, etc. This will influence rural industrial development at a later stage of the pandemic.

Postponed progress of rural infrastructure projects

In rural areas, the lagged water, electricity, road, network, living environment, and public service infrastructures are notable shortcomings for a moderately prosperous society in all respects. After the outbreak, rural production shutdown measures postponed infrastructure construction projects that were already under way or about to commence. During epidemic prevention and control, resumption of these projects faced multiple difficulties, and the general lack of capacity influenced overall progress of rural infrastructure construction.

Difficulty in epidemic prevention. Most rural construction businesses are local or nearby micro, small, and medium-sized enterprises. These generally face shortages of supplies for epidemic prevention and also lack capacity in this respect. People gathering after recovery of construction increases pressure on epidemic prevention and increases cost expenditure.

Difficulty in employment. According to a survey, about 20 percent of villagers are worried about the pandemic and stopped working in the fields and going out for work or non-agricultural business.[28] This creates employment challenges for rural businesses. Project construction businesses also face employment challenges; in particular, it is difficult for non-local technical personnel and project management personnel to return to work.

Difficulty in transport. When transport is restricted for the purpose of epidemic prevention and control, the green channel for rural material transport is mainly for agricultural materials, agricultural products, and necessities; this does not include building materials, apparatus, etc. required for project construction. During epidemic prevention, many villages just "ban" all persons and vehicles that do not belong to their own villages and implement policy of keeping the main roads open but denying access to the villages.

Difficulty in funds. Micro, small, and medium-sized construction businesses lack funds. As the pandemic continues, the wages of hired labor and transport costs in rural areas will increase significantly; the price of raw materials might also rise. Undoubtedly, this will increase financial pressure. Under impact of the pandemic, economic and financial revenues in most places show negative growth; in the local general public budget in China from January to May 2020, revenue decreased by 10.4 percent YoY,[29] while financial expenditure pressure increased. There is a huge financing gap for rural construction and resumption of production, which will influence financial investment levels for rural infrastructure construction, which in turn will affect progress of follow-up infrastructure projects.

Emerging shortage of rural public service capacity

The outbreak exposed weak links in rural public services that were not fully considered previously.

Shortcomings of rural public health service capacity. Although township hospitals and village clinics are generally present, the level of medical facilities available, the disease prevention and control system, and the professional quality and serviceability of personnel are obviously insufficient to cope with an epidemic.

Shortcomings of rural social mobilization capacity. At the early stage of the outbreak, primary organizations mobilized villagers mainly via traditional broadcast loudspeakers. This imperfect rural emergency response mechanism responds slowly to public safety events, and it is not linked to the main way villagers receive information. According to a survey, villagers gather information about the epidemic mainly via network media (88 percent) and broadcast television (63 percent), clearly more prevalent than receipt of information via the village loudspeaker (23 percent).[30] The construction of a rural social mobilization system has been neglected for a long time. Organization for such a system, including procedure setting, staffing, and setting up equipment and facilities for social mobilization, is practically nonexistent.

Shortcomings of rural infrastructure management capacity. After the outbreak, due to village and road closures and worry about infection, waste
transfer, and toilet maintenance were affected in many villages, and this led
to waste accumulation and unusable toilet in villages. This reveals the insufficient operation and maintenance capability of rural infrastructures.

Shortcomings of primary organizations' use of new media. Use of online
social media platforms and smartphones has been highly popularized in
rural areas, reaching deep into all aspects of villagers' lives. But few primary
organizations actively utilize online platforms to carry out relevant activities,
mainly because of lack of awareness and ability.

Difficult new challenges for poverty alleviation

It is still a tough battle to lift the remaining 5.51 million poor out of poverty
and to uncap 52 poor counties and 2,707 poor villages in 2020.[31] A sudden outbreak brings new difficulties and challenges for poverty alleviation. Although
the pandemic is not serious in poverty-stricken areas, due to the weak industrial base and lack of endogenous driving force, consolidation of the results of
poverty alleviation is urgent. This outbreak will undoubtedly further increase
the difficulty of getting rid of poverty and the risk of repoverty.

First, it affects increases in income among the poor population and those
who have just risen out of poverty from migrant work. According to statistics
from the State Council Poverty Alleviation Office, 27.29 million poor laborers
went out to work in 2019 in China, and about two thirds of the income of
their families came from migrant work, involving about two thirds of the
poor population.[32] Thus, continual increase of employment income is of great
importance to get rid of poverty. The outbreak meant that some of the poor
had to remain at home and could not go out to work. As of March 27, 2020,
more than 20 million poor laborers in 25 provinces of China went out to work,
5 million poor laborers did not go out to work for the time being, 5.6 million
poor laborers were willing to go out to work, and 2.1 million laborers in 52
poor counties still in poverty went out to work, accounting for 83 percent of
the number of migrant workers in 2019.[33] The global pandemic will add to
the impact of pandemic and international trade deterioration and influence
industry sectors that create more jobs for the poor population, so migrant
work opportunities for the poor population will become unstable and they
will face higher risk of decreased income. Statistics show that the rural labor
force in poverty-stricken areas obtained significantly less wage income than
normal in February 2020, but benefited from the return to work and ability to
go out to work organized by local governments as a priority. Per capita wage
income of rural residents in poverty-stricken areas reached 1,192 Yuan in the
first quarter of 2020, a nominal growth of 0.3 percent, but the growth rate was
10.6 percent lower than that in the same period of 2019.[34]

Second, the outbreak restricts stimulation of industry development for
poverty alleviation. Most industry projects for poverty alleviation involve

characteristic agricultural products, which should be sold immediately after being produced and have high dependency on external market and service support. During epidemic prevention and control, since people's mobility and logistics and production services were negatively affected, consumer demand dropped substantially, some characteristic agricultural products of poverty-stricken areas appears became unsaleable, and the benefits of industry projects for poverty alleviation declined. Poor households themselves have weak operating capacity and will face more serious difficulties from service shortages and lagging sales, and more difficulties in recovery. Per capita net business income of rural residents in poverty-stricken areas was 1,037 Yuan in the first quarter of 2020, a nominal growth of 0.1 percent, of which per capita net business income of secondary and tertiary industries was 339 Yuan, a nominal decrease of 10.4 percent.[35]

Third, the outbreak postponed the resumption/commencement and construction progress of poverty alleviation projects. During epidemic prevention and control, due to restrictions on mobility of people and logistics, some poverty alleviation projects were in shutdown or lacked the capacity to operate and could not proceed as planned. Under dual pressure of epidemic prevention and control and poverty alleviation, government departments and two committees representing the villages in poverty-stricken areas have insufficient organizational strength to maintain partner assistance and east/west collaboration for poverty alleviation as normal.[36] This will slow the progress of poverty alleviation projects. According to data released by the Joint Prevention and Control Mechanism of the State Council on April 1, 2020, 22 provinces in the midwest arranged 370,000 poverty alleviation projects; 220,000 of them commenced, but the operating rate was only 60 percent.[37] This was far lower than the operating rate of over 98 percent for industrial enterprises above designated size in China.

Fourth, the outbreak increases the risks that the population already out of poverty will go back into poverty and that people who are near-poor will fall into poverty. According to preliminary investigation in different places, nearly 2 million people in the population emerging out of poverty face the risk of going back into poverty, and nearly 3 million people in marginalized populations face the risk of falling into poverty.[38] Among the districts already out of poverty, some have a weak industrial base and only a single, unstable channel to increase income. Thus, the impact of the pandemic will undoubtedly increase risks of falling back into poverty or falling into poverty for the first time. In particular, in areas of extreme poverty that have just been lifted out of poverty, and where industry development is just starting, farmers' income source is not yet stable, and they are particularly sensitive to external impacts. The impact of the pandemic might lead to a premature end of industry development and decreased household income. We should be on high alert for areas that may fall back into poverty, or fall into poverty for the first time, due to the pandemic. It should be pointed out that under the strong support of government policies, poverty alleviation work has returned to normal gradually. As of May 31, 2020, 27.5 million poor laborers in 25 provinces went out to work, accounting for 100.79 percent of the total number of migrant workers last year; 2.7 million laborers in 52 supervised counties went out to work, accounting for 107.45 percent of total migrant workers last year; 22 provinces in midwest China arranged an operating rate of poverty alleviation projects up to 89.9 percent; the work resumption rate in poverty alleviation enterprises was up to 98 percent; and the work resumption rate of poverty alleviation workshops was up to 98.6 percent.[39]

Countermeasures for Epidemic Control to Support Agriculture, Rural Areas, and Farmers

Requirements for securing a decisive victory in building a moderately prosperous society in all respects and alleviating poverty will not be weakened because of the impact of the pandemic. Since the outbreak, General Secretary Xi Jinping has emphasized many times that we should set out a unified plan for epidemic prevention and control and economic and social development, make efforts to realize annual economic and social development target tasks, secure a decisive victory in building a moderately prosperous society in all respects, and win a decisive battle against poverty alleviation.[40] To make this happen, we must set out a unified plan for epidemic prevention and control and agriculture, rural areas and farmers. We should introduce overall policy measures, give priority to developing agriculture and rural areas comprehensively, prioritize meeting the requirements of human, financial, and material resources for poverty alleviation and remedy of rural shortcomings, vigorously promote increase of income for farmers from employment and entrepreneurship, go all out to compensate losses caused by the pandemic, and complete poverty alleviation and building a moderately well-off society in rural areas as scheduled. We should look from the present and take a long-term perspective, paying attention to the aspects described in this section to deal with the impact of the COVID-19 pandemic on agriculture, rural areas, and farmers in the context of scientific and accurate rural epidemic prevention and control.

Multiple policies to quicken rural industrial development

Having achieved positive results in terms of epidemic prevention and control, governments from the central to local should take measures towards unified planning for future epidemic prevention and control and economic development, restoration of economic order, and reduction of the negative impacts of the pandemic. At present, agricultural and rural economic order has basically been restored in China. We should formulate and implement policy measures to support development of agriculture and rural industry and to help rural businesses pull through. We should create a good development environment by stabilizing and stimulating investment in agriculture and rural industries, and inject more power into rural industrial development under normalized epidemic prevention and control.

Restore agricultural and rural economic order as soon as possible

We need to embrace a new development concept unswervingly, deepen structural reform on the agricultural supply side, restore agricultural production and rural business activities in different districts at different levels, and quickly restore agricultural and rural economic order corresponding to epidemic prevention and control. We should adjust and optimize prevention and control measures in the resumption of work and production according to local conditions, and we should cancel emergency prevention and control measures that were taken at an early stage but are incompatible with current restoration of production and social order. While maintaining required prevention and control materials and emergency response capacity, we should restore the flow of rural workers, logistics, and funds; ease the employment, funding, and raw material supply issues of rural businesses; strengthen epidemic prevention guidance services for rural businesses; establish normalized epidemic prevention and control mechanisms that can be adapted to agricultural production and rural business activities as soon as possible; strengthen production and market operation scheduling of important agricultural inputs; guarantee spring farming, seeding, and management and year round supply of agricultural materials for agricultural production; formulate unified planning of production development, marketability, circulation transport, market regulation control, quality safety, and other works; and strengthen technical support services and solve production bottleneck problems in a timely fashion.

Ensure grain security and supply of major agricultural products

With the global COVID-19 pandemic, many countries have been "closed," and some countries have promulgated policies to restrict and even prohibit the export of agricultural products such as grain. In response, we should adhere to the national grain security strategy: "we take the initiative, based on [the] domestic market, ensure capacity, import properly, supported by science and technology"; implement a system in which the provincial governor takes responsibility for grain security; fully mobilize grain growing by farmers and grain collection by local government; stabilize the area for sowing of grain and the yield; increase comprehensive productivity and quality of grain; and improve the efficient and effective supply of grain. Meanwhile, we should implement a system in which mayors take responsibility for shopping basket products, guaranteeing stable supply and stable market price for agricultural products such as meat, eggs, milk, aquatic products, vegetables, and fruits. In particular, we should implement measures for prevention of an African swine fever epidemic; stabilize and increase confidence in poultry businesses; provide more policy support in relation to fiscal matters, taxation, finance, insurance, land, etc.; and promote fast recovery and development of the live pig industry and go all out to guarantee effective supply in the pork market.

Promote quick development of new types of agricultural businesses

On the one hand, while helping new types of agricultural businesses to restore capacity and get through the rough patch as soon as possible, we should also improve their risk response capability and overall competitiveness; provide support measures in fiscal matters, credit, guarantees, insurance, etc.; offset operating losses caused by the pandemic; prevent a flood of bankruptcies caused by capital chain rupture; take effective measures to improve operator quality and capability of new types of agricultural businesses; and address nonstandard management, incomplete systems, and other problems associated with new types of agricultural businesses. We should guide new types of agricultural businesses to adjust and optimize production structure; sign medium- and long-term transfer contracts with rural households; popularize interest distribution methods such as physical object renting currency settlement, dynamic rental adjustment, pooling of land as shares and guaranteed dividends; form stable land rent, protect the lawful rights and interests of both parties of the transfer.[41]

On the other hand, we should quicken the development of agricultural productive services; mobilize stronger service providers to provide united, standardized, professional services; give critical support to key aspects such as providing centralized seedlings, mechanized transplanting, and managed services for agricultural production such as agent seeding and transplanting, and agent plowing and planting; strengthen professional services in aspects of nutrition, breeding, veterinary services, big data application, etc.; popularize new models such as online contract signing and live broadcast supervision services; and promote the role of collective economic organization and farmers' cooperative organization for connecting rural households. We should organize the cross-region work of service providers; ensure unimpeded roads and smooth connections; and address the insufficient capacity of agricultural machinery in some districts. We should subsidize services in different links or provide tax cuts and exemptions so as to solve the problem of increased service costs caused by the pandemic.

Speed up cultivation of new industries and new business forms and models

We should grasp the opportunities brought about by emerging new industries and new business forms and models after the outbreak; develop rural industries to enrich local people; target key links of the industry chain; strengthen whole agricultural industrial chains; form competitive industry clusters; promote integrative development of rural primary, secondary, and tertiary industries; and add new power to rural industry revitalization. We should encourage employment, entrepreneurship, and innovation in hometowns; provide more convenient policy and service support for entrepreneurship by those who return to and remain in hometowns; and improve employment capacity of rural new industries and new business forms for people nearby. We should support sales enterprises to unite with production bases; integrate high-quality resources on the production end; form complete agricultural industrial chains that are highly efficient and have smooth connections; popularize recycle agriculture with combined farming and animal husbandry; cultivate a model of online sales and offline distribution; expand new industries such as rural tourism, leisure agriculture, and healthcare for the elderly; and create more economic value for farmers.

Create a good environment to promote investment in rural industries

Stable investment is critical to steady growth. To offset the impact of pandemic, we should create a good development environment; promote and stimulate investment in rural industries; enhance the confidence of investors; and stabilize agricultural and rural economic growth. With respect to the current pandemic, we should set special support policies for new types of businesses and service providers; further extend tax incentives; offer loan support; postpone renewal periods; promulgate reduction and exemption policies for fees for rental, water, electricity, gas, etc.; and cancel redundancy requirements for small and micro businesses and for individual businesses to acquire policies. In combination with the construction of rural comprehensive service centers, we should integrate the service force of town/township governments and primary organizations; provide policy advice and project application, resource connection, tax payment, accounting agency, and other services for rural businesses; and reduce their operating costs and development resistance.

Do everything possible to increase farmers' income sustainably

The loss of income due to the pandemic is irretrievable. To ensure sustainable increase of farmers' income, we must speed up income growth for this group on the basis of stable income sources. This requires creation of conditions for stable employment and re-employment of outgoing rural migrant workers; more employment opportunities for rural migrant workers who stay in their hometowns; support to increase agricultural and non-agricultural business benefits; and effective guarantees for extremely poor group and groups that have suffered heavy losses under the pandemic.

Stabilize employment income of rural migrant workers

In current and future periods, stable employment support policy should focus on migrant worker groups to strengthen the connection between output area and input area of rural migrant workers. We should provide point-to-point, district-to-district, one-stop transport work; eliminate unreasonable travel restrictions; and help rural migrant workers return to work or find new jobs as soon as possible. Employment incentives should be promulgated to support employment of rural migrant workers, encouraging employers to employ rural migrant workers through project support, tax cuts and exemptions, purchase services, etc. We should support the employment of disadvantaged groups; create jobs in poverty-stricken areas; launch employment training programs for rural migrant workers to promote job transfer; strengthen dynamic employment monitoring of rural migrant workers; and provide support for rural migrant workers to safeguard their rights and interests, preventing wage arrears and other infringements.

Expand nearby and local employment opportunities

In rural areas, we should establish public welfare jobs, such as cleaner, plumber, trackman, eco-ranger, with a labor force from low-income and poor families and marginalized groups. We should provide special rewards for family farms, large and specialized agricultural family operations, farmers' cooperatives, and agriculture-related enterprises that offer more jobs during the pandemic, linking support policy with employment. We should provide more training for new types of farming and encourage rural migrant workers who are willing to go back home to run a business. To encourage nearby and local independent entrepreneurship, we should increase support for property tax, financing, etc. of rural entrepreneurship and simplify approval processes and provide business coaching.

Promote the role of policy in stabilizing income

We should expand subsidies for grain producers; increase agricultural support protection subsidies; adjust and optimize subsidy structures; improve new types of agricultural subsidies oriented to high-quality green development; and improve the income incentive role of agricultural support and protection policy. We should target new types of agricultural businesses and service providers; provide temporary subsidies for businesses or links that have significant effect on stable yield and efficiency improvement; lead small rural households to adopt modern agriculture; and share increment income of agricultural chains. We should explore incentive mechanisms against emergency events. Rewards should be provided for rural residents who participate in epidemic prevention and control. We should provide subsidies for rural low-income groups by issuing coupons in some places to guarantee basic living standards for farmers in difficulties, and we should incentivize rural products and services so as to expand rural consumer demand effectively.

Strengthen efforts to remedy shortcomings in building a moderately prosperous society in all respects

The key to remedying shortcomings in rural infrastructure and public services is to quickly catch up on the work delayed by pandemic as well as noting work needed to address new shortcomings exposed by the pandemic. This needs more human, financial, and material resources. Therefore, we must centralize more resources; fully utilize the rural migrant workers still in hometowns to speed up rural infrastructure and public service projects; and consider enhancing rural epidemic prevention and control capacity and other public safety resources as a whole.

Speed up rural infrastructure construction

To formulate unified planning of COVID-19 pandemic prevention and control and stable economic and social development, central government has decided to speed up the construction of major projects and infrastructure in national planning. Currently, agriculture infrastructure, rural public service facilities, information facilities, and living environment facilities are weak links, and the state should provide support in the form of investment and policy as a priority. In relation to agriculture infrastructure, we should provide critical support to high-quality farmland construction, updating of irrigation and water conservancy facilities, standardized animal housing construction, etc. so as to lay a foundation for quick recovery after the pandemic. In terms of rural public services, we should list the shortcomings in public health service facilities and integrated emergency capacity exposed by epidemic prevention and control as critical elements for rural infrastructure construction. In terms of rural living environment, construction of village roads, underground pipe networks, waste and sewage treatment facilities should be high on the agenda. In relation to information provision in rural areas, we should speed up the construction of agricultural big data platforms and smart agriculture and smart village facilities. In addition, we should also quicken the progress of infrastructure projects under construction; encourage collective economic organization and farmers' cooperatives to undertake the projects that may be constructed by villages independently; explore independent construction of "home entry" facilities by rural households; guide the participation of stranded rural migrant workers; increase the operation management capacity of rural infrastructure; establish specialized, normalized operations management teams; and cultivate public welfare service organizations.

Quickly remedy the shortcomings of rural public services

Rural public services represents a serious shortcoming in building a moderately prosperous society in all respects, while rural emergency management is a shortcoming within this. Therefore, in the unified planning for epidemic prevention and control and economic and social development, we should focus on enhancing rural integrated emergency capacity. First, increase rural public health service capacity. We should establish rural emergency material reserves systems, improve rural public health service systems, strengthen rural public health team building. Second, improve rural emergency organization systems. We should strengthen linkage and coordination among departments. As part of this we should define functional assignment of counties, towns/townships, and villages—using a three-level linkage mechanism, construct "unified planning at county level, [a] responsibility system at town/township level, dominant action at village level." We should also promote sinking of key emergency management works. Third, intensify rural safety risk prevention. There are many disasters, accidents, conflicts, and disputes in rural areas, and we should establish plans for early warning of rural emergency; this would involve risk survey and safety protection for different types of emergency events according to their features and driving factors. Fourth, improve rural disaster rescue systems. We should establish special fiscal relief funds and mobilize the market to participate in rescue systems, and we should form an interactive disaster rescue system including government, enterprise, and market. Fifth, improve the ability of primary organizations to use new media applications. In combination with construction of service platforms at village level, we should popularize Internet information platforms; encourage primary organizations to provide public services via new media; promote integration of rural governance with new media; and improve governing capacity of primary organizations.

Implement policies in a unified way to realize poverty alleviation targets

To win the fight against poverty as scheduled is a solemn promise of the Party Central Committee to the whole nation, an important basis for implementing a rural revitalization strategy, and also a baseline requirement for building a moderately prosperous society in all respects. To address the adverse impact of the pandemic on poverty alleviation, we should consider village conditions and implement policy according to the district and local requirements; formulate unified planning for epidemic prevention and control and targeted poverty alleviation; quicken the progress of poverty alleviation projects; complete remaining poverty alleviation tasks to a high standard; improve the quality of poverty alleviation actions; and realize poverty alleviation goal as scheduled.

Complete remaining poverty alleviation tasks to a high level

In poverty-stricken areas, we must grasp both epidemic prevention and control and poverty alleviation, and formulate unified planning and connections.[42] While strengthening epidemic prevention and control, we should restore production and social order quickly; comprehensively complete remaining poverty alleviation tasks to a high standard; and make efforts to minimize the impact of pandemic. Further, we should focus on the "three regions and three prefectures" and other areas of extreme poverty; increase funding and policy support; provide extra funds to districts more heavily affected by the pandemic; actively create conditions to promote resumption of work and production in rural dilapidated house transformation, irrigation, and water conservancy projects as well as in other enterprises and poverty alleviation workshops; encourage key resumption enterprises to hire poor laborers as a priority; help poor laborers return to local and nearby jobs; transfer employment through multiple channels; access opportunities for more national investment in pandemic control and for laborers currently staying at home; implement and start one batch of poverty alleviation projects quickly; help the remaining poor rural population out of poverty and end poor counties; and concentrate on fighting extreme poverty.

Enhance stability and sustainability of poverty alleviation

Preventing back to poverty and new poverty is critical to improving the quality of poverty alleviation and fundamental to the fight against poverty. To improve the quality of poverty alleviation comprehensively, for the poor population already out of poverty, we should keep continuity of policies for a certain period, making sure that although they are out of poverty, they are still supported—help people to get on their feet and then support them for a time; intensify support after relocation for poverty alleviation by improving poverty alleviation based on industry, employment, and support for ambition and wisdom; form competitive long-term poverty alleviation as well as a long-acting mechanisms of sustainable and stable income growth and poverty reduction; enhance self-development capacity among the population out of poverty; eliminate the sources of back to poverty and new poverty; further strengthen monitoring and early warning of populations at risk of back to poverty or becoming new poor; formulate timely and appropriate support policy; establish dynamic support mechanisms to prevent back to poverty and falling into poverty; and realize sustainable poverty alleviation.

Notes

1 Coordinated epidemic prevention and control and economic and social development achieved remarkable results, with decline in major economic indices narrowing significantly in March, National Bureau of Statistics of China, April 17, 2020: www.stats.gov.cn/tjsj/zxfb/202004/t20200417_1739327.html
2 The summer harvest is a foregone conclusion, *Farmers' Daily*, June 16, 2020, page 1.
3 National investment in fixed assets (excluding rural households) decreased by 16.1 percent from January to March 2020, National Bureau of Statistics of China, April 17, 2020: www.stats.gov.cn/tjsj/zxfb/202004/t20200417_1739329.html
4 National Database of the National Bureau of Statistics: data.stats.gov.cn/easyquery.htm?Cn=A01
5 National Database of the National Bureau of Statistics: data.Stats.Gov.cn/easyquery.htm?Cn=A01
6 Online survey by the Rural Organization and System Research Team at the Rural Development Institute, Chinese Academy of Social Sciences, February 11–14, 2020.

7 Family Farm Development Monitoring Research Team at the Institute of Rural Development, Chinese Academy of Social Sciences, *Impact of COVID-19 on Family Farm Production and Management and the Countermeasures*, Research Report of the Think Tank of the Chinese Academy of Social Sciences on Urban-Rural Integration, 3rd issue, 2020.

8 Liu Changquan, Wang Shukun, and Han Lei, *The Impact of COVID-19 on Dairy Farming in China and the Countermeasures*, Research Report of the Think Tank of the Chinese Academy of Social Sciences on Urban-Rural Integration, 3rd issue, 2020.

9 Household consumer price increased by 4.3 percent YoY in March 2020, National Bureau of Statistics of China, April 10, 2020: www.stats.gov.cn/tjsj/zxfb/202004/t20200410_1737879.html

10 Online survey by the Research Team on Rural Organization and System, Rural Development Institute, Chinese Academy of Social Sciences.

11 Zhang Ruijuan and Dong Ying, The impact of COVID-19 on agricultural socialized service organizations, *China Development Observation*, issue 3–4, 2020.

12 Family Farm Development Monitoring Research Team, *Impact of COVID-19 on Family Farm Production and Management and the Countermeasures*.

13 Zhang Weihua, Deputy Director of the Industry Department of the National Bureau of Statistics, explains the profits of industrial enterprises, National Bureau of Statistics of China, March 27, 2020: www.stats.gov.cn/tjsj/sjjd/202003/t20200327_1735115.html

14 Ban Juanjuan and Zhong Yuan, Resumption rate of work and production in small and medium-sized enterprises exceeded 30 percent, a new round of policies to help small, medium and micro businesses will be implemented, Xinhua Net, February 28, 2020: www.Xinhuanet.com/politics/2020-02/28/c_1125636614.htm

15 Che Kemeng, Ministry of Industry and Information Technology, Work resumption rate of small and medium-sized enterprises in China reached 76.8 percent, *People's Daily Online*, March 30, 2020: finance.people.com.cn/n1/2020/0330/c1004-31654104.html

16 Zhang Yi, Unemployment rate rises under impact of the pandemic, implementation of coordinated policies will improve the employment situation, National Bureau of Statistics of China, March 16, 2020: www.stats.gov.cn/tjsj/sjjd/202003/t20200316_1732415.html

17 In the first four months of this year, 3.54 million new urban jobs were created, and more than 90 percent of migrant workers returned to work, China News Net, May 24, 2020: backend.Chinanews.com/cj/2020/05-24/9193227.shtml

18 Coordinated epidemic prevention and control and economic and social development achieved remarkable results, decline in major economic indices narrowed significantly in March, National Bureau of Statistics of China, April 17, 2020: www.stats.gov.cn/tjsj/zxfb/202004/t20200417_1739327.html

19 In April, the main indicators of national economic performance continued to improve and showed positive changes, National Bureau of Statistics of China, May 15, 2020: www.stats.gov.cn/tjsj/zxfb/202005/t20200515_1745627.html; in May, the national economy continued to recover, National Bureau of Statistics of China, June 15, 2020: www.stats.gov.cn/tjsj/zxfb/202006/t20200614_1760155.html

20 Personal income and consumer spending in the first quarter of 2020, National Bureau of Statistics of China, April 17, 2020: www.stats.gov.cn/tjsj/zxfb/202004/t20200417_1739334.html

21 Ye Xingqing et al., Assessment of the impact of COVID-19 on agricultural and rural development in 2020 and recommendations for response, *Issues in Agricultural Economy*, 3rd issue, 2020.

22 Online survey by the Rural Organization and System Research Team at the Rural Development Institute, Chinese Academy of Social Sciences, February 11–14, 2020.

23 In the past, the custom of "New Year goods" in rural areas was strong. After entering the late lunar month, people would prepare sufficient food for family daily life and entertaining relatives and friends from New Year's Eve to the fifteenth day of the first month or even the second day of the second month of the second lunar year.

24 National Database of the National Bureau of Statistics: data. Stats. Gov.cn/easyquery.htm?Cn=A01

25 Household consumer price increased by 3.3 percent YoY in Apr. 2020, National Bureau of Statistics of China, May 12, 2020: www.stats.gov.cn/tjsj/zxfb/202005/t20200512_1744707.html; Household consumer price increased by 2.4 percent YoY in May 2020, National Bureau of Statistics of China, June 10, 2020: www.stats.gov.cn/tjsj/zxfb/202006/t20200610_1755399.html

26 Total retail sales of consumer goods decreased by 15.8 percent in Mar. 2020, National Bureau of Statistics of China, April 17, 2020: www.stats.gov.cn/tjsj/zxfb/202004/t20200417_1739331.html; Total retail sales of consumer goods decreased by 7.5 percent in Apr. 2020, National Bureau of Statistics of China, May 15, 2020: www.stats.gov.cn/tjsj/zxfb/202005/t20200515_1745631.html; Total retail sales of consumer goods decreased by 2.8 percent in May 2020, National Bureau of Statistics of China, June 15, 2020: www.stats.gov.cn/tjsj/zxfb/202006/t20200614_1760159.html

27 Personal income and consumer spending in the first quarter of 2020, National Bureau of Statistics of China, April 17, 2020: www.stats.gov.cn/tjsj/zxfb/202004/t20200417_1739334.html

28 Online survey by the Research Team on Rural Organization and System, Rural Development Institute, Chinese Academy of Social Sciences.

29 Fiscal income and expenditure in May 2020, Ministry of Finance, June 18, 2020: gks.Mof.Gov.cn/tongjishuju/202006/t20200618_3534764.htm

30 Online survey by the Research Team on Rural Organization and System, Rural Development Institute, Chinese Academy of Social Sciences.

31 The State Council Information Office held a press conference on the decisive battle against poverty, Chinese Government Net, March 12, 2020: www.gov.cn/xinwen/2020-03/12/content_5490339.htm

32 Xi Jinping, Speech at a Symposium on the Decisive Battle against Poverty, *People's Daily*, March 7, 2020 Edition 2.

33 On Apr. 1: the Joint prevention and control mechanism of the State Council introduced the work of poverty alleviation and civil affairs during the epidemic control period, Chinese Government Net, April 2, 2020: www.gov.cn/xinwen/gwylflkjz77/index.htm

34 Fang Xiaodan, Nominal income of rural residents in poor areas continued to grow in the first quarter of this year, National Bureau of Statistics of China, April 20, 2020: www.stats.gov.cn/tjsj/sjjd/202004/t20200430_1742608.html

35 Fang Xiaodan, Nominal income of rural residents in poor areas continued to grow in the first quarter of this year.

36 Guo Xiaoming and Gao Jie, *The Impact of COVID-19 on Poverty Alleviation and its Countermeasures*, Research Report of the Think Tank of the Chinese Academy of Social Sciences on Urban-Rural Integration, 5th issue, 2020.
37 On April 1: the Joint prevention and control mechanism of the State Council introduced the work of poverty alleviation and civil affairs during the epidemic control period.
38 Xi Jinping, Speech at a Symposium on the Decisive Battle against Poverty.
39 The latest progress made in the recent priority work of poverty alleviation (as of May 31), State Council Poverty Alleviation Office, June 5, 2020: www.cpad.gov.cn/art/2020/6/5/art_624_125701.html
40 Xi Jinping, Speech at the Meeting on the Coordinated Implementation of COVID-19 Prevention and Control and Economic and Social Development, *People's Daily*, February 24, 2020, Edition 2.
41 Family Farm Development Monitoring Research Team, *Impact of COVID-19 on Family Farm Production and Management and the Countermeasures*.
42 Wei Houkai, Make three overall plans to win the battle against poverty under impact of the pandemic, *China National Conditions and Strength*, 2nd issue, 2020.

3 Impact of the COVID-19 pandemic on China's industrial economy and countermeasures

Shi Dan, Deng Zhou, Huang Yana, and Yu Chang

The COVID-19 pandemic has been a major public health emergency featuring the quickest spread, the most extensive scope of infection, and the highest degree of difficulty for prevention and control since the founding of New China in 1949. It is also the most serious global pandemic in this century. The outbreak hit China's industrial economy unprecedentedly in the first quarter of 2020, and its impacts on future development depend on the duration of the global pandemic, the effectiveness of anti-epidemic measures in different countries, as well as the policies in each country to restore the economy after the outbreak. This chapter analyzes the short-term impacts and medium- and long-term impacts of the pandemic on China's industry in two scenarios according to the existing forecasts of the epidemic trend, and it puts forward policy suggestions for China's industrial economy to turn crises into opportunities and enhance the toughness of industry development based on the main risks and opportunities during the pandemic.

Research foundation and analysis

The COVID-19 pandemic in China peaked in January and February 2020[1] and took a turn for the better in March; from April, the prevention work was refocused to the control of imported cases,[2] basically consistent with some early epidemiological research (Shen et al., 2020).[3] According to the judgment of epidemiologists, containment of the pandemic still needs to continue in China; as a perfect and powerful monitoring system has been established and put into operation, the possibility of a second outbreak in China will not be high. However, although the pandemic has been basically contained in China and is spreading slowly in Asian countries and some European countries, there has been no sign of slowdown of the pandemic in the world's largest economy, the United States, and the pandemic has even been relapsing in some countries. A Harvard epidemiologist utilized the epidemiologic Susceptible–Exposed–Infectious–Recovered model to simulate the COVID-19 epidemic dynamics and concluded that COVID-19 would not disappear in the short term and that the social distancing policy in the United States should be extended or executed at intervals up to 2022. Uncertainties about

DOI: 10.4324/9781003184447-4

the prospects of containing the pandemic are also based on the duration of the immune antibody obtained from the COVID-19 in the human body, and there would be the possibility of a second outbreak in the winter of 2020 (Stephen et al., 2020).[4] This forecast has also been consistent with the conclusions of most mainstream economic research institutes. For example, Morgan Stanley predicted further outbreaks of COVID-19 in the winter of 2020 and in the spring of 2021, even till the end of 2021, and the outbreak might cause global economic recession (Morgan Stanley, 2020).[5]

The pandemic has endangered the safety of human life, and its direct and indirect impacts on the economy have been considered the secondary disasters of the outbreak; however, as this pandemic has caused the greatest global economic recession since the end of the World War II, the level of concern about potential economic impacts of the pandemic was next only to worries about the pandemic itself (Luo Zhiheng, 2020; An Guojun and Jia Fuwei, 2020).[6] This document explores the impacts of the COVID-19 pandemic on China's industrial economy, including short-term impacts and medium- and long-term impacts based on the predicted duration of the pandemic in epidemiological studies. Specifically, short-term impacts mean direct damage to China's industrial economy caused by domestic and foreign outbreaks, where statistical data were used to summarize the industrial economic operation in the first quarter of 2020; medium- and long-term impacts have been measured by simulation of the trend of China's industrial economic operation affected by the pandemic before the end of 2021, using external impacts. According to the forecasts of domestic and foreign institutions and epidemiologists on the global pandemic, and from the perspective of the impacts of the pandemic on industrial economy, it has been argued that the global pandemic trend might be illustrated in two scenarios: Scenario 1 represents an optimistic forecast, and Scenario 2 represents a pessimistic forecast.

Scenario 1: The global pandemic has been contained in the short term. China has not loosened its control over the pandemic, and it harnessed domestic transmission of the pandemic nationwide before June 2020; under the leadership of the World Health Organization, all countries are advised to participate actively in global joint prevention and control, and the global pandemic has been basically contained without apparent rebound in October 2020.

Scenario 2: In countries other than China, the global pandemic continues and has rebounded many times. All countries have taken different countermeasures against the pandemic, having found it hard to choose between the loss caused by economic shutdown and the tough prevention and control measures. While the pandemic has been contained in some countries, it is still spreading widely in countries with a weak economic base, poor sanitary conditions, and unresolved prevention and control measures. It will recur over and over again after work resumption of work and personnel mobility in these countries until the COVID-19 vaccines and new drugs have been developed successfully and passed clinical trials for mass vaccination and targeted treatment. In such a scenario, the global pandemic may be basically contained just in 1–2 years.

If the pandemic is controlled totally in China in June 2020 and comprehensively around the globe in October 2020, its impacts on China's industrial economy will be short term; however, if the pandemic continues into 2021, there will be a high possibility of global economic crisis and recession, thus leading to profound medium- and long-term impacts on China's industrial economy at several levels.

Short-term impacts of the pandemic on China's industrial economy in the first quarter of 2020

In the first quarter of 2020, the outbreak and control measures for the COVID-19 pandemic brought unprecedented impacts on China's industrial economy. In January and February, all industrial sectors had been hit by the pandemic; in March, China's industrial operation had been restored gradually with mitigation of the domestic pandemic situation, regardless of the worsening situation of the pandemic overseas. On the whole, the pandemic has caused unprecedented damages to China's industrial economic operation; consequently, enterprises in different sectors, in different districts, and of different types have been hit to different degrees.

Overall impacts of the pandemic on China's industrial economic operation

The COVID-19 pandemic has caused unprecedented short-term damage to China's industrial economic operation, with a rate of decline in industrial growth far beyond the rate of decline during the SARS (severe acute respiratory syndrome) outbreak in 2003 and during the international financial crisis in 2008 (as shown in Figure 3.1). China's industrial growth declined precipitously in February 2020 when the heaviest hit of the pandemic occurred; the industrial added value decreased by 25.9 percent year on year in that month and by 26.6 percent on a month-on-month basis, the biggest one-month drop after the monthly indicators had been included in statistics; the manufacturing Purchasing Managers Index fell to a record low, and manufacturing economic activities contracted sharply; the industrial production time of industrial enterprises was compressed significantly and more enterprises were running under their production capacity, leading to very low industrial capacity utilization.[7] Meanwhile, industrial investment demand and demands for non-necessities and exports decreased simultaneously, cutting the number of new orders, slowing the product sales rate and the inventory turnover rate of finished products, and increasing the business inventories. Both the production and marketing of industrial enterprises had decreased,

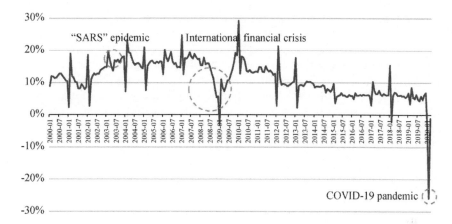

Figure 3.1 Changes in the growth of industrial added value in the same months year-on-year since 2000.

Source: National Bureau of Statistics of China

but their employment, depreciation, amortization costs, finance charges, and other rigid expenditures had not; the costs for epidemic prevention increased greatly, and the decline in profit was far higher than decline in income; as a result, in January and February, the operating revenues and total profit of industrial enterprises above designated size decreased by 17.7 percent and 38.3 percent year on year, respectively, the number of loss-making enterprises increased by 32 percent year on year, and 36.4 percent of enterprises suffered from losses. In addition, the cross-conduction of negative impacts via the supply chain and industry chain among sectors and regions has finally led to nationwide paralysis of the industrial supply chain network, sales system, and logistics system. In January and February, the added value of 39 sectors in 41 major industrial categories showed negative year-on-year growth, and the industrial added value in 31 provinces, districts, and cities showed negative growth. Under dual impacts of the pandemic both at home and abroad, imports and exports of goods declined significantly in the first quarter, and the industrial export delivery value decreased by 19.1 percent year on year in January and February.

With effective control of domestic outbreak in China, the negative impact of the pandemic has weakened quickly. In March 2020, the operating conditions of industrial economy improved notably, the industrial added value grew 32.1 percent on a month-on-month basis, and the industrial output scale approached the level in the same period of last year. On the supply side, the pandemic caused insignificant damage to the latent production capacity in China. In early February 2020, some industrial sectors started orderly resumption of work, employees successively returned to their jobs, the logistics system operated more smoothly, industrial capacity utilization ascended steadily, and domestic supply chains recovered. On the demand side, though demands for industrial investments and durable consumer goods had been postponed by the pandemic, most did not vanish. After the pandemic was contained, huge demands for products revitalized the industrial market. In March, however, industrial investment decreased greatly, by 21.1 percent year on year, only 6.4 percent less than that in January and February. The value of retail sales of automobiles, home appliances, furniture, and other products still dropped significantly on a year-on-year basis, so it will take a long time for demand to recover in China.

Impacts of the pandemic on different sectors, districts, and types of enterprises

The pandemic has had huge impact on the entire industrial economy of China, though the degree of impact on each sector may vary. On the whole, greater impact was found in sectors with more complicated supply chain systems, longer industry chains, and more intensive labor, with the greatest impacts occurring downstream of industry chains and in sectors producing durable goods and capital goods. As shown in Figure 3.2, from January to February 2020, about half of China's industrial sectors were heavily hit by the outbreak, including automobiles, furniture, textiles, clothing, mechanical equipment, etc., with added value falling by 20 percent and more year on year. About a quarter of sectors were moderately hit, including food and beverage, electronic information manufacturing, etc., with added value falling by 10–20 percent year on year. Of the remaining sectors, some were hit slightly, including medicine, chemical fuel, iron and steel, etc., with added value falling by less than 10 percent year on year, and some experienced positive growth.

The degree of impact of the pandemic on China's industrial economy in different districts depended on the local severity of the epidemic and the local industry structure. As shown in Figure 3.3, from January to February 2020, the pandemic's impacts in the more economically developed eastern and central regions were obviously greater than those in the northeast and western regions. The greatest impact was found in Chongqing, Guangdong, Jilin, and Shanghai (Hubei is not included in Figure 3.3), and the slightest impacts were found in Xinjiang, Ningxia, Yunnan, Gansu, and Inner Mongolia. Resumption of work also accelerated in China's developed areas in March, with industrial added value falling less than 1 percent year on year in the eastern and central regions.

The degree of impact of the pandemic on enterprises has been linked directly with their capability for work resumption and their resistance to fund risks, regardless of the sector where they operate. With better production and fund conditions, a large enterprise could resume work earlier[8] and have stronger resistance to the risk of capital chain rupture, so the impact

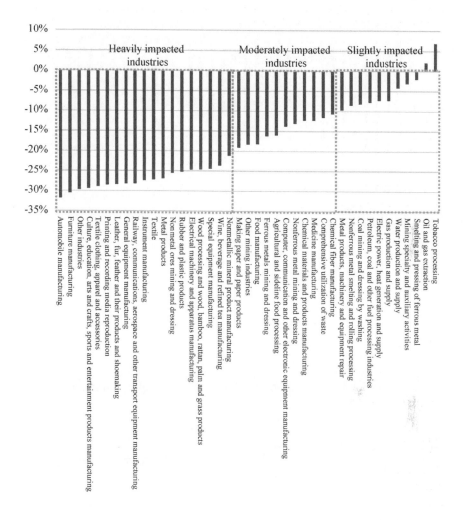

Figure 3.2 Year-on-year growth in January and February of added value of industries above designated size.

Source: National Bureau of Statistics of China

of the pandemic would be less than that on micro, small, and medium-sized enterprises.[9] Standing upstream of the industry chain and having high capital intensity and low labor intensity, a state-owned enterprise would be hit much less than a foreign-funded or privately operated enterprise (as shown in Table 3.1).

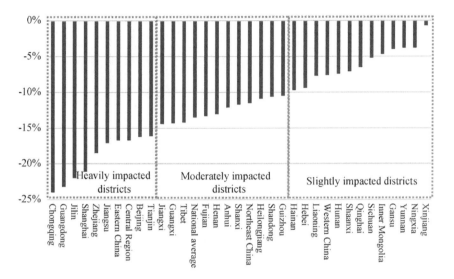

Figure 3.3 Year-on-year growth in January and February of industrial added value in affected provinces (except Hubei).

Source: National Bureau of Statistics of China

Medium and long-term impact mechanisms of the global pandemic on industrial economic operation

The medium- and long-term impacts of the pandemic on China's industrial economy depend on three interactive factors: (i) the global pandemic trend, epidemic prevention and control measures, and economic incentive policy; (ii) the duration of direct impacts of the global pandemic, determined by the pandemic trend and prevention and control measures; and (iii) the speed of the industrial economic recovery determined by the economic incentive policy after mitigation of the pandemic. Due to huge uncertainties about these three factors, it is currently hard to accurately predict the degree of the pandemic's impacts on industrial economy; however, it is certain that these impacts are no longer limited to the short term. Therefore, we should stay on high alert to avoid the potential medium- and long-term impacts.

Basic factors affecting the degree of impact from the pandemic on China's industrial economy

Global pandemic trend

The global pandemic trend is a primary variable determining the duration of direct impacts and the degree of damage caused by the pandemic. At present,

Table 3.1 Operating conditions of industrial enterprises in main ownership types in January and February

Industry category	Year-on-year increase of industrial added value	Year-on-year increase of operating revenue	Year-on-year increase of total profit	Year-on-year increase of number of loss-making enterprises	Year-on-year increase of total loss of enterprise	Proportion of loss-making enterprises
Industry totals	−13.5	−17.7	−38.3	32.0	24.3	36.4
State holding enterprises	−7.9	−11.5	−32.9	19.6	27.7	48.4
Joint-stock enterprises	−14.2	−16.9	−33.6	31.9	21.0	35.1
Foreign-invested enterprises and enterprises invested in by Hong Kong, Macao, and Taiwan merchants	−21.4	−21.7	−53.6	31.7	34.9	49.3
Privately operated enterprises	−20.2	−20.5	−36.6	35.3	20.3	32.8

Source: National Bureau of Statistics of China.

due to inadequate understanding of COVID-19, no consensus has been reached by domestic and foreign epidemiologists, public health experts, and infectious disease experts on the future global pandemic trend, so the duration of the pandemic's impacts remains unknown. There are two critical questions about the global pandemic trend. First, will large-scale spread of the pandemic continue? Due to regional seasonal differences, the peaks of the pandemic may vary; currently, there is a trend of multipoint outbreaks, and due to shortage of specific medicines and vaccines, it's difficult to control the global pandemic effectively. Second, will there be new waves of the outbreak? High transmissibility of COVID-19 has aggravated worries about new waves all over the world.

COVID-19 prevention and control policies of all countries

When it comes to COVID-19 prevention and control policies, all countries face a tough choice between short-term economic loss and pandemic control.

With respect to epidemic prevention and control strategy, China has fought "a quick battle" to annihilate the coronavirus without considering short-term economic costs, while European and American countries have fought a "protracted war" to flatten the fat-tail curves of the outbreaks. The global dual-track system for epidemic prevention has not been fully implemented in all countries; after containing the pandemic rapidly at a huge cost, China faces a risk of imported cases. If China strictly controls personnel flow into China, it will be more difficult to restore foreign economic activities, and the risk of global supply chain disruption will continue to rise.

Economic incentive policies of all countries

In order to minimize the impact of reduced economic activities on individuals, enterprises, and financial systems, to alleviate the long-term destructive effect of economic depression, and to ensure quick recovery of the post-pandemic economy, all countries have launched a series of economic incentive policies in succession. Proactive fiscal and monetary policies may effectively boost industrial demand and create favorable conditions for industrial economic recovery: first, personal consumption subsidies and government purchases are expanded to boost personal consumption and government consumption, and, second, money supply is eased and low interest rates are provided to boost industrial investment. However, in the short term, the pandemic trend will still play a crucial role in global economic recovery, so it is difficult to evaluate the effect of economic incentive policies in different countries. Meanwhile, in order to first promote industrial economic recovery in their own countries, all countries might further strengthen manufacturing revival and trade pro-tection. China's industrial economic recovery is not only contingent on its stimulus policies, but also prone to policy games with other countries.

General process and degree of impact of the pandemic on China's industrial economy

The COVID-19 pandemic has impacted China's industrial economy on both the supply side and the demand side (see Figure 3.4). As compared with other sectors, the industrial sector is a tradable sector that produces material goods and has longer supply chains and industry chains; thus the pandemic's impacts may easily trigger cross-conduction among sectors via the supply chain and trigger cross-conduction among countries via international trade and cross-border investment. Though complex and diverse, the impact of the pandemic can be generally divided into four stages: full impact, recovery, full recovery, and profound adjustment.

Stage I: full impact

The pandemic has generated drastic external impacts on China's industrial supply and demand, leading to a widespread halt of industrial economy

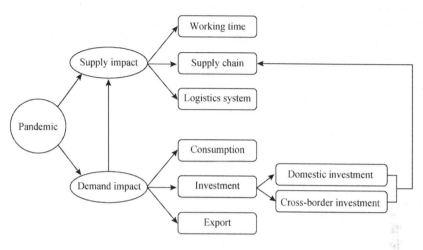

Figure 3.4 Impacts of the pandemic on China's industrial economy.

operation. This stage has a short duration, generally one to two months from the start of the outbreak to the appearance of a "knee point" of existing confirmed cases, and the impact in this stage has mainly come from domestic outbreaks. At this stage, the industrial output growth has declined precipitously, much lower than the trend line before outbreak. From the perspective of the impacts of the pandemic on supply, the prevention and control policy of mandatory quarantine and lockdown has compelled industrial enterprises to stop work and production. This is the main reason for significant decline in industrial output at this stage. From the perspective of the impacts of the pandemic on demand, the consumption of non-necessities has been hit heavily, enterprise cash flow has tightened, industrial investment has slumped, and demand for capital goods has declined sharply. In addition to negative impacts on supply and demand, the rigid demand for epidemic prevention supplies has boosted the capacity and output of very few relevant industries, which become the only weak growth points at this stage.

Stage II: recovery

The mitigation of local outbreaks in China has weakened the pandemic's impacts on industrial supply and demand and helped the recovery of the industrial economy by stages. However, the mitigated outbreaks of the pandemic both at home and abroad led to extension of the time required for recovery, though this duration could not be determined. At this stage, industrial output growth has picked up again, but is still lower than the trend line before the outbreak. From the perspective of the pandemic's impacts on supply, adverse factors influencing working time, the domestic supply chain, and the logistics system have been basically eliminated; most industrial enterprises have resumed work quickly and are ready to increase capacity utilization in a short time, making it possible to realize overall repair of supply. Backlog of orders at an early stage has brought about transitory stable output after resumption of production. However, the supply chain trade in relation to the global production network is the epitome of the global division of labors, making possible the "contagion" of the pandemic's impacts via the global supply chain (Baldwin & Lopez-Gonzalez, 2015).[10] Halting of production by overseas suppliers as well as restrictions on cross-border materials and personnel mobility have hindered intermediate products trade, and the risk of supply chain disruption has increased with the continuous extension of the global pandemic duration. At this stage, the pandemic's heavy impact on the existing global supply chain and industry chain pattern has foreshadowed the remodeling of the division of labor in the global supply chain. From the perspective of impact of the pandemic on demand, the lag in recovery of demand behind the recovery of supply has led to weak consumption and reduced investor confidence, and enterprises have maintained their capacity utilization at a low level due to insufficient orders after work resumption, a phenomenon called "resumption of work without resumption of production." First, domestic consumer demand in China has been released slowly; however, as the pandemic still exerts heavy impacts on the income and spending power of some people, consumer discretionary demands can be only partially satisfied, with few new consumer demands being generated. Second, due to the weakening of enterprise profitability and internal financing capacity and the generally pessimistic economic outlook, industrial investment has increased slowly and foreign direct investment has declined. Third, external demand has been weak in China for a long time due to the global economic recession, leading to sluggish growth in sectors with high dependency on external demands, but there has been huge export of materials used in epidemic prevention. With the dual impacts of the global supply chain bottleneck and sluggish demands, the recovery of China's industrial economy will be a long process.

Stage III: full recovery

With the direct impacts of the pandemic on industrial supply and demand vanishing after the slowdown in global pandemic transmission, the sustained increase in supply and demand has driven full recovery of the industrial economy. The retaliatory rebounds of industrial output growth have exceeded the trend line before the outbreak, but the absolute value of industrial output remains significantly lower than the trend line before the outbreak. This stage, where the impacts of the pandemic are indirect, is a critical period for the post-pandemic adjustment of the domestic industry structure and global supply chain. From the perspective of the impact of the pandemic on supply, as all countries have begun comprehensive resumption of production, the risk of global supply chain disruption has been removed, and adjustment has accelerated in the global supply chain. The COVID-19 pandemic has made non-economic impact an important consideration in the adjustment of the global supply chain. Therefore, transnational corporations will re-evaluate and remeasure the efficiency of the global division of labor and the security of the supply chain (He Jun, 2020),[11] and the governments of all countries will treat supply chain security as a major systematic risk and take strategic countermeasures. From the perspective of the impact of the pandemic on demand, complete recovery of consumer and investor confidence has triggered a surge in demand postponed by the outbreak. The consumer discretionary sectors have seen significant rebounds, and the domestic industrial investment structure has been inclined to sectors involved in homemade substitute goods production and digital transformation. External demand has also come back on track. Robust demand both at home and abroad has become the core impulse for full recovery of all industrial sectors.

Stage IV: profound adjustment

The COVID-19 outbreak has profoundly changed economic ideas and people's behavior, giving rise to the lasting impacts of "backlash against globalization" and adjustments in the global supply chain. Due to the increasingly fierce global industry competition and the deteriorating external environment for China's industrial development, industrial economy growth will fall back to a level slightly lower than that before the outbreak, despite a sudden rise in demand after the pandemic was contained. In recent years, there has been a mounting backlash against globalization and readjustments in the global value chain specialization in the world economy. Under the guidance of trade protectionism, explicit and implicit barriers have been set for flows of goods, capital, and labor among nations (Tong Jiadong et al., 2017).[12] The international division of labor has indicated trade slowdown and loose connections in the global value chain. The increasingly prominent indigenization in countries such as the United States and Germany has hindered the deepening of global value chain specialization (Peng Zhiwei and Zhang Bowei, 2018; Aslam et al., 2018).[13] The COVID-19 outbreak has inspired populism, undermined mutual understanding in politics, and broken the consensus of major powers on economic globalization (Li Xiao and Chen Yu, 2020),[14] and China faces more uncertain factors in the global trade and investment environment. More importantly, the global supply chain was designed for long-term demand, and any adjustment will have a profound influence. Localization of the global supply chain will reduce the benefits of developing countries from capital flows related to the global value chain and deprive them of the opportunities to obtain human capital and knowledge from the international market, thus crippling developing countries' industrialization through integration into the global value chain in future years (IMF, 2020).[15] Meanwhile, slowdown and decline in the international trade growth of intermediate products will bring about major changes in the paradigm of the global value chain specialization based on trade in intermediate products. This has not only posed new challenges to China's export-oriented manufacturing, but also provided new opportunities for homemade substitute goods and upgrading of China's industrial structure.

Forecast of China's industrial economic development in the two scenarios

According to the two scenarios of global pandemic mentioned above as well as the general rules of the pandemic's impacts on industrial economy, we created a curve for the COVID-19 pandemic and domestic industrial growth from January 2020 to December 2021 (Figure 3.5) and divided the industrial economy trend after May 2020 into an optimistic Scenario 1 and a pessimistic Scenario 2.

As shown in Figure 3.5, if it is assumed that industrial economic growth maintained stable before outbreak of the pandemic, the trend line of output growth is g. When the outbreak occurred in China, a great deviation appeared immediately on the industrial economic growth path. If the outbreak had not evolved into a global pandemic, the industrial economic growth path in China should be graphed as curve 1; that is, the path may absorb the pandemic's

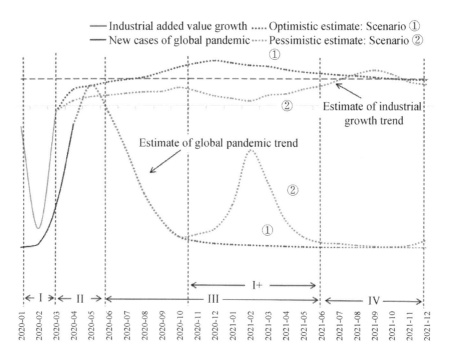

Figure 3.5 COVID-19 pandemic trend and domestic industrial growth.

Note: The number of new cases of the global pandemic from January to April 2020 and the year-on-year growth of the industrial added value from January to March in China are based on actual data, and the subsequent trend lines are based on estimates.

impact in a short time and then come back to its original growth path; however, while the outbreak was contained in China, the global outbreak was out of control; due to imported cases and external impact, the industrial economic growth path in China has been changed to curve 2, indicating a longer time to restore the industrial economy and a slowdown in growth rebounds. Besides this, output growth has declined slightly compared with that before the outbreak as a result of the permanent deviation in the industrial economic growth path due to the deteriorating external environment after the outbreak. If a second outbreak of the COVID-19 pandemic occurs, its impacts on the industrial economy will be repeated.

The staged impacts of the outbreak on China's industrial economy in the two scenarios are shown in Table 3.2.

In the optimistic Scenario 1, China's industrial economy entered the full recovery stage in the third quarter of 2020, and most industrial sectors, except some related directly to epidemic prevention and control, have seen a growth rate slightly lower than that before the outbreak. Due to the huge damage caused by the outbreak to the global industry chain and industrial economy of major countries, even if overall work resumption has been basically realized in China in the second quarter of 2020, the full recovery stage will last until the second quarter of 2021. This is because, after the outbreak has been preliminarily controlled, the industrial production and consumption backlogged by the outbreak will become an important power to activate industrial growth, and central and local government policy measures to stimulate economy will continue to invigorate industrial economic growth. Policy effect on the outbreak will weaken from the third quarter of 2021, and the permanent impact of the outbreak on the global industry chain will emerge; consequently, China's industrial economy will begin to enter the profound adjustment stage. With China's overall industrial growth stabilizing, tremendous changes might take place in the industry structure, market structure, trade structure, and supply chain system.

In the pessimistic Scenario 2, China's industrial economy saw a limited recovery in the third quarter of 2020 because the outbreak continued in main trade partner countries and the international market remained sluggish. More seriously, a second outbreak of the pandemic might peak in some countries and import cases into China in the fourth quarter of 2020 and in the first two quarters of 2021, dealing a blow to the originally vulnerable industrial economy of China. Unlike Scenario 1, from the third quarter of 2020 to the second quarter of 2021, China's industrial economy may enter a painful adjustment stage and recover with difficulty under repeated pandemic outbreaks. The outbreak will be controlled from the third quarter of 2021; however, since the global pandemic will have lasted for one year and exerted severe permanent impacts on the industrial economy of major countries, there will be a high possibility of global economic recession. As the industrial investments are squeezed out by the huge cost of containing the pandemic, China's industrial economy growth will step down markedly compared with

Table 3.2 Staged impacts of the outbreak on China's industrial economy: Two scenarios

	I	II	III	IV
Scenario 1	2020 Q1 Full impact stage	2020 Q2 Recovery stage	2020 Q3–2021 Q2 Full recovery stage	2021 Q3–Q4 Profound adjustment stage
	Large-area shutdown and halt of production; sudden expansion of production capacity of emergency products	Capacity recovery and demand release; but affected by global supply chain disruption and insufficient external demand, industrial growth declines	Global supply chain is restored gradually; industrial investment is restored slowly; international market rises again slowly	Permanent effect of global division of labor and market starts to present; overall development trend is smooth
Scenario 2			III 2020 Q3 Painful adjustment stage	IV 2021 Q3–Q4 Profound adjustment stage
			Supply chain adjustment; industrial investment slows down; international market is sluggish	Global economic recession; sluggish industrial investment; step down of industrial growth
			1+ 2020 Q4–2021 Q2 Second outbreak occurs; the world enters economic depression; industrial investment and international markets are influenced severely	

that before the outbreak. If there is any unbreakable barrier in vaccine development and production, the possibility of a third outbreak at the end of 2021 will not be ruled out, thus dealing even more severe blows to the industrial economy globally and in China.

Of course, the two scenarios represent extreme estimates. The actual trend lines of the global pandemic are more likely to rest between the two scenarios, and the pandemic's impact on China's industrial economy will also be somewhere in the middle.

Main risks and opportunities for China's industrial economy before the end of 2021

According to the most optimistic estimates, direct impacts of the pandemic on the global industrial economy will last at least until the first half of 2021, and full recovery of the industrial economy will not occur earlier than the end of 2021. As a whole, before the end of 2021, China's industrial economic operation will face many risks, but there are also opportunities for economic development and transition.

Negative impacts on export-oriented industrial sectors

The European Union and the United States, the worst-hit regions, have accounted for more than one third of China's export market. Economic shutdown and recession in these countries and regions have exerted huge negative impacts on China's goods exports, and export-oriented manufacturing enterprises relying heavily on external demand have been hard hit (as shown in Figure 3.6). The demand side of two sectors are facing huge pressure: (i) consumer discretionary sectors with greater elasticity of demand, such as clothing, furniture, home appliances, consumer electronics, and automobiles[16]; capital goods required for production, including mechanical equipment, instruments, and apparatus.

Risk of international supply chain disruption and opportunities for homemade substitute goods

Industrial shutdown in major countries has aggravated the risk to the industrial economy supply chain in China. Despite constant declines, the processing trade has accounted for one quarter of China's foreign trade, and China's key industrial sectors have maintained close supply chain relations with Japan, South Korea, the European Union, the United States, and other countries or regions (as shown in Figure 3.7). The spread of the COVID-19 pandemic in these countries and regions has led to interrupted supply, delayed delivery, and price rise risks for raw materials, components, and parts in the upstream of the industry chain and brought uncertainty to cross-border transportation, restricting work resumption of Chinese

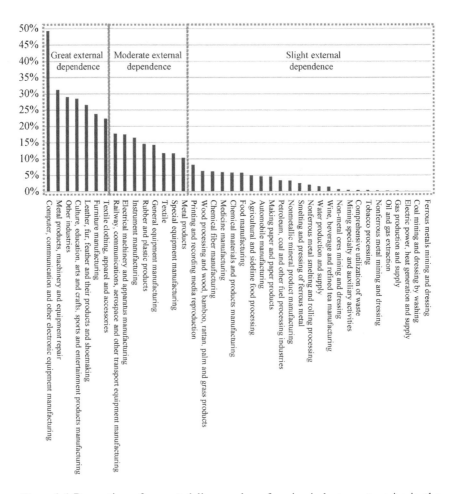

Figure 3.6 Proportion of export delivery value of major industry categories in the operating revenue of 2019.

Source: National Bureau of Statistics of China

enterprises downstream of the industry chain. At the moment, industries with high dependency on foreign suppliers in pandemic-affected countries are generally suffering an impact on supply, and the downstream industries of high-tech products that have high technological content and added value and where homemade substitute goods cannot be found in the short term are suffering the greatest loss, including automobile, mechanical equipment, and semiconductor industries.

While the global supply chain disruption impacted the downstream industries in China, the outbreak of the global pandemic has also objectively created opportunities for China's potential competitors to enter domestic and

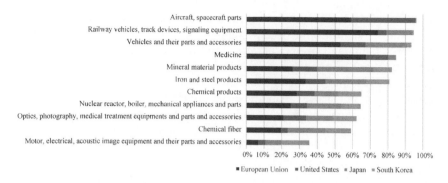

Figure 3.7 Proportion of imported products from the most-affected countries in 2019.
Source: General Administration of Customs

foreign industrial supply chains. In order to cope with foreign suppliers' shutdown and supply interruption, some Chinese downstream enterprises have sought alternative solutions to supply chain breakdown. In the first quarter of 2020, an increasing number of orders were placed to medium and high-end domestic suppliers to semiconductor, optical image, auto parts, and medical device manufacturers, and considerable gains were reaped by components and parts manufacturers with strong independent innovation. With the spread of the global pandemic leading to delayed resumption of production and work in some countries, Chinese enterprises at the upstream of industries may take the advantage of early work resumption to accept international orders so as to integrate into the global supply chain system while entering the domestic high-end supply chain.

Risks intensified by the backlash against globalization and opportunities for adjustments in the international division of labor

In recent years, so as to increase the domestic employment rate and stimulate development of the real economy, quite a few developed countries have introduced policy measures relating to "manufacturing comeback" or revitalizing domestic industry. Catalyzed by the pandemic, the manufacturing comeback trend might be further enhanced in developed countries. For example, in order to solve the contradiction between supply and demand of masks in the United States, the US government has asked relevant medical protection enterprises, including well-known mask manufacturers 3M and Honeywell, to bring jobs back to the US homeland.[17] If the pandemic lasts for a long time, in order to stabilize domestic employment and quicken economic recovery, changes may take place in the division of the global industry chain and in the industry layout that originally pursued comparative advantage of high efficiency and low cost, thus reinforcing de-globalization. Under the multiple impacts of populism, trade protectionism, and the COVID-19 pandemic, some manufacturers might move their industrial capacity out of China.

As the number one industrial power and the largest goods trade country in the world, China has been integrated into the division of labor in the global industry chain. Despite the weakening of the labor cost advantage, China has far surpassed some developed countries and other developing countries with respect to comprehensive capabilities, including industrial capacity, supporting systems, technology integration, independent innovation, and international market expansion. During the COVID-19 outbreak, China's huge capacity for industrial supply, fast adaptability, and strong ability for restoration have not only guaranteed material supply and the relatively smooth functioning of Chinese society during the pandemic, but also provided solid material production guarantees for global pandemic control. The pandemic has increased the international reputation of "Made in China" while illustrating the comprehensive capacity of China's industrial economy. China will be an indispensable player in the post-pandemic adjustment of the international division of labor.

Accelerating the implementation of China's major industrial development strategies

In recent years, China has successfully launched its major industrial development strategies, including "Made in China 2025," "high-quality development," "innovation-driven development," "manufacturing going abroad," "smart + manufacturing," and "servitization of manufacturing." These strategies have focused on supply-side structural reform and laid a policy foundation for the quick and steady development of China's economy in the medium and long term. In the next 1 to 3 years, China's major industrial development strategies will be implemented continuously and profoundly. Shortcomings in China's industrial economy exposed during the pandemic will enhance industrial transformation and upgrading and facilitate the optimization, adjustment, and implementation of major industrial development strategies.

First, industrial digital transformation will be accelerated. During the COVID-19 pandemic, digital technology and tools played a significant role in every aspect of China's social economy as a guarantee to rapidly control the pandemic in China. Industrial sectors and enterprises with a higher degree of informatization were able to allocate factor resources, better satisfy demand, and resume production and work earlier during the pandemic. Some of them even seized the opportunities to realize growth against the existing trend. This has fully verified the great significance and positive role of industrial digital transformation in response to the non-economic impact. Shortcomings in China's industrial economy during the pandemic will also provide an important basis for the innovation of digital technology application scenarios and for the deep integration of new-generation information technology with industries.

Second, the elements of high-quality industrial development will be richer. In light of the lessons learned at the early stage of the COVID-19 outbreak about large-area industrial shutdown and halt of production, China's high-quality industrial economy should include not only optimization of economic structure, improvement of resource utilization, enhancement of technological innovation capacity, and growth of labor productivity, but also enhancement of the overall "resilience" of China's industrial economy system so as to realize more stable operation when facing non-economic impacts such as a major public health event.

Third, we will encourage more enterprises to "go abroad." Based on the post-pandemic situation in China, although China is a big power in foreign industrial investment, it has relatively weak control over the global capacity and industry chain; besides, Chinese industrial enterprises scattered in different places all over the world cannot achieve effective coordination to relieve the pressure arising from domestic industrial shutdown at the early stage of the outbreak. In response to these problems, the risk of non-economic impact should be fully considered in China's "going abroad" strategy and related measures so as to enhance the capacity to integrate the supply chain, market, and information around the world and increase the accessibility of material channels between production bases in different countries and the degree of flexibility of capacity adjustment.

Policy thoughts for promoting resumption of industrial production, turning crises into opportunities, and reinforcing the resilience of industrial economy

Despite uncertainties about the trend and duration of the global pandemic, it is certain that the pandemic will exert profound impacts on the industrial economy of China and the world in medium and long term. Therefore, we should implement the policies of guaranteeing resumption of industrial production and reaching design capacity in the near term; promulgate contingency policies in response to the crises and opportunities caused by the pandemic in the short and medium term; summarize experiences and lessons of domestic and foreign industrial economic operation during the pandemic in the medium and long term; and enhance the inherent resilience of industrial economy by adjusting policies so as to prevent and cope with a rebound of the COVID-19 pandemic as well as any possible non-economic impact in the future.

Promoting safe resumption of industrial production in the near term

First, we should formulate and implement burden reduction and compensation policies for industrial enterprises. In addition to routine burden reduction policies, we should extend the duration of tax cuts and exemptions and provide direct subsidies and other rewards to enterprises that responded to the national call to switch to/expand production of epidemic prevention materials during the outbreak. Second, we should fully utilize information technology to strengthen monitoring of domestic and overseas markets and realize steady resumption of production. The industrial management department, government statistics department, industry research institution, hlwjd. cn, and big data companies should cooperate for collection and analysis of domestic and overseas market information in real time and provide a reference for enterprises to formulate plans for resumption of production and work. Third, we should utilize government strategic reserve and household reserve consumption to alleviate adverse impacts of the supply and demand fluctuation of anti-epidemic products. We should also summarize the lessons from shortage of some products at the early stage of the outbreak and strengthen strategic reserves of important materials at both central and local levels; at the same time, we should learn from the emergency material reserve scheme for Japanese households and encourage households to reserve relevant materials. Fourth, we should normalize industrial epidemic prevention, strictly implement epidemic prevention measures in the process of production resumption, gradually standardize anti-epidemic works, and enforce them in industries as an important part of safe production.

Implementing the policy of "turning crises into opportunities" in the short and medium term

We should bring together policy power and relevant resources to help industrial enterprises dissolve risks. First, we should improve the force majeure certification system and establish a special support fund. The commercial and judicial departments should establish green channels for force majeure certification in industrial contracts during the pandemic and provide legal assistance for micro, small, and medium-sized enterprises. We should guide financial institutions to provide financing and insurance services for industrial enterprises during the pandemic, moderately extend loan periods and reduce loan rates, and encourage local industry to allocate part of its capital for special aid against the pandemic. Second, given that some transnational corporations increased their order quantities or sought new supply channels in other countries during the pandemic, we should strengthen international dialog, enhance the comprehensive competitive advantages of China's industries, and prevent industrial capacity from transferring out quickly during the pandemic on the basis of work resumption as soon as possible. Third, with respect to the challenges of interrupted flows of personnel and materials caused by the pandemic, we should coordinate relevant resources and optimize allocation of these resources to guarantee steady advancement of key major industrial construction projects, major technology R&D projects, and demonstration projects as well as major overseas market expansion projects.

While helping enterprises dissolve various risks, we should grasp opportunities in the pandemic to launch stimulus policies. First, we should take advantage of being the first country to resume production and work; strengthen cooperation among industrial manufacturers, transport enterprises, and customs and quality supervision departments by utilizing China's advantageous capacity and associated systems; and increase export of medical devices, everyday necessities, and other anti-epidemic products. Second, we should grasp opportunities in new markets, promulgate associated policies to stimulate consumption, and continuously release new demands and new demand models that emerged during the pandemic to form new industrial growth points. Third, we should seize the opportunity of industry upgrading to promote the construction of projects such as smart factories, the industrial Internet of Things, smart supply chains, and smart industrial parks.

Enhancing the resilience of all-round industrial economy in the medium and long term

We should make enhancement of resilience of the industrial economy an important part of our major industrial development strategies, including high-quality industrial development, construction of industrial power, and innovation-driven industries. Specifically, the resilience of China's industrial economy is embodied by: (i) resilience in production capacity—the ability to expand capacity rapidly under special conditions and restore capacity at a lower cost; (ii) resilience in economic structure—the capacity to realize the product structure adjustment of the same production line and the structure adjustment in the same production area in a short period; (iii) resilience in the supply chain—the capacity to form interactive, networked, and multi-channel supply systems among different areas, different industries, and different enterprises; and (iv) resilience in the market—the capacity to maintain overall stability of the industrial products market in special periods.

We should continually improve the emergency mobilization capability of China's industrial economy. During the pandemic, China's industrial sectors showed powerful anti-strike capability and quick adaptability and restorability as a whole; however, some shortcomings and deficiencies were also exposed at the early stage of the outbreak, and severe short-term shortage of some products occurred in some districts. For such problems, we should construct and improve our industrial emergency mobilization system, realize optimal allocation of critical materials and factors at the national level in case of serious non-economic impact, avoid waste of resources congested in some fields and districts, and guarantee normal operation of key industrial sectors. Meanwhile, we should conduct regular drills in response to main non-economic impacts at different levels in different industries, simulating scenarios in which we are trying to maintain industrial production and material circulation in case of a public health event, terrorist attack, or natural disaster so that we can constantly identify defects and make timely corrections.

We should continually reinforce our industrial economy's production reserve capacity and capability for emergency implementation of policy. We should locate new major industrial projects in underdeveloped areas, such as mid and western regions, optimize China's industrial material reserve structure and layout, and enhance logistics coordination in industrial agglomeration areas. Policymaking bodies should formulate an emergency policy system plan in response to main non-economic impacts and should start to develop corresponding mechanisms and execute corresponding emergency policy in case of any such impact.

We should reinforce our capacity to allocate and distribute international materials and to improve capacity for international cooperation in special periods. Non-economic impacts may have different influence on different countries and regions; for example, the COVID-19 pandemic occurred first in China and other East Asia and Southeast Asian nations, then broke out in Europe, Oceania, North America, and South America. With regard to this nature of non-economic impact, international material allocation and international capacity cooperation may be utilized to reduce the impact on the industrial economy in terms of supply and demand. To support international cooperation, we need to establish a rapid customs clearance system and a transportation channel for multinational materials in case of emergency. Meanwhile, the possibility of non-economic impact should be fully considered in industrial investment, industrial infrastructure construction, and industrial capacity layout of countries along the Belt and Road Initiative route so as to guarantee normal circulation of materials and capacity allocation between production bases all over the world after the impact occurs.

Notes

1 The first case appeared on December 8, 2019. Wuhan began implement strict travel restrictions on January 23, 2020, and the number of newly confirmed cases reached the peak in early February.
2 As of 22:00 on April 24, 2020, there were 1,406 confirmed cases in China, with 318 of the 344 cities reporting zero cases.
3 In January 2020, Professor Zhang Lei and Associate Professor Shen Mingwang from the School of Public Health, Xi'an Jiaotong University, Professor Xiao Yanni from the Institute of Mathematics and Statistics, and Professor Peng Zhixing from the School of Public Health, Nanjing Medical University, cooperated on a mathematical model to predict the epidemic trend of COVID-19 in China, concluding that the pandemic would peak in late February or early March or 5–14 days earlier if control measures are strengthened.
4 Stephen M. Kissler, et al.,2020, "Projecting the transmission dynamics of SARS-CoV-2 through the post-pandemic period", *MedRxiv*; Stephen M. IK, Christine T., Edward G., Yonatan H. Gradand M. L., 2020, "Projecting the Transmission Dynamics of SARS-CoV-2 through the Post-pandemic Period", *Science*, https: // science.sciencemag.org/content/early/2020/04/24/science.abb5793.
5 Morgan Stanley, 2020, *Global Macro Briefing: The Great Covid-19 Recession aka GCR*, New York, April 3.
6 Luo Zhiheng, 2020, "The Impact of COVID-19 on Economy, Capital Markets and National Governance and the Response", *Financial Economics*, No. 2; An

Guojun and Jia Fuwei, 2020, "Analysis of the Impact of COVID-19 on Economy and the Research on Countermeasures", *Financial Theory and Practice*, No. 3.

7 The utilization rate of industrial capacity in the first quarter was 67.3 percent, 8.6 percent lower than that in the same period of 2019, a record low.

8 According to the data from the Ministry of Industry and Information Technology, the average operating rate of industrial enterprises above designated size reached 98.6 percent as of March 28, 2020, while that of small and medium-sized enterprises was only 76 percent.

9 According to the manufacturing PMI in February and March 2020, large enterprises had the best performance, followed by medium-sized enterprises and finally small enterprises.

10 "Supply chain contagion" is the effect of a supply disruption in one country on the manufacturing output in other countries.

11 He Jun, 2020, "From Efficiency to Safety: Global Supply Chain Adjustment and Response to the Impact of the Pandemic", *Study & Exploration*, 1–11[2020-04-28]. http://kns.cnki.net/kcms/detail/23.1049.C.20200422.0943.002.html.

12 Tong Jiadong, Xie Danyang, Bao Qun, Huang Qunhui, Li Xiangyang, Liu Zhibiao, Jin Bei, Yu Miaojie and Wang Xiaosong, 2017, "Anti-globalization" and the Transformation and Upgrading of Real Economy, China Industrial Economics, Issue 6.

13 Peng Zhiwei and Zhang Bowei, 2018, "The Evolution and Determinants of China's International Division of Labor Benefits." *China Industrial Economics*, Issue 6; Aslam A, Boz E, Cerutti E, et al., 2018, "The Slowdown in Global Trade: A Symptom of a Weak Recovery?". *IMF Economic Review*, 66(3).

14 Li Xiao and Chen Yu, 2020, " World Economy under the Impact of the Pandemic and China's Countermeasures", *Northeast Asia Forum*, 1–15[2020-04-29]. https://doi.org/10.13654/j.cnki.naf.2020.03.004.

15 IMF, Global Uncertainty Related to Coronavirus at Record High, April 4, 2020, (https://blogs.imf.org/2020/04/04/global-uncertainty-related-to-coronavirus-at-record-high/); IMF, Maintaining Banking System Safety amid the COVID-19 Crisis, March 31, 2020, (https://blogs.imf.org/2020/03/31/maintaining-banking-system-safety-amid-the-covid-19-crisis/); IMF. World Economic Outlook, April 2020, https://with.imf.org/zh/Publications/WEO/Issues/2020/04/14/weo-april-2020, 2020-4-14.

16 Take the automobile industry as an example: IHS and other market institutions have significantly lowered their 2020 global auto sales forecast. Although China's whole vehicle export volume is small, auto parts play an important role in the global supply chain system. In March, hundreds of whole vehicle manufacturing factories around the world stopped work, which sharply reduced the demand for China's auto parts.

17 Foreign media reported at the end of February 2020 that the United States had a demand of 300 million masks for medical workers, but only 30 million masks were available, a gap of 270 million. To address the perceived supply and demand conflicts at home, the United States asked medical protection companies invested in by Asia's largest economy, including well-known mask makers 3M and Honeywell, to come back to the US homeland and open factories there.

4 From efficiency to safety

Adjustments in the global supply chain under the impact of the COVID-19 pandemic and countermeasures

He Jun

More than two-thirds of global trade has been realized by industrial organization based on global division of labor; that is, raw materials or parts of finished products have crossed the border of one country or several countries before final assembly.[1] Global manufacturing has increased the allocation efficiency and dynamic efficiency of the global economy through global resource reallocation and knowledge diffusion and recombination, and has become an important power of global economic growth in the past 20 years. However, due to value distribution structure, relative cost fluctuation of factors in different countries as well as the escalating de-globalization policy in some countries, the overall global manufacturing system has entered the stage of contraction and adjustment in recent years.

Although the pandemic itself, as an exogenous short-term impact, could not change the cost structure and technological capability of each country, the pandemic has led the United States and Europe to be truly concerned about supply chain security at a strategic level and intensified the urgency of the United States and Europe to change the "China-oriented global supply chain system," which has interacted with Sino-US trade conflicts and promoted the development of the global supply chain system in a diversified and decentralized direction.

Global supply chain adjustments after the COVID-19 outbreak were most probably triggered by the following two fuses: localized production of pharmaceuticals, medical devices, and protective supplies; and escalating suppression by the United States on China's high-tech industry and enterprises. Both factors will further aggravate protectionism and trigger quick adjustment in the global supply chain through demonstration effect and counter effect. Facing localization and diversification challenges to the global supply chain, China should quicken the rhythm and efficiency of supply chain recovery in the short term, take "integrating into localization" as the main strategic line, comply with localization and diversification requirements of the global supply chain in the long term, and ensure minimum loss and maximum gain of China's manufacturing industry in the process of global supply chain adjustments.

DOI: 10.4324/9781003184447-5

Global supply chain adjustment and its economic logic

From the perspective of scale change of direct investment and structural adjustment characteristics of the global supply chain,[2] global supply chain adjustment has roughly experienced two stages since 2000: the deepening of the global supply chain before 2007 and the contraction and closing of the global supply chain after 2007 (financial crisis). (i) At the deepening stage, global direct investment increased rapidly; at the contraction stage, the growth of global direct investment slowed down notably. After 2008, global foreign direct investment became sluggish. If deducting one-off factors such as US tax reform and unstable fund flow, the annual average growth rate of global foreign direct investment was just 1 percent in 10 years after 2008; in 2018, the global foreign direct investment flow decreased by 13 percent to USD 1.3 trillion, which was the third year of decrease. From 2000 to 2007, the annual average growth rate of global foreign direct investment was 8 percent, which had risen above 20 percent before 2000.[3] (ii) At the deepening stage, the degree of participation in global supply chain increased continuously; at the contraction stage after the financial crisis, the degree of participation in the global supply chain presented a downward trend as a whole. According to the classification of the global value chain made by the World Bank,[4] the added value of a country may be broken down into pure domestic added value, traditional trade (a product is produced in one country and consumed in another country), trade based on the simple global value chain (raw materials or parts of finished products have crossed the national border of a country before production) as well as trade based on the complicated global value chain (raw materials or parts of finished products have crossed the national border of several countries before production). According to calculation based on this classification, the growth rate of the global value chain, especially of the complicated value chain, exceeded the growth of other components of global gross domestic product (GDP) from 2000 to 2007. The global value chain contracted during the 2008 financial crisis, then recovered quickly in the period of 2010–2011, but basically slowed down thereafter (except in 2017; see Table 4.1).[5]

The decrease in the global direct investment growth and global supply chain participation has shown that factors driving the global supply chain to open were weakened while factors suppressing the opening of the global supply chain were intensified gradually. In the more than 20 years before the financial crisis in 2008, under the combined action of a variety of technical and economic factors, the opening of global trade and investment had experienced a continuously deepening process from the inter-sector division of labor to the division of labor within a sector, and further to the division of labor in a product, and the supply chain system had become more and more complicated and globalized.

Reasons for such structural changes are as follows: (i) improvement of the global infrastructure and rapid development of the information technology

Table 4.1 Forward global value chain participation index variation (proportion of added value)

	Degree of participation in global value chain			Simple global value chain			Complicated global value chain		
	2000	2007	2017	2000	2007	2017	2000	2007	2017
High technology sector	25.3	30.7	28.8	13.8	16.1	15.6	11.5	14.6	13.2
medium technology sector	22.5	21.6	23.7	14.5	16.4	14.7	8.0	9.7	9.1
Low technology sector	12.4	15.8	15.3	7.9	9.9	9.5	4.5	5.9	5.8

Source: World Bank, *Global Value Chain Development Report 2019*: www.worldbank.org/en/topic/trade/publication/global-value-chain-development-report-2019

have reduced the costs for cross-border production and for transportation and management of trade, so the tradability of goods increased notably; (ii) development of the electronic information technology and technological innovation in main industrial countries have driven the modular product design and production, thus significantly increasing the economic efficiency of the vertical breakdown of manufacturing and decentralized global production; and (iii) under the background that the global manufacturing efficiency space driven by first two factors were opened, all countries began to adopt more open trade and investment policies one after another, further accelerating the opening and division of labor of global manufacturing. Especially in electronic information, automobiles, and other complicated product fields, since the product architecture became more complicated, the production process has required higher special skills, and the globalized market required enterprises to have more flexible capacity; all these have led the manufacturing industry in more and more developed countries to adopt the outsourcing form for global sourcing and production; therefore, a complicated global manufacturing system was formed in which suppliers utilized their suppliers' network for multistage production.

However, after the 2008 financial crisis, the de-globalization trend intensified constantly. First, under the impact of the financial crisis, the United States hoped to promote manufacturing comeback by means of cutting taxes, popularizing smart manufacturing, and taking more protective trade investment policies so as to strengthen US economic growth and employment. Second, after Trump took office, in order to inhibit the technological progress and industry catch-up of China, he took tariff, non-tariff, and even political means to continuously destroy the World Trade Organization (WTO)-oriented multilateral trade and investment system on the grounds of information security and industry security, and he further promoted de-globalization and protectionism, so the global supply chain has been on the verge of being contracted and closed. The outbreak of COVID-19 and the subsequent disruption of the global supply chain have further aggravated worries in the United States and Europe about supply chain security; as a result, both the United States and Europe have further promoted localization of the supply chain and diversification of sourcing areas under the policy slogan of industry chain security and public health security, thus speeding up the closure and contraction of the global supply chain.

How should we interpret relative changes of the two forces that influenced the paradigm of the global manufacturing supply chain as well as changes in US policy on the global supply chain system before and after the 2008 financial crisis at the theoretical level? Economic discussions on trade liberalization and trade protection have never stopped. The confrontation in classical studies has not been perceived as cognitive differences in logic and main influencing variables, but as disagreement on critical assumptions that have influenced trade benefits. The following two theories are especially important for us to understand the changes in US global trade and investment policies since 2000. Scholars' claims, represented by Grossman, Helpman, and Feenstra, in favor of a global supply chain asserted that trade globalization in the form of outsourcing would have benefits for the United States. Outsourcing has converted the original non-tradable activities of the United States to tradable services; in the meantime, the products outsourced to or imported from China, India, and other developing countries by the United States were generally low-value products, while the United States has provided products or services with high added value to other countries as it possessed core technology, complicated integration, and branding capacity. Therefore, based on the net value of US import/export trade in the outsourcing process, there is no doubt that the United States is the winner in global manufacturing. The United States also pointed out possible risks in global outsourcing; for instance, technology spillover in the outsourcing process might enhance technical capacity of China, India, and other developing countries, thus causing adverse impact on US trade conditions. However, since the United States may continuously develop new technologies and new products to increase its economic efficiency, damages to US trade caused by later-developing countries may be outweighed by its trade benefits.[6]

But it was to this very point that Samuelson and other "conditional protectionist" scholars raised objections. They argued that globalization has not always increased US benefits and may hurt US benefits under specific conditions. The specific conditions here mainly refer to relative technological capability of the United States and its trade partner countries. Samuelson analyzed three possible scenarios of US-China free trade: (i) both sides would gain benefits from the bilateral free trade; (ii) the United States would unilaterally gain benefits but China would suffer losses; and (iii) China would unilaterally gain benefits by improving its productivity via trade—that is, if China increased its productivity at a faster speed through technology learning and catch-up, the Sino-US division of labor in manufacturing would damage the benefits to the United States.[7] If policy reasoning was conducted based on such theory, the United States should, on the one hand, quicken the development of new products and new industries to ensure its productivity advantage and, on the other hand, adopt strategic policy in the process of utilizing the global supply chain system to suppress technological catch-up by later-developing countries, which was the core content of the Trump administration's economic policy towards China. Therefore, different judgments on the relative speed of technical capacity between later-developing countries and developed countries (mainly China and the United States) have constituted the basis of economic theories on the supply chain globalization. The fundamental reasons for the United States to promote protectionism and de-globalization include that following: (i) China has significantly enhanced its forward design capacity and original innovation on the basis of long-term technology learning and accumulation of technological capacity, and it has ceaselessly created substitutes for the United States' high-tech and high added value products; and (ii) the United States has inhibited China's technological catch-up. One point that needs to be added is that mainstream economics has analyzed the issue of supply chain globalization mainly from relatively stable and "routine" cost–benefit factors such as labor cost, technological capability, and market scale, while management science has further introduced emergent risk factors (e.g. an earthquake, the COVID-19 pandemic) and the corresponding issue of supply chain security into analysis of the paradigm and adjustment of the global supply chain. This point provides an important theoretical supplement for a more comprehensive understanding of the issue of adjustments in the global supply chain.

From efficiency to safety: The COVID-19 pandemic accelerated localization and diversification of the global supply chain

The impact of the COVID-19 pandemic on the global supply chain has been manifested at three interconnected levels: (i) delayed delivery of orders due to the suspension of work and production in upstream enterprises and the decrease in the capacity and efficiency of logistics; (ii) decline in the scale and efficiency of production caused by disrupted upstream supply or sluggish downstream demand; and (iii) adjustments by enterprises in the supply chain structure and relationship for strategic consideration of supply chain security, including increase or replacement of suppliers/buyers and adjustment of the global investment paradigm. The impact of the pandemic on the global supply chain has been mainly manifested as delay of order delivery and decrease in production scale in the short term and as deep changes of the supply chain structure and relationship in the long term.

Short-term impact: Continually increasing the risk of a disrupted global supply chain

According to the spread of the pandemic and changes in policies of all countries in response to the pandemic, the impact of the pandemic on the global supply chain can be roughly divided into three stages. The first stage extends from the end of 2019 with the outbreak in to the middle of March 2020 when the outbreak was controlled effectively in China but with large-scale outbreaks occurring in other countries. At this stage, after China's supply chain was suspended, the supply chain system in China slowed down and was even blocked out, leading to rapid impact on the global supply network. In addition to suspension of work and production, the insufficient service capacity of transportation (especially sea transportation and air transportation) has further affected the impact of China's supply chain block out on the global supply chain. According to analysis of trading volume and payment data on the world's largest business collaboration platform, Tradeshift, the overall trade activities in China decreased by 56 percent, the number of orders between Chinese enterprises decreased by 60 percent, and the transaction volume between Chinese enterprises and international corporations decreased by 50 percent in the week from February 16 to 23, 2020, without considering the influencing factors before and after the Spring Festival from January to February 2020. According to the results of a questionnaire survey by the Council of Supply Chain Management Professionals with US enterprises in mid-February 2020, 62 percent of enterprises surveyed encountered delay of order delivery from China, 53 percent could not get supply chain information from China, 48 percent encountered delay of goods transport from China, and 46 percent encountered delay of shipment at Chinese ports. At the beginning of February, due to shortage of parts from China, the production line of the Hyundai Motor Company in South Korea was out of production across a large area, and part of the production lines of the Nissan Motor Company in Japan were also suspended in mid-February. Due to supply disruption of parts in China, some Nissan and Toyota factories in Japan had to stop production. For enterprises producing consumer electronics in the United States and Europe, such as cell phones and computers, the average delivery time of orders from China was delayed 4 to 6 weeks compared with normal operations. As a whole, the impact of the pandemic on the global supply chain at this stage has been manifested as the block out of the supply chain in China and China's one-way negative impacts on the global supply chain, such as late delivery and decreasing order numbers.

The second stage started from mid-March 2020 when the block out in overseas supply chain and the decline in demand had an adverse impact on supply chain security and efficiency in China. After March, the pandemic brought huge tests and challenges for Japan, South Korea, and then Italy, Germany, France, the United States, and most other European and North

American countries. In mid-March, some motor companies shut down their production in Europe and North America, one after another. China saw a quick recovery of production and work. According to survey data released by the Ministry of Industry and Information Technology on March 17, the work resumption rate of industrial enterprises above designated size in China (except Hubei) reached 95 percent, and it was nearly 100 percent in Zhejiang, Jiangsu, Shanghai, Shandong, Guangxi, and Chongqing. However, due to the disrupted supply chain and decreasing orders in foreign countries, the negative impact of the global pandemic on the supply chain started "flowing backward" to China; henceforth, the negative impacts on China's supply chain started interacting with those on the global supply chain. Meanwhile, because of the highly decentralized and complicated global manufacturing network, enterprises and governments could not monitor the potential risks in the supply chain, so it became very difficult for them to make accurate judgments and decisions to maintain a stable supply chain. On account of the global pandemic and the continuously deteriorating expectations of the trend of the pandemic, global production and investment contracted on a large scale. According to the prediction of the United Nations Conference on Trade and Development (UNCTAD) in March,[8] the COVID-19 pandemic would decrease global foreign direct investment by 40 percent, a record low in the past 20 years.

With the spread of the global pandemic, its impact on the global supply chain moved gradually from the second stage to the third stage. The third stage involved major changes taking place in the nature and direction of the impact of the pandemic on the global supply chain that would not only cause more severe delays to goods delivery and an even greater decrease in orders, but also lead to broad disruption of the global supply chain, thus exerting a fundamental impact on the global supply chain system with regard to the supply chain structure and supply chain relationship. According to the results of a questionnaire survey by the Council of Supply Chain Management Professionals with US enterprises in mid-March 2020, 36 percent of enterprises surveyed encountered supply chain disruption, and 28 percent were looking for alternative suppliers in other countries (this figure was 8 percent at the early stage of the outbreak). It may be seen that with the spread of the pandemic, its impact on the global supply chain has been escalating gradually from short-term impact to long-term impact.

Long-term impact: Speeding up the process of global supply chain localization and diversification

Despite its exogenous short-term impact, the COVID-19 pandemic has not changed the cost structure and technological capability in all countries. The factor cost of all countries and the trend of Sino-US trade conflicts have remained the main factors that will influence the trend of the global supply chain in the future, but the long-term impact of the pandemic has promoted

American and European entrepreneurs, researchers, and policymakers to pay close attention to the supply chain security factor at a strategic level, specifically to the so-called "China-oriented global supply chain system" pattern. In the long run, the adjustments in American and European supply chain strategy will inevitably deeply influence the dominant position of China's supply chain, though this is just a prime concern for China in terms of its strategic adjustment and policy deployment in the future.

Although the United States dominates the global innovation system, it is undeniable that the center of the global manufacturing system is located in China: China is the largest manufacturing center in the world, with its industrial added value accounting for nearly one quarter of global industrial added value, and its proportion in the global intermediate market up to one third. China is the largest trading partner of more than 120 countries, and the largest source of imports of approximately 65 countries. Since entering the WTO, China has gradually developed a dominant position in the global supply chain system and has intensified this continuously. Also, the degree of China's dependency on the global supply chain has decreased continuously, while the degree of the global supply chain's dependency on China's supply chain has increased gradually. An analysis of the global value chain shows that although the United States and Germany are still the most important hubs in the complicated global value chain network, China, as the supply and demand center in the traditional trade and simple global value chain network, has become more and more important in the global manufacturing network.[9]

In the Broad Economic Catalogue of the United Nations Commodity Trade Statistics Database, international traded goods are divided into intermediate goods, capital goods, and consumer goods. From 2003 to 2018, the proportion of China's import/export scale of goods in these three categories in the import/export scale of similar global goods increased significantly: the proportions of the value of imports of intermediate goods, capital goods, and consumer goods increased by 7.8 percent, 2.1 percent, and 3.1 percent, respectively; and the proportions of the value of exports increased by 7.1 percent, 15.2 percent, and 7.6 percent, respectively. From the perspective of China's import and export goods structure, from 2003 to 2018, the proportion of total imports and exports of China's intermediate goods and capital goods in total imports and exports decreased by 2.7 percent, but the proportion of the value of exports increased by 13 percent. This shows that China has changed gradually from relying on external inputs to export of supply capacity during its further integration into the global supply chain (see Figure 4.1). In addition, almost every district in China has been deeply embedded in the global supply chain system. Take as an example the epicenter of the pandemic in China, Wuhan: according to the statistics of Dun & Bradstreet, a US business information company, about 51,000 companies in the world have one or more of their direct suppliers in Wuhan, and 938 of Fortune 1000 Companies have their Tier 1 or Tier 2 suppliers in Wuhan.

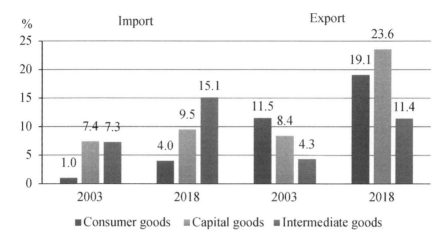

Figure 4.1 Proportion of global imports and exports for China's consumer goods, intermediate goods, and capital goods in 2003 and 2018 (%).

Source: United Nations Commodity Trade Statistics Database: https://comtrade.un.org

Due to extensive and deep participation of Chinese enterprises in the production systems of Asia, Europe, and North America, the supply chain security and even the public health security of all countries (e.g. pharmaceutical and protective supplies) have highly relied on China's supply chain. Even before the global outbreak in mid-February, according to predictions by the World Health Organization, the global demand for medical protective supplies had already increased 100-fold, and the prices had increased 20-fold. When the global pandemic occurred in mid-March, all countries in Europe and Asia banned the export of critical protective supplies, including masks, gloves, and protective clothing. Some American and European countries even intercepted the protective supplies of other countries. The shortage of epidemic prevention supplies was evident. After mid-March, Chinese enterprises gradually started resumption of work and production, and China became practically the only hope to solve global shortage of protective supplies. That is to say, at the first stage of the outbreak, the block out of China's supply chain caused a block out of the global supply chain; at the second stage of the outbreak, global public health security relied heavily on medical supplies from China. In this context, the American and European governments and enterprises were more concerned about the high dependence of their supply chain security and public health security on "Made in China" products. Bruno Le Maire, French Minister of Economy and Finance, even said:

> This pandemic is a "game changer" of globalization, because it exposes the vulnerability of international supply chain. The pandemic has exposed our "irresponsible and unreasonable" dependence on China. The

global supply relationship, especially the supply relationship of medical and automotive industries, needs to be reconsidered.

Therefore, the long-term impact of the pandemic on the global supply chain system is that supply chain security will gradually become an important commercial concern for American and European enterprises, pushing them to adjust the global industry chain layout, while ensuring domestic industry security and public health security will guide future policy changes by American and European governments.

The strategic measures of the United States and Europe to improve supply chain security in the future include two aspects. On the one hand, modern manufacturing technology will be utilized to increase manufacturing responsiveness. During the COVID-19 pandemic, American and European high-tech companies exhibited extremely high manufacturing flexibility and set benchmarks for global manufacturing enterprises. Siemens, General Electric, Boeing, and other companies have utilized 3D printing technology to produce masks. HP, the world's largest 3D printer supplier, has utilized its printer groups in the United States and Spain to produce mask adjusters, face masks, and other medical apparatus. Aenium, an aerospace parts enterprise, had capacity to change products and start supplying the urgently needed surgical mask filtering layer within about two weeks. This company utilized its laser technology for producing ultralight metal parts to develop four filtering layers made of hospital-grade polymers, which may be put into 3D printed masks developed by HP and may also be used for ventilators. We may anticipate that after the pandemic, American and European countries and enterprises will further quicken the application and popularization of new manufacturing technologies, including 3D printing, smart manufacturing, and reconfigurable production systems, so as to enhance timely adjustment and the capacity of the supply chain to respond to major outbreaks and disasters.

On the other hand, more importantly, the United States and Europe will push to change the current "China-oriented global supply chain system"; that is, enhancing their supply chain security by adjusting the structure of the global supply chain. First, they will promote the diversity of global sourcing and increase the diversity of the supply chain by adding sources of procurement other than mainland China or through multinational investment so as to reduce the risk of collective purchase from China. For example, they may increase procurement and production in Vietnam, Indonesia, Thailand, India, and other Asian economies. An important way that American and European countries expand diversified sourcing is to expand production and supply in neighboring countries and shorten the supply chain while increasing the diversity of the supply chain so as to simultaneously increase supply chain security and supply chain efficiency. For example, the United States has transferred more procurement and production to Mexico, Brazil, and other Latin American countries, while Europe has transferred more procurement and production to Eastern Europe and Turkey. Dun & Bradstreet has utilized

Table 4.2 Products that the United States imports most from China and possible alternative supplier countries

Products	Possible alternative supplier countries
Electrical machinery, equipment, and parts	Brazil
Nuclear reactor, boiler, and parts	Chile, Singapore
Furniture and parts	Mexico
Toys, games, and sports necessities	Mexico, Brazil
Plastic and plastic products	Mexico, Brazil
Motorcycle and parts	Chile, Columbia, India
Clothing and clothing accessories	Brazil, Canada
Optical, medical, and surgical instruments	Columbia, Brazil, India

Source: US Dun & Bradstreet website: www.dnb.com

economic data from the United Nations to calculate the products that the United States has imported most from China as well as the most promising supplier countries that can produce substitutes for these imported products (see Table 4.2).

Second, they will promote a manufacturing comeback with localized production. In fact, the United States and Europe had strong policy demands for localized manufacturing before the outbreak of COVID-19 globally. Both the German National Industrial Strategy 2030 and the Franco-German Manifesto for a European Industrial Policy Fit for the 21st Century, issued at the beginning of 2019, regarded supply chain security and production localization as important aspects of industrial policy adjustment. A manufacturing comeback has been key in the United States initiating Sino-US trade conflicts. Trump put forward the objective of a manufacturing comeback during his presidential campaign in 2016, and he launched a tax reform plan for this purpose and encouraged transnational corporations to move their business back to the United States. But, could American and European policy adjustments really lead to a large-scale manufacturing comeback? Take the United States as an example: Although some US enterprises were driven by Trump's adjustments in tax and trade policy and moved part of their manufacturing capacity back to the United States to meet domestic demands, there has been no large-scale manufacturing revival so far. By the end of 2019, employment in the US manufacturing industry accounted for 8.5 percent of total employment, falling back 0.1 percent compared with the previous year and decreasing by 0.3 percent compared with the average during Obama's tenure, a record low in the past 80 years. By the end of the third quarter of 2019, the proportion of manufacturing value added in the US GDP was 11.0 percent, falling back 0.3 percent compared with the previous year and 0.8 percent lower than the average during Obama's tenure, a postwar record low. Additionally, the China Business Climate Survey Report issued by the US-China Business Council in August 2019 showed that most US enterprises would continue to stay in the Chinese market, even if they transferred their investments out of China, and that more enterprises would move to other districts, with the proportion of enterprises moving back to the United States even decreasing by 1 percent compared with 2018.

Therefore, the changes of factor cost in different countries and the Sino-US trade conflicts will promote decentralized and localized development of the global supply chain, while the COVID-19 pandemic will further accelerate this process. As a whole, however, due to high manufacturing costs in American and European countries, there will be slim possibility of large-scale comeback of the manufacturing industry, especially the labor-intensive and capital-intensive manufacturing industry; nevertheless, decentralized production or diversification of the supply chain will become an important aspect of adjustments in the global supply chain in the future. In the past few decades, with the fast rise of China's manufacturing industry, the global supply chain tended to be more and more centralized. We have used the export share of industrial products of 29 countries and regions (28 main industrial countries, other countries are deemed as one region) to calculate the export Herfindahl-Hirschman Index (HHI) of global industrial products, the results of which show an uptrend in both the share of China's industrial products in global exports and the export HHI of global industrial products. The uptrend in the global HHI has become more evident after China entered the WTO in 2000 (see Figure 4.2). However, due to rising factor costs in China as well as changes in US trade policy and the COVID-19 pandemic, in the future, the

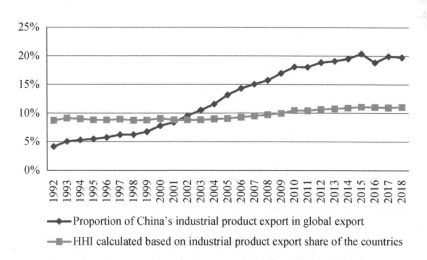

Figure 4.2 Changes in proportion of global imports and exports for China's intermediate goods and capital goods, 1992–2018 (%).

Source: World Bank and National Bureau of Statistics of China

increasingly prominent industry chain security factor will drive decentralized adjustment and evolution of the global supply chain, and the HHI will show a downtrend. In particular, while the United States transferred its manufacturing to Mexico, Brazil and other Latin American countries, and Germany, France, England, and other European countries transferred their manufacturing to Eastern Europe, Turkey, and other countries, the so-called "peripheral production" will probably become a strategic focus of the United States and Europe for localization and production of the global supply chain in the future. On the one hand, these geographically adjacent countries could increase economic efficiency of the supply chain; on the other hand, the United States and Europe, as industrial powers, will have very strong political influence on those countries to which they moved their factories, so as to secure supply chain security.

Domino effect: Conjecture on the future adjustment mechanism in the global supply chain

After analyzing the possible impact of the COVID-19 pandemic on the global supply chain adjustment, we have an interesting ensuing question: will concerns about supply chain security really drive American and European governments and enterprises to make adjustments in the global supply chain? In fact, external impacts on the global supply chain will not be the main influence. When the devastating tsunami and earthquake occurred in Fukushima, Japan, in 2011, many high-tech companies located in Fukushima were key producers in the global supply chain; for instance, about 22 percent of 300 mm semiconductor silicon wafers, 60 percent of key auto parts, and a large number of lithium battery chemicals and conductive film for tablets, PCs, and liquid crystal displays have been made by Japanese manufacturers located in Fukushima, many of whom were single sources for American and European enterprises. When American and European supply chains were affected by the disaster, there was heated discussion about supply chain security in American and European academic and business circles. However, after Japanese enterprises in Fukushima gradually resumed production, it was evident that supply chain security had not driven the diversification of American and European enterprises' supply chains. Why have American and European senior management not learned lessons from the Fukushima earthquake and nuclear disaster? It is because American and European enterprises, as profit-seeking capital, will not sacrifice supply chain efficiency and competitiveness for an event of very small probability.

So we can't help but ask: is the worry about supply chain security at this time only a momentary uproar among American and European enterprises in case of a temporary disruption in the global supply chain caused by the global COVID-19 pandemic? Once the global COVID-19 pandemic is controlled effectively, the global supply chain will restore its normal operation, and American and European enterprises will still continue with the existing supply chain; therefore, the so-called China-oriented global supply chain system will not change fundamentally. Our answer: the COVID-19 pandemic is most likely to be an important turning point of adjustment in the global supply chain system; that is, the COVID-19 pandemic will promote American and European governments and more American and European enterprises to reconstruct the supply chain. Under the influence of the Sino-US trade conflicts and other factors, the global supply chain system will develop in a diversified and decentralized direction. Adjustment in the global supply chain after the COVID-19 pandemic will probably be triggered by the following two factors: (i) localized production of pharmaceuticals, medical devices, and protective supplies; and (ii) escalating suppression of China's high-tech industries and enterprises by the United States. Both of these factors will aggravate the protectionism of American and European trade and investment policies and trigger quick adjustment in the global supply chain through demonstration effect and counter effect.

First, the COVID-19 pandemic will promote pharmaceuticals and medical devices and other industries to initiate localization of the global supply chain, while American and European concerns about public health security will likely expand to industry security and even national security, thus generalizing the supply chain security problem and finally leading to the deglobalization process and localization of the global supply chain system. The shortage of medical supplies such as medicines, ventilators, protective clothing, surgical masks, gloves, and disinfectants has become the most serious challenge facing all countries in the epidemic protection process. Even the United States and Germany, as manufacturing powers, have had to purchase protective products from China or violate international rules by intercepting aid materials and orders of other countries to guarantee their domestic medical protective supplies. During the outbreak, Stephen Hahn, Food and Drug Administration (FDA) Chief, said in a declaration that the United States has encountered a shortage of 20 drugs, bulk drugs, or finished products of these drugs imported from China. According to statistics from China's Ministry of Commerce, pharmaceutical raw materials, intermediate products, or final products of 95 percent of ibuprofen, 91 percent of cortisol, 70 percent of acetaminopher, 40 percent of heparin, and 45 percent of penicillin imported by the United States in 2019 came from Chinese manufacturers. According to FDA statistics in 2018, with respect to medicines on the US market, 88 percent of bulk drugs came from abroad, with China's share accounting for 14 percent; 24 percent of finished drugs and 31 percent of bulk drugs came from India, but 70 percent of Indian pharmaceutical raw materials came from China. In view of public health security, the former FDA chief once gave a special report to the Senate in which he suggested that Congress grant relevant permissions to the FDA so that it could impose compulsory requirements on American pharmaceutical enterprises to evaluate and submit potential risks of their supply chain. Bruno Le Maire also publicly said: "We shall not continue to rely on China for 80 percent to 85 percent of active pharmaceutical ingredients." It may be expected that after the pandemic, the political pressure from public health security will drive European and American governments to quicken localization of pharmaceuticals and medical devices industries. Once localization of these industries has become a trend in America and Europe, and efficient local industry chains have been gradually developed, the demonstration effect of adjustments in the global supply chain of these industries will probably induce adjustment in American and European industrial policies and business policies, so as to form a decentralized and localized global supply chain.

Another important reason for accelerated localization and decentralization of the global supply chain after the COVID-19 pandemic is that the United States will further suppress China's high-tech industries on the grounds of industry security and information security. Before the COVID-19 pandemic, the United States has already started suppression of China's high-tech industry development and technological catch-up by raising tariffs. The fundamental cause for the United States to initiate trade war was not to reduce trade deficit, but to change the relative share of benefits from Sino-US trade, just as revealed above in the "conditional protection theory" put forward by Samuelson. Such change has been determined by relative technological capability of the two countries; therefore, suppressing China's technology has been the fundamental objective of the United States to further aggravate Sino-US trade conflicts and the fundamental impetus for adjustments in the global supply chain in the future. According to a latest report issued by the World Intellectual Property Organization, China submitted a total of 58,990 applications through the Patent Cooperation Treaty (PCT) of the World Intellectual Property Organization in 2019 (53,345 applications in 2018), surpassing the United States for the first time since the establishment of the PCT in 1978 and ranking first in the world. The United States ranked second in the world based on 57,840 applications in 2019 (56,142 applications in 2018). Facing the accelerating technological catch-up of China, once the pandemic is controlled effectively, US policy priorities will surely turn quickly from containing the pandemic to curbing China's progress. After Trump took office, the United States rapidly upgraded the focus from supply chain security to industry chain security at a national level. With the new strategic focus of curbing China, the US government has changed the traditional system by which its industrial sectors gave a decentralized response to the industry chain security of different fields. It has also developed a whole-of-government system to establish and strengthen relevant institutions across sectors (e.g. the Committee on Foreign Investment in the United States, the Supply Chain Working Group) or to establish a regular coordination mechanism across sectors (e.g. emerging and underlying technology prediction mechanism), so as to include the systems that generated industry chain security problems into sector policies and ensure overall visual field and comprehensive coordination of all sectors. While continuously strengthening the management system of industry chain security, the United States has accelerated its crackdown on China's high-tech industry. Once this crackdown on China's high-tech industry, especially 5G technology, touches the core benefits of China maintaining technological progress and industry development, the US suppression and China's countermeasures in ICT and other high-tech industries will probably be upgraded to a large-scale technology war and trade war, thus accelerating adjustment in the paradigm of the global supply chain, value chain, and innovation chain.

That is to say, the global supply chain reconstruction of pharmaceuticals and medical devices driven by the COVID-19 pandemic, along with the crackdown of the United States on China's high-tech industry, will probably intensify global protectionism and lead to the domino effect of more and more localized and decentralized industry supply chains.

Short-term policy and long-term strategy for adjustment in the global supply chain

The pandemic itself has short-term impact, but its impact on the global supply chain will last for a long time. Facing decentralization and diversification challenges of the global supply chain, China should quicken the recovering rhythm and efficiency of the supply chain, strengthen unified planning and deployment of foreign investment and technology strategy, and fundamentally improve its active adaptability to adjustments in the global supply chain in the long term.

Short-term policy responses: Speeding up collaborative recovery of the industry chain

With respect to the impact of the COVID-19 pandemic on the supply globally and in China, China should aim at a quick recovery of the operating efficiency of its supply chain in the short term, strengthen the resilience of China's supply chain and fast responsiveness to international demands, and minimize the negative impact of the pandemic on China's supply chain as far as possible. First, China should quicken orderly resumption of work and production, strengthen disclosure of foreign manufacturer-oriented information, fully exhibit the resilience and vigor of China's supply chain system, maintain and strengthen the vantage point of China in the global supply chain system, and grasp the "time lag" between domestic and foreign supply chain recovery to turn crises into opportunities. As the pandemic deteriorates, more and more American and European countries will take more severe lockdown and quarantine measures (e.g. Italy stopped production activities from March 23, 2020), and the local supply chain systems in the United States and Europe will be disrupted more seriously. If China controls the pandemic, demands on American and European markets for Chinese industrial products will rise significantly. Particularly, with respect to electronics and automobile industries in the complicated supply chain system, and petrochemical and pharmaceutical industries, American and European enterprises at the downstream of the supply chain will even introduce strategic reserve and procurement policies to ensure their production continuity, thus further increasing demand for Chinese industrial products. If Chinese enterprises can resume work and production in a timely and orderly manner, the demand growth in American and European markets will result in a quick recovery and even an upgrade of China's supply chain. In view of this, on the one hand, Chinese government at all levels should strengthen policy coordination and guarantees, repair the supply chain as soon as possible, enhance the modernization level of the Chinese industry chain, climb to the high end of the value chain, and occupy a more advantageous position in the global supply chain. On the other hand, China will fully utilize existing e-commerce platforms of the United States, Europe, and China, hold an online China Import and Export Commodities Fair to transfer positive information about industrial resumption in China to American and European markets, fully exhibit the resilience and recoverability of the Chinese industrial system in case of major outbreaks and disasters to offset the negative impact of diversified supply chains of American and European enterprises, and create another miracle in terms of the rise, rather than fall, of China's supply chain since the outbreak of SARS (severe acute respiratory syndrome) in 2003.

Second, China will actively establish a more comprehensive and systematic cooperation and control mechanism against COVID-19 with the international community. During collaborative anti-epidemic efforts, China should further promote the development of an international cooperation system and control mechanism for the global supply chain and enhance the right to speak and the imitativeness of China in the global supply chain system. On the one hand, China should quicken recovery of production capacity, improve global supply guarantees for epidemic prevention supplies, and powerfully support global epidemic prevention. On the other hand, China should promote international cooperation in the supply chain security field, including issuing a joint statement of supply chain security with main trade partners, creating a multichannel and multilevel supply chain security system, proposing the "supply chain anti-terrorism partner program," and making the "counterplan for the supply chain against natural disaster." China should establish a long-term cooperation mechanism with the World Customs Organization, International Maritime Organization, Universal Postal Union, and other international organizations in maritime affairs, shipping, postal service, and other fields to build a transregional resilient supply chain. China should organically combine global supply chain cooperation with the Belt and Road Initiative, encourage Chinese enterprises to "go abroad" through foreign direct investment to lay out the supply chain in the world, link the localized response of China's supply chain to the appeals of the United States and Europe for localized production, reduce the "zero-sum game" with other countries, and develop highly coordinated, friendlier cooperative strategic partnership in the supply chain.

Third, China will provide more policy supports for micro and small businesses, and it will improve weak points to ensure the immunity of China's supply chain. Compared to big enterprises, micro and small businesses may be vulnerable in the supply chain due to their weaker financial strength, supply chain management capacity, and order bargaining power. If the impact of the COVID-19 pandemic on the global supply chain lasts till the end of the second quarter, closedown and bankruptcy of a large number of micro and small businesses may occur. To keep healthy operation of the Chinese industry chain, specific services and policy supports should be provided for micro and small businesses, including extending loan duration, renewing the term of repayment for micro, small, and medium-sized enterprises facing repayment difficulties, guiding insurance institutions to provide insurance on resumption of work and production and business lockdown and insurance for employees with notifiable diseases in micro and small businesses, and setting up a labor supply and demand platform on the enterprise service cloud.

Long-term strategic adjustment: Actively promoting "integrating into localization"

Facing an irreversible trend of decentralization and localization of the global supply chain, China should adjust its foreign strategy and technological innovation strategy, actively adapt to adjustment in the global supply chain, try to occupy a more positive position in the global supply chain adjusting process, and minimize its negative impact on China.

First, we should take integrating into localization as a main line of strategy and quicken strategic foreign investment of China's manufacturing industry. Facing big challenges of adjustment in the global supply chain, we should consolidate regional attraction to China as a global manufacturing center by building a more open and fair environment for competition and investment. In our opinion, the policy orientation of maintaining China's global factory position, further increasing attraction to China for investment, will surely be important, but it is undeniable that as American and European awareness of supply chain security after the COVID-19 pandemic was strengthened and a new round of technological revolution and industrial revolution with intelligent and automatic production was prioritized, the space for China to further increase its participation in the global supply chain has become very narrow because localization and decentralization will be an irreversible trend of the global supply chain in the future. On this basis, the core of China's strategy in the future global supply chain should be targeted at accelerating the foreign direct investment of Chinese manufacturing enterprises, and Chinese enterprises should go abroad and meet the localization demand in the global supply chain so that China's manufacturing industry can reap maximum benefits with minimum loss in the adjusting process of the global supply chain. Therefore, China should actively promote foreign direct investment of the manufacturing industry in the future. Although China has accelerated

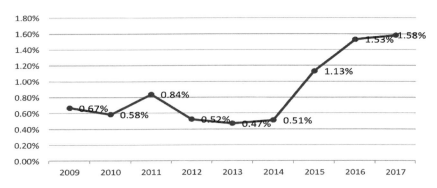

Figure 4.3 Ratio of China's foreign investment in the manufacturing industry to investment in fixed assets of the manufacturing industry.

Source: World Bank and National Bureau of Statistics of China

its foreign direct investment in recent years, its manufacturing capacity has remained highly centralized in mainland China since Chinese manufacturing enterprises were too dependent on the domestic market or too dependent on exports to occupy foreign markets. The relative scale of China's foreign investment in the manufacturing industry has remained small. Statistical data show that the relative growth of China's foreign direct investment in the manufacturing industry started to increase after 2014, and the ratio of China's foreign direct investment in the manufacturing industry to investment in fixed assets of the domestic manufacturing industry was merely 1.58 percent in 2017 (see Figure 4.3). To choose foreign investment destinations, with the slowdown of direct investment of American and European enterprises in China, Chinese enterprises have found it more and more difficult to absorb and study technologies in mainland China. Therefore, the entry of Chinese enterprises into American and European markets should be in the form of direct investment, becoming deeply embedded in the global innovation network dominated by the United States and Europe by occupying high-end or leading markets, and ensuring their strong position in the global innovation network. On the other hand, for the traditional labor-intensive manufacturing industry and low-skill links with the high-tech industry, China should actively enter Eastern European, Southeast Asian, and Latin American markets via direct investment and fully utilize the relative labor cost advantage of these countries. While encouraging foreign direct investment in the manufacturing industry, China should strengthen the construction of "mother factories" in mainland China and rely on these factories for sustainable innovation and upgrading of advanced manufacturing technology and process capacity in China.

Second, in the face of the escalating technology crackdown from the United States, the Chinese technological innovation environment will change fundamentally in the future. China must speed up the improvement of its own technological innovation system and enhance initial innovation capacity of its manufacturing industry. The key to strengthening the Chinese response to adjustments in the global supply is to increase Chinese technological capability; with more difficulties in technology learning caused by the technology crackdown by the United States, it is particularly important for China to build a more effective national innovation system, open new technology innovation routes, and increase initial innovation capacity and independent innovation ability. According to theories of Grossman and other scholars, the boundary of division of labor between developed and developing countries has remained clear: developed countries are engaged in high-value activities, while developing countries are engaged in low-value activities. However, once technological dynamics is introduced into the analysis of global value chain specialization, the boundary of division of labor between late-developing countries and developed countries will not remain static. When the technological capability of late-developing countries has accumulated more and more quickly and is approaching the technology frontier, benefits of developed countries from trade may be damaged. Though this is just the condition in the "conditional protection" theory emphasized by Samuelson, under which trade hurts developed countries. In the final analysis, increasing technological innovation capacity may be fundamental for developed countries or late-developing countries to occupy a favorable position in the global supply chain system and the value chain system. However, with adjustment being made in the global manufacturing system and innovation system, the technological capability of late-developing countries will be transferred from absorption capacity to initial innovation capacity. Requirements for these two capacities in late-developing countries' innovation systems and policy paradigms are different. When China gradually enters the stage of initial innovation capacity, on the one hand, it will strengthen intellectual property protection and encourage initial innovation rather than technical imitation; on the other hand, it will improve its scientific research system in national laboratories, generic technology research and development institutions, and research universities, and actively promote cooperation of research institutions with enterprises to strengthen fundamental research capacity and, in turn, develop independent innovation and an innovation-oriented policy system. It should be emphasized that in the period when global trade protectionism and de-globalization prevail, special attention should be paid to increasing China's independent innovation ability by market means and competition in order to prevent the evolution of countermeasures against the United States into severely conservative domestic industrial and innovation policies, thus leading to excessive government intervention and abuse of concentrating resources on major undertakings.

Third, China will improve its industry chain security management system. China should establish its early warning long-acting mechanism of supply chain security assessment and risk, and set up a National Industry Chain Security Committee for strategic decision-making and deployment of Chinese industry chain security issues caused by diplomatic incidents, foreign technology blockades, and major disasters and epidemics. This committee should be led by the State Council, with its members selected from the Ministry of Industry and Information Technology, the Development and Reform Commission, the Ministry of Foreign Affairs, the Ministry of Commerce, the Ministry of Finance, the Ministry of Science and Technology, the Intellectual Property Office, and other relevant departments. The Ministry of Industry and Information Technology should act as the executive agency. China should increase investment of funds and personnel, form a team and institution for professional industry chain security assessment, organize economists, technical experts, industry experts, and legal experts to form a professional committee on industry chain security assessment for long-term, sustainable, systematic, scientific, and rigorous research on the industry security chain, establish the knowledge system and method system for assessment of the Chinese industry chain, form a response strategy library for Chinese industry chain security, and develop a counterplan for different industry chain security circumstances at the levels of technology, market, capital, industrial policy, and diplomacy. China should improve its supply chain assessment and early-warning system for scientific assessment of the spillover effect and conduction effect of major events and disasters on China's supply chain and analyze and assess impact resistance of its supply chain as a whole in key fields and districts (clusters) to prevent against the pandemic and other force majeure events so that Chinese decision-making on industry chain security management may be more scientific and systematic. China should improve timely feedback of industry chain security monitoring data and information to supply chain participants, strengthen industry chain coordination, and improve the resilience and cooperation of China's supply chain to fight major disasters and epidemics.

Notes

1 World Bank, 2019, *Global Value Chain Development Report 2019: Technological Innovation, Supply Chain Trade, and Workers in a Globalized World.* Washington, DC: World Bank Group. www.worldbank.org/en/topic/trade/publication/global-value-chain-development-report-2019
2 Industrial chain, supply chain, and value chain are interrelated but not strictly defined concepts. In our opinion, the supply chain refers to the input–output trading relationship between enterprises and industries; the value chain refers to the interaction among production, research and development, marketing, financing, and other value-creating activities; while the industrial chain is a more general concept that includes supply chain and value chain.
3 UNCTAD, 2019, *World Investment Report 2019: Special Economic Zones.* Geneva: United Nations. https://unctad.org/webflyer/world-investment-report-2019
4 Although the World Bank report uses the concept of value chain, since its analysis of data is based primarily on value added in the input–output sense, we believe that it is actually analyzing the supply chain rather than the value chain issue.

5 World Bank, *Global Value Chain Development Report 2019*.

6 Gene Grossman and Elhanan Helpman, 2005, "Outsourcing in a Global Economy," *Review of Economic Studies*, Vol. 72, No. 1: 135–159; Robert C. Feenstra, 1998, "Integration of Trade and Disintegration of Production in the Global Economy," *Journal of Economic Perspectives*, Vol. 12, No. 4: 31–50.

7 Paul A. Samuelson, 2004, "Where Ricardo and Mill Rebut and Confirm Arguments of Mainstream Economists Supporting Globalization," *Journal of Economic Perspectives*, Vol. 18, No. 3: 135–146.

8 UNCTAD, 2020, *Investment Policy Monitor*, Issue 23. https://unctad.org/en/PublicationsLibrary/diaepcbinf2020d1_en.pdf

9 World Bank, *Global Value Chain Development Report 2019*.

5 Tertiary industry under the COVID-19 pandemic

Impact and response

Xia Jiechang

The COVID-19 outbreak is the major public health emergency with the quickest propagation speed, most extensive infection scope, and highest difficulty in prevention and control since the founding of new China in 1949. This outbreak spread all over the world and has become a global pandemic in almost all countries and regions in the world and a public health crisis that occurs once in a century. As of July 4, 2020, global cumulative confirmed cases exceeded 11 million persons, with a death toll of over 530,000. The tertiary industry (service industry) accounts for half of China's national economy, its contribution rate to gross domestic product (GDP) reaching 59.4 percent. Analysis of how the pandemic is influencing the tertiary industry is of important theoretical value and practical significance for innovating the tertiary industry development mode, finding countermeasures, promoting restorative growth of tertiary industry, and enhancing development toughness of tertiary industry.

Tertiary industry under the pandemic: Impact and differentiation

Serious impact on specific service sectors that rely on passenger source and physical premises

During this pandemic, service industries that rely heavily on passenger source and physical premises, especially closed physical premises, including catering, aviation, tourism, entertainment, and retail, have been severely impacted by the pandemic, causing sharp decline in earnings of such enterprises and temporary unemployment of relevant employees. Since the 2020 Spring Festival, the total number of passengers dispatched by railway, roads, waterways, and civil airlines has decreased significantly compared with the same period last year; in the meantime, sectors involved in culture and entertainment, sports, and tourism (travel agencies, hotels and scenic spots, etc.) were almost closed down. Due to the nature of different categories in the service sector, the impact of the pandemic on the sector is different from that on other sectors. Based on limited relevant data, only four sectors—aviation, entertainment,

DOI: 10.4324/9781003184447-6

catering, and tourism—were selected to estimate possible economic losses resulting from the impact of the pandemic. As service sectors featuring highly centralized and flowing populations and requiring specific physical premises or even closed physical premises for customers, these four sectors were the most severely affected by the pandemic. Therefore, these four service sectors were selected for analysis because of their relevance.

Civil aviation enterprises suffering huge losses

People are most easily infected with the coronavirus in closed physical spaces. Airports, as public places with strong public services and intensive passenger flows, have higher risk of viral infection during the pandemic, so effective measures must be taken to enhance safety management and public health and epidemic prevention and to reduce passenger flow in these specific places. Airports, airlines, and relevant enterprises suffered severe losses in February and March 2020. According to relevant data from the Statistics of Main Production Indicators of Chinese Civil Aviation, in February 2020, tourist traffic of domestic routes in China decreased by 84.8 percent year on year, and international routes decreased by 82.4 percent. At present, as the pandemic has been significantly alleviated in China, airlines in China are likely to restore normal operation after May. However, due to the global pandemic, all countries have chosen to close borders and issue flight bans one after another; as a result, international flights have declined significantly and even entered a state of shutdown. According to the Civil Aviation Administration news spokesman Xiong Jie, due to the impact of the COVID-19 pandemic, the total turnover volume of air transportation decreased by 46.6 percent year on year in the first quarter of 2020, and air passenger traffic decreased by 53.9 percent year on year, causing an accumulated loss of RMB 39.82 billion, to which airlines contributed RMB 33.62 billion.[1] It was estimated that if the pandemic could be controlled at the end of April and normal operation of airlines restored gradually in May 2020, the total income loss for the year for the aviation industry in China might be RMB 90–100 billion.

Impact of the pandemic on the entertainment industry

According to relevant data in the 2019 White Paper on China's Pan-Entertainment Industry issued by the Ministry of Industry and Information Technology, the output value of China's pan-entertainment core industry was about RMB 415.5 billion in 2019. As the lasting impact of the pandemic on entertainment enterprises could not be mitigated and this sector would possibly be the last to resume work, the loss incurred by this sector would be RMB 138.5 billion, though this was calculated using data from just 4 months. According to the result of a survey by CEIBS Business Review, entertainment enterprises were commonly short of cash flow: 34.0 percent had cash in hand for only 1 month, 33.1 percent for only 2 months, and 17.9 percent for only

3 months. If the pandemic could be controlled before April 2020, almost 67 percent of entertainment enterprises would face the risk of bankruptcy. Even if only 30 percent of the enterprises faced the risk of bankruptcy, the final impact of the pandemic on the sector in the year would be RMB 83.1 billion. Therefore, shutdown and bankruptcy of enterprises would lead to an economic loss in the entertainment industry up to RMB 174.1 billion for the year.[2] This clearly indicates the severe impact of the pandemic on the entertainment industry.

Impact of the pandemic on the tourist industry

As an important industry in the national economy, the tourist industry involves travel, delicacies, accommodation, shopping, and recreation. The COVID-19 pandemic hit both the domestic market and the international market. Earnings of the tourist industry may be divided into two categories, domestic tourist income and international tourist income. Affected by the pandemic, many countries have suspended domestic flights and announced travel alerts, which has led to a sharp decline in the international tourist income. Foreign exchange earnings from international tourism were USD 127.1 billion in 2018, and calculated according to the lasting impact of the pandemic over 4 months, international tourist income will decrease by at least USD 42.4 billion in 2020, roughly equivalent to about RMB 296.8 billion.[3] It now seems that the global pandemic might impact international tourism for more than 6 months, causing the international tourist income to decrease by USD 63.6 billion, roughly equivalent to RMB 444.8 billion. In addition, the total annual tourist spending in China was RMB 5.1 trillion in 2018; after the outbreak in 2020, based on a conservative estimate of the pandemic's impact over 4 months, the annual domestic tourist income would probably decrease by one third, or RMB 1.7 trillion.[4] Shrinkage of the tourism market seemed inevitable in 2020 as services such as conferences and exhibitions, meetings, study tours, business travel, sports tourism, and medical tourism would have to be postponed or cancelled. The impact of the pandemic on the tourist industry also had a "long-tail effect" with a certain time lag. Hit by the pandemic, consumers could not eliminate psychological fear in the short term, and the tourist inclination would probably dip downward. In response to the global pandemic, European and American countries have had less time for control measures; therefore, outbound travel and inbound travel might see a downturn for nearly 1 year, with the degree of the pandemic's impact on both outbound and inbound travel depending on the severity of the pandemic, overseas response measures, and the implementation of a tourism revival plan.

Impact of the pandemic on the catering industry

Food is regarded as the primary item among human daily necessities. China is a country full of various delicacies, so the catering industry has occupied a special position in China. With increased income levels, more and more Chinese people have chosen to have meals in restaurants, causing the spending on a single consumption to rise. Catering is a typical labor-intensive service industry and plays an important role in creating jobs in the service sector and in paying local taxes. As takeout service has become popular, food delivery services may help reduce partial losses for the catering industry during the pandemic, unlike the story in the air transportation, tourism, and entertainment industries. In China, earnings in the catering sector amounted to RMB 4.7 trillion from January to December 2019, averaging RMB 389.2 billion monthly. The period before and after the Spring Festival has generally been the quickest income growth period for the catering industry, but affected by the pandemic, large-scale hotels, chain catering enterprises, and small restaurants all over China suspended business in February and March. Even if the pandemic can be alleviated in the future, due to psychological fear and other factors, consumers' high enthusiasm for eating out will cool down, and the established habit of dining together will probably be discarded. Normal operation of the catering industry might be fully recovered after overall elimination of the pandemic. Considering the degree of development of takeout services, based on a 50 percent loss in 3 consecutive months, the loss incurred by the catering industry in this period was approximately RMB 583.8 billion. If financial pressure of 3 months and bankruptcy of some catering enterprises is taken into consideration, the annual economic loss for the catering industry would be likely to exceed RMB 1 trillion.[5]

The COVID-19 pandemic has been controlled effectively in China since March 2020, with "zero cases" realized in most districts and production and markets restored gradually. However, the pandemic broke out in countries and regions other than China. As of April 26, 2020, confirmed cases of the COVID-19 pandemic exceeded 2.8 million, with a death toll over 200,000. If the global pandemic is controlled effectively in a short time, the Chinese service industry will quickly restore normal operation; if so, there will be no evident change in the fundamentals of the service market, such as supply and demand, service factor mobility, and resource allocation, and restorative growth of services will probably be realized in the second half of the year. If the global pandemic cannot be controlled in the near term, and it spreads to Africa, South America, and Southeast Asia, international flow of service factors will be further obstructed. Advancement in information technology has changed the nature of services (i.e. local production for local consumption), greatly promoted service globalization. But shrinkage of the international market has led inevitably to shrinkage of the domestic market, domestic service enterprises being hit heavily for a second time, and a setback in the boom in service trade that occurred in recent years. Therefore, we should take precautions to fully utilize the huge domestic market, expand domestic demand, and slow down loss of service industry during the pandemic.

Differentiated impact of the pandemic on traditional service industry and emerging service industry

The pandemic has directly hit supply and demand or production and marketing sides of the service industry. In general, we may divide the service industry into the traditional service industry and the emerging service industry. The pandemic hit the traditional service industry on the demand side. Negative impact of the pandemic on transport, tourism, catering, hotels, and other traditional services appeared to be more direct and evident, inevitably leading to a short-term negative growth of the service industry. Proof of this was the negative growth of 5.2 percent of the Chinese service industry in the first quarter of 2020. The Chinese service industry has accounted for more than half of economic aggregate; service employees make up about 47 percent, but serious impact of the pandemic might cause tens of millions of service employees to lose their jobs temporarily. After elimination of the pandemic's impact and restorative growth of services, these persons might return to their jobs, but they may also have few employment opportunities due to transform- ation and upgrading of their original enterprises, or some of them may lose their jobs due to enterprises taking bankruptcy in this period, leaving workers to face very serious employment pressure. The traditional service industry, such as transport, logistics, tourism, and conference and exhibition services, that requires nonlocal flow of personnel to provide services, may remain almost stagnant due to strict local quarantine or control measures; service industries that require space for gathering and leisure time, such as catering, sports events, and entertainment industries, have been out of service or open in limited periods due to worry about virus transmission in crowds.

However, the COVID-19 pandemic had a slight positive impact on digital services. Network and digital technology have alleviated the impact of the pandemic on new services and provided new development opportunities and environments for digital services. The COVID-19 pandemic occurred in a network and digital era in which the digital economy, sharing economy, and platform economy based on modern information technology have developed rapidly, and the network information technology and digital technology economy have been deeply integrated into services development in an all- round way; in addition, the technological progress and business innovation models have reconstructed the traditional services and created many emerging service business models. At present, digital reconstruction and upgrading of services have gained attention in China, as service supply and consumption patterns are being reconstructed. Digital transformation of services may miti- gate some economic losses of services because consumption behaviors and production activities that originally had to be realized through movement of persons or nonlocal consumption may now be realized remotely via the Internet in the form of "contactless service."

Since network and digital technology have greatly reduced service costs, remote services may become more prosperous during the pandemic; for example, distance learning, online entertainment, online advertising, network live broadcasts, video conferencing, cloud conferences and exhibitions, and cloud tourism. In addition, the pandemic has brought about development opportunities for service activities in cyberspace, which are further forming their own competitive advantage in relevant Chinese service sectors, upgrading technology and innovating products continuously so as to obtain better development opportunities. For example, under the impact of this pandemic, service sectors such as hotels, scenic spots, and other tourist attractions have launched online booking, robot services, and other contactless services. Once the pandemic was basically controlled in China, scenic spots were opened in an orderly way to prevent overcrowding, and more reliance has been put on contactless services that made disruptive change in the industry. This could enhance quality, open up new business forms, and cultivate new growth points for the tourist industry. With the Internet and network technology, some tourist destinations have launched cloud tourism activities during the pandemic so that consumers could enjoy famous scenic areas in China on WeChat or Weibo platforms while staying at home. According to a survey, 71.5 percent of interviewees went out to travel for a time after the pandemic, and 20.7 percent chose not to travel before the pandemic was controlled. Online tourism programs can strengthen offline tourism. From online viewing to interactive live broadcasts, various forms of cloud tourism have offered fresh ways to upgrade tourism quality and will create huge tourist flows for offline tourism after full recovery of the tourist industry.[6] In another example, during full quarantine after the 2020 Spring Festival in China, traditional film and television companies lost popularity, but online film and live broadcast videos developed rapidly in this situation. Gaming, live broadcasting, and short video industries have seized new development opportunities; for instance, the number of cell phone game users increased 30 percent compared to before the outbreak.[7]

Data on service industry development in the first quarter from the National Bureau of Statistics of China verified the above-mentioned analysis and judgment. In the first quarter of 2020, China's service industry decreased by 5.2 percent, but the information service and public health service increased quickly, offsetting the decline in the traditional service industry to some extent. For example, during the pandemic prevention and control period, both the information demand for e-commerce, online education, web conferencing, remote diagnosis and treatment, and the information service industry based on Internet technology have increased rapidly, with the information service industry seeing a year-on-year increase in added value of 13.2 percent. However, the traditional service industry suffered big losses, with the added value of accommodation and catering, wholesale and retail, and transport storage and postal services decreasing by 35.3 percent, 17.8 percent, and 14.0 percent year on year, respectively.[8] It is clear that the impact of the pandemic on China's service industry was enormous, but the structural signs remained particularly obvious. China's service industry will probably experience differentiation and fission in its development process under the pandemic, so we should improve the situation, grasp the trend of structural upgrading, and continuously improve service supply and consumption patterns.

Serious impact of the pandemic on the employment capacity and pattern of the service industry

Quarantine is the most effective action against the COVID-19 pandemic. However, long periods of quarantine or social distancing have adverse effects on production, investment, market trading, business contacts, and everyday life, and some employees, especially those involved in transport, culture and entertainment, sports events, catering and hotel industries, might lose their jobs. The scale of employment in China's service industry was about 360 million in 2018; if about 6 percent of employees in the service industry lose their jobs or remain underemployed due to this outbreak, there would be about 20 million workers out of work. Of course, if the pandemic is controlled quickly and market and business activities are restored, most employees who lose their jobs will return to their original jobs or look for new employment opportunities.

As the COVID-19 pandemic prevailed, service sectors such as catering, tourism, and hotel accommodation have almost closed down, leaving many workers idle and suddenly increasing employment pressure in labor-intensive industries. With huge demands being transferred to online services, online orders have risen suddenly and sharply. There appeared to be a shortage of employees in local takeout enterprises, logistics, and other life services industries. During the pandemic, different types of service enterprises shared their employees to alleviate employment pressure to some degree, or they innovated new employment forms. During the pandemic, remote online offices emerged, and online collaboration became a common mode of operation, introducing changes in employment patterns after work resumption. It may be expected that change in operation modes during the pandemic as well as development of the platform economy and sharing economy will lead to informal employment such as "flexible employment" and "self-employment" becoming new patterns in many service sectors, continuously enriching employment forms and alleviating employment pressure.

Scarce capacity of China's service industry in response to the impact of the COVID-19 pandemic

Weak supply chain affects sustainability of the service industry

The digital service industry boomed during the pandemic, implying digitalization of the service industry has become a main transformation and innovation against public health emergencies. To realize digital transformation of the service industry, the key lies in timely supply and efficient distribution of offline production and logistics to consumers. The spread of the pandemic has hit the supply chain and distribution chain of the service industry directly, thus leading to market shrinkage and a sharp drop in consumption. This was a serious challenge that the service industry had to face during this pandemic. For example, a survey of national couriers by the State Post Office Bureau in 2019 shows that 76.31 percent of couriers came from rural areas, 15.89 percent from counties, and only 7.80 percent from cities. Under dual pressure from epidemic prevention and control and the volume of people returning to hometowns during the Spring Festival, these couriers could not or were reluctant to return from their hometowns to their places of work. As a result, overall work resumption of express enterprises was postponed. For example, YTO Express declared official resumption of work from January 28, but hard-hit areas were excluded; Deppon Express started mutual express services from February 3; STO Express declared overall work resumption from February 10; but some even did not issue an explicit time schedule for overall work resumption.[9] Logistics has been seen as a core link in the supply chain or as the hub linking production and consumption; but if logistics is impeded, the resumption of work and production would not be implemented.

Rigid man-hour system suppresses the efficiency of resumption of the service industry

The service industry has faced increasingly individualized and undetermined changes in demand, including changes due to the external impact of the pandemic. However, most Chinese service industries (traditional service industry and emerging service industry) have adopted a fixed man-hour system and fixed production mechanism and staffing mode. China has lagged far behind developed countries in employment flexibility; the employment system and mechanism of China's service industry have been seriously rigescent, thus suppressing the flexible employment response, quick rebound, and flexible growth capacity of the service industry under exceptional circumstances, and fixing the labor cost of enterprises. So we are in urgent need of an adjustment mechanism and policy support; for example, a more flexible treatment scheme for the arrangement of social security and labor relations. During epidemic prevention and control, in order to reduce personnel gathering, service enterprises intending to resume production should be encouraged to take flexible employment measures, create conditions for remote interactive collaboration to enable flexible offices, or negotiate with employees for flexible work time, such as staggered office hours, flexible commuting, etc. This has played an important role in the feasibility and improved efficiency of work and production resumption, and this has been verified by international experience. Therefore, it's very necessary to reform employment to create more resilient and flexible employment patterns.

Extensive decrease in the rebound strength of the service industry

Emerging services, including digital services (such as online tourism, online booking, etc.) have been important in offsetting the impact of the pandemic, but they have suffered the dual restraints of capital shortage and personnel shortage under the impact of the pandemic. Modern services, whether online or offline, have been reliant on creative content and innovative products to realize growth. At present, most network platform services and online services in China have improved circulation efficiency but lacked content innovation. Online booking, food ordering, or shared rental and shared accommodation services have expanded their operating channels via networks, but there has been no substantial difference in service quality and content. The impact of the pandemic has further highlighted the need for breakthroughs in service content and product innovations in China's service industry. China's service industry should utilize specific national circumstances and industry features to find ways to rapidly increase creative content and innovative products, so as to resist the impact of external emergencies and improve its own capacity for restoration.

Medical allocation distorts and weakens the balance effect of the service industry

From the perspective of supply, as medical services output was treated as public goods or quasi-public goods with obvious externalities, fully publicly owned medical services have placed a heavy burden on government and led to low efficiency, while fully privately owned services have caused market failure and had a negative effect on consumer welfare.[10] Through years of reforms, some improvement has been achieved in China's medical health system, but the performance and resource allocation of public health services have been unequal, with market failure and unfair distribution not solved fundamentally.[11] Therefore, the Chinese government should assume main responsibility for the construction of a medical services system, adopt public–private partnership to alleviate shortages of medical resources, promote availability of medical services, and meet diversified demands of medical services. In an equilibrium state of mixed provision, private medical services have met high-end demands and public health services have met basic needs; compared with strict private provision, mixed provision has improved employee welfare, and at a lower cost than pure public provision.[12] At present, China's medical services rely mainly on public hospital resources, and the market pricing mechanism is inappropriate for lack of private medical services with incentive and supervisory measures as a supplement. Therefore, in the case of sudden epidemic outbreak, there will be a lot of uncertainties in disease morbidity and prominent conflicts between significantly increased medical demand and shortage of medical services provision.[13] From the perspective of the configuration of medical resources in China, the "inverted triangle" structure has not matched the pathogenesis of the coronavirus. The World Health Organization reported that allocation of public medical resources should be structured according to a "regular triangle": about 80 percent of patients should be given access to primary medical institutions, and high-end health facilities should mainly focus on difficult and complicated diseases. After the outbreak of COVID-19, a huge number of patients crowded into high-end health facilities while very few patients visited primary medical institutions. This was because medical health resources were misallocated and patients had low confidence in community health service workers, thus leading to overcrowded high-end health facilities and seriously unused community health service resources.

Low efficiency of community services and management weakens the capacity of the service industry to contain the pandemic

Consumer services, which refer to service activities that meet the final consumption demand of residents and are important components of the modern service industry, can drive economic development, increase social employment, and improve living standards of residents. Generally speaking, consumer services have been targeted for and rooted in communities to meet above 75 percent of basic livelihood needs of the residents.[14] However, as one community is governed independent of another in China, community services have always been a shortcoming in the development of the service industry. Take elderly care as an example: as the provision of relevant service factors has been basically separated from community management, the elderly care service industry that should be vibrant within the community has become less so, thus severely suppressing consumer demand for community elderly care. The elderly were most severely hit by the coronavirus and in urgent need of community management, community services, and elderly care. For a long time, little has been done in this field, and it could not provide strong support in the "anti-epidemic" work. To increase community governance and the level of community services, we must increase consumer services that reflect community needs (especially the needs of the elderly population), continuously innovate the consumer services model, and actively promote a diversified, convenient, secure, and radiated circle of community business.

Stabilizing the uptrend of the tertiary industry

Facing up to the severe impact of the pandemic on the service industry

As the most serious global public health event after World War II, the COVID-19 pandemic has had an inestimable impact on the normal operation of the global economy and personnel mobility, and on China's economic and social development. This is verified by macroeconomic data for the first quarter of 2020 made public by the National Bureau of Statistics of China on April 17, 2020. GDP in the first quarter of 2020 decreased by 6.8 percent year on year, of which primary industry decreased by 3.2 percent, secondary industry decreased by 9.6 percent, and tertiary industry decreased by 5.2 percent. Other macroeconomic indicators also declined dramatically. However, we should not simply compare current economic data with previous data, nor should we judge whether China's economy has depressed or encountered economic and financial crisis from this time on. China's fight against the pandemic has achieved staged victories, with local outbreaks harnessed, economic operation restored to normal, resumption of work and production fully promoted, and business and market activities recovered gradually. According to the data publicized at the press conference of the National Development and Reform Commission on April 20, 2020, power consumption, freight volume, and other physical indicators have been restored since March. For example, the industrial decline in March was 12.4 percent, less than that in January and February; the service production index dropped 3.9 percent; and the power consumption in early April increased 1.5 percent year on year. In March, the manufacturing Purchasing Managers Index and non-manufacturing business activity index increased again by 16.3 percent and 22.7 percent, respectively, both rising above the threshold again.[15] This means that China's economy has come out of the pandemic, and that a restorative growth of the service industry could be expected soon.

It is undeniable that the pandemic has seriously hit China's economic and social development, especially the service industry that has accounted for half of China's economy. However, through more than 40 years of reform and opening up, China's service industry has been developed greatly with powerful tenacity and adequate space. The impact of the pandemic is an exogenous factor, and short-term sharp decline does not change the solid foundation of development in the service industry. The impact of the pandemic on China's service industry has been mainly structural. With quick promotion of the "Internet +" development mode, service sectors such as catering, travel, hotels, tourism, household management, public baths, and financial insurance will be closely connected with the Internet, and new service forms, such as contactless takeout, fresh food at home, online entertainment, online education, Internet finance, video conferencing, and cloud conferences and exhibitions will be widely accepted in society.

Stabilizing the uptrend of the tertiary industry regardless of the COVID-19 impact

In 2019, China's GDP per capita exceeded USD 10,000 for the first time, marking a new phase of development of living standards in China. International experience has shown that GDP per capita of USD 10,000 is a gateway to a new phase of consumption upgrade and service upgrade, and China's service industry has a historic opportunity. Online and offline services have been integrated deeply by endless new models and business forms and continuous innovation of business forms and content, offsetting the impact of the pandemic to a certain degree. Relying on the huge domestic market, more permeable technological advances, easing of market access mechanisms as well as abundant human resources and a stable, innovative, and upgraded service industry may still be expected in China; and the sustainable, stable, and healthy development pattern of the service industry has remained unchanged. In the course of history, human society has experienced severe pandemics that exerted huge and far-reaching effects on economy and society, but the COVID-19 pandemic is unlikely to halt social and economic activities and progress.

What is more important, modern information technology used to fight the COVID-19 pandemic will probably reverse the "inverse Kuznets process" in structural adjustment of these years. Simon Kuznets regarded industrial structural change in economic development as a process of movement of labor force and other factors from a low productivity sector to a high productivity sector, achieving continuous improvement in labor productivity. Therefore, the process of increasing productivity with industrial structural change is known as the "Kuznets process," while industrial structural change failing to increase productivity is the inverse Kuznets process.[16] In recent years, according to the basic trend of economic restructuring in China, the proportion of the tertiary industry has been constantly higher than that of the secondary industry, but the productivity of the tertiary industry has been always lower than that of the secondary industry, despite a narrowing gap. The fundamental cause for lower productivity of the tertiary industry was the gap in technological progress and scale economy. This pandemic has changed the production and delivery mode of the service sector. As modern information technology is more widely used, the productivity of the tertiary industry has improved. This is exactly the high-quality development goal that we have been pursuing. Therefore, we should face up to the huge impact of the pandemic and seek chances to "turn adversity into opportunity" as far as possible, promoting the development of the service industry in a new phase.

New drivers for restorative growth of the tertiary industry

Promoting a digital, platform-based, and intelligent service industry

The technological change based on new-generation information technology will inevitably lead to the Fourth Industrial Revolution, featuring ubiquitous Internet, greatly improved mobility, and extensive utilization of big data and artificial intelligence (AI).[17] The technological revolution has been restructuring the service industry and quickening the innovative development of the service industry. China's service industry is marching toward a "new service" era. Driven by technological revolution and change of business model, innovations in the service mode, scope of service, service delivery, and service experience are not only objective requirements for high-quality development of the service industry, but also new driving forces to promote restorative growth of the service industry.

Quickening digital reconstruction of the service industry

QUICKENING DIGITAL RECONSTRUCTION OF THE SUPPLY SIDE OF THE SERVICE INDUSTRY

On the basis of developing information communication service industry, China should vigorously promote "Digital China" construction, especially focusing on the integrative development of digital technology in service sectors such as finance, technology services, design creativity, modern logistics, human resource development, and after-sales service. We should develop the "Internet +" production service system, promote the revolution of production modes and organization forms, and form a digital and coordinated industry development pattern. Digital consumer services are also important and urgent. The COVID-19 pandemic has further highlighted the importance of provision of digital consumer services. Digital consumer services could not only increase the consumption convenience and efficiency of urban and rural residents, but also foster accurate production based on consumption data at the demand side. Big data on the Internet consumption platform may support industrial Internet development and realize personalized customization or flexible manufacturing. It's also increasingly urgent to utilize and popularize digital technology in the public service field. China should strengthen digital reconstruction of public services, realize more convenient and efficient provision of public services such as basic education, basic medical care, and social elderly care, better meet people's expectation for a decent life, and improve the well-being of its people.

PROMOTING TRADE IN DIGITAL SERVICES

Great changes have taken place in the global economic pattern and the mode of trade. Entering the state of digital transformation, developed countries have promoted the trade in digital services and seized new strategic competitive points.[18] As a large trading country with a big digital economy, China has ranked first in the world in the population of netizens. China's information infrastructures have been improved notably and met the fundamental conditions for quick development of digital trade. Digital service was originally non-tradable for enterprises or residents, but now it has become tradable and interchangeable, easy for people's purchases, consumption, and payment for cross-border services and data. In the era of the digital economy, and with innovative development of the mobile Internet, big data, AI, cloud computing, and other new-generation information technologies, digital trade has become critical for main economies to compete for control power or commanding point.

ACTIVELY PROMOTING DEEP INTEGRATION OF ONLINE AND OFFLINE SERVICES

Digital reconstruction of the service industry means integrative development of online and offline services rather than online or on-cloud supply and demand of all services. While hitting some services negatively, the COVID-19 pandemic has also generated new market opportunities, quickened the integrative development of online and offline services, promoted the growth of emerging service forms such as online shopping, online entertainment, network teaching, remote offices, cloud conferences and exhibitions, and cloud tourism. Online consumption is not a new thing today, but the impact of the pandemic has enabled it to prevail; therefore, we should take this as an opportunity to continuously improve the "Internet + consumption" ecosystem. Online consumption should not be a cloud castle, but needs offline support and coordination, especially in the construction of logistics and distribution, smart store, and smart block. The bonding points of integrative online and offline development are "exhibition" and "experience." Therefore, to provide new scenarios for service consumption, China should encourage cities and enterprises to construct online and offline integrated consumption exhibition halls and consumer discovery halls if conditions permit.

Platform economy is leading the transformation and upgrading of the service industry

Driven by network technology and big data, the supply and demand sides of the service industry have been more reliant on the platform economy. On the platform, supply and demand of mass services can provide diversified choices for both parties and reduce trading costs and magnify trade size exponentially. The platform economy has become an important force to promote the transformation, upgrading, better quality, and efficiency of the service industry.

PLATFORM-BASED PRODUCER SERVICES

Platform-based development is an important means to enhance control power of producer services. We should encourage leading enterprises to create an Internet-based development platform for producer services, guide upstream and downstream enterprises to participate in the construction of an online service platform that integrates information, purchase, logistics, finance, e-commerce, etc. so as to integrate logistics, fund flow, information flow, and workflow, and increase the coordinated development capacity of R&D, manufacturing, and service sectors.

PLATFORM-BASED CONSUMER SERVICES

With the development of modern information technology including big data, mobile Internet, and AI, the platform-based consumer services have become more and more important. With the consumer service platform, service supply and demand will allow separation of space and time to match decentralized mass supply and demand for transactions, increase the efficiency of resource allocation, and expand the boundary between service and transaction. The development of platform-based consumer services has also increased the technical content of consumer services and improved the people's service experience, so it is an important breakthrough in the transformation and upgrading of consumer services.

GOVERNANCE MODE OF INNOVATION IN THE PLATFORM ECONOMY

To create a good environment for innovative development of the service industry, we should construct an ecosphere favorable to the development of the platform economy. Extensive utilization of network technology and big data has actively imposed government fulfillment of economic regulation, market supervision, social governance, and other basic functions, but it has also brought about major issues and challenges. To comply with the new trend of service economy development, we should reform our supervisory thinking, innovate the governance mode, rebuild the supervisory system of service industry on the principles of unified, efficient, open, inclusive, and multiparty participation, and advocate supervision of the platform economy and other emerging service forms on the principles of "government management, self-discipline, and multiparty participation in shared-governance."[19]

Improving the intelligence level of the service industry

FULLY RECOGNIZING THE STRATEGIC SIGNIFICANCE OF AN INTELLIGENT
SERVICE INDUSTRY

Since the Report on the Work of the Government 2019 officially put forward the "intelligent +" strategy, AI technology has extensively permeated the service industry. The AI alternative service has been widely used in the data-intensive sectors, including transport, finance, retail, medical care, education, and network security, and in the labor-intensive sectors, including legal services, human resource management, and translation. The positive effect and possible impact of intelligent service has been recognized and accepted by society, so it is urgent for us to cultivate an AI industrial ecosphere.

ACTIVELY PROMOTING PENETRATION AND INTEGRATION OF TECHNOLOGIES AND
SERVICES, INCLUDING BIG DATA ANALYSIS, MACHINE STUDY, AND THE INTERNET
OF THINGS

AI technology has been used widely in data-intensive sectors, including finance, retail, medical care, and education, and it has achieved a preliminary effect. Next, China should promote AI-based services such as human resource optimization, auxiliary prediction, assets pricing, and personalized customization services, promote large-scale intelligent services, enrich mobile intelligent service content, utilize intelligent services to upgrade quality of services, enrich household consumption patterns, optimize consumption structure, broaden consumption fields, and increase productivity of the service industry.

Developing a flexible and efficient employment structure

Flexible employment depends on the organic combination of industry, technology and worker skills, all of which are indispensable. The service industry has gradually become a leading industry in China's economy. It is very different from traditional manufacturing industry in terms of organizational structure and mode, as its organization is more flexible. From a technical point of view, professional labor market resources have become increasingly rich in China. With the continuous improvement of education, the labor market level and quality in China have been improved greatly and the proportion of professional technicians in the service industry has increased continuously, providing a solid foundation for development of the flexible and efficient employment structure.

Clarifying the category, property, and functions of flexible employment in the service industry

Flexible employment refers to the sum of employment forms other than traditional regular or standard employment forms in aspects of work time, labor remuneration, workplace, etc. It includes, for example, self-employment, part-time employment, temporary employment, part-time jobs, remote employment, independent employment, and contract employment. Due to business operation requirements of the service industry, it is of great importance to develop and advocate for flexible labor employment. First, the human cost and wage model has been higher in the traditional fixed employment pattern than in the service industry due to seasonal and rhythmic features of the service industry, leading to surplus and waste of labor resources. Second, with continuous development of the sharing economy and digital economy, flexible employment and flexible offices may save time, increase work efficiency, and thus increase productivity. Third, the unemployment rate has risen continuously due to the depressive employment market. In addition to creating jobs and promulgating policy for vigorously increasing employment, the government should also change people's employment concept and encourage the labor force to enter the flexible employment market so as to alleviate pressure on the employment market overall.

Improving relevant laws and regulations for flexible employment in the service industry

The development of the service industry structure and Internet platforms has spurred new work patterns. Besides the well-known didichuxing.com and meituan.com platforms, with the development of Internet technology, relevant digital culture industry platforms have also incubated many work forms different from those in traditional employment, including pan-entertainment live broadcasts, game live broadcasts, and e-commerce live broadcasts. To encourage flexible employment in the service industry, laws and regulations based on labor force surveys should be established, providing set standards for flexible employment. For this purpose, local governments have been advised to establish a "service AI improvement pilot area" according to their requirements and explore normalized development of flexible work in the service industry.

Remodeling the talent training concept and training system for the service industry

We should carry out reform of our education and training system, adapt to the new economy, new services, and new business forms, and coordinate the cultivation of composite and flexible talents. We should offer special rewards to innovative jobs in the service field. Local government may promulgate the "service industry rebounding index" together with third parties, guide industry confidence, stabilize the rate of missing employees, and guarantee the health and safety of the service personnel closely related to people's livelihood and supplies in household services, wholesale markets, vegetable markets, and supermarkets.

Stabilizing the supply chain system of the service industry

The key to sustainable development of the service industry lies in whether seamless connection as well as timely supply and efficient allocation could be realized among offline production, consumption, and logistics. Therefore, efforts should be made on both the industry supply side and the policy supply side.

RESUMING WORK IN AN ORDERLY WAY TO MAINTAIN A STABLE SERVICE
INDUSTRY CHAIN

Service enterprises should first go all out to resume production relating to people's livelihoods, restore the supply chain of daily necessities, and maintain stable service industry chains under the conditions of containing the COVID-19 pandemic. Fifty percent of unemployment insurance expenses actually paid in the previous year may be returned to the insured enterprises with no or few layoffs. For insured enterprises with no or few layoffs but which have faced temporary business difficulties and are willing to recover production, the standard for reimbursing unemployment insurance expenses may be determined according to the local monthly per capita unemployment insurance benefits over 6 months and the number of insured workers. The standard of unemployment insurance benefits may be raised to 90 percent of local minimum wage.

First, we should make efforts to reduce tax, reduce and exempt the value-added tax of service sectors severely affected by the pandemic (especially transport, tourism, catering, and accommodation) in the first quarter of 2020, and use the loss amount to deduct the amount of income tax reduction in profit-making months. We should further reduce the insurance contribution rate of consumer services; for example, reducing the contribution rates of pension and medical insurance by 1 percent and 2 percent, respectively. Finance discounts have been granted to service industries that suffered losses in two consecutive quarters. We should also increase government subsidies and constructive expenditures.[20]

Second, we should organize personnel relating to consumer services to return to work as soon as possible, implement local "aids for enterprise jobs" policy and take specific measures to increase job opportunities and solve the expensive employment problem in current labor-intensive consumer services, and stabilize enterprise employment to the maximum extent possible. If all other conditions are equal, it is advisable that the government accept applications of pandemic-affected small and medium-sized service enterprises for social insurance subsidies, job subsidies, and on-the-job training subsidies, focus on tackling their temporary operation difficulties, and prioritize approval of their applications on examination of eligibility.

Third, we should strengthen financial support for industry enterprises that were significantly affected by the pandemic, flexibly utilize renewal of loans without repayment of principal and emergency on-lending to support relevant enterprises, especially micro, small, and medium-sized service enterprises, to stabilize granting of credit, and offer extensions or renewals for due loans. We should prevent against the occurrence of capital chain rupture, continue reducing the cost rate of transport, catering, tourism, sports, education and training, and clothing service enterprises that were significantly hit by the pandemic, and take measures to reduce financing costs for micro and small businesses on a year-over-year basis; for example, implementing a loan market quotation interest rate, an internal fund transfer pricing discount, and reduction and exemption of service fees. At the same time, we should optimize business processes, open green service channels, increase online transaction efforts, simplify credit granting application formalities, shorten credit approval times, and provide high-quality shortcuts and efficient financial services for enterprises.[21]

Constructing a long-acting mechanism for development of the tertiary industry and enhancing its capacity to contain the pandemic

Now, we are focusing on how to cope with the impact of the pandemic and achieve restorative growth of services. But in the long run, we should construct a long-acting mechanism, promote high-quality development of the service industry, and enhance its capacity to contain the pandemic.

Deepening reform in the service industry and policy innovation under the guidance of opening up based on rules and related institutions

Reform of the service industry in China has entered "deep water," so extraordinary forces are required to help us find the way out. The most effective force is opening up based on rules and related institutions. The boundary between government functions and market functions must be clarified for efficient and high-quality development of the service industry. Each should play its own role to ensure the basic position of competition policy, avoid excessive industrial policies influencing factor allocation and flow in the service market, and develop a unified open market environment. We should quicken the opening up of the service industry to the outside world, significantly reduce policy and access barriers in services trade, and promote the mobility of various service factors. We should promote mutual recognition of standards and occupational qualifications with developed countries in relevant fields, enhance recognition and degree of participation of Chinese service enterprises in the international market, drive growth of service enterprises during participation in international competition, deeply integrate into the global industry chain, supply chain, value chain, and innovation chain, and improve competitiveness and innovative upgrading of the service industry.

Planning of the digital service development strategy

The tertiary industry is the largest industry in China's national economy. However, most enterprises of the tertiary industry still rely heavily on the traditional service mode. As digital transformation has taken place only in some sectors, the overall competitiveness and risk tolerance of the tertiary industry remain weak. During this pandemic, digital services has played an important role in fostering new services with strong digital and networking capacity. During the COVID-19 pandemic, people have cooperated with government calls for home quarantine, remote offices, and minimizing unnecessary going out and gathering together. Although offline restaurants, tourism, hotels, and banks were hit to different degrees, multiple new service modes have emerged as required by the times. With the development of the Internet, digital services have been accepted gradually; for example, contactless delivery, online cloud tourism, remote teaching, and other services have developed well and been widely accepted during the pandemic. The government should guide large-scale Internet platforms to fulfill their social responsibility, give full play to their advantages in resources, science and technology, and data, constantly strengthen infrastructure construction of digital services in the whole service industry, and realize transformation of the service industry toward digital networking.

Taking our response to the COVID-19 as an opportunity, the government should further integrate digital technologies including automated AI technology and information technology with modern service industry, enrich 5G technical application scenarios based on services, and drive end consumption of e-commerce, e-government affairs, and network culture. Taking our response to the pandemic as the starting point, the government should, through propaganda of the digital concept, establish healthy lifestyles, enrich people's connotation of a wonderful life, and expand the digital consumption market for healthcare, sports and leisure, green villages, fitness centers, and outdoor sports facilities.

Data are a core factor of digital, platform-based, and intelligent services, so a good data ecosystem is a fundamental support for the development of innovative services based on digital economy and for the transformation and upgrading of the service industry. In essence, Internet data originate mainly from R&D, design, simulation, purchase, production, sales, supply chains, finance, logistics, consumption, orders, payments, and social communication processes. These data have played a large role in customized production and precision marketing, in better matching of supply and demand, and in reduction of transaction costs; but to which businesses these data should belong—manufacturer, consumer, Internet operator, or data collector—should be defined at policy and legal levels. The government should establish laws and policy rules for the rights, transactions, and sharing of data adaptive to Internet development, construct a good data control environment, establish a national center for service industry Internet big data, find access to various data sources, normalize data formats and interfaces, collect relevant data, and form an available data set and corresponding data resource directory oriented to application features for sharing and use among manufacturers, service providers, Internet operators, and research institutions, so as to create a force for development.

Promoting the community governance system and the community service system

As the basic social unit of a city, community is the cornerstone for the modern construction of China's system and capacity for governance. Studies by foreign scholars have shown that people's well-being depends to a large extent on community governance. In countries with low level of community governance, the efficiency of public health expenditure is relatively low. A low-quality community endangers the health of its residents.[22] Therefore, China should reconstruct its community governance system in the future to enhance community governing capacity, combine community intelligent facilities, foster the public health service and consumer service platform economy, actively promote construction of "intelligent community" and "digital community," improve social governance at the community level, and build the micro-foundation for continuous and steady development of the service economy.

The construction of intelligent community should be based on basic applications within the community and should include community-oriented government administrative services and government-dominated public services, such as community public security, elderly care, education, health, and public space management, and commercial services oriented to the life of community residents, such as neighborhood services, food, clothing, housing, transport, and other services required by community residents. For example, we should establish a uniform e-commerce network platform and convenient vegetable service in community, realize online purchase and unified distribution services, meet the demand of residents for clean vegetable distribution services, and remove barriers in business information transfer and logistics networking, so as to help consumption break through time and space barriers and fundamentally improve community services.

In addition, we should explore household management, laundry, and other life services, provide e-commerce applications, drive coordinated development of household management and other industries by complementing residential property management and household services and chain services in the community, and further promote diversified development of community life services, so as to facilitate the transition of traditional services to modern services.

Improving energy efficiency of the public health service system to fight against the pandemic

Establishing a public–private complementary health and medical service market

The public–private partnership model of medical service provision has been used to solve problems such as unreasonable allocation of medical resources, serious underinvestment of government in public hospitals, and low operation efficiency of public hospitals. Advantages of the public sector and the private sector should be fully utilized to develop partnerships, making use of the strong points of each and not benefitting only the government or the service provider. Meanwhile, the management sector should build performance targets to improve the performance of medical and health sectors.[23] Sound governance is the core to improving performance of medical services, while standard information, incentives, and responsibilities are of great importance for governance.[24]

Quickening the technological progress of the medical system and improving the anti-epidemic capacity of the public health service system

Society's fight against diseases, including the coronavirus, involves system engineering that requires a solid economic base and effective social governance, yet technological progress is the most critical factor. Technological progress in information technology and life science technology have been seen as key national resources to improve public health support capacity and the response to epidemic diseases. In the fight against the COVID-19 pandemic, technological progress represented by new-generation information technology has played an extremely important role.[25] We should rely on science and technology to quicken technology R&D, make more efforts to develop medicines and vaccines, and provide science and technology support for public health. We should accelerate application of AI, big data, and other new technologies in the field of public health, including epidemic prevention and control, to ensure timely and complete reporting of public health system information, monitor possible outbreaks, improve anti-epidemic capacity of the public health service system, and bring benefits for people's livelihoods and well-being.

Notes

1 Civil Aviation Administration, In Q1 of 2020, the Accumulated Loss of the Whole Civil Aviation Industry was RMB 39.8 Billion, sina.com, April 15, 2020: http://finance.sina.com.cn/stock/relnews/hk/2020-04-15/doc-iirczymi6521935.shtml

2 Lu Yang and Xia Jiechang, The Impact of the Pandemic on the Service Industry and the Countermeasures, *China Economic Times*, March 2, 2020.

3 Lu Yang and Xia Jiechang, The Impact of the Pandemic on the Service Industry and the Countermeasures.

4 Xia Jiechang and Feng Xiaoxu, The Impact of COVID-19 on Tourism and the Countermeasures, *China Business and Market*, 3rd issue, 2020.

5 Lu Yang and Xia Jiechang, The Impact of the Pandemic on the Service Industry and the Countermeasures.

6 Liu Xuying, "Cloud Tourism" Builds New Consumption Scene, comnews.cn, March 20, 2020: www.comnews.cn/article/ibdnews/202003/20200300041214.shtml

7 Fan Zhou, Small, Medium and Micro Enterprises in the Cultural Industry Usher in a Period of Development Opportunities by Using Live Broadcasting Technology, *China Business Journal*, March 20, 2020.

8 Fu Linghui, Some Views on the Change of Some Indicators in the First Quarter, National Bureau of Statistics of China, April 20, 2020: www.stats.gov.cn/tjsj/sjjd/202004/t20200420_1739722.html

9 Yang Xia, Express Industry under the Pandemic: Difficult Full Resumption of Work in the Short Term, High Pressure at Joined Outlets, Sohu.com, February 9, 2020: https://www.sohu.com/a/371749978_313745

10 S. G, Karsten, Health Care: Private Good vs. Public Good, *American Journal of Economics and Sociology*, 54(2), 1995, 129–144.

11 Zhao Jianguo and Li Xianru, Has the Regulatory Reform of Investment Improved the Quality of Public Medical Services? *Research on Financial and Economic Issues*, 11th issue, 2019.

12 M. Jofre-Bonet, Health Care: Private and Public Provision, *European Journal of Political Economy*, 16, 2000, 469–489.

13 M. Rothschild and J. E. Stiglitz, Increasing Risk: I. A definition, *Journal of Economic Theory*, 2, 1970, 225–243.

14 Xia Jiechang, Create a New Pattern for the Development of Modern Service Industries, *Finance & Trade Economics*, 12th issue, 2015.

15 Development and Reform Commission, Negative Growth of China's Economy in the First Quarter: No Historical Comparison, sina.com, April 20: http://finance.sina.com.cn/roll/2020-04-20/doc-iirczymi7317912.shtml

16 Cai Fang, Population, Government, and Public Services in Urban Development, *Social Sciences Abroad*, 2nd issue, 2020.

17 Cai Fang, How Does Economics Embrace the New Technological Revolution? *Studies in Labor Economics*, 2nd issue, 2019.

18 Xia Jiechang and Tan Hongbo, Commercial Presence of Trade in Services: Scale, Competitiveness, and Industry Characteristics, *Research on Financial and Economic Issues*, 11th issue, 2019.

19 Liu Yi and Xia Jiechang, The Theory and Policy Research Trends of Sharing Economy, *Economic Perspectives*, 4th issue, 2016.

20 Wei Xiang and Xia Jiechang: Reduce Losses and Costs to Help Small and Medium-Sized Enterprises to Turn the Corner, *Economic Daily*, February 9, 2020.

21 Wei Xiang and Xia Jiechang, Reduce Losses and Costs to Help Small and Medium-Sized Enterprises to Turn the Corner.

22 A. S. Rajkumar and V. Swaroop, Public Spending and Outcomes: Does Governance Matter? *Journal of Development Economics*, 86, 2008, 96–111.

23 Hu Shanlian, Strengthen the Capacity Building of the Medical and Health Care Systems under the Framework of National Governance System, *Health Economics Research*, 1st issue, 2020.

24 M. Lewis and G. Pettersson, *Governance in Health Care Delivery Raising Performance*, World Bank Development Economics Department & Human Development Department, Policy Research Working Paper 507, 2009.

25 Liu Yi, Building a Public Health Safety Net with Big Data: Application Prospects and Policy Recommendations, *Reform*, 4th issue, 2020.

6 Impact of the COVID-19 pandemic on the demand side and countermeasures

Zhang Xiaojing

Impact of the once-in-a-century pandemic: "To be, or not to be?"

"To be, or not to be, that is the question." It may sound ridiculous for common people to bark out "to be or not to be" when facing a general economic depression or financial turbulence, but this memorable quote from Shakespeare has resonated with people facing this "once in a century" pandemic. Why? First, the pandemic has caused tens of thousands of deaths every day. As of July 1, 2020, global cumulative confirmed COVID-19 cases reached 10,563,221, and the cumulative number of deaths reached 513,032. The more than 500,000 deaths from COVID-19 reflect the original meaning of "to be or not to be." Second, many people were affected by the pandemic, especially the low-income vulnerable group of people who were struggling to survive. They could not survive without jobs and income for one or two months or quarters, or even longer. Third, quite a few enterprises were affected by the pandemic because of the strict closedown or lockdown measures to contain the pandemic, which suspended economic activities and crippled all leveraged enterprises' payment of wages or debts. Survival has become a problem for enterprises. Therefore, from the perspective of "to be or not to be," the economics of the pandemic is radically different from the economics of generic economic and financial crisis: survival comes first, then the conflict between epidemic prevention and control (protection of lives) and resumption of work and production (survival of enterprises) when discussing the impact of the pandemic on economy.

The outbreak of COVID-19 at the beginning of 2020 and its subsequent impacts were unexpected. The COVID-19 pandemic can be likened to the Spanish Flu pandemic 100 years ago. Many researchers have concluded that the impact of COVID-19 could be more catastrophic than that of the Spanish Flu, so its occurrence could be described as "once in all history."

The outbreak must be contained in all countries, including China. Countermeasures have varied from country to country. The containment policies for preventing the spread of the pandemic, either social distancing or shutdown and lockdown, have inevitably brought direct negative impacts on

DOI: 10.4324/9781003184447-7

both the demand side and the supply side of economy. From the perspective of economic performance, decline in both consumption and output was unavoidable.

Barro's[1] research has shown that the Spanish flu pandemic caused gross domestic product (GDP) to fall by 6 percent and consumption to fall by 8 percent in typical countries. According to limited data, the short-term impact of this pandemic on the financial market would go beyond the Spanish flu pandemic in 1918, the Great Depression in 1929, and the international financial crisis in 2008.

According to the forecast submitted by the Organisation for Economic Co-operation and Development (OECD) to the G20 Summit at the end of March 2020, the annual GDP growth dropped by 2 percentage points in a month in which the containment policy was implemented; therefore, over the year, containment actions would have an adverse effect on one fourth of the total GDP of main economies (see Figure 6.1). The tourism sector alone would see a decline of up to 70 percent. Many economies would slip into recession.

According to the prediction by the International Monetary Fund (IMF) in its flagship World Economic Outlook report on April 14, 2020, global growth dropped to −3 percent in 2020, 6.3 percentage points down compared with its prediction in January. It also predicted that this would be the most serious economic depression since the Great Depression and far beyond the financial crisis in 2008. The prediction of the World Economic Outlook in June 2020 degraded global growth to −4.9 percent, 1.9 percentage lower than the prediction in April 2020. Negative impact of the COVID-19 pandemic on economic activities in the first half of 2020 was more severe than expected, indicating a slower recovery than suggested by the previous prediction. Global growth

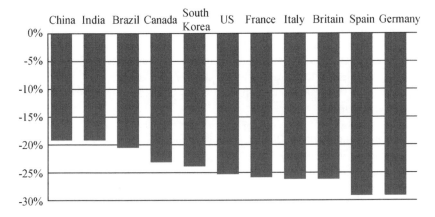

Figure 6.1 Preliminary effect of pandemic containment measures in different countries (proportion of GDP).

Source: OECD updates to the G20 summit on outlook for global economy

in 2021 is expected to be 5.4 percent. Generally speaking, this means GDP in 2021 will be 6.5 percent lower than the prediction before the outbreak of the pandemic in January 2020.

We compared the data predicting the impact of the pandemic in the World Economic Outlook in June 2020 with data on the Great Depression and the Great Recession, taking developed economies as the reference (see Figure 6.2). This shows that developed economies were hit more heavily in the Great Depression and the Great Recession. According to comparison results, the pandemic caused the greatest decline in economic output, much greater than in the Great Recession of 2008, but there would be a V-shaped rebound. In contrast, the Great Depression featured the longest duration, followed by the Great Recession and then the pandemic. This comparison indicates that the COVID-19 pandemic generated a very deep but less broad impact on economic output. This is because the mechanism of the crisis caused by the pandemic is different from that of crisis relating to the economic and financial system itself. The economic shutdown caused by the pandemic and the containment measures may be temporary and economies have not been damaged fundamentally, whereas the Great Depression and the Great Recession occurred due to the problems of the economies themselves.

Bernank, former Federal Reserve chairman, regards the COVID-19 pandemic as a natural disaster (like a snowstorm), not like the Great Depression in the 1930s.[2] In fact, Bernank argues that the impact brought about by the pandemic was almost the opposite to that of the financial crisis. At that time, problems in the banking system influenced the overall economy; but

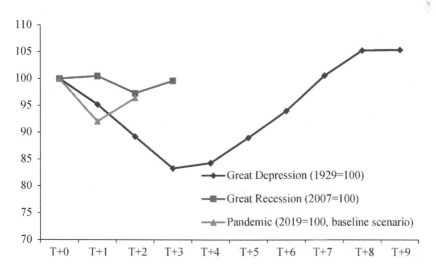

Figure 6.2 Impact of the Great Depression, the Great Recession, and the COVID-19 pandemic on the output of developed economies.

Source: Maddison (2010)[5]; International Monetary Fund

the COVID-19 crisis brought about problems to the real economy, which "infected" banks.

Some scholars even hold the view that the impact of this pandemic is not the same as that of the global financial crisis in 2008, because the former was an exogenous risk while the crisis in 2008 was an endogenous risk. In other words, internal interaction among market participants contributed to the global systemic financial crisis in 2008, the root cause of which stayed in the financial system itself. While the COVID-19 pandemic imposed an external impact on the economy, the root cause was outside the financial industry. Therefore, it was generally believed that if the pandemic was not controlled, any solution concerning the financial system would fail. The United States launched a series of rescue measures in March 2020, but the market gave no heed to it at the early stage of pandemic transmission. This is one of the peculiarities of the pandemic economics.

Fundamental mechanism of the impact of the pandemic on economy

The COVID-19 pandemic hit the economy on both aggregate demand and aggregate supply. On the supply side, when the pandemic exposed workers to the risk of coronavirus infection, they responded by reducing labor supply. On the demand side, when the pandemic exposed people to the risk of coronavirus infection while purchasing commodities or services, they responded by reducing consumption. The interaction between reduced supply and reduced demand has led to continuous recession.[3]

For a more detailed description of the fundamental mechanism for the impact of the pandemic on economy, see Figure 6.3. The modern economy is a complicated network of interrelated parties, such as employees, companies, suppliers, consumers, banks, and financial intermediaries. Everyone

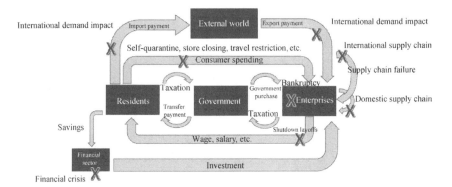

Figure 6.3 Fundamental mechanism of the impact of the pandemic on the economy
Source: Baldwin (2020)[6]

is an employee, customer, or creditor of others. If any link in the relationship between buyers and sellers is broken due to disease or quarantine policy, the result will be a series of disruptions. Figure 6.3 shows a type of revenue cycle flow chart that may be found in most introductory economics textbooks. In its simplified form, first, a household has capital and labor force and sells these to an enterprise; then, the enterprise utilizes the capital and labor force to manufacture products for the household's daily use; further, the household spends their revenue earned from the enterprise on purchasing the products manufactured by the enterprise; finally, a complete economic cycle is formed to keep economic growth.

Now, let's investigate how the impact of the pandemic leads to a disrupted economic cycle flow and generates a transmission effect. Let's start from the impact on the demand side. Look at the "household" on the left, and move our eyes clockwise; we find that the household who did not receive wages has encountered financial difficulties, so it chooses to reduce expenditures. Next, the impact on domestic demand has led to a decrease in imports and out-flow of income to foreign countries. Although this did not decrease domestic demand competition, it has reduced foreign income, and thus reduced external demand (see the cross in the top right corner of Figure 6.3). The decrease in demand and/or direct impact on supply might lead to disruption of the international and domestic supply chain (see the two crosses on the rightmost side). In this way, a large number of enterprises had to close down or lay off workers in order to meet requirements for containing the pandemic. Some enterprises have suspended production and waited for resumption of work only after the pandemic is controlled effectively. Of course, this story may also be told from the perspective of the enterprises on the supply side (on the right-most side). In order to prevent the spread of the pandemic, enterprises have suspended production and laid off some employees (two crosses), causing decreases in employees' income and expenditure, in domestic consumption, and in expenditures on imported products; meanwhile, the story described above continues.

The above analysis on the demand side and supply side is made only to facilitate understanding of economic operation, regardless of a particular order. In the real economy, the pandemic's impact on demand and supply has occurred simultaneously and reinforced each other.

In order to better understand the action mechanism of the pandemic's impacts on economy, the impacts may be divided into three categories or three waves.

The first wave was direct impact on domestic consumption and produc-tion, as illustrated in Figure 6.3. The first wave of impacts, whether in the household sector or in the business sector, have always been discussed first. The subsequent transmission mechanism involves the second and even the third wave of impacts.

The second wave of impacts acted on the external channel, leading to con-traction of external demand, disruption of the international supply chain, and fluctuations in the international financial market. With rapid spread of the pandemic worldwide, it has further influenced China's domestic situation from outside in the aspect of international trade, hindering global economic growth, influencing external demand for trade in goods, causing international route disruption or decline, reducing passenger sources of the international tourist industry, and affecting trade in services. At the level of international capital flow, with the increase of uncertainty and suspension of economic activities, drastic revaluation of value has been made in the financial market, with funds flowing into traditional safe harbors and countries hit by the epidemic facing capital flight. If the pandemic continues, even foreign direct investment and other long-term funds will evacuate quickly. In terms of the supply chain, many domestic industries or enterprises have made a global arrangement for their supply chain, as foreign production or international logistics disturbed by the pandemic have inevitably influenced the normal production and operation of domestic enterprises in the same industry chain.

The third wave acted on the balance sheet. For the sake of simplicity, an important aspect has been neglected in the chart in Figure 6.3—the amplification effect of enterprises' balance sheets, including: (1) financial market turmoil and devaluation of resident's assets, which has further compressed consumption; (2) enterprises affected by the pandemic confronted with suspension of production, shortage of cash flow, and tight liquidity due to loaners' worry about enterprises' insolvency and refusal to expand line of credit; and (3) financial intermediaries' performance of asset liquidation that caused assets dumping to meet fund withdrawal requirements of investors due to the collapse in prices of financial assets caused by the pandemic. In order to meet the capital adequacy ratio and other supervisory requirements, financial institutions had to shrink their balance sheets, thus aggravating the liquidity crisis on financial market. This perhaps is an important reason for the US financial market collapse in March 2020.

Impact of the pandemic on the demand side

We may fully analyze impact of the pandemic on China's economy based on the impacting mechanism in Figure 6.3. Here we will mainly discuss the impact of the pandemic on the demand side.

Economic and social development data in the first quarter of 2020 fully reflect the strength of impact of the pandemic on aggregate demand. According to initial estimates, GDP fell 6.8 percent year on year in the first quarter of 2020. This quarterly fall was probably the biggest drop since the reform and opening up in China in 1978. However, compared with previous prediction of the parties concerned, these data were better than expected. Resumption of work and production in March 2020 has played a critical supporting role in China's economic performance. However, the sharp decrease in consumption investment and a further decline in producer price suggest that the future road of economic recovery will be full of thorns.

Impact on consumption

According to the data publicized by the Bureau of Statistics, in the first quarter of 2020, the total retail sales of consumer goods decreased by 19.0 percent year on year, down 15.8 percent in March, 4.7 percentage points narrower than that in January and February; and commodity retail decreased by 12.0 percent in March, 5.6 percentage points narrower than that in January and February. In terms of consumption types, the catering sector's income decreased by 44.3 percent, and commodity retail decreased by 15.8 percent; however, commodities closely related to daily life witnessed an increase in earnings, such as cereals and oils, food and beverage, and traditional Chinese and western medicines of enterprises above designated size, rising by 12.6 percent—4.1 percent, and 2.9 percent, respectively, 2.9 percentage points, 1.0 percentage points, and 2.7 percentage points quicker than those in January and February, respectively. It must be pointed out that consumption data have improved since March. In May, the total retail sales of consumer goods decreased by 2.8 percent year on year, 4.7 percentage points narrower than last month, and the volume of retail sales decreased by 0.8 percent, approaching the level in the same period of last year. There has also been increase in consumption of basic necessities, retail of automobiles, furniture, and housing, and transportation products. Consumer sectors suffered the most negative effect of the pandemic, especially highly contact-intensive industries, such as catering, accommodation, transport, tourism, and cinema. However, the pandemic has also made new growth points possible, such as the "contactless economy"; just as severe acute respiratory syndrome (SARS) made great development of e-commerce possible in 2003. According to Figure 6.4, national cumulative online retail sales increased

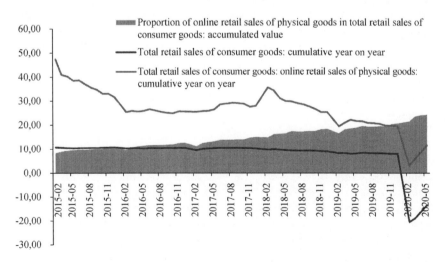

Figure 6.4 Year-on-year cumulative changes in total retail sales of consumer goods (%).
Source: Wind database

5.9 percent year on year in March 2020 (the cumulative total retail sales of consumer goods decreased by 19 percent year on year), 2.9 percentage points quicker than that in January and February, which accounted for 23.6 percent of total retail sales of consumer goods, 2.1 percentage points higher than that in January and February. From January to May, online retail sales increased by 11.5 percent year on year, 2.9 percentage points quicker than that from January to April, which accounted for 24.3 percent of total retail sales of consumer goods, 5.4 percentage points higher than that in the same period of 2019. As compared with other suspended economic activities, the contactless economy developed very quickly during the pandemic. According to third-party data monitoring, the trade size of local online life services in China exceeded RMB 1.5 trillion in 2018, increasing by 56.3 percent over the preceding year. The consumption scale of current online life services exceeded RMB 2 trillion. According to the 2020 China Mobile Network Spring Report released by QuestMobile, in the first quarter of 2020, sectors involved in entertainment, education, offices, public welfare, medical care, and information during the pandemic have quickly become online and on cloud, with the number of monthly active users of mobile Internet up to 1.138 billion during the Spring Festival of 2019 and over 1.156 billion in March 2020. At the same time, the monthly per capita service duration in a single day increased by 28.6 percent, from 5.6 hours in 2019 to 7.2 hours in 2020. Affected by the pandemic, user information, lifestyle and entertainment, and other demands were transferred to online operations, leading to a 1.5 percent year-on-year growth of the mobile Internet and an increase of 17 million in monthly active users compared to the end of 2019.

Besides the pandemic itself, factors that have restricted consumption include resident income. Due to a large gap in income, the rich have stronger spending power, but lower marginal willingness to spend and higher willingness to save, so the releasable consumption potential has been limited; the poor have higher marginal willingness to spend, but lower income and higher liquidity constraints, so they could not increase their spending power, which was a critical factor that has restricted the growth of total consumption. According to the special survey by the Survey and Research Center for China Household Finance, Southwestern University of Finance and Economics,[4] the pandemic has led to pessimistic expectations among residents for the employment situation and income growth, and this might increase overall precautionary savings. Due to lack of financial liquidity of family assets, the impact on lower-income groups was greater. Affected by the above-mentioned factors, the expected total household consumer spending in 2020 would decrease by 11 percent. As a whole, the pandemic has influenced employment, reduced income, and led to underconfidence of consumers, so it's not an optimistic outlook for quick recovery of total consumption growth of the society. From this perspective, stabilizing employment and subsidizing low-income groups by transfer payments (or cash payments or coupons) support not only social policies, but also policies on the aggregate demand of consumption.

Impact on investment

In the first quarter of 2020, national investment in fixed assets (excluding rural households) was RMB 8.414 trillion, decreasing by 16.1 percent year on year, 8.4 percentage points narrower than that in January and February; and private investment in fixed assets decreased by 18.8 percent, 7.6 percentage points narrower than that in January and February. Investment in infrastructure decreased by 19.7 percent, investment in manufacturing decreased by 25.2 percent, and investment in real estate development decreased by 7.7 percent—10.6 percentage points, 6.3 percentage points, and 8.6 percentage points narrower than in January and February, respectively (see Figure 6.5). Investment in primary industry decreased by 13.8 percent, investment in secondary industry decreased by 21.9 percent, and investment in tertiary industry decreased by 13.5 percent, and private investment amounted to RMB 4.780 trillion—decreasing by 18.8 percent, 11.8 percentage points, 6.3 percentage points, 9.5 percentage points, and 7.6 percentage points narrower than in January and February, respectively. From January to March, national investment in fixed assets (excluding rural households) amounted to RMB 8.414 trillion, decreasing by 16.1 percent year on year, 8.4 percentage points narrower than that in January and February.

Affected by the pandemic, overall investment decreased greatly. But investment in some sectors, such as the high-tech industry and anti-epidemic sectors, showed a certain "resilience." Investment in the high-tech industry decreased by 12.1 percent, 4.0 percentage points below total investments, of which investment in high-tech manufacturing and high-tech services decreased by 13.5 percent and 9.0 percent, respectively. In the high-tech manufacturing industry, investment in the manufacturing of computer and office equipment increased by 3.2 percent. In high-tech services, investment in e-commerce services increased by 39.6 percent, investment in professional technical services increased by 36.7 percent, and investment in the commercialization of research findings increased by 17.4 percent. However, investment in social fields decreased by 8.8 percent, of which investment in the health field decreased by 0.9 percent, 15.2 percentage points lower than total investments. Investment in biological drug product manufacturing and anti-epidemic industries has kept growing, and the construction of key epidemic prevention projects has accelerated. On a month-on-month basis, investment in fixed assets in March (excluding rural households) increased by 6.05 percent compared with the last month.

From January to May, investment in fixed assets (excluding rural households) decreased by 6.3 percent year on year, 4.0 percentage points narrower than that from January to April, of which, investment in infrastructure decreased by 6.3 percent, 5.5 percentage points narrower. Investment

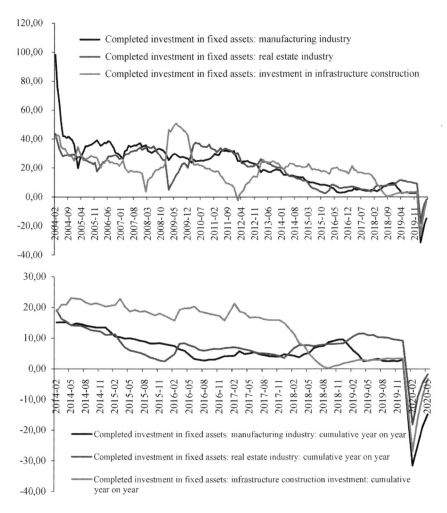

Figure 6.5 Investment in the manufacturing industry, the real estate industry, and infrastructure construction.

Source: Wind database

in the high-tech industry and social sectors changed from fall to rise. The Purchasing Managers Index (PMI) is a barometer of economic activities. With the pandemic control and orderly resumption of work and production, the PMI saw a sharp rebound in March 2020. Data have shown that the manufacturing PMI was 52.0 percent, 16.3 percentage points higher than in the last month (see Figure 6.6). The non-manufacturing business activity index was 52.3 percent, 22.7 percentage points higher than in February. In May, the manufacturing PMI was 50.6 percent, and the non-manufacturing

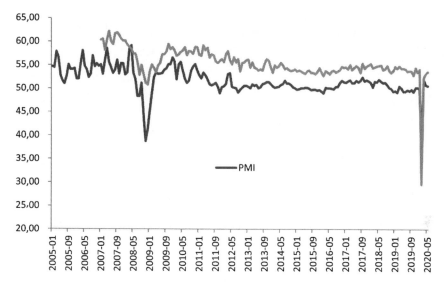

Figure 6.6 Purchasing Managers Index.
Source: Wind database

business activity index was 53.6 percent, both rose above the critical point for 3 consecutive months. The manufacturing business expectations index and the non-manufacturing business activities expectation index were 57.9 percent and 63.9 percent, respectively—3.9 and 3.8 percentage points higher than in last month, respectively.

Impact on external demand

According to the latest IMF prediction (April 2020), the pandemic would lead to a global output loss up to USD 9 trillion. This reflects the decline in global aggregate demand and undoubtedly means a sharp fall in external demand.

Affected by the sharp fall in external demand, in the first quarter of 2020, China's import and export of goods decreased by 6.4 percent year on year, of which, imports/exports decreased by 0.8 percent year on year in March, 8.7 percentage points narrower than that in January and February, and exports decreased by 3.5 percent, imports increased by 2.4 percent, and the general trade imports increased by 4.0 percent. In the first quarter, exports decreased by 11.4 percent, and imports decreased by 0.7 percent (see Figure 6.7). After offsetting imports/exports, the trade surplus amounted to RMB 98.3 billion.

With respect to regional distribution of exports, most regions in which external demands were reduced have been hit severely by this pandemic, while regions where the pandemic developed mildly or was controlled effectively

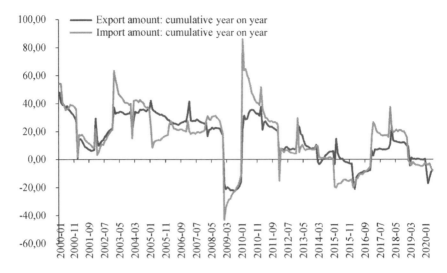

Figure 6.7 Cumulative year-on-year growth of imports and exports (%).
Source: Wind database

have become a main force to recover export demand of China. Specifically for data in March, as compared with January and February, China's exports rose again significantly in the regions of mild spread of the pandemic; for example, in Association of Southeast Asian Nations (ASEAN) countries and Japan, exports to ASEAN countries rose again to 7.7 percent, driving overall exports to rise 1.6 percent, and exports to Japan rose again to −1.4 percent, driving overall exports to rise 1.4 percent. In the latter half of March, when pandemic outbreaks mainly occurred in Europe, and European economies successively took quarantine measures, starting with Italy, the growth of China's exports to the European Union fell 24.3 percent in March, driving overall exports of China to rise by 1.0 percent.

While the pandemic raged, the global economy and trade saw a sharp fall. In the second quarter, the World Trade Organization barometer of trade in goods was 87.6, a record low; the United Nations Conference on Trade and Development predicted that the value of global commodity trade in the second quarter would decrease by 26.9 percent compared with that in the first quarter. Nevertheless, since March, China's export decline has been narrowed from −13.3 percent in March to −7.7 percent in May, but import decline expanded from −2.9 percent in March to −8.2 percent in May, to some degree reflecting the weak domestic demand.

Although the decline in external demand was smaller than predicted from the data, indicating the resilience in China's foreign trade growth, attention should still be paid to three points. First, the contribution rate of external demand (based on net export) to growth decreased continuously in these years (and was even negative in some years), but this did not mean that external demand was unimportant. In particular, the export sector has created a large number of jobs. If exports decreased due to weak external demand, unemployment would become worse. Second, perhaps the contraction of external demand has not been fully demonstrated. Because the pandemic is still ongoing in Europe and America, while it has been controlled in China (not excluding the possibility of a second wave, though the probability is much smaller), the end time of the pandemic in Europe and America would be much later than China. Since it was uncertain whether the pandemic could be controlled in Europe and America before the third quarter, the strength of economic recovery in the second half of the year was also highly uncertain. It might take nearly 2 years for Europe and America to return to the GDP level before the pandemic, so it's difficult to realize a V-shaped rebound. Third, with respect to impact on external demand, attention should not only be paid to Europe, the United States, and Japan, but also to emerging economies. Under the impact of the pandemic and subsequent international financial market turmoil, emerging economies have become more vulnerable in aspects of currency devaluation, capital flight, excessive corporate leverage, and currency mismatch (more foreign currency debt), which might trigger a crisis and arouse the attention of China in import/export diversification process.

Policy responses: Broadening consumption and focus on new "growth pole"

While hard-hit by the pandemic, all industrial sectors have found it incredibly difficult to maintain growth. Various imaginative policy suggestions have been put forward; for example, formulating systematic recovery planning, the "new 4 trillion," and a Chinese version of modern monetary theory (a core viewpoint of which is monetization of fiscal deficit). The general direction of maintaining growth is definitely correct, but the questions are how to maintain growth, to what degree, and whether to maintain growth "at all costs." Many people thought, after all, that economic upheaval should not happen and economic growth should not slow down, so any means can be used for this purpose. Here, words like cost, price, and sequelae sound too pedantic.

In our opinion, although it is not known when the pandemic will end, especially since the overseas spread has brought about risk of importation, a V-shaped rebound could not be expected from the decline of 6.8 percent in the first quarter of 2020. As most economic data have improved since March 2020, economic growth should not collapse. Considering endless arguments on maintaining a minimum percentage of national economic growth before the New Year, now it is widely thought that GDP growth up to 2 percent is an optimistic scenario (the IMF gave a prediction on China's GDP growth of 1 percent in June 2020). From the pandemic outbreak at the beginning of 2020 on, evolution of the outbreak and its impact on economy and finance at home and abroad have continuously "refreshed" the forecast judgments of the parties concerned, showing serious underestimation of the situation. Therefore, on the one hand, we should seek truth from facts and weaken the growth target; and on the other hand, we should guarantee employment and people's livelihoods, expand domestic demand, enhance effectiveness of countercyclical regulation, and make efforts to realize steady growth.

Pro-consumption should be placed in a more important position

First, pro-consumption should be given more attention. Above all, the impact of the pandemic has been greater on consumption. Data for the first quarter of 2020 show that the pandemic has led to a decrease in total retail sales of consumer goods by 19.0 percent, and a decrease in investment in fixed assets by 16.1 percent. According to the data as of May 2020, resumption of work and production was relatively successful in China, but demand recovery remained sluggish. Demand (especially consumer demand) was a main source of conflict. Stabilizing investment was undoubtedly necessary, yet problems included small investment incentive multiplier, low efficiency, an evident crowding-out effect, and restricted financing channels. Compared with promoting household consumption, investment expansion could more easily lead to structural distortion and debt accumulation risks. Moreover, consumption has become a key driver of China's growth. Household consumption accounted for nearly three quarters of final consumption; during 2015–2019, the average contribution rate of final consumption to China's GDP growth was 61.5 percent.

Second, the key to broadening consumption is service consumption. In 2019, service consumption accounted for 50.2 percent of household consumption in China, compared to about 60 percent in developed economies, so there is a great development space. From the perspective of services trade deficit in recent years, development of the service industry has been one of our shortcomings. Service consumer demand remained weak because service provision did not match it, especially in quality. There were two factors restricting high-quality provision of services: monopoly and control in finance, telecommunications, railway and aviation as well as in education, medical care, elderly care, and other fields; and lack of systems and standards that should be emphasized more for the development of the service industry. In this aspect, there are many deficiencies. Therefore, to expand service consumption, we should lay stress on double upgrade of consumption and industry, promote opening of the service industry to the inside and outside from the supply side, improve standard services systems as soon as possible, and continuously increase the public service level of education, medical care, culture, and sports.

Third, the "contactless economy" is a new growth point. To promote faster development of the contactless economy, we should formulate relevant standards, including contactless service standards and criteria for takeout, express delivery, remote services, and other industries, as well as online educational curriculum certification, family doctor e-signing, and other systems. We should also set up contactless economy infrastructure and supporting platforms. Finally, we should promote the development of contactless social services, promote integrative online and offline consumption development of education, medical care, elderly care, child care, household management, culture and tourism, sports, and other services, expanding service content and service coverage.

Fourth, there is still potential for automobile consumption. Difficulty in automobile sales in recent years does not equal a saturated auto market. In our opinion, there is still great potential for automobile consumption. For one thing, per capita car population is not high in China. Car population per thousand persons was 619 in Japan and 450 in South Korea in 2018, and up to 811 in the United States in 2017; in 2020, car population per thousand persons is only 179 in China, lower than developed countries including the United States and Japan and developing countries including Iran and Thailand. In combination with the experience in Japan and South Korea, automobile consumer space still exists in China. Current per capita car population in China is only equivalent to the level of Japan in 1970 and South Korea in 1994, and these two countries maintained long-term growth of automobile sales volume for about 20 years after reaching this per capita car population level. In addition, the current impact of the pandemic may be a new opportunity for automobile consumption. Similar to the SARS outbreak in 2003, many people purchased vehicles in order to avoid infection, so auto sales in the same year increased by 70 percent year on year. In addition, the impact of this pandemic has led to a collapse in the oil price, which will, at least in the short term, promote automobile consumption. Therefore, we should relax restrictions on vehicle purchase, reduce vehicle purchase tax, expand automobile consumer credit services, and attach importance to county auto markets and other policies so as to release potential automobile consumption.

Fifth, we should increase public consumption properly. The current public consumption rate (proportion of public consumption in GDP) is relatively low in China, approximately 2 percent lower than the world average level, 3 percent lower than in OECD countries, and nearly 6 percent lower than in the eurozone. However, considering that the proportion of final consumption in GDP in developed economies is far higher than in China, the proportion of public consumption in final consumption up to 27.5 percent in 2018 was not low. Therefore, increasing public consumption should be "proper," so we should mainly expand resident-oriented social public services and consumer spending, including increasing public consumer spending in social healthcare as well as increasing consumption subsidies of low-income groups, rather than expanding consumption of government itself.

Large-scale investment stimulus plan should not be launched

Under the impact of the pandemic, economic downward pressure has increased, so expanding investment is a must, but we should not launch a large-scale investment incentive plan.

First, investment efficiency has decreased. We generally use Incremental Capital-Output Ratio (ICOR) to measure investment efficiency. The higher the value, the less the incremental output brought by incremental capital becomes and the lower the investment efficiency. Before the Asian financial crisis, in the period from 1981 to 1997, the annual average ICOR was 2, and in the period from 1998 to 2008, it rose to 3.7. Since this crisis, in the period from 2009 to 2019, the annual average ICOR reached 7.9. From the 1980s up to the present, ICOR has increased continuously and investment efficiency has declined; the decline of investment efficiency has been especially significant since 2009 (see Figure 6.8). In this case, excessive reliance on investment and even the "new 4 trillion" stimulus plan might be inappropriate.

Second, there was a crowding-out effect of government investment. In 2009, growth rate of fixed capital was almost twice that before the crisis, and the contribution of investment in the same year to GDP growth approached 90 percent. Although this stimulated economic growth, it has led to a crowding-out effect on private economy. On one hand, the new 4 trillion yuan and top ten industrial revitalization plan allowed all-out attack of

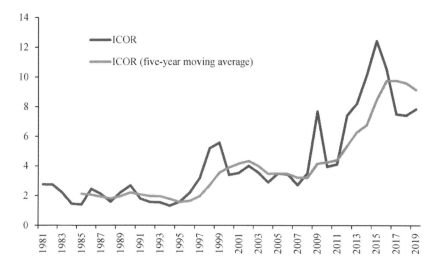

Figure 6.8 Changing trend of ICOR, 1981–2019.
Source: Wind database

state-owned economy, competing with private economy for resources and markets; on the other hand, finance credit resources were inclined to state-owned economy, so private economy could only obtain funds at a higher cost from shadow banks and other channels, thus aggravating private enterprises' difficult and expensive financing problems. Estimates by the Research Center for National Balance Sheet at the Chinese Academy of Social Sciences show that the proportion of state-owned enterprise assets in the business sector has been increasing since 2010, reflecting the crowding-out effect brought about by the 4 trillion yuan investment stimulus plan.

Third, we should stimulate private investment and avoid "Japanization." Japanization has multiple meanings. Here, it mainly refers to relying on the increase of government debt and expansion of government investment to support economic growth in case of insufficient internal impetus of the market. The problems brought about by Japanization include significantly rising public sector debt, risk accumulation, and concentration. On a global scale, the private sector's leverage is far higher than that of the public sector, with a difference of more than 60 percent. In Japan, since a qualitative and quantitative easing program was implemented at the beginning of this century, public sector leverage started to be higher than private leverage, and the gap is up to about 70 percent now. In China, public sector leverage is currently nearly 40 percent higher than private sector leverage. As far as the current development stage of China is concerned, the vigor of the private sector should also be stimulated, and internal impetus of the market should be utilized to support growth by allocating more resources to the private sector. If resource allocation of the public sector emphasizes risk prevention, then resource allocation of the private sector will put more emphasis on efficiency principles and steady growth. So to stimulate investment, more private investment should be stimulated: on one hand, from the perspective of efficiency, private investment has its advantages; and on the other hand, active participation of private investment will promote market sharing of risks, favorable to mitigating the high leverage of the public sector. Therefore, we should further promote market opening, public–private partnership, and mixed-ownership reform, and provide a larger development space for private economy; at the same time, we should substantially promote protection of private property rights, stabilize expectations, give confidence to private entrepreneurs, and stimulate entrepreneurship and vitality of private investment.

Focus on urban clusters/metropolitan areas and create a new "growth pole"

Since the reform and opening up, optimal configuration of factor resources has driven China's growth. First, factor mobility between urban and rural areas, especially labor migration from the so-called traditional sectors to modern sectors, has increased labor productivity greatly, which is the source of growth at the beginning of reform and opening up. Since the 1990s, especially since the establishment of the socialist market economy and export-oriented economic development, more and more factor resources are diverted to the tradable sector, so export-orientation has become a new growth engine. Occurring simultaneously with the above two processes is the transfer of factor resources from state-owned sectors to non-state-owned sectors, which has also increased efficiency. At present, we encounter certain bottlenecks in three aspects: (1) scale of agricultural labor transfer will not be as large as that in the past, and urban–rural integration, rural revitalization, and factor resources do not flow in one direction any longer; (2) since the 2008 international financial crisis, trade expansion of the global value chain has been hindered, and due to reverse globalization and trade war between the United States and China, export-oriented economic development has to be adjusted; and (3) before the crisis, there was a great era of development in the private economy as a whole, but after 2008, this changed significantly as the development space for private economy is restricted.

It now seems that an important "structured bonus" at the next stage will appear on optimal space configuration of factor resources. So we should focus on urban clusters/metropolitan areas to create a new growth pole. Focusing on urban clusters/metropolitans area may (1) pull investment into infrastructure construction of urban clusters and smart cities, and facilitate population migration and housing construction surrounding urban clusters and metropolitan areas; (2) promote consumption due to an income effect brought about by major cities; and (3) increase productivity via a scale effect and a concentrating effect. Focusing on urban clusters/metropolitan areas is a new direction of regional development strategy in the new era, and it emphasizes complementary advantages, promotes concentration of industry and population to dominant regions, develops sources of growth in main urban clusters/metropolitan areas, and increases overall economic efficiency. This is an adjustment of the "balanced" development strategy of the past, and it embodies a new development concept of dynamic balance. Expanding domestic demand must be based on this important strategic change to release new growth drivers.

Major urban clusters and metropolitan areas are the main force for current consumption and a potential force for future consumption in China. Morgan Stanley forecasts that by 2030, China's urbanization rate will increase from 60 percent currently to 75 percent, that the number of urban residents will increase by 220 million, and that half of the urban population will reside in five metroplexes (the Yangtze River Delta, the Beijing-Tianjin-Hebei Region, the Guangdong-Hong Kong-Macao Greater Bay Area, the middle reach of the Yangtze River, and the Chengdu-Chongqing Region). Average population size in these five metroplexes will exceed that of most EU countries. In terms of reform of the household registration system, the mutual recognition of cumulative years of registered permanent residence in the same city in the Yangtze River Delta, the Pearl River Delta, and other urban clusters will be favorable to the flow of population towards urban clusters/metropolitan areas. Based on big data on the Jingdong platform, in recent years, consumption of 12 metropolitan areas has accounted for above 80 percent of total national consumption. All 13 non-resource-based cities whose GDP per capita has exceeded USD 20,000 are now located in the Yangtze River Delta, the Pearl River Delta, the Beijing-Tianjin-Hebei Region, the middle reach of the Yangtze River, and other urban clusters, which are key areas for future consumption growth.

Investment has been centralized in infrastructure for important urban clusters and metropolitan areas. This includes the integrated transport system of highways, railways, shipping and aviation, cross-regional energy infrastructure construction of the electric power and natural gas network, interprovincial major water conservancy construction projects for flood control and water supply, information infrastructure construction of fiber optic broadband and the 5G network, as well as construction of social housing and improvement of basic public services. Investment in this aspect is of great importance for stabilizing current growth and improving long-term development capacity. Therefore, more support in the form of land and funds should be given to support the regional development strategy. In March 2020, approval for land use was carried out in eight provinces and cities: Beijing, Tianjin, Shanghai, Chongqing, Jiangsu, Zhejiang, Anhui, and Guangdong. Governments at provincial level have been required to assume more responsibility for use of the urban–rural development land occupation index for creating a new growth pole, because these pilot provinces and cities practically cover the most important urban clusters. Approval for land use has been always a key constraint in implementing investment projects, so unbinding land through pilot works will quickly increase investment in these areas and promote economic growth.

Notes

1 R. J. Barro, J. F. Ursúa, and J. Weng, *The Coronavirus and the Great Influenza Pandemic. Lessons from the "Spanish Flu" for the Coronavirus's Potential Effects on Mortality and Economic Activity*, NBER Working Paper 26866, 2020.
2 M. J. Belvedere, Bernanke: Coronavirus Disruptions 'Much Closer to a Major Snowstorm' than the Great Depression, CNBC, March 25, 2020: www.cnbc.com/2020/03/25/bernanke-says-this-is-much-closer-to-a-natural-disaster-than-the-great-depression.html
3 Martin S. Eichenbaum, Sergio Rebelo, and Mathias Trabandt, *The Macroeconomics of Epidemics*, NBER Working Paper 26882, March 2020.
4 The Impact of COVID-19 on Engel's Coefficient and Household Consumption Behavior: http://finance.sina.com.cn/zl/China/2020-04-17/zl-iirczymi6918895.shtml
5 A. Maddison, Historical Statistics of the World Economy, 1-2008AD, 2010: www.ggdc.net/maddison
6 R. Baldwin, Keeping the Lights On: Economic Medicine for a Medical Shock, Voxeu, March 13 (2020): https://voxeu.org/article/how-should-we-think-about-containing-covid-19-economic-crisis

7 Impact of the COVID-19 pandemic on the supply side and countermeasures

Huang Qunhui

The COVID-19 pandemic has had an all-round impact on the global economy. Whether in the economic dimensions of production, distribution, exchange, and consumption, or the economic analytical framework of supply and demand, all economic activities have been heavily hit by the pandemic in the short term, and a profound impact may also be felt gradually in the long run. In terms of the short-term impact of the pandemic, for supply-side analysis of the impact of the pandemic on the economy, we should recognize the short-term impacts of lockout, enterprise close down, and supply chain disruption. We should also give attention to long-term impacts of technological change, production mode change, and policy implications.

Mechanism and characteristics of the pandemic's impacts on economic supply

After the 1960s, many doctors and health policy analysts thought that microbial diseases had been eliminated thoroughly, in essence due to the use of antibiotics, vaccines, and other therapies. But at the end of the 20th century, as the directory of human infectious diseases developed continuously (including acquired immune deficiency syndrome (known as AIDS), legionnaires' disease, Lyme disease, bovine spongiform encephalopathy (known as BSE or mad cow disease), Ebola, Rift Valley fever, severe acute respiratory syndrome [SARS], avian influenza, monkeypox, Nipah virus, rabies, and the Chandipura virus), it was generally believed that the aim of eliminating infectious diseases was too optimistic. At the end of the 20th century, approximately 6 million people died of various infectious diseases every year; in developing countries, one in every two deaths was caused by infectious diseases[1]; what is more, with globalization, infectious diseases in fact began to threaten human society more seriously. "The global migration of human beings, animals and plants has brought about economic prosperity, cultural integration and social transformation, but there was a price, i.e. diseases spread at an unprecedented speed and scope."[2] This has been proved by the global COVID-19 pandemic in 2019. Before vaccines were developed, the most effective way to resist epidemic disease was to reduce person-to-person contact, though the impact of

DOI: 10.4324/9781003184447-8

this anti-epidemic method on economy was undoubtedly huge. It's very hard to make a choice between life and death and the economy. Although life is priceless, we should go all out to fight against the pandemic and protect life, but we should still analyze the impact of the pandemic on the economy and achieve maximum anti-epidemic effect at a minimum economic cost.

Analysis of the mechanism of the pandemic's impacts on economic supply

The impact of the unexpected pandemic on the economy brought three changes in economic operation: change in economic trends, change in economic circle, and change of external impacts. The most direct impact of the pandemic was the threat to human life as well as the change of human behaviors to protect life and reduce person-to-person contact. The labor force is the most basic factor of economic supply; undoubtedly, the impact of the pandemic on the economy was directly manifested as impact on supply, not only in terms of manufacturing shutdown caused by insufficient labor supply, but also the stoppage of consumption in the service industry. The stoppage of consumption in the service industry may still impact supply in some way. In fact, apart from continuous process manufacturers, most manufacturers had some inventory of goods and so were given a buffer of time to cope with the impact of the pandemic; however, due to the instantaneity of consumption, the service industry was hit first. Most external impacts were imposed on demand and then transferred to supply; for example, the impact of Sino-US trade conflicts. While the economic impact of the pandemic was first manifested as supply constraints of factors of production due to various constraints on labor force behavior, a series of passive contractions has appeared on the supply side. Of course, with continuous impact of the pandemic on supply, investment, consumption, and exports, the demand side would also contract passively, leading to impacts on demand, supply, and consumption, which interacted and finally caused an economic depression.

In economics textbooks, impact on supply generally refers to an event that influences enterprise production costs, and thus influences cost to the enterprise to provide products and services. Impact on supply may be divided according to its impact on output at the established price level, favorable or positive impact on supply, and adverse or negative impact on supply. Impact on supply would move the aggregate supply curve and the Phillips curve, positive impact on supply would enable a rightward shift of the aggregate demand curve and a left shift of the Phillips curve, and negative impact on supply would enable a leftward shift of the aggregate demand curve and a rightward shift of the Phillips curve. Of course, the precondition for these changes has been the short-term nature of impact on supply.[3] Impact of the pandemic was a typical negative impact on supply, due to the substantial drop in the supply of labor force and other factors of production in the short term, the supply of substances, and the decline in labor. This is why the aggregate supply curve has generated a leftward shift. Theoretically, the leftward shift of the supply curve meant an increase in unemployment, while a decrease in the supply quantity of goods and services also meant an increase in commodity price and inflation rate. Impact on supply triggers a high unemployment rate and high inflation rate, and short-term give-and-take lines of inflation rate and unemployment rate; that is, the Phillips curve would move towards the right. That is to say, impact on supply caused by the pandemic could trigger a short-term stagflation and cause an economic depression. In order to solve this macroeconomic stagflation problem, corresponding fiscal policy and monetary policy have been required to maintain stable economic operation. This explains why governments of all countries continuously introduced various fiscal policies and monetary policies to repair the impact of the pandemic on supply after the outbreak was basically controlled.

Impact on labor supply caused by the pandemic can be broken down into three levels. First, direct loss of labor force; that is, personal casualty caused by the pandemic, which led to labor shortage. Modern medicine, public health, and epidemic prevention systems prevented huge population loss, which moved the aggregate supply curve to the left; .in contrast, the Black Death in Europe in the 14th century led to the deaths of one third to two thirds of the European population. Some studies even concluded that because the Black Death caused a shortage of labor and relative abundance of capital and land, it had promoted the collapse of the European feudal economy and generated the historical Great Divergence.[4] This fully reflects the huge influence of impact on supply at this level.

The second impact is job transfer of labor force; that is, a large number of workers transferred from original jobs to jobs related to fighting the pandemic, such as direct frontline medical rescue, production and transport of medical facilities, materials, and necessities of life, population quarantine, preserving order, and other social governance works, which has generated a structural change of labor force, accompanied by a lot of costs.

The third impact is disrupted supply of labor factor; that is, elimination of person-to-person contact in order to avoid spread of the pandemic, which meant that many workers suspended provision of labor, with the exception of provision of daily necessities. From the economic circular flow diagram between firms and households, households would not provide labor factor to firms via factor markets, nor would firms provide products and services to households via product and service markets, except for provision of daily necessities and economic activities requiring no person-to-person contact. This has disrupted the input–output flow and monetary flow of many firms and households, and suspended mass production and service activities. In the current highly coordinated modern economic system based on division of labor, anti-epidemic requirements of home quarantine and social distancing have caused decrease or disruption of labor supply as a production factor of firms, and would rapidly lead to decrease or disruption of fund flow and logistics in firms, poor coordination and even disruption in the industry chain and supply chain, and abnormal operation of the fund cycle and input–output cycle in the economic circular flow diagram. If the pandemic lasts for a long time and government provides weak assistance, it will lead to bankruptcy of many firms, unemployment, and overall economic recession. With specialization of the global value chain, impact of the pandemic on one economy's supply side might be extended rapidly to the global industry chain and supply chain, thus exerting huge impact on the global economy. Apparently, the third level of impact of the pandemic on labor supply has hit the economy most seriously, and we should analyze the impact of the pandemic on economy on the supply side. This is also indicated by previous epidemics; for example, above 90 percent of the socioeconomic losses brought about by SARS in 2003 were attributed to change of human behavior patterns, not to the direct loss of life and property brought about by the epidemic.[5]

Basic features of the COVID-19 pandemic's impact on supply

Based on the above, further analysis of the economic impact of this pandemic from the supply side has required a basic judgment on the scope and degree of the pandemic's impact on supply. It now seems that the pandemic's impact on supply has three basic features: short-term impact, global impact, and high strength.

Short-term impact on supply

Although we cannot judge the duration of the pandemic accurately now, based on the following reasons, we may judge that the pandemic's impact on supply will be short term. First, the duration of the pandemic has been generally no more than a year. The actual evolution of the pandemic in mainland China also proved that the pandemic may be basically controlled in a region in about half a year by banning social activities and taking social distancing measures, including bans on gatherings and large-scale group activities, stay-at-home orders, mandates to keep social distance, closing shops and schools, and reducing and even suspending flights. More critically, if the pandemic lasts for more than a year, vaccines will be available to finally end the pandemic, which means that the pandemic cannot last long.

Next, impact on labor supply caused by social distancing will generally be shorter than the duration of the pandemic. Slack demand caused by impact on supply and demand suppression, if not the inherent problem of the economic system, will also generally end along with the end of the pandemic. There will be the possibility of economic "blowout" after the pandemic has ended, due to suppression of demand for some time and relevant government stimulus policies. In addition, considering asymptomatic patients and other factors, epidemic prevention and control might be normalized at this time, and the existing strict social distancing and other prevention and control measures will not be long term.[6] Human society should explore the options for production and lifestyle coexisting with the pandemic, and formulate unified planning for epidemic prevention and social and economic development, which will also gradually smooth the impact on supply caused by strict quarantine of existing labor force. This means that the pandemic's impact on supply would not be permitted to become long term, though the fight against the epidemic has been normalized. It may be seen from China's economic data that although economic growth in the first quarter of 2020 decreased by 6.8 percent as a whole, if we compare data for March with data for January and February, we can see that all economic indicators, including added value of tertiary industry, employment, investment, and consumption, have witnessed a rebounded growth and even significant narrow declines. This shows that although this impact was very strong, it was a short-term external impact as compared with the impact in January and February, and a quick recovery trend has shown up in March.

Finally, historically, such a disastrous external impact of pandemic on supply is not long-term if economies do not have inherent structural economic problems and are not affected by economic trends and periods. For example, the 1918 Spanish Flu, the 1957 Asian Flu, the 2003 SARS, and the 2001 9/11 event did not exert a long-term impact on the economy.[7] Of course, we cannot exclude the long-term impact of a disaster event on the economy and society in the future, which could even change production and living habits. In a word, due to its short-term nature, the pandemic would not generate long-term economic depression similar to the 1929 Great Depression or the 2008 international financial crisis if there were no problems in the economic structure itself.[8]

Global impact on supply

The World Health Organization has defined the global outbreak as a "global pandemic." In the age of globalization, although different countries have taken social distancing and other prevention and control measures at different times, the results of these measures had only minor differences, such as the impact on labor supply due to reduction of social communications. Today, with the specialization of the global value chain, the global pandemic will quickly destroy the global industry chain and supply chain, thus leading to a global impact on supply.

Now it is worth worrying about the wave of de-globalization due to disruption of the global industry chain and supply chain.[9] According to the spread of the pandemic and changes in the response policies of all countries, and from the point of view of industry chain and supply chain, the pandemic's impact on supply will roughly experience three stages. At the first stage, according to the outbreak in China, China's economy saw a huge impact on supply, including suspension, slowdown, and even block out of the domestic industry chain and supply chain, impact on the global supply network, and widespread late delivery and order reduction. At the second stage, as the pandemic spread overseas, supply chain obstruction and drop in demand in some countries had further economic impact on supply in China. After March 2020, countries and regions including Japan, South Korea, and then Italy, Germany, France, and other European countries and North America faced huge tests and challenges from the pandemic. In mid-March, some motor manufacturers closed their factories in Europe and North America. Although work resumption rate increased continuously in China, the supply chain has not been fully recovered, and as the external impact of the pandemic came to affect China, a negative interactive effect appeared between the impact on supply of China and impact on supply of other countries. At the third stage, the disrupted global supply chain and industry chain led to impact on global economic supply.

With respect to the global manufacturing network, the world manufacturing industry may be divided into three networks: the North American Free Trade Area (the United States, Canada, and Mexico), the Eurozone (mainly Germany, France, the Netherlands, and Italy), and the East Asian region (China, Japan, and South Korea). After mid-March, 2020, the three global manufacturing networks were hit hard. With the specialization of the global value chain, impacts on supply and demand were superimposed on each other. As the nature and direction of the pandemic's impact on the global supply chain has been changing fundamentally, the pandemic will not only lead to more delays of goods delivery and reduction of orders, but also large-scale disruption of the global supply chain, thus resulting in impact on global supply.

Large impact on supply

This was experienced directly in large-area enterprise shutdown, unemployment, and large-scale disruption of the industry chain and supply chain in many countries. China's manufacturing Purchasing Managers Index (PMI) was 35.7 in February 2020, a record low; merely from the perspective of PMI, this was a record impact. After the pandemic entered Europe and America, Italy's PMI was only 17.4 in March, another all-time low. The initial PMI value of manufacturing and service industries was only 49.2 and 39.1, respectively, in the United States, 44.8 and 32.7, respectively, in Japan, and 48 and 35.7, respectively, in the United Kingdom—all below thresholds. Affected by the pandemic, the Service Production Index and industrial added value decreased by double digits in China in January and February, by 13 percentage points and 13.5 percentage points year on year, respectively. Based on the report of International Labor Organization issued on April 7, 2020, 81 percent of the 3.3 billion workers in the world were affected by the COVID-19 pandemic, with their workplaces completely or partially closed.[10]

Considering the huge impact on supply, all countries launched strong economic rescue or stimulus measures. As of the first quarter of 2020, US President Trump signed a USD 2 trillion economic rescue package to support small and medium-sized enterprises and low- and medium-income residents;

as a result, the scale of economic rescue exceeded that for the 2008 international financial crisis by far, becoming the largest ever economic rescue plan, and various aid stimulus plans have since been released. On March 17, 2020, Britain unveiled a GBP 330 billion government loan scheme, and provided enterprises with a GBP 200 tax cut and exemption and financial aid. On April 7, 2020, the Japanese government also launched an unprecedented JPY 108 trillion emergency economic stimulus plan, with the scale equivalent to 20 percent of Japanese gross domestic product (GDP), thereby exceeding the USD 2.2 trillion US stimulus package which was 10 percent of US GDP.

Impact of the pandemic on the supply side of China's economy: Short term and long term

Although impact of the pandemic on supply was short term, for such a strong global external impact, this was by no means merely a short-term increase in labor stoppage and unemployment. With high risk of enterprise closure and bankruptcy and high probability of supply chain disruption, the pandemic will also influence long-term technological progress and production modes, and even influence the country's position in the global system of division of labor.

Impact of the pandemic on the supply side of China's economy: Short-term perspective

On the supply side, the impacts of the COVID-19 pandemic on the economy may be divided into three levels: factor, enterprise, and industry.

Factor level: The "cliff effect" and the "substitution effect"

The impact on supply is due to inability of the labor force to provide face-to-face contact or to gather during the pandemic. On the one hand, there was a drop in labor supply—a cliff effect; on the other hand, supply of technology, funds, and other factors has made up for insufficient labor supply, and the employment structure has changed due to substitution of different types of labor—a substitution effect.

With respect to the cliff effect, based on data from the National Bureau of Statistics of China, 1.08 million persons got new urban jobs in China in January and February. In February, the urban unemployment rate was 6.2 percent, about 1 percentage point higher than in normal conditions. In March, the urban unemployment rate was 5.9 percent, down 0.3 percentage points compared with February, but still significantly higher than in normal conditions. The PMI of manufacturing and non-manufacturing industries were 31.8 and 37.9, respectively, in February 2020, record lows; although PMI recovered quickly in March, it was still below the normal operation level.[11] Research has shown that based on the work resumption rate of small and medium-sized enterprises, the total lost workdays in the first quarter was about 22.5 days, accounting for 36.9 percent of the original 61 work days in the first quarter. If production and economic operation activities could fully return to normal in all districts other than Hubei in the second quarter, the actual work days would be 228.5 days in 2020, a drop of 8.6 percent of working time compared with 2019.[12]

With respect to the substitution effect, all countries have taken fiscal and financial measures to provide sufficient funds to enterprises to ensure basic cash flow in case of a cliff drop of labor supply and inability of enterprises to maintain normal production and operation. This can be interpreted as substitution. Additionally, new technology was used to decrease labor force participation and reduce production activities that require contact. The most typical practices were substituting online activities for offline activities and holding online meetings rather than meeting face-to-face. However, from the perspective of labor employment, under the impact of the pandemic, many enterprises could not restart production and generated a lot of occupational replacements. Take as an example the takeout service: from January 20 to February 23, 2020, 75,000 new takeout riders joined the Meituan platform; 18.6 percent of these additional riders were former factory workers, 14.3 percent were former sales personnel in enterprises, 19.2 percent were former service workers, and only 14.3 percent had been unemployed before the Spring Festival. This means that most of them changed their previous occupation to that of takeout rider because original factories, restaurants, and service stores hadn't been open to business; their only option was to change jobs.[13]

Enterprise level: From rapid production shutdown to resumption of production and work

The requirements for social distancing and other epidemic prevention and control measures led to rapid large-area shutdown of enterprises, so production supply fell greatly or was partially disrupted, and many enterprises suspended their production and operation activities. According to analysis of transaction payment data from Tradeshift, the world's largest business collaboration platform, and the intercept data for the week starting February 16, it is clear that China's overall trading activities decreased by 56 percent and orders among Chinese enterprises decreased by 60 percent, while the number of transactions between Chinese enterprises and international corporations decreased by 50 percent.[14] Losses caused by such rapid shutdown were huge. According to a survey by the China Enterprise Confederation on the top 500 service enterprises in China from March 3 to 5, 2020, the pandemic exerted an adverse impact on operation in these enterprises in the first quarter. Among those enterprises that assessed losses, almost all were affected. About 55 percent suffered heavy losses, and about 90 percent suffered decrease in operating revenue in the first quarter.[15] Such an impact might be more fatal for small and medium-sized enterprises. Perhaps a large number of small and medium-sized enterprises faced bankruptcy and closure. According to a survey by the Business Model Innovation Center Survey Team at the School of Economics and Management, Tsinghua University, of 1,506 low- and middle-income enterprises in early February 2020, 31.81 percent of the enterprises reported an estimated decrease of more than 50 percent in operating revenue in 2020, and 27.22 percent reported an estimated decrease of 20–50 percent; therefore, a total of 59.03 percent expected to face decrease in annual revenue of 2020 of more than 20 percent. If the pandemic lasts for a long time, 85.74 percent of small and medium-sized enterprises will not survive.[16] Considering that the pandemic was not so widespread at that time, its actual impact on small and medium-sized enterprises were greater than these data suggest. As a whole, for industrial enterprises, industrial capacity utilization has reflected the degree of enterprise shutdown. As shown in Figure 7.1, industrial capacity utilization dropped sharply to 67.3 percent in the first quarter of 2020, 10.2 percentage points less than in the fourth quarter of 2019. Given the impact on the Spring Festival, compared with industrial capacity utilization in the first quarter of 2017, 2018, and 2019, decreases of 8.5 percent, 9.2 percent, and 8.6 percent, respectively, were evident, still showing a cliff drop effect.

Although the COVID-19 pandemic hit Chinese enterprises very hard, compared with European and American countries, certain favorable factors remained in China, including the number of Chinese enterprises that have

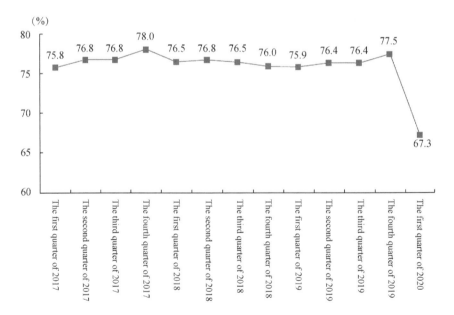

Figure 7.1 Quarterly industrial capacity utilization, 2017 to 2020.

Source: National Bureau of Statistics of China, April 17, 2020: www.Stats.Gov.Cn/tjsj/zxfb/202004/t20200417_1739333.Html

recovered from the pandemic and the coincidence of the outbreak with the Chinese traditional Spring Festival holiday. Enterprises in most industries will generally stop production for a vacation of one week during the Spring Festival; exceptions are continuous production, catering, tourism, transport, and other consumption services. This means that most industries were not affected by social distancing for about a week, thus reducing the loss arising from impact on supply. For enterprise production supply, the true impact of the pandemic came with the inability to resume work and production after the Spring Festival holiday due to control measures for prevention and quarantine. Enterprises could not carry out normal production operations, so production supply decreased sharply. The nature of the impact of the pandemic at enterprise level was whether work and production could be resumed rapidly after closedown had occurred.

However, as the old saying goes "illness comes on horseback, but goes away on foot," and it was very difficult for enterprises to resume work and production. The reasons include the large number of employees being unable to return to work on schedule due to different quarantine periods, transport controls, closures, and other prevention and control measures in different places, but also the impeded transport logistics, insufficient epidemic prevention supplies, difficulties in delivery of products downstream to the industry chain, high pressure on capital chains, difficulties in order fulfillment and continuation, inability to promote projects, significant increase in costs, and impact on international trade. These reasons come down to epidemic prevention requirements, enterprise operation, and enterprise supply chain. Results of a questionnaire survey covering February 14 to 17 on work resumption and reasons for not resuming work among 542 enterprises after the Spring Festival found that small businesses (less than 100 employees) and catering, accommodation, culture, tourism, construction, and manufacturing businesses were more readily affected by the hard-and-fast rules of government ban on work resumption. Also, in terms of enterprise operation difficulties, small private enterprises were more challenged by fund shortages and employees being unable to return to work as normal because of epidemic prevention requirements in their hometowns or the location of the company. In terms of the supply chain, construction, processing, and manufacturing enterprises were more affected by upstream enterprises that had not resumed work or had insufficient supply of production materials.[17]

Impact of the pandemic on enterprise production supply varied significantly with enterprise scale. Compared with big enterprises with strong resistance to impact, small and medium-sized enterprises faced a higher risk of closure and bankruptcy because resumption of work and production was affected by the pandemic. Research has shown that the smaller the scale of enterprise, the lower the probability of work resumption. With increase in scale, the enterprise would be more likely to resume production. Compared with enterprises with 50 and fewer employees, the probability of work resumption in enterprises with 50–100 employees, 100–500 employees, 500–1,000 employees, and 1,000 employees was, respectively, 20.8 percent, 18.7 percent, 19.4 percent, and 36.9 percent higher than the average. Compared with enterprises with an operating revenue lower than RMB 5 million, the probability of work resumption of enterprises with operating revenue of RMB 5–20 million, RMB 20–100 million, RMB 100–500 million, and RMB 500 million was, respectively, 15.9 percent, 17.4 percent, 31.2 percent, and 45.2 percent higher than the average.[18] In fact, many big enterprises resumed work and production very early on. According to a survey by the China Enterprise Confederation on China's top 500 manufacturers, as of February 20, the work resumption rate of these enterprises was up to 97 percent, the average work participation rate of employees was 66.17 percent, the average operating rate of subsidiary enterprises was 75.24 percent, and the average capacity utilization was 58.98 percent.[19] This survey also shows that the overall resumption of work and production in state-owned enterprises was better than that in private enterprises.

Although enterprises encountered numerous difficulties during resumption of production and work, as epidemic prevention and control became more effective in China, enterprises have sped up this process. China's PMI rose again on the basis of a sharp decrease in the last month, and manufacturing PMI was 52.0 percent, up 16.3 percentage points over previous month. The non-manufacturing business activity index was 52.3 percent, 22.7 percentage points higher than the last month. As of March 25, among procurement enterprises in China, the work resumption rate of medium and large enterprises was 96.6 percent, 17.7 percentage points higher than in February.[20] As of mid-April, the work resumption rate of industrial enterprises above designated size was nearly 100 percent, indicating short-term impact on supply.

Industry level: Higher risks of supply chain disruption and industry chain relocation

In the modern global value chain specialization system, each enterprise is a point in the world industry chain and works with other enterprises to ensure survival and development in the complicated dynamic global industry eco-system. As the center of the global manufacturing system, China's industrial added value accounts for nearly a quarter of global industrial added value, and China's share in global intermediate market is up to a third. China is the largest trading partner of more than 120 countries and the largest country of origin of approximately 65 countries.[21] This means that the pandemic's impact on China's manufacturing industry would exert huge influence on the global supply chain. Due to their different characteristics, all industries were affected by the pandemic to different degrees, but with the spread of the pandemic worldwide, the pandemic's impact on the global supply chain has been manifested as large-area delivery delays and order reductions, and risks of disruption to the global supply chain and migration of China's industry chain will increase continuously.

For the chemical industry with typical process manufacturing, upstream refining and chemical sectors were less affected by the pandemic due to continuous production during the Spring Festival. However, as upstream sectors of the chemical industry belong to heavy capital industry with large development inertia, the industry chain had strong stickiness, and the supply chain became closer. Once scattered, it would be difficult for the industry chain to restore the market. Thus, enterprises must have guarantees against major financial risks. Small and medium-sized enterprises have been dominant in fine chemical sectors downstream of the chemical industry, and most of them have adopted the order system to meet the increasing demand for epidemic prevention chemicals. Yet for some industrial chemicals in the middle reach of the industry chain, such as rubber and plastics, China has highly relied on Japan, South Korea, the United States, Italy, and Germany, which will influence the Chinese industry chain as the pandemic develops. It should be noted that due to too high specificity of fine chemical terminal products, the impact of the pandemic will bring about large demand fluctuations. Generally speaking, the opportunity brought by the pandemic for the chemical industry has outweighed the impact. The key is to resume production in a timely and comprehensive way and to seize opportunities to promote high-quality development of the chemical industry.

The pandemic has exerted a great impact on discrete manufacturing industries, including automobiles, electronics, machinery, home appliances, and clothing. From the perspective of the industry concentration ratio in Hubei and Wuhan, automobiles, new-generation electronic information technology, and biological medicine will be subject to greater impact. Take the automobile industry as an example. The impact on the supply chain of the auto industry in Hubei would be most prominent; Hubei is one of the four automobile production bases in China, and the gathering place for auto parts enterprises. There are 1,482 auto enterprises above designated size, and their entire vehicle output in 2018 was 2.2 million, accounting for 9 percent of national output. Auto parts production in Hubei accounted for 13 percent of national production. The first wave of the pandemic's impact on China's auto industry has exerted huge influence on the global automobile supply chain. On February 10, all five full vehicle enterprises in South Korea suspended overseas production because the parts supplied by China were used up; on February 14, both production lines of Nissan Motor Co., Ltd. in Kyushu factory in Japan stopped production. With the drastic impact of the pandemic on European and American enterprises, several enterprises declared shutdown. This has also hit the automobile and auto parts imports of China, causing incalculable impact on the global automobile supply chain and disruption of the global supply chain. Generally speaking, China's industries whose supply chain had a big impact on the global supply chain included textile clothing, furniture as well as electronics, machinery, and equipment industries.

Analysis of the pandemic's impact from outside on the Chinese industry chain (where China acts as the supply side) concluded there were reduced orders in such sectors as clothing, semiconductors and integrated circuits, optical and precision instruments, chemicals, air conditioners, toys, and home appliances. As the demand side, China's electromechanics, chemicals, optical instruments, transportation facilities, and rubber and plastics industries have relied heavily on Japan, South Korea, the United States, Italy, Germany, and other countries, vulnerable to the impact of a more serious pandemic. Sectors that import from COVID-19-affected countries and, thus, facing risk of disruption of the supply chain included optical imaging, medical devices, vehicles and parts, semiconductors and integrated circuits, high added-value parts and equipment. But this was also an opportunity for China in terms of innovation and upgrade. From the geographical perspective, the spread and persistence of the pandemic would develop along two main lines: emerging markets around China and developing countries; and European and American developed countries. This may lead to disruption of the global supply chain and cause a "grey rhino" impact on the global economy.[22]

Faced with increasing risk of disrupted global supply chain, all countries have adjusted their supply chains to ensure supply chain security, which will inevitably aggravate the trend of de-globalization. Affected by trade protectionism and a new round of scientific and industrial revolution in recent years, the global supply chain has shown trends of localization, regionalization, and decentralization, and the huge impact of the pandemic on the global manufacturing network has aggravated such trends. The layout of the global supply chain might face big adjustment. China's global supply chain and its global position will be greatly challenged. Now, American and European countries are making efforts to change the "China-oriented global supply chain system." On the one hand, they have increased the diversity and flexibility of the supply chain by adding sources of procurement other than mainland China or through multinational investment; on the other hand, they have moved their companies in China back to the home countries so as to increase the response capability of local supply by strengthening local production and production in neighboring countries. During the pandemic, both the United States and Japan issued some measures to encourage the return of their enterprises. In the stimulus plan to counter the pandemic's impact publicized by Japan, JPY 220 billion (RMB 14.2 billion) would be utilized to subsidize Japanese enterprises to move their production lines from foreign countries back to Japan, and JPY 23.5 billion (RMB 1.5 billion) would be utilized to subsidize Japanese companies to move their production to countries other than China.[23]

Impact of the pandemic on the supply side of China's economy: Long-term perspective

Often, historically, disasters, wars, and unexpected large-scale changes in the social and economic environment have become opportunities to promote technological innovation, institutional innovation, and management innovation. Economic theory suggests that factors of production are closely correlated. In case of shortage of labor factor supply, the increase in equilibrium supply price, capital and innovation factors will play a more important role due to decrease in equilibrium price. The pandemic will, on the one hand, stimulate some emerging industries, business forms, and new business models; on the other hand, it will catalyze some new industries, new business forms, and new business models to mature. The economic value added of new industries, new business forms, and new models in China occupied 15.7 percent of GDP in 2018. Under the pandemic, the proportion will further increase. Studies have predicted that under the impact of the pandemic, digital economic growth might slow down by 2.2–3.8 percent in 2020, but digital economy would be the optimal choice to alleviate impact of the pandemic and drive economic growth. Based on different durations of the pandemic, digital economic growth will be about 2.8–3 times the GDP growth.[24]

Under the impact of the pandemic, social economy will have deeper and wider demand for digital technology, including online demand for medical and health public services, community governance, education and shopping, and intelligent production in manufacturing enterprises. This will promote digital transformation of enterprises and the economy, helpful in upgrading industry toward informatization and intellectualization, and it will also drive investment in the construction of digital, intelligent infrastructures, accelerating replacement of economic drivers in China to some degree. From the perspective of the existing impact of the pandemic on technical factor supply, the applications of future digital and intelligent technological innovation are shown in Table 7.1.

The pandemic's long-term impact on China's economic supply side has promoted not only technological innovation, but also institutional innovation. Huge impact of the pandemic has enabled people to reflect on corresponding system loopholes in the entire economic society and carry out institutional innovation to make up for these. Also, in response to the short-term huge external economic impact, a series of relevant system and policy measures have been promulgated during the pandemic, including a series of short-term policies to reduce enterprise burden, such as cost reduction measures in aspects of taxation, finance, social insurance, and logistics. After tentative implementation during the pandemic, some effective measures may be changed to long-term policies, thus objectively promoting the deepening of structural reform on the supply side. On April 10, 2020, the Central Committee of the Communist Party of China and the State Council issued the Opinions Concerning the Building of Institutional Mechanism for More Perfect Market-Oriented Factor Allocation, which put forward a series of institutional designs to promote market-oriented land factor allocation, guide reasonable, smooth, and orderly flow of labor factor, promote market-oriented capital factor allocation, and quicken development of the technology factor market, cultivation of the data factor market, and market-oriented factor price reform. Although these institutional innovations were

Table 7.1 Application of digital and intelligent technological innovation during the pandemic and possible future development

Field	Application during the pandemic	Application cases during the pandemic	Possible future development
Business offices	The pandemic rapidly and significantly raises demand for remote coordinated offices, and cloud service enterprises provide quick online office services.	DingTalk meeting software of the Alibaba Group, Coordinative Lark software of ByteDance, corporate WeChat and Tencent Meeting, etc. followed up rapidly for business promotion. On February 3, 2020, the work resumption date, tens of millions of enterprises had nearly 200 million persons using DingTalk remote office. Tencent provided online services for more than 250,000 enterprises.	During the pandemic, promote online offices and coordinative production, and further accelerate digital, networked, intelligent development of production management. With epidemic control being normalized, users will develop remote office habits gradually, and this will further promote remote business office technology to mature and improve supply and quality of such technology.
Government and community governance	To strengthen control of social distancing and acquire personal health information, vigorously promote application of AI technology in government governance and community management.	"Health code," personnel health verification, trajectory tracking, and pandemic alarms were implemented. Major telecommunication companies and network enterprises provided accurate population movement route maps according to user data.	With respect to future development, government governance and community management will be more intelligent, and there will be further construction and improvement of the social credit system. Under a legal framework, using smartphones as the main medium, acquire tracking, social communication media, smart video recording, associated articles and other data, convert them into biometric identity, behavior, social communication network, and other information, and develop important means of social credit construction and legal supervision.

Productive services	During the pandemic, integrate deeply with productive services—for example, Internet and education, medical care, finance and transport; a large number of online service platforms are produced, and many online service models are innovated.	In terms of online medical care, as of February, 191 public medical institutions and 100 enterprise Internet hospitals increased free online treatment against the pandemic. In terms of online education, during the pandemic, the Ministry of Education and Ministry of Industry and Information Technology launched a national middle and primary school network cloud platform. More than 100 online education platforms were added. Tencent provided 100,000 courses (Teacher Top Speed Version) to users all over China.	Digital, intelligent producer services will be promoted extensively in the future, and online medical care, online education, virtual banking, smart transport, and other business models and technologies will be developed continuously. Technological innovation and business model innovation will improve the efficiency of producer services.
Consumer services	During the pandemic, home quarantine control measures enable a large number of contactless service models. A stay-at-home economy has been developed rapidly. Internet and artificial intelligence are deeply integrated with consumer services.	Shanghai Municipal Bureau of Culture and Tourism launched online virtual reality exhibition halls for art galleries and museums, and constructed smart exhibition halls. "Contactless delivery" orders accounted for 80 percent of activity on Meituan, Jingdong, and other e-commerce platforms. Experiments with unmanned aerial vehicle delivery, smart robots, and other highly intelligent modes began. Online orders on Hema Fresh, Su Fresh, Dingdong Maicai increased greatly.	The intelligence level of consumer services will be further improved. Unattended retail, unattended catering, virtual reality entertainment, and "zero contact service" business models may have more development opportunities. The position of the takeout service industry will be consolidated. Offline enterprises will innovate various online service models.

(continued)

Table 7.1 Cont.

Field	Application during the pandemic	Application cases during the pandemic	Possible future development
Manufacturing	During the pandemic, the significance of smart manufacturing is further expanded. It is not only the way forward for advanced manufacturing and efficiency, but also an effective way to reduce risk. Industrial Internet, cloud manufacturing platforms, and industrial robots are used more extensively.	During the pandemic, market orders for disinfection robots increased by 7–8 times; Lenovo Wuhan production base utilized 5G sensing and Internet to improve production safety and quality. The Ministry of Industry and Information Technology promulgated measures to support small and medium-sized enterprises to promote digital transformation and smart manufacturing during the pandemic.	Smart manufacturing represents the development direction of the manufacturing industry and is the core technology of a new round of scientific and industrial revolution. With continuously improved 5G network, artificial intelligence, industrial Internet, Internet of Things, data centers, and other new-generation information infrastructures, smart manufacturing will be more popular in the future and truly bring a new round of industrial revolution.

Source: the author, based on relevant data.

not temporary measures promulgated after the outbreak, they will play an active role in the response to the impact of the pandemic, stabilizing market expectations and promoting economic recovery. The pandemic itself is a huge test field for institutional innovation and has long-term impact on economic development on the supply side.

The global pandemic has not only promoted institutional innovation in China, but will also have long-term major influence on global economic and political order. The pandemic might quicken the evolution of "great changes unseen in a hundred years." Actually, before the outbreak, some major industrial trends had appeared in economic globalization. On one hand, new industrial revolution weakened the role of traditional comparative advantage centered on labor cost for globalization, and the direction of evolution and dynamic mechanism of globalization changed profoundly. On the other hand, the global value chain has shown a trend of major structural adjustment. With the rise of China's manufacturing industry value chain, the expansion of the global value chain has gradually become stagnant and unfavorable to multilateral global governance rules based on cooperation, mutual benefit, and negotiation, posing serious challenge to the multilateral trading system and greatly affecting the efficiency and authority of the World Trade Organization.[25] The spread of this pandemic and short-term disruption of the global supply chain might cause all countries to think about how to seek economic development balance between self-reliant security and efficiency in case of global division of labor in the long run. No definite answer can be given now as to whether the pandemic will become the last straw that breaks up economic globalization or another nail to seal the economic globalization coffin, or whether US-oriented economic globalization will change to China-oriented economic globalization. It is sure that under the impact of the pandemic, as an institutional supply, the economic globalization order faces huge opportunities for innovation.

Response to the pandemic's impact on supply: Bailout and innovation

With respect to the high external impact of this pandemic on supply and the huge supply-side impact on factors of production, enterprises, and industries of China, it has become necessary and urgent for government to issue short-term fiscal and monetary policies and social assistance policies. However, in design of policy to cope with the pandemic's impact on supply, the requirements of economic structure adjustment and the long-term economic development trend in China must also be considered. Short-term impact response policies should coordinate with long-term reform and development policies. The future economic trend would be the result of short-term impact response policies and long-term economic reform and development policies. On one hand, we should actively utilize macro policy to help enterprises to pull through difficulties; on the other hand, we should attach importance to the long-term policy trend of China, where focus on economic growth changes to high-quality development, and to the deepening of supply-side structural reform. This has required short-term response from policymakers in the form of fiscal and social policies to act as a "bailout" to protect people's livelihoods and enterprises, especially small and medium-sized enterprises. In the long term, institutional innovation and technological innovation should still be carried out to replace old growth drivers with new ones for high-quality economic development, and particular attention should be paid to avoiding excessive use of financial stimulus policy; otherwise, the financial system will become over-leveraged and have a huge negative impact on China's economic restructuring. Short-term enterprise bailout and long-term stimulation of innovation should be balanced in the current policy package.

First, the normalized epidemic prevention and control mechanism has promoted enterprises' resumption of work and production, and actively alleviated difficulties of enterprises, especially small and medium-sized enterprises.

Quick and overall resumption of enterprise production is critical to tackling the pandemic's impact on supply. We should persist in a combination of emergency response and normalized prevention and control, and actively promote resumption of enterprise production under the guidance of classified guidance and zoned policy implementation. Central and local governments have formulated and issued a series of measures to help resumption of work and production, and support enterprises to pull through difficulties. On one hand, various local government policy measures for manufacturing enterprises should be implemented from global and systematic perspectives, including tax cuts and exemptions, interest reduction and exemptions, loan extensions, business operation cost subsidies, smooth logistics, and convenient customs clearance. On the other hand, we should focus on key links, key enterprises, and key problems to actively promote resumption of work and production and ensure normal operation of the whole industrial chain. This specifically includes helping enterprises to solve difficulties and problems in recruiting workers, delivery and transport of raw/auxiliary materials and products, supply chain connection, promoting coordinated work resumption of upstream/downstream industry chain, strengthening interregional industry coordination and cooperation mechanisms, and guaranteeing smooth and efficient logistics. We should increase support for small and medium-sized enterprises, and especially protect stable operation of "little giant" enterprises that have grasped core technology in key industry chains. In terms of health and epidemic prevention, we should strengthen support for small and medium-sized enterprises in public welfare, increase their health and epidemic prevention capacity, and allow them to resume work and production as soon as possible. We should encourage these industries and enterprises to innovate their business models and expand their online and personalized service models as far as possible. We should give full play to the role of public platform and large-scale platform enterprises as service supporters of small and medium-sized enterprises, reduce the operating costs of small and medium-sized enterprises, and increase their operation convenience. We should establish central and local bailout funds for micro, small, and medium-sized enterprises, the fund source of which may be financial contributions of local governments or chartered local long-term bonds. The fund may be set up according to the specific industry and should take as reference the average tax payment, five insurance payments, and other indicators from the past 3 years. The fund should be paid in cash to micro, small, and medium-sized enterprises at one time or at several different times. The fund may especially be used for financial crisis remedies triggered by overdue or default of micro, small, and medium-sized enterprises. Finally, we should encourage local governments, enterprises, and various social organizations to actively explore coordinated rescue mechanism for micro, small, and medium-sized enterprises and fully utilize taxation mechanisms, financial mechanisms, insurance mechanisms, state-owned corporate social responsibility mechanisms, and house property rental mechanisms to construct a diversified bailout rescue mechanism for the whole society.

Second, we should strengthen trans-industrial and trans-regional coordinated work resumption of the whole industry chain and increase the security level and modernization level of the Chinese industry chain.

As the risk of China's supply chain disruption and industry chain relocation increased continuously during the pandemic, from the perspective of industry chain, China has faced two major economic tasks. On one hand, we will resume work and production of the whole industry chain as soon as possible and restore the industry chain hard-hit by the pandemic. On the other hand, we will construct the security and modernization system and mechanism of the Chinese industry chain in the long term. Therefore, efforts should be made in the following aspects: classified management of the industry chain based on the degree of impact of the pandemic on the industry chain and characteristics of the industry itself. The Ministry of Industry and Information Technology should take the lead to establish a trans-industrial, interprovincial coordinated work resumption mechanism for industry chains as soon as possible and promote coordinated work resumption of small, medium, and large enterprises. For integrated circuits, basic software, network security, and other strategic industries, we should provide new specialized core parts enterprises with directional support in terms of raw materials guarantee and employment and logistics. For chemicals and other process manufacturing industries, we should grasp the opportunity of the global oil price drop to resume production in a timely and comprehensive way and seize the opportunity for high-quality development of the chemical industry. For textile, clothing and other labor intensive industries, we should restore professional market and logistics system as soon as possible, and drive overall recovery of domestic supply chain. Also, government should help enterprises to restore the industry chain from the perspective of supply chain finance. For wholesale and retail, accommodation, catering, logistics, transportation, culture-oriented travel, automobile manufacturing, electronic information, textile clothing, and other industries significantly affected by the pandemic, we should establish a key monitoring mechanism. For enterprises and projects with development outlook, we should not blindly take back, stop, or delay loans; instead, we should extend loan periods and reduce fees and interest. We should exempt old loans of debtors affected by disasters through out-of-court settlement, exempt compensation obligations of guarantors, and avoid damage to credit due to relevant defaults. Government should coordinate the relationship among core enterprises, supply chain enterprises, and financial enterprises, promote core enterprises for transaction rights verification, reduce costs of financial institutions, and reduce the lending rate for small and medium-sized enterprises. Also, government should cultivate core enterprises and industry platforms in the industry chain, improve core enterprises and industry platform to coordinate with upstream/downstream partner enterprises, gather various factors of production, and promote efficient allocation of resources. On one hand, government should create an industry chain with stronger innovation capacity and higher added-value by improving innovation ability of these core enterprises; on the other hand, government should increase digital capacity of core enterprises to drive the management informatization, modernization, and systematization of the entire supply chain. Government should target at digital construction, promote a new round of infrastructure construction, support enterprises to strengthen digital management capacity of supply chain process, utilize digital technology to offset uncertainty in the supply chain, and promote evolution of supply chain management. In addition, as a major task of industrial base reconstruction, we should improve the Chinese industry chain security management system and establish a long-acting mechanism of industry chain security assessment and early warning of risk for different industries and districts. We should also establish a national industry chain security committee to make strategic decisions and deployment for Chinese industry chain security issues caused by diplomatic incidents, foreign technology blockade, major disasters, and epidemics, strengthen industry chain coordination, and improve the resilience and cooperativity of China's supply chain when facing major disasters and epidemics. Also, we should strengthen global joint anti-epidemic work, actively participate in international cooperation and governance of the global value chain, support Chinese enterprises to quicken "going global," guarantee the security of the global supply chain, establish a multichannel and multi-level supply chain security system, and coordinate to promote the construction of the global industry chain and the Belt and Road Initiative.

Third, we should grasp intelligent technological innovation opportunities during the pandemic to promote new infrastructure construction and replace traditional economic drivers with new ones.

We should fully utilize the impact of the pandemic to stimulate technological innovation and increase supply. We should then take the development opportunities of new industries, new business forms, and new models—especially further deep application of digital, intelligent technologies in social governance, business offices, manufacturing, and lifestyle consumption fields—so as to promote replacement of traditional economic drivers with new ones and accelerate high-quality economic development in China. As the digital and intelligent direction of development will be dominant in a new round of scientific and industrial revolution as well as transformation and upgrading of industry structure in China, more advanced digital information infrastructures are required to accelerate application and development of digital and intelligent technologies. Since the Central Economic Work Conference in 2018, Chinese central government has required development of the powerful domestic market, quickening of the pace of commercial 5G, and strengthening of the construction of new-generation information infrastructures. Under the impact of the pandemic in 2020, the central government has emphasized quickening the construction of new infrastructure. Although new infrastructure construction could really expand domestic demand and maintain growth, it should not be regarded as a government stimulus plan against the pandemic, but as built-in, high-quality development of China, so that it can objectively expand domestic demand and promote growth. Specifically, new infrastructure should be developed at three levels: new industrialization, new urbanization, and a modern economic system. The new infrastructure construction should serve for the high-quality industrialization and urbanization strategy and adhere to supply-side structural reform, avoiding going back to the old "indiscriminate" path.[26] New infrastructure means new industrialization, and the so-called new industrialization includes information-based, digital, networked, intelligent, and green traditional industrialization. It is the result of application of information technology, intelligent technology, and new energy technology in a new round of scientific and industrial revolution. New infrastructure not only includes new-generation intelligent information infrastructure and new energy infrastructure, but also reconstruction of traditional infrastructure on the basis of information-based, intelligent, and green facilities. New infrastructure construction should support the high-quality urbanization strategy. On one hand, it has laid out all new information-based, intelligent, and green urban infrastructure; on the other hand, it has utilized new-generation information technology and green technology to integrate transport, energy water conservancy, municipal environmental protection, public health, and other traditional urban infrastructures such as transport and information infrastructure between cities where urban clusters and metropolitan areas have been constructed. In addition, we should adhere to supply-side structural reform in new infrastructure construction. The new infrastructure construction investment and projects should respect the reactive results of market rules and market mechanisms, rather than the stimulating result of large-scale investment by government through selective industrial policies. The new infrastructure construction should be guided by government, but government should not intervene in it directly or excessively. Especially under the current influence of the pandemic, we should be on the lookout for any build up of pressure in achieving macroeconomic targets and high enthusiasm of local government for investment. As central government requires quickening the new infrastructure construction, we should understand and recognize this requirement from the perspective of high-quality economic development of China and actively promote new infrastructure construction. We should keep in mind the main lines of supply-side structural reform and start from the prioritized and full utilization of market mechanisms.

Notes

1 Lois N. Magna, *The History of Medicine*, by master translator Liu Xueli, Shanghai People's Publishing House, Edition 2, 2017, page 472.
2 Prateik Chakrabarti, *Medicine and Empire: A Global History of the Birth of Modern Medicine*, translated by Li Shangren, Social Sciences Academic Press, Edition 1, 2019, pages 174–175.
3 N. G. Mankiw, *Principles of Macroeconomics*, translated by Liang Xiaomin and Liang Li, Peking University Press, Edition 5, 2009, page 302.
4 Sevket Pamuk, The Black Death and the Origins of the "Great Divergence" across Europe, 1300–1600, *European Review of Economic History*, 11(3): 289–317.
5 Xu Feibiao, What is the Outlook of the World Economy under Impact of the Pandemic? *China Comment*, 6th issue, 2020.
6 From an economic point of view, if the economic loss caused by strict quarantine is greater than the economic loss of life caused by not strict quarantine, then strict quarantine measures should be lifted. Preliminary estimates suggest that sequestration in the United States would reduce the loss of life by USD 8 trillion, or 40 percent of GDP, in 2019, so it makes sense before it falls to −40 percent and causes a great recession. Similarly, China's quarantine policy in the first quarter saved between USD 25 trillion and USD 40 trillion in lives, while the economic quarantine policy caused about USD 2.5 trillion in economic losses. The quarantine policy was very successful (see Chen Yuyu, Less Loss of 40 Trillion! How was China's "Epidemic Account" Calculated, April 1, 2020: www.sohu.com/a/384887496_99982005). Of course, life is priceless, so such estimates cannot be accurate. But they must be considered. If economic recession is caused by excessively strict epidemic prevention and control, this will further affect epidemic prevention and control, and cause even more social, economic, and national security problems. The timing and extent of resumption of work and production based on the epidemic curve and the order and strength of a package of economic policies are the key to overall planning for the epidemic response and economic and social development (see Cai Fang, Five Characteristic Facts about Economic Response Policies under Impact of the Pandemic, April 14, 2020: http://finance.sina.com.cn/zl/China/2020-04-14/zl-iircuyvh7793923.shtml).
7 Xue Qiu, What Can We Learn from the Six Disasters in the Past 100 Years? Barron's, April 4, 2020: https://xueqiu.com/9487181048/146068566
8 Teng Tai and Liu Zhe, The Economy Will Not Suffer a "Great Depression", Rescue Measures Should Be Taken Quickly, *The Economic Observer*, April 1, 2020.
9 He Fan et al., Will Globalization Reverse Under the Quadruple Impact of COVID-19? *Finance and Economics*, March 18, 2020.

10 Ling Xin and Chen Junxia: International Labor Organization, The Pandemic Has Affected More than 80 Percent of the World's Working Population: http://finance.sina.com.cn/roll/2020-04-08/doc-iimxyqwa5704636.shtml

11 Service Industry Survey Center, National Bureau of Statistics, China Federation of Logistics and Purchasing, PMI Performance in China in Mar. 2020, March 31, 2020: www.stats.gov.cn/tjsj/zxfb/202003/t20200331_1735877.html

12 Zhang Ping and Yang Yaowu: Shifting Growth Paths and Supporting Policies Under Impact of the Pandemic—Based on the Analysis of the Unbalanced Impact on Enterprises, *Economic Perspectives*, 3rd issue, 2020.

13 Meituan Research Institute, Monthly Increase of 75,000 Registered Riders, Takeout Has Become a Reservoir of Employment—Meituan New Rider Employment Report During COVID-19 Outbreak, Survey Report of Meituan Research Institute, No. 14, March 8, 2020.

14 Liu Qiudi, The Impact of the Outbreak on Global Supply Chain Restructuring, *China Newsweek*, March 16, 2020.

15 China Enterprise Confederation Research Group, More than Half of China's Top 500 Service Companies Suffered Significant Losses and Most Were Optimistic about the Second Quarter, March 31, 2020: www.somac.org.cn/article/849/2.htm

16 Business Model Innovation Center Survey Team, School of Economics and Management, Tsinghua University, How to Help Small and Medium-Sized Enterprises in the Face of the Pandemic, *Guangming Daily*, February 14, 2020.

17 Quoted from Zhang Ping and Yang Yaowu, Shifting Growth Paths and Supporting Policies Under Impact of the Pandemic—Based on the Analysis of the Unbalanced Impact on Enterprises.

18 Zhang Ping and Yang Yaowu, Shifting Growth Paths and Supporting Policies Under Impact of the Pandemic—Based on the Analysis of the Unbalanced Impact on Enterprises.

19 China Enterprise Confederation Research Group, China's Top 500 Manufacturing Enterprises Resumed Production with 97 Percent Work Rate and Nearly 60 Percent Capacity Utilization Rate, *21st Century Business Herald*, February 22, 2020.

20 Service Industry Survey Center, National Bureau of Statistics, China Federation of Logistics and Purchasing, China PMI Performance in March 2020.

21 Cai Tingyi et al., Global Supply Chain Volatility: Vulnerability and Resilience, *Finance and Economics*, 5th issue, 2020.

22 Xu Qiyuan et al., Dealing with the Global Supply Chain "Grey Rhino" Shock, *Finance and Economics*, 5th issue, 2020.

23 Marginal Laboratory, Details of Japan's Economic Stimulus Plan Have Been Released: Allocate Funds to Support Enterprises to Withdraw from China, April 9, 2020: https://baijiahaoBaidu.com/s?Id=1663460652158652650&wfr=spider&for=pc

24 Sun Ke, What is the Impact of the Pandemic on the Development of Digital Economy and Macro Economy? February 12, 2020: www.smartcn.cn/208052.html

25 Huang Qunhui, The Industrialization Process of New China from the Perspective of Centenary Goals, *Economic Research Journal*, 10th issue, 2019.

26 Huang Qunhui, New Infrastructure Construction from the Perspective of High-Quality Development, *Study Times*, March 18, 2020.

8 Process and countermeasures for resumption of work and production

Du Yang

COVID-19 has become a global pandemic disease. As cases have been basically controlled in China, the most important task now is to promote resumption of work and production, minimize the impact of the pandemic, and make efforts to realize economic and social development targets. However, facing this once-in-a-century pandemic, the difficulty in restoring economic activities has exceeded many people's expectation, so countermeasures should be formulated according to the features of pandemic development and changes in the economic situation.

Features and stages of the pandemic's impact

Pandemic prevention and control and recovery of economic activities have been interdependent and interactional. The impact on economic activities has come from the COVID-19 pandemic; therefore, the strength and the epidemiologic features of the pandemic have become the main factor that will influence the process and mode of resumption of work and production.[1] After entering the 21st century, epidemic diseases such as severe acute respiratory syndrome (SARS), Middle Eastern respiratory syndrome, Ebola, etc., have attacked populations many times. However, the COVID-19 pandemic has wide scope, high casualties, and a deep impact that goes far beyond other pandemics. The scope and degree of this pandemic's impact may be comparable with the global impact of the 1918 Great Influenza; therefore, it's not an exaggeration to call this a "once in a century" event.

For the moment, the pandemic is hitting our economy. It has caused short-term slack demand and destroyed the supply capacity of some productive industries; however, if it is controlled in a short time, the pandemic will not damage the fundamental mechanism of economic development. Considering the shocking and short-term features of the pandemic, attention must be paid to the timeliness of corresponding policy measures. At the same time, only decisive and powerful countermeasures could restrict the impact of the pandemic to a short-term impact and prevent it from becoming a factor that will influence the long-term trajectory of social economy. The degree of

DOI: 10.4324/9781003184447-9

the pandemic's impact will determine the process of work and production resumption and the strength of the support policies taken.

As the pandemic is running rampant all over the world, and especially when the international spread of the pandemic and the impact of imported cases are still serious, it is difficult to specifically assess the degree of impact. Some economists argue that the impact of the 1918 Great Influenza on the macroeconomy provides a basis for estimating the impact of this pandemic, and an upper limit to analyze the impact of the pandemic on the macroeconomy.[2] The 1918 Great Influenza caused a decline of 6–8 percent in gross domestic product (GDP) and consumption in countries affected. However, the world has changed dramatically compared with 100 years ago. On the positive side, revolutionary progress has been achieved in mankind's technological capacity. Molecular biology, gene detection, and other technological means have enabled people to quickly and accurately identify virus characteristics, and advances in medical treatment has significantly reduced mortality. In addition, there have been abundant macroeconomic governance means in which demand management is dominant. These means may iron out the impact of the pandemic on the economy to a certain degree. On the negative side, the pandemic might have a multiplier effect on all economies in the world as they are connected more closely, so extension of industry chains may lead to a "butterfly effect" in world economies. As the country first hit by the pandemic, China has suffered economic losses arising successively from the domestic outbreak and imported cases; as a result, the economic fluctuations and uncertainties in resumption of work and production increased greatly. From the outbreak of COVID-19, the impact of the pandemic on economic activities and resumption of production and work may be roughly divided into three stages, described in the remainder of this section.

Impact at the early stage of the COVID-19 outbreak

The period from lockdown in Wuhan to the end of the Spring Festival holiday is considered the early stage of the COVID-19 outbreak. It may be thought of as the first stage of the pandemic's impact on economic activities. At this stage, the whole of China worked as one to fight against the novel coronavirus, and going all out to fight against the pandemic was seen as an overwhelming central task at that time. At the early stage of the pandemic, during 2020 Spring Festival, the impact of the novel coronavirus on economy and labor market[3] was mainly in the service sector. Differences existed in the influencing mechanisms of the pandemic on economic activities of secondary industry and tertiary industry. For secondary industry, the impact was mainly centralized on the supply side (production), which would require an elastic recovery and follow-up remedy. By contrast, the impact of the pandemic on tertiary industry was centralized on the demand side, causing direct subsequent losses that could not be restored. Due to strict quarantine measures, hard-hit industries included tourism, catering, accommodation, culture and entertainment, wholesale and retail trade, and transport, which should have been in their high season of sales or services. Quarantine measures decreased demand in the service sector and directly influenced its operating revenue. The contracted need for final services inevitably led to a sharp decrease in need for employment.

The suspension of economic activities and the concentrated fight against the pandemic have clearly influenced employment. It is inappropriate to consider the unemployment problem caused by restrictions to social mobility during the fight against the pandemic under the analytical framework of traditional labor market. As this outbreak occurred during the Spring Festival holiday, the negative impact on the labor market was alleviated to some degree; however, continuous impact on economic activities during the pandemic and in the subsequent period has inevitably caused job losses.

In tertiary industry, mostly micro and small businesses and individual businesses were hard hit at the first stage of the pandemic. Apparently, in contrast with big enterprises, these businesses were too weak to resist risks, so they were more likely to suffer from the initial impact and subsequent effect of the pandemic. We can calculate the average employment scale of the hard-hit industries using China's Fourth National Economic Census data. As shown in Table 8.1, of these industries, the average size of individual businesses was less than 3 persons, and the average employment scale of legal entities was less than 10 persons, indicating that a large number of micro and small businesses were engaged in these industries. According to the results of the Ant Group's Online Survey on Small and Micro-Sized Enterprises, based on 20,000 questionnaires administered to enterprises, tertiary industry were most likely to be severely affected by the pandemic (i.e. "unable to run business and might shut down"); accommodation, catering, culture and education, entertainment, transport logistics, people's livelihood service as well as wholesale and retail trade all had results exceeding 70 percent. There were 8.6 million legal entities in the six industries. Based on the survey data, approximately 6 million enterprises were unable to sustain business at the first stage of the pandemic.

Table 8.1 Average scale of enterprise in hard-hit industries (persons)

	Legal entity	*Individual business*
Wholesale and retail trade	6.17	2.02
Transport, storage and postal services	24.87	2.02
Accommodation and catering	16.40	2.94
Lease and commercial services	8.98	2.29
Residents service, repair and other service industries	8.71	2.38
Culture, sports and entertainment	7.40	2.85

Source: calculated according to Fourth National Economic Census data.

According to the survey results, from the perspective of the scale of operating revenue, the smaller the scale, the more severe the impact on micro and small operators. In micro and small operators with operating revenue below RMB 100,000, up to 46.4 percent estimated a decrease in operating revenue in the first quarter by more than 80 percent year on year. According to the Fourth National Economic Census data, there were 51.3 million businesses in the six industries. Based on the work resumption rate of 40 percent at the first stage, according to the survey results, over 30 million individual businesses were hit at the first stage of the pandemic.

Simultaneous epidemic prevention and control and economic recovery

The second stage of resumption of production and work started roughly from February 10, 2020, when the Spring Festival holiday was over and the pandemic broke out worldwide (at the time when the World Health Organization (WHO) officially declared COVID-19 a global pandemic disease). On February 4, 2020, new confirmed cases of COVID-19 decreased for the first time in districts of China other than Hubei, and the downtrend of new cases has continued in these districts since then. After the Spring Festival holiday, both epidemic prevention and control and resumption of work and production became possible in some districts. Orderly resumption of work and production was very necessary for the following reasons.

First, the pandemic was still very serious in Hubei at this stage, and Hubei, as a main battlefield, required continuous material support from other districts of China. With the increase of confirmed and suspected cases, demand for medical supplies increased significantly. Merely from the perspective of medical production and supply, due to increasingly specialized production links, many districts were involved in the product production chain; consequently, continuous large-scale supply of medical supplies could not be guaranteed without full coordination of upstream/downstream industry chain. The economy in Hubei Province was basically in a state of shutdown during the pandemic. With the passage of time, higher quantity, more categories, and wider scope of means of livelihood and other articles were required. The reserve and inventory of these supplies could not meet the requirement. Therefore, where conditions permitted, other districts fully utilized their production capacity to guarantee material supplies for Hubei's epidemic prevention and control.

Next, the scale of the pandemic in the rest of the world was unclear at that time, and the global economy was in normal operating state. As one of the three centers of global value chain besides the United States and Germany, China assumed responsibility for maintaining the stability of the global supply chain. Different from the SARS outbreak in 2003, when China had just joined the World Trade Organization, when COVID-19 broke out, China's economy was highly integrated in the global economy, and the latter relied heavily on China's manufacturing sector. From the periodicity of orders, March and April after the Spring Festival became a peak period of new orders. As shown

Table 8.2 PMI new export order index

	2016	2017	2018	2019
Annual average	49. 4	50. 9	49. 1	47. 5
Annual maximum/month	50.3/	52.0/	51.3/	50.3/
	November	June	March	December
March (deviation)	50.2 (0.8)	51. 0(0. 1)	51.3 (2.2)	47.1 (−0.4)
April (deviation)	50.1 (0.7)	50.6 (−0.3)	50.7 (1.6)	49.2 (1.7)
March, month-on-month basis	2.8	0.2	2.3	1.9

in Table 8.2, the Purchasing Managers Index (PMI) new export order index saw a large month-on-month growth in March after the Spring Festival, higher than the annual average in March and April. This means that in the global supply chain, the seasonal procurement and production plan has been arranged according to the Chinese lunar Spring Festival.

At the second stage, with positive progress of pandemic prevention and control, people of all walks of life gradually became more optimistic about recovery of economic activities. However, according to data sources, difficulties in recovery of economic activities were far greater than expected. Recovery of traffic may be used to calculate the extent of recovery of economic activities. The estimated national average work resumption rate was only 42 percent on February 14. The overall operating rate of merchants in the second week after the Spring Festival was only 52 percent, of which the offline operating rate was 51 percent and the online operating rate was 68 percent. These figures were much lower than in the same period of 2019, indicating a slow recovery of economic activities at the second stage. Main factors that restricted work resumption were unrecoverable personnel mobility under the Level 1 local response mechanism for epidemic prevention and control, and enterprises' difficulty in finding workers, which became a major obstacle restricting resumption of work and production at that time. This issue will be discussed later.

Contraction of external demand caused by outbreak of the COVID-19 pandemic globally

The third stage of the outbreak was characterized by the impact of imported cases on China's economy. Roughly, we may regard March 11 as the beginning of the third stage; this is when the WHO officially declared the COVID-19 as a global pandemic. The pandemic spread all over the world at an unexpected speed and degree, and it had a sudden strong impact on China's economy and resumption of work and production.

First, since the pandemic was running rampant outside China, the pressure on the control of imported cases increased continuously. When COVID-19 was basically controlled in China, priorities shifted to recovery of economic activities, but the increase of imported cases disrupted the original rhythm of work and production resumption in some districts and postponed the process to a certain degree. The repeated outbreaks in Beijing in June 2020 reflect the variability and complexity of the COVID-19 virus and the increased uncertainty in economic recovery.

Next, countries hit hard by the pandemic were developed economies closely related to China's economy, including the United States, the European Union, and other main trade partners of China. Slack demand in these countries due to the impact of the pandemic reduced foreign trade orders placed on China, and the loss of the foreign supply chain would also affect relevant industries in China in the era of economic globalization.

At present, the impact of the global pandemic on China's economy continues, so China should pay close attention and design active response policies against similar crises in the future.

Process and influence of work and production resumption

Resumption of work and production refers to the process in which economic activities change from the stagnant state during the epidemic prevention and control period to the normal state of economic operation. A comprehensive index system is required for overall measurement of the economic recovery. As mentioned above, the impact of the pandemic is extremely variable, so the traditional statistics cannot reflect the impact of the pandemic on economic activities in a timely way. By contrast, timely observation of personnel mobility, logistics, use of factors of production, and changes of indexes closely related to economic activities may serve as the basis from which to deduce the work resumption process. At present, big data sources are very extensive, including payment data, transport and travel data, electricity usage data, and light data, which may reflect changes in economic activities from different sides. Of course, each category of data may only reflect a certain feature of economic activities. Separate use of each category of data cannot prevent hasty generalization; rather, they may complement each other to approach the appearance of facts as far as possible.

CMB Wealth Management's ICRIN has utilized satellites to observe changes in night lights of hundreds of industrial parks in mainland China and developed a domestic industrial capacity recovery index to reflect recovery of industrial capacity in China after the Spring Festival holiday. We can utilize the night lights index to assess the recovery of industrial capacity to some degree. As the basis for calculation, ICRIN took night lights data in the downtime of 2020 (from January 24 to February 2) and night lights data before the period of shutdown. This index started from February 17, 2020, and formed a comparable time series. Figure 8.1 shows the changes in the night lights index after the 2020 Spring Festival holiday. As of February 24, industrial capacity had recovered by about 50%; as of April 4, it had recovered to 76 percent of the

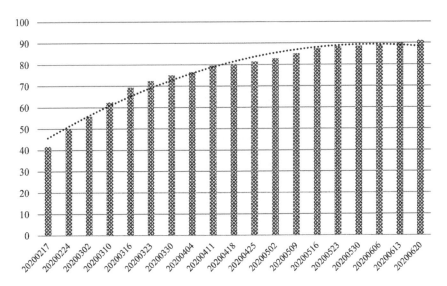

Figure 8.1 Changes in the night lights index for industrial parks after the 2020 Spring
Festival.

Source: Wind Financial Database

level in the reference range. The trend of work resumption in this figure shows
that recovery of industrial capacity first recovered quickly and then slowed
down gradually. In the first week, starting February 17, 2020, industrial production recovered most rapidly, and the index increased by 8.3 percent. In the
three weeks following March 11, 2020 (when the WHO declared COVID-19 a
global pandemic), the light index of industrial parks slowed down, up 3.1 percent, 2.6 percent, and 1.4 percent, respectively. As of January 20, 2020, the
industrial capacity of the samples observed had recovered to 91 percent in the
reference range, remaining in the negative growth section.

Restricted by data, we cannot observe the difference in work resumption
among different industries. It was reported that on February 23, when nearly
half of enterprises had resumed work and production, the biopharmaceutical
industry related to the pandemic saw a relatively high work resumption rate,
followed by the manufacturing and processing industries. The overall operating rate of the chemical industry was low, averaging at about 30 percent (Ma
Chuanmao, 2020).[4]

Due to the direct correlation between recovery of economic activities and
urban transport, transport and travel data may reflect the process of resumption of production and work from another perspective. The urban travel
intensity data provided by Baidu can be compared to the year-on-year travel
changes in cities so as to reflect the degree of recovery of economic activities. In order to reflect year-on-year changes more accurately, according to

changes of holiday policy during the pandemic, we compared the changes in transport and travel intensity on corresponding work days of 2020 and 2019. Specifically, the 2020 Spring Festival holiday was extended to the ninth day of the first lunar month (February 2, 2020); that is, the statutory Spring Festival holiday was over on February 3. Although this was the most anxious period of epidemic prevention and control with limited recovery of economic activities, after the statutory holiday, some important economic sectors started to recover activities. Therefore, we took the first day after the Spring Festival holiday as the starting point for data observation; that is, the starting date was the seventh day of the first lunar month in 2019 and the tenth day of the first lunar month in 2020 (February 3). We compared the year-on-year changes in transport and travel on the corresponding date in the 2 years, and we selected several of the most developed cities in China[5] for observation, including Beijing, Shanghai, Hangzhou, Suzhou, Guangzhou, Shenzhen as well as other cities in several developed areas so as to reflect changes in economic activities of the most important provinces for China's economic growth, including Zhejiang, Jiangsu, and Guangdong.

Since urban transport and travel intensity varies greatly on work days and weekends, we observed the year-on-year changes on work days and weekends in 2020. The transport recovery on work days better reflects the recovery of productive economic activities, while the transport and travel intensity on weekends reflects the recovery of daily life and consumption. Figure 8.2 shows the year-on-year changes in travel intensity in six cities on work days after the 2020 Spring Festival. The recovery was up to 90 percent on the 30th work day after the Spring Festival holiday in Suzhou and Hangzhou, and this quickly recovered to the level in the same period of 2019. The figure also approached 95 percent of the level in the same period of 2019 on the 30th work day in Shenzhen. Among first-tier cities, recovery was lowest in Beijing, only 71.1 percent on March 27 (the 34th work day), 95.5 percent in Shanghai, and 82.0 percent in Guangzhou.

The year-on-year recovery of transport on weekends better reflects the recovery of consumption. The higher the recovery of consumption, the higher the recovery of transport and travel on weekends. But Figure 8.3 shows that the impact of the pandemic on consumption has exceeded the impact on productive economic activities. Recovery of travel intensity on weekends started gradually from the second weekend (February 15) after the Spring Festival holiday in all the cities. On the sixth weekend (March 15), travel intensity was almost fully recovered in Suzhou and Hangzhou, though at 90.4 percent and 85.6 percent, respectively, this was not up to the level in the same period of 2019; travel intensity was 79.7 percent in Shenzhen. The recovery of travel intensity on weekends was even lower in Shanghai (77.3 percent), Guangzhou (74.9 percent), Beijing (53.6 percent), and other supercities.

Although analysis of the overall work resumption process based on professional data resembled the blind men and the elephant, consensus has been achieved from all kinds of data, including the following.

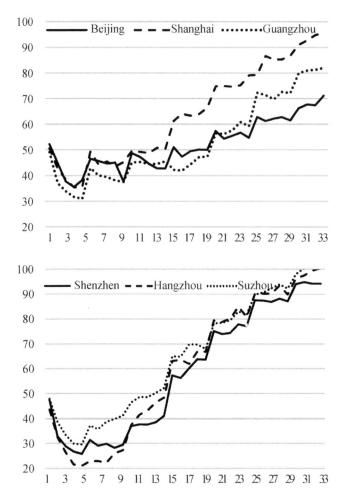

Figure 8.2 Year-on-year travel recovery on work days after the 2020 Spring Festival (%).
Source: Baidu Travel Database

First, as of the end of the first quarter, the overall recovery of economic activities was less than 80 percent, with a large regional disparity. The corresponding economic recovery was even lower in cities where more rigorous epidemic prevention and control measures were taken, even though the main developed provinces were dedicated to restoring economic activities as soon as possible. Due to the instability and complexity of the evolution of the pandemic, especially with the increasing uncertainty generated by reverse flow of international pandemic cases, economic recovery work in China remained arduous.

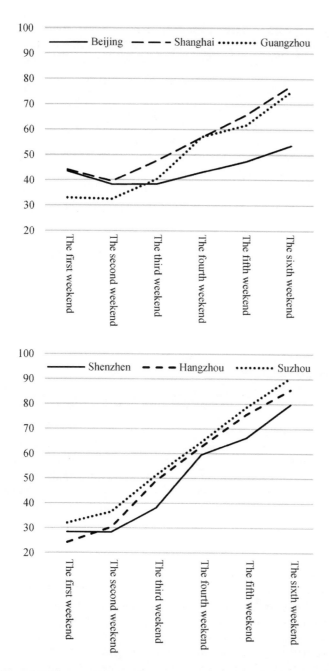

Figure 8.3 Year-on-year travel recovery on weekends after the 2020 Spring Festival (%).
Source: Baidu Travel Database

Second, due to different industry features, the manufacturing sector recovered rapidly, with higher elasticity; in contrast, sectors involving services in tertiary industry were obviously affected by the pandemic and found it more difficult to recover economic activities. Whether or not economic activities of the service sector could be restored as soon as possible would determine the success or failure of the "economic battle." The service industry has become a main source of employment growth; therefore, recovery and development of tertiary industry played a decisive role in stability of employment. What is more, compared with secondary industry, micro, small, and medium businesses and individual businesses were more centralized in tertiary industry, so continuous loss of this industry would bring more serious livelihood problems. In addition, continuous contraction of tertiary industry would exert a negative effect on final demand, which could be transmitted to manufacturing and other sectors, thus affecting the entire economy profoundly and extensively.

China's future regulation control policies should be based on actual features of resumption of work and production, especially the employment and livelihood problems of tertiary industry caused by the pandemic. A corresponding plan should be implemented to shorten the duration and reduce the degree of impact of the pandemic as far as possible.

Insufficient work resumption, slack employment demand, and cyclical unemployment

Insufficient recovery of economic activities is transmitted to the labor market, leading to slack employment demand and unemployment; that is, cyclical unemployment. The impact of COVID-19 on employment was evident. The urban unemployment rate was 6.2 percent in February, 1.05 percentage points higher than the monthly average in 2019. The unemployment rate featured cyclical unemployment, so the "keep employment stable" policy should start from the demand side and focus on the governance of cyclical unemployment.

In terms of drivers of unemployment, cyclical unemployment and structural unemployment were the two forms that exerted greatest influence on unemployment policy. As a whole, China's economic development has entered a period of rapid economic restructuring, so structural unemployment is always a dominant factor of unemployment. However, COVID-19 exerted a progressive impact on the economy at different stages, mentioned above, featuring cyclical unemployment caused by aggregate demand contraction, mainly in the following aspects.

First, the sudden surge of unemployment broke through the normal level of full employment and featured cyclical unemployment. From January 2017 to December 2019, the average monthly urban unemployment rate was 5.04 percent, and the standard deviation was only 0.15 percent; meanwhile, at this level of unemployment, China's economy maintained a medium to high rate of growth, and the price level also remained stable as a whole. This shows that the unemployment rate of 5 percent reflected a stable unemployment level under the economic growth conditions, and this may also be seen as full employment.

For unemployment under full employment, governance measures should be based on medium- and long-term policies to, for example, improve the labor market system environment, increase the operating efficiency of the labor market, and reduce frictional unemployment. The level of human capital of workers should also be improved so that they can adapt to continuous adjustment requirements of the economic structure. These policies concerning the labor market system and labor supply have represented the main content of long-term active employment policies.

However, since the outbreak of the COVID-19 pandemic, the change in unemployment rate has broken up the medium- and long-term trajectory of the labor market, and the urban unemployment rate in February jumped by 1.16 percent compared with the average monthly unemployment rate in the previous 36 months. The urban unemployment rate was still at a high level of 5.9 percent in May 2020. The undercapacity of secondary industry and limited recovery of tertiary industry caused by the pandemic led to contraction of aggregate demand and very evident cyclical unemployment. Although a more thorough calculation requires more trend data, through comprehensive assessment of the employment, price level, and economic growth, we think that this approximate 1.2 percent unemployment rate has indicated cyclical unemployment.

Next, the cyclical unemployment originated from insufficient resumption of work and production caused by the progressive impact of the pandemic on aggregate demand. If a decisive and specific economic rescue plan is not implemented, residents' income might further decrease, causing further contraction of consumer demand, which may be transmitted to the labor market and generate further unemployment.

The nature and origins of cyclical unemployment and structural unemployment are quite different, so means of addressing these may vary greatly. Government should launch pertinent measures to boost the economy and expand demand according to the scale and features of current cyclical unemployment caused by the pandemic, so as to make up the employment losses at the first and second stages mentioned above, and it should prevent the third stage by taking effective economic stimulus measures in a timely way.

Estimates of the scale of cyclical unemployment caused by insufficient work resumption could help us assess the strength and scale of short-term stimulus policies in macroeconomic control. As mentioned above, if the deviation of the current unemployment rate from the long-term steady unemployment rate is cyclical unemployment, then, considering the slight fluctuation of unemployment rate over the previous 36 months, the scale of current cyclical unemployment would be about 1.0 percent to 1.3 percent. Based on the urban employment scale of 442 million in 2019, assuming that the labor force participation rate did not change, additional urban unemployed population caused by cyclical unemployment would be roughly 4.7 million to 6.1 million.

The foregoing analysis in this chapter shows that the Spring Festival holiday took place just at the first stage of the pandemic, and there was limited year-on-year impact on secondary industry, including manufacturing. The impact on tourism, catering, wholesale and retail, transport, entertainment, and other service sectors was evident; in particular, micro, small, and medium-sized enterprises and individual businesses were seriously affected. Therefore, we may assume that the cyclical unemployment was mainly caused by loss of the service industry. According to year-on-year changes of total retail sales in February 2020 (down 20.5 percent year on year) as well as changes of the urban unemployment rate in the same period, we have calculated the elasticity of urban unemployment rate relative to total retail sales to be −0.83. This shows that recovery of service activities as soon as possible would effectively promote job growth. So only when governance of cyclical unemployment is regarded as a key part of the "keep employment stable" policy can the policy be successful.

In combination with the current situation of resumption of work and production, we think that direct distribution of one-off subsidies to all citizens is the most powerful weapon to enhance effective demand, control cyclical unemployment, promote economic development, and safeguard and improve people's livelihoods. Basic income subsidy plans have been discussed a lot in developed countries. Although based on national conditions in China, this approach is not mature enough to be implemented as a long-term plan. With respect to the huge impact generated by the worldwide pandemic, it's absolutely necessary to implement it as a temporary and one-off plan. It's perfectly possible to increase the fiscal deficit rate by 1.5 percent and distribute a per capita income subsidy of RMB 1,000 to all citizens according to the impact of the pandemic and financial capacity.

First, it's pertinent to implement a one-off subsidy plan for all people to control cyclical unemployment. The foregoing analysis in this document shows that the increase in the unemployment rate was mainly caused by the huge impact on main sectors in tertiary industry that absorbed employment. Therefore, boosting consumption would have an immediate effect on promoting employment. Based on data from the National Bureau of Statistics of China, rural residents' average propensity to consume was 0.85, while this was 0.66 for urban residents. To calculate according to 60 percent of the urbanization level at the end of 2019, the income subsidy of RMB 1.4 trillion may generate RMB 554 billion of consumption in urban areas and RMB 476 billion of consumption in rural areas. Since the marginal propensity to consume of the low-income group is higher, the actual consumption effect may be even higher if high-income group is encouraged to donate one-off subsidies to those on a low income.

If the above-mentioned RMB 1.03 trillion of consumption is realized within 3 months, the subsequent consumer demand may add 6.8 million jobs if other conditions remain unchanged, and offset the employment loss brought about by the pandemic at the early stage. What's more important, a large number of micro, small, and medium-sized businesses and individual businesses would achieve continuous operating capacity and turn the economy and people's livelihoods back to their normal track.

Next, the income subsidy plan for citizens is an effective supplement to the already launched investment plan. "New infrastructure construction" and other medium- and long-term investment plans might have a time lag in developing effective final demand. The income subsidy plan may start consumer demand in a timely manner to reduce cyclical unemployment before effective demand for investment is generated. Since it's a one-off plan, policy exit is not connected with investment plan so there is no echelon effect in the combination of a short-term plan with a medium- and long term plan.

Third, the previous investment plan will lead to reconstruction of the economic structure and will have a crowding-out effect on private investment, adverse to optimization of the economic structure. The one-off income subsidy plan has reduced policy links, so it may directly generate consumer demand and be more favorable to solving the difficulties of micro, small, and medium-sized businesses and individual businesses. The subsequent employment effect will also be obvious.

Finally, some scholars were worried that an income subsidy for all people would increase price levels. The main subject of this plan is low- and middle-income groups that might drive the price of basic consumer goods up, but the sense of happiness gained by the low-income group from consumption would be sufficient to offset the negative impact of price fluctuations. Existing research shows that the impact of unemployment on citizens' overall sense of happiness was double the impact of price rises.[6] Therefore, a comprehensive policy effect will be more likely.

Summary and prospects

This COVID-19 pandemic has exerted a huge negative impact on social economic life, and its subsequent impact will persist. On one hand, we should continue to give active policy response to its dynamic effects on economic recovery according to the how the pandemic evolves so as to reduce the shock generated by the pandemic; on the other hand, we should take a long-term perspective to optimize the social governance structure according to the development shortcomings exposed by the pandemic and in the work resumption process, thereby converting the crisis into opportunities.

Public service aspect of epidemic prevention and control

With progressive recovery of economic activities, the task to prevent and control the pandemic remains arduous, especially preventing the relapse of domestic cases as well as imported cases. This exerts a high pressure on economic recovery. The government should strengthen provision of public services and ensure successful implementation of economic activities. The following actions may be considered.

First, we should strengthen the digital and technological aspects of epidemic prevention and control management. With the development of digital technology and Internet technology, we should provide full support for digital management of epidemic prevention and control. Since the outbreak, some leading technology companies assumed social responsibility and showed high technological capability. Relevant government departments may entrust the software and hardware support required for digital management of epidemic prevention and control to some world-leading technology companies in China so as to improve governing capacity of the whole society.

Next, we should increase our capacity to provide a virus detection service, improve detection levels, and enhance implementation of the "early detection, early quarantine and early treatment" principle. After this pandemic outbreak, some biotech companies have responded quickly to greatly improve technological capability and serviceability of detection services, enhance the capacity of detection services in the form of government purchase service, and provide detection services as public goods in unusual times, thus supporting normal performance of economic activities.

Finally, we should reserve emergency response capability against the pandemic and make preparations for evolution of the pandemic after economic activities resume. The Xiaotangshan Hospital model may be a component of the long-term infrastructure and major emergency mechanism in developed areas, and reserve construction may be carried out to increase prevention and control capacity and play a key role in economic recovery.

Emphasize coordination of a rescue policy and economic recovery plan

This pandemic has exerted a continuous and large-scale impact on the economy. Based on the severity of impact and the process of recovery of economic activities, a short-term rescue plan should be implemented to provide special help for the hard-hit service industry, micro and small businesses, individual businesses, and the unemployed; this would keep employment stable, benefit people's livelihoods, and boost growth. An economic recovery plan should also guarantee continuous economic development capacity. Therefore, the following should be considered in formulation and implementation of policies.

First, the policy for cyclical unemployment should be mainly macroeconomic control policy. The short-term, timely, and countercyclical features of the policy should also be considered for timely exit when cyclical unemployment disappears. Therefore, some one-off and temporary policy instruments may be used. From the perspective of policy means, as compared with monetary policy, fiscal policy will help to target groups and enhance the timely effect of policy, with more controllable side effects.

Next, newly launched stimulus policies should be complementary to the already launched control policies or the control policies being considered. For example, the policy to be launched for quickening new infrastructure construction should aim at the main direction of Chinese economic restructuring and strategic commanding point of international competition in the future, help to optimize the economic structure, improve supply level, and enhance medium- and long-term supply level and quality of China's economy. It will also solve the structural unemployment problem to a certain degree. But we should see that the impact of short-term slack demand on the labor market needs to be solved now, and some short-term and timely plans are also urgently needed to boost demand and recover jobs.

Finally, it is noted that it was micro, small, and medium-sized businesses and individual businesses that suffered employment demand loss; therefore, this rescue policy should have a real effect on these businesses. For the unemployed in these industries, the social security net should strengthen unemployment rescue plans.

Reform the defect of incomplete urbanization

In the process of pandemic prevention and control and subsequent work resumption, the difference between the registered population and the resident population has caused incomplete urbanization and increased the cost of social functioning and the difficulty of recovery of economic activities. Reform of the household registration system should be carried out to coordinate the urbanization process with social and economic development.

The urbanization process is incomplete, as it has always taken labor migration rather than comprehensive population movement as a carrier. Such incompleteness has been embodied in two aspects: first, in urban economy, floating population mainly worked on the supply side, and their demand was suppressed; second, separation of production behavior from consumption behavior in terms of space has generated a reciprocating flow of personnel and increased the operating costs of the labor market and economy. Fundamental measures to solve these conflicts include quickening improvement of the household registration system and reform in relevant fields, and realizing citizenization of the floating population.

In recent years, it has become an important direction for reform to narrow the gap between the urbanization rate of the registered population and the urbanization rate of resident population so as to realize more complete urbanization. However, actual progress has been slow since citizenization of the floating population involved wide areas, multiple fields, and complicated interest relationships. During the period of the Thirteenth Five-Year Plan, this gap has not narrowed, remaining at 16.15 percent in 2016 and 16.22 percent in 2019. Considering that regionally redefined urbanization (e.g. changing a village to a residential community) accounted for a large proportion (nearly 40 percent) of urbanization growth in recent years, the actual progress of floating population citizenization might be slower.

When economic operation is in a normal state, the incomplete urbanization process will raise the operating cost of the labor market and the entire economic system, and damage economic efficiency; but such influence is also observable in normal years, and the potential economic operating cost is also immeasurable. This pandemic has exposed the incomplete urbanization more directly. We should utilize the "final exam" of this pandemic to solve the problems that should have been solved through more comprehensive and thorough reform, so as to realize healthier and more complete urbanization.

It may be seen from the pandemic prevention and control and recovery process after effective control of the pandemic that incomplete urbanization has increased the cost of social governance and economic operation in two aspects. First, even in normal years, large-scale personnel mobility during the Spring Festival causes a huge social operating cost. To estimate the cost, we can use monitoring data on rural migrant workers in combination with other data published by the National Bureau of Statistics of China: about 160 million rural migrant workers moved into the eastern region, and about 46 million rural migrant workers returned to their hometowns during the Spring Festival. Such a large-scale seasonal flow has brought greater difficulties for pandemic prevention and control. Even in normal years without impact of the pandemic, reciprocating flow of the labor force between the work place and hometown may also increase the time cost. It has taken about 3 weeks on average for rural migrant workers to be fully back to their jobs after the Spring Festival holiday, half a month longer than the statutory holiday. Therefore, if complete urbanization is realized, there will be a rise in the proportion of family migration, a decline in personnel flow, and an increase in effective labor input of rural migrant workers, which may help to increase the gross output level.

Second, large-scope personnel mobility has intensified the difficulties in recovery of economic activities after the outbreak. Required by epidemic prevention and control, personnel mobility was restricted substantially after the 2020 Spring Festival, and a large number of rural migrant workers chose to stay in their hometowns, thus failing to meet employment demand. At a later stage of the pandemic in China, a "barrier lake" formed by impeded labor migration became the biggest obstacle for resumption of work and production. Under the special conditions of the pandemic impact, incomplete urbanization has weakened the elasticity of labor market adjustment and increased difficulties in recovery of economic activities.

Over a longer term, the complete urbanization process will improve the social governance structure and promote economic development after the pandemic.

First, promoting the citizenization-dominant urbanization process is helpful to improve productivity. Previously, the negative view of the low-skilled population in urban development was an important barrier to further promotion and deepening of citizenization reform of rural migrant workers. It may be seen from the course of development in China and the development experience of other countries that an open and inclusive urban labor market could improve the degree of specialization of the urban labor market by attracting low-skilled labor. This process has not only increased employment of low-skilled workers, but also enabled highly skilled workers to focus more on their jobs, thus increasing productivity and promoting economic development through more effective social division of labor.

Next, complete urbanization is helpful to alleviating current employment difficulties. Due to the impact of the pandemic on China's economy and its lasting impact on the world economy, the "keep employment stable" policy faced huge challenges. In this grim situation, urbanization should play a special role in solving employment conflicts. Cities have the advantages of centralized industry distribution, scale effect, and sufficient information flow for the labor market, so they play a leading role in job creation. Increase of the urban population itself will generate a job creation effect. What is more, gathering of various types of groups in cities will form a multilevel labor market and diversified employment demand. So, under the impact of the pandemic, to better resist unemployment risk, we should gather more of the population in cities rather than workers being scattered in different areas.

An important condition for keeping urban job creation capacity is to absorb population continuously through free flow of the labor force. When economic growth was hit by the pandemic, external demand contracted sharply. We should pay special attention to the coordination of urban management policy and labor market policy in major cities, implement active employment policy, and prevent some measures that may restrict population movement and segment the labor market from damaging job creation.

Notes

1 In 2020, there was a consensus that the novel coronavirus is less serious than other viruses in harming the human body, but more contagious and hidden. This characteristic of the virus is an important reason why COVID-19 has become a global pandemic.
2 R. J., Barro, J. F Ursúa, and J. Weng, *The Coronavirus and the Great Influenza Pandemic: Lessons From the "Spanish Flu" for the Coronavirus's Potential Effects On Mortality and Economic Activity*. National Bureau of Economic Research Working Paper Series, No. 26866, 2020.
3 Some people think that the epidemic most comparable with this outbreak is the SARS epidemic in 2003. However, when SARS broke out, the leading industry in China's economic structure was secondary industry. In 2003, the added value of secondary industry accounted for 45.6 percent of GDP (40.3 percent in industry),

this was 42 percent for tertiary industry. According to preliminary results from the National Bureau of Statistics, the added value of secondary industry accounted for 39.0 percent of GDP in 2019, while the added value of tertiary industry accounted for 53.9 percent of GDP.

4 M. Chuanmao, Surveillance Data from More than 170 Satellites – Nearly 50% of Industrial Enterprises Have Resumed Work, *Securities Times*, February 27, 2020.
5 Data from other cities are being processed.
6 R. Di Tella, R. J. MacCulloch, and. A. J. Oswald, Preferences Over Inflation and Unemployment: Evidence from Surveys of Happiness, *American Economic Review*, 91, 335–341, 2001.

9 Impact of the COVID-19 pandemic on foreign trade and countermeasures

Zhao Jin

The COVID-19 global pandemic has spread to more than 200 countries, and with its epicenter in the developed economies of Europe and America, it has become a major event influencing the international political and economic landscape in this century. The International Monetary Fund, the United Nations Conference on Trade and Development, the World Trade Organization (WTO), and the International Labor Organization predicted that COVID-19 would generate a huge impact on the world economy, international investment, international trade, and global employment. China is the largest trading country of goods in the world and the center of Asia's global value chain (GVC). From the perspective of GVC, the COVID-19 global pandemic will hit China's export of finished products, textiles, information and communication technology (ICT), and services trade. If the epicenter of the pandemic shifts from Europe and America to Asia, China's foreign trade will be hit hard, and the employment of hundreds of millions of people will also be affected. As responses to the impact of the COVID-19 global pandemic on China's foreign trade, in the short term, we should use property tax, finance, facilitation of trade investment, and other policy instruments to guarantee stable supply chains, smooth logistics, and the development of small and medium-sized enterprises; in the long term, we should quicken government digital service and enterprise digital transformation to improve the level of digital trade and promote high-quality development of trade.

Adverse impact: Great impact on China's trade and employment

In a new era of GVC, we cannot rely on traditional net imports to measure the influence of trade impact on China's economy comprehensively. China is the second-largest trading country in the world, the largest trading country in goods, and the center of the Asian GVC. Closedown of global important economies and major trading countries, supply chain disruption, and decrease in international market demand will exert important influence on China's trade, investment, and employment.

DOI: 10.4324/9781003184447-10

The impact on international trade

Overall impact on international trade

At early stage of the pandemic outbreak in China, transnational corporations evacuated their personnel from China, factories were closed and out of production, stores, restaurants, and hotels were not in service, products could not be delivered on time, and foreign orders had to be cancelled one after another. Double-digit decline occurred in both imports and exports of China from/ to its important trade partners, such as the United States, Germany, Britain, and France. In the first quarter, the China's imports/exports from/to the traditional US, EU, and Japanese markets decreased by 18.3 percent, 10.4 percent, and 8.1 percent, respectively.

Since China is at the center of traditional trade and a simple GVC network, while American and European developed countries are at the center of a complex GVC network,[1] low- and medium-tech industries might be affected by the expanded pandemic in China and Asia, and high-tech industry might be affected more by the pandemic in American and European developed countries. However, as a whole, the export of finished products has been hit hardest by the pandemic, and the import of intermediate products has been hit more by the Asian pandemic. (1) From the perspective of exports, in 2017, China superseded Japan and became the global supply center of finished product trade in Asia. China has important trade links with other centers (the United States and Germany) and has important links with Asian neighbors (Japan, South Korea, and almost all other Asian countries), China Taipei, and other emerging economies (Russia, Brazil, and India). The COVID-19 global pandemic hits China's finished product export hardest. But in simple GVC and complex GVC networks, since China is a regional supply center, without direct contact with European and American centers, export of China's intermediate products will be hit more by the pandemic in Asia. (2) From the perspective of imports, in 2017, in simple GVC and complex GVC networks, China is a regional demand center, and its import of intermediate products is mainly hit by the Asian pandemic.

Impact on trade in goods

At early stage of the COVID-19 outbreak in China, with the Spring Festival affected, foreign orders were cancelled, some countries took trade protection measures against China, import and export of trade in goods decreased, and trade surplus was narrowed. According to customs statistics, from January To March, China's total imports and exports of trade in goods decreased by 6.4 percent compared with the same period of 2019: exports decreased by 11.4 percent, imports decreased by 0.7 percent, and trade surplus decreased by 80.6 percent.[2]

After the outbreak of the global pandemic, data from the Ministry of Commerce show that from January To May 2020, China's imports/exports decreased by 4.9 percent: exports decreased by 4.7 percent, imports decreased by 5.2 percent. Trade surplus was narrowed. In terms of value chain appreciation, since different industries of China have different positions in the GVC and different links with the European, American, and Asian GVC centers, impact of the pandemic on these industries has varied in Europe, America, and Asia.

First, looking at the impact on the textile industry, China's exports of textile products will be hit hard by the COVID-19 global pandemic, while imports will be affected more by the pandemic in Asia. (1) From the perspective of exports, China's textile industry was upgraded from a regional GVC center in 2000 to a world GVC center in 2017. China is the world supply center regardless of traditional trade or simple/complex GVC network. No matter if the COVID-19 global pandemic spreads from Europe and America to Asia or not, it will hit China's export of textile products hard. (2) From the perspective of imports, in 2017, in the traditional trade network, Asia had no demand center. The United States is an important global demand market, and Chinese, Japanese, and Korean products were exported to the United States directly. Compared with Japan, the proportion of China's export to the United States was not high. In a simple GVC network, as a regional demand center, China imported from Japan, Australia, South Korea, and India, then exported to the US market. In a complex GVC network, trade links of Europe, Asia, and North America are centralized in regional trade partners. China is a regional market demand center of Asia and has few links with European and American regional centers. Therefore, product import will be mainly affected by the pandemic in Asia, and less affected by the pandemic in Europe and America.

Second, looking at the impact on ICT industries, exports are affected by the pandemic in the United States and Europe, as well as South Korea, Japan, and Taipei in Asia. Imports of low- and medium-tech products will be affected by the pandemic in Europe and Asia, and high-tech products will be affected by the pandemic in Asia. (1) From the perspective of exports, in 2017, China substituted Japan and became the supply center for traditional trade, simple GVC and complex GVC in the Asian Pacific Region, and South Korea, Japan, and China Taipei became subcenters in the Asia Pacific Region. Export of China's ICT products will be affected by the pandemic in Europe and America, as well as the pandemic in South Korea and Japan. (2) From the perspective of imports, in 2017, China became a regional demand center for three trade networks. In traditional trade and a simple GVC network, China imported from Germany, Japan, South Korea, and Taiwan, and then exported to the United States; China's ICT imports are thus affected by the pandemic in Europe, Japan, South Korea, and Taipei. In a complex GVC network, American, European, and Asian centers are separated from each other, regional centers in Germany, China and the United States have no direct or indirect correlations. China's imports of ICT are mainly affected by the pandemic in Asia.

Impact on services trade

In 2019, the top ten partner countries (regions) of China in services trade were China Hong Kong, the United States, Japan, Singapore, Germany, Britain, South Korea, Australia, Canada, and China Taiwan. These contributed a total of USD 526 billion, accounting for 70 percent of services trade, mainly in Asia.

At the early stage of the COVID-19 outbreak in China, suspension of flights and visa and other relevant measures taken by foreign countries on China affected outbound travel, aviation, transport, commercial services, etc. directly in the short term, and traditional services trade decreased. The data issued by the Ministry of Commerce show that, affected by the pandemic, from January to February, total imports and exports of services decreased by 11.6 percent year on year: exports decreased by 6 percent, and imports decreased by 14.6 percent. In the structure of services trade, traditional services trade was severely affected by the pandemic, and import/export volume of travel, transport, and building services decreased by 23.1 percent, 4.4 percent, and 28.4 percent, respectively.[3]

With the COVID-19 global pandemic, export of services trade will be mainly affected by the pandemic in the United States and Asia, while imports will be mainly affected by the pandemic in Asia. (1) From the perspective of exports, in 2017, in a traditional trade network, China was the production network center for Asia and mainly exported to Japan, South Korea, and other Asian countries and to the United States. In a simple GVC, China is the service provision center for the Asian region and has established service contact with the United States. It is mainly affected by the pandemic in Asia and the United States. In a complex GVC, the three centers are independent from each other, and China's service export is mainly affected by the pandemic in Asia. (2) From the perspective of imports, in 2017, China was a regional demand center of traditional trade in a simple GVC network and a complex GVC network. For traditional trade and the simple GVC network, the United States is the only global service demand center, China's service import demand mainly comes from the Asian Pacific Region, and Europe does not influence China greatly. In a complex GVC network, China's service demand comes from South Korea, Japan, Singapore, etc. in Asia, and from the current view, the pandemic in Europe and America does not influence China greatly. If the epicenter of the pandemic changes from European and American developed countries to Asia, this will exert an important influence on China.

Impact on direct investment

At the early stage of the COVID-19 outbreak in China, affected by the Spring Festival, enterprise shutdown occurred in a large area, and the overall scale of foreign investment funds decreased. According to statistics from the Ministry of Commerce, from January To March 2020, foreign investment in actual use was RMB 216.19 billion in China, which decreased by 10.8 percent year on year. Finds decreased by 25.6 percent and 14.1 percent in February and March, respectively.[4]

Europe and America became global pandemic epicenters, while the epidemic trend was unclear in Japan, South Korea, and other Asian countries. As China has coped with the pandemic successfully, provides services to foreign-funded enterprises with priority for overall resumption of work and production, and actively promotes the progress of major industries and projects, it has become the safest investment destination in the world today. On March 25, 2020, the American Chamber of Commerce in China published the findings of a questionnaire survey on the impact of the COVID-19 pandemic on member enterprises; nearly half of the members indicated great impact of the pandemic on their operations in China, with income and market demand decreasing for most enterprises. However, while half of the companies surveyed could not judge whether the pandemic would influence their investment strategy in China, and one third said there would be no impact, many companies said they would maintain existing investment levels and only 3 percent would consider exiting the Chinese market completely.[5]

Impact on employment

China is the second-largest trading country in the world, with a population of 1.4 billion. Compared with other major trading countries, proportion of domestic employment driven by export is not high, but contribution of export to domestic employment is far beyond other countries. As shown in Figure 9.1, in 2015, the proportion of export-driven domestic employment was only 12.7 percent in China, higher than only the United States among nine major trading countries in the world, but it drove employment up to nearly 100 million persons (including export-driven indirect employment of 64.06 million persons and direct employment of 33.19 million persons). In the same period, export-driven employment only involved 14.69 million persons in the United States and 12.20 million persons in Germany. Contribution of trade to employment was about 180 million in China in 2019. The impact of the COVID-19 global pandemic on China's employment will be far beyond the impact on developed countries.

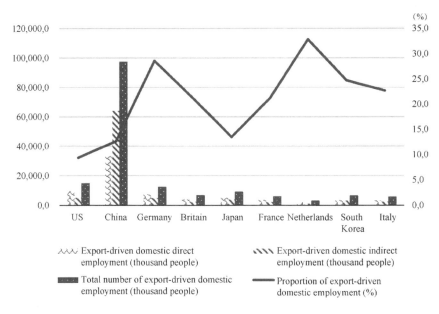

Figure 9.1 Comparison of export-driven employment in nine major trading countries.
Source: OECD

Beneficial effects: Improving digital level of China's trade and optimizing trade structure

Under the contemporary GVC specialization system, China's economy is deeply integrated with the global economy, and the pandemic has exerted adverse impact on China's trade in the short run and employment faces huge pressure. But in the long run, China's economic development shortcomings exposed in the pandemic as well as the emerging new growth points portend a new direction of trade development in the future and will provide new opportunities for high-quality trade development in China.

Optimization of trade structure and narrowing of trade deficit

With the COVID-19 pandemic in China and the rest of the world, enterprises face decrease in foreign trade orders and undercapacity, and they have to adapt to the market trend of digital consumption, accelerate digital and intelligent transformation, and quicken industrial restructuring to handle new changes such as a long-term pandemic and insufficient supply in the medical product market. This has several benefits.

First, it is conducive to the optimization of export structure. The pandemic has led to increased purchase of pandemic-related masks, protective clothing, and medical equipment. While other countries have restricted the export of epidemic prevention and control equipment and products, China has become an important global exporter of anti-epidemic materials. As of April 4, 74 countries and 10 international organizations negotiated commercial procurement with Chinese enterprises, of which 54 countries/regions and 3 international organizations signed medical supplies procurement contracts with Chinese enterprises.[6] From January to May, masks led to an increase of 25.5% in textiles, and there were increases in medical devices and Chinese medicinal herbs by 33 percent and 8 percent, respectively. Meanwhile, homeworking has also brought an increase in the international market's demand for small home appliances and other consumer goods, and Chinese household appliance enterprises have rapidly increased their export orders to the United States and Europe. In the first 2 months, the export volume of all kinds of home appliances of Galanz, an independent brand, to North American markets such as the United States and Canada increased by 102 percent.[7] From January to May, affected by the pandemic, exports of clothing, bags and cases, shoes, furniture, and other labor-intensive products decreased by 20.3 percent, but the export of integrated circuits and computers increased by 14.5 percent and 1.8 percent, respectively.[8]

Second, it is conducive to the optimization of international market layout. Pandemic epicenters are centralized in European and American developed countries, which is conducive to forcing companies to open up markets in Asia and countries along the route of the Belt and Road Initiative. From January to May, the exports to the traditional market fell by 6.5 percent, and its proportion dropped to 50.3 percent. The exports to the emerging market fell by 2.9 percent, and its proportion rose to 49.7 percent. Exports to ASEAN countries did not decline, but rather increased, with exports increasing by 2.8 percent, and ASEAN became the largest trade partner of China.[9]

Third, it is conducive to the optimization of the mode of trade. In the first quarter, import/export of China's processing trade fell by 12.4 percent, accounting for 23.8 percent. Import/export of general trade fell by 5.7 percent, accounting for 60 percent of total foreign trade. Affected by the pandemic and subsequent supply chain disruption, to ensure the development of the whole industry chain, China transferred supply of intermediate products from international to domestic supply after resumption of work and production, which might lead to a decrease in the proportion of processing trade and an increase in the proportion of general trade.

Fourth, it is conducive to the optimization of services trade structure and the narrowing of trade deficit. Affected by the pandemic, from January to May, the import/export volume of China's services trade fell by 14.6 percent year on year, but knowledge-intensive services trade bucked the trend and grew by 8.7 percent; its proportion in total imports and exports of services trade increased by 9.3 percent, up to 43.3 percent. Compared with imports, export of knowledge-intensive services realized double-digit growth of 11.2 percent, and its proportion in total service exports reached 56.8 percent. The fields of quick export growth include royalties for intellectual property (38.4 percent), telecommunications, computer, and information services (19.7 percent), and insurance services (15.6 percent). Since the decline in imports (21.5 percent) was far beyond the decline in exports (2.3 percent), from January to May, services trade deficit decreased by 44.9 percent year on year, and the trade deficit decreased by RMB 285.15 billion.[10]

As the world's largest trading country in goods, China has had goods trade surplus and services trade deficit for a long time. Services trade deficit mainly originates from the travel service. In 2019, services trade deficit was USD 261.1 billion, of which travel trade deficit was up to USD 218.8 billion; the proportion of travel trade deficit was up to 83.8 percent. The global pandemic has led to a decline in the number of domestic outbound travelers, travel services deficit has narrowed, and the services trade deficit will fall. China's trade deficit will narrow as a whole.

Improvement of China's digital level of trade and development of new business forms

With the COVID-19 global pandemic, China's foreign trade enterprises face the cancellation or delay of orders and difficulties in signing new orders, forcing the government and enterprises to accelerate digital transformation, innovate new development models of international trade, and add new drivers of trade development to realize high-quality development of trade.

First, we should develop new business forms of foreign trade. In the first quarter, import/export of cross-border e-commerce increased by 34.7 percent, and export in market purchase mode increased by 50. 9 percent. On April 7, the State Council adapted to changes in the pandemic by adding 46 new comprehensive experimental zones for cross-border e-commerce. The 105 comprehensive experimental zones, covering 30 provinces, cities, and autonomous regions of China, will accelerate the development of new business forms of international trade.

Second, we should innovate new models of trade transaction. The Ministry of Commerce decided to hold the 127th Guangzhou Fair online in mid/late June, and it created a 10X 24-hour all-weather online foreign trade platform, which will initiate "cloud trade" and "cloud contract signing."

Third, we should improve the public service platform for foreign trade. The pandemic has pushed government affairs service centers in the pilot free trade zones in Guangdong, Jiangsu, and Shangdong provinces to adopt "contactless" "online office, palm-top office, [and] telephone office" to provide enterprise services and promote paperless international trade documents at customs.

Boosting investor confidence in the international market in China and the optimization of investment structure

The COVID-19 pandemic has spread to more than 200 countries. Facing this unprecedented pandemic, the Chinese government has responded successfully based on the concept of People First, resumed work, production, and markets in an orderly way, and boosted investor confidence in the international market in China. Although affected by the pandemic, foreign investment in actual use was RMB 355.2 billion from January to May in China, a year-on-year decrease of 3.8 percent (excluding banks, securities, and insurance); yet in April, foreign investment in China showed recovery growth, and in May, foreign investment in actual use was RMB 68.63 billion, a year-on-year increase of 7.5 percent. At the same time, investment structure and regional layout have been optimized.

First, in terms of the growth of high-tech industry, from January to May, a year-on-year increase of foreign investment in actual use in China's high-tech industry was 2 percent: e-commerce services, R&D and design services, and information services showed double-digit rapid growth, with growth rates of 67.9 percent, 49.8 percent, and 42.3 percent, respectively.[11]

Second, there was robust growth of investment in Shanghai and other pilot free trade zones. From January to February, the foreign investment in Shanghai and Guangdong pilot free trade zones increased by 13 percent and 12.8 percent, respectively; the foreign investment attracted by Hainan, Fujian, and Zhejiang pilot free trade zones increased by 230.2 percent, 149.5 percent, and 140 percent, respectively.[12] In the first quarter of this year, the foreign investment in actual use in 18 free trade zones of China was RMB 28.9 billion, accounting for 13.4 percent of the whole country.

Third, in terms of the optimized regional layout, some economies and countries have increased investment in China steadily. From January to May, the actual amount of foreign investment from ASEAN countries and the countries along the Belt and Road Initiative saw a year-on-year increase of 10.1 percent and 6 percent, respectively.

Countermeasures in China: Relying on high-quality trade development to turn danger into opportunity

To cope with the impact of the COVID-19 global pandemic on China's foreign trade, the central government launched property tax, finance, credit insurance, trade and investment facilitation, and other policies, which have played important roles in stabilizing supply chain, smoothing logistics, and developing small and medium-sized enterprises in the short term. The global pandemic will pass. In the long run, China should utilize this window of tremendous change and adjustment in the world economy, seize new opportunities brought by the pandemic in the development trend of international trade, and focus on high-quality trade development to turn danger into opportunity and promote sustainable foreign trade.

First, we should seize the opportunities of digital transformation and digital innovation in enterprises emerging during the pandemic, create "digital trade demonstration areas," improve the digital level of trade, and quicken the development of digital trade.

With all people at home during the pandemic, this changes people's consumption patterns (online consumption, quality consumption, digital consumption) and work patterns (remote offices). Enterprises have started digital transformation: Evergrande Group has utilized virtual reality for online house sales and, Tongcheng-Elong, a leading tourism enterprise, has utilized virtual reality technology for digital marketing of scenic spots as part of "cloud tourism"; to quicken digital innovation of enterprises, Alibaba, Baidu, Tencent, and other enterprises have provided online medical services, and an affiliated research institution of Alibaba has utilized AI technology for detection; to improve digital services of enterprises, Ali DingTalk, Corporate WeChat, Tencent Meeting, and other remote office software have been used extensively; to promote digital upgrade services, Alibaba has upgraded the Alipay digital life open platform; and since 80 percent of Chinese service enterprises are not digitalized, Ali will "partner with 50,000 service providers to help 40 million service merchants [with] digital upgrade in the three years to come," creating "new infrastructure construction" of digital service.

Contemporary digital technology development has promoted digital innovation, digital production, and digital services in enterprises, and it has also accelerated global digital consumption. Digital globalization has promoted revolutionary changes of international trade. This is evident in the change of international trade structure. Digital technology has turned non-tradable services to tradable ones, changed trade structure, and increased the proportion of services trade. In terms of the change of international trade models, digital technology has changed the people's consumption habits, consumers have realized online transactions via apps, and new models of e-commerce international trade have emerged. In terms of the change of international trade content, the products traded have expanded from tangible goods to intangible digital products (e.g. electronic games, music, movies, streaming media), trading subjects of international trade have changed from finished product trade and intermediate product trade to digital trade. In terms of the change of services trade provision mode, since marketing, pension insurance, finance and intellectual property rights, professional services, etc. may be provided remotely via communication technology networks, in the future, services trade will be available via M1 cross-border provision rather than M3 commercial presence and M4 movement of natural persons.

In the new era of the Fourth Industrial Revolution and digital economic development, in order to realize high-quality trade development, China should promote organic integration of trade with the Internet, Internet of Things, big data, artificial intelligence, and block chain to foster new drivers of trade development. Although the US–China trade conflict in 2019 has decreased overall exports of China to the United States, exports by AliExpress to the United States increased, relying on the cross-border e-commerce. We should seize the opportunities of digital consumption, enterprise digital transformation, and digital innovation created by the pandemic and utilize the window of major changes in the world economy. China should create digital trade demonstration areas in Zhejiang Province, Guangdong Province, Hainan

Province, and Shanghai City, and Beijing City to improve the digital level of trade and development of digital trade, and empower high-quality trade development.

Second, we should seize the opportunities of demand expansion in information services, remote medical care, distance learning, etc. brought by the pandemic, promote the transfer of factors of production to high-end services, and vigorously develop services trade.

The global pandemic first hit services trade (e.g. travel, aviation, logistics) and then trade in goods (with enterprise shutdown due to supply chain disruption). But at the same time, the pandemic has also brought demands for information services, remote medical care, distance learning, etc.

In international trade, the proportion of trade in goods to services trade has been 80:20 for a long time. In 2018, the proportion of trade in goods was 77.7 percent, and the proportion of services trade was 22.2 percent. Industry is the foundation of trade. In the creation of GDP, the proportion of added value of the service industry is 65 percent in the world, while this proportion is nearly 70 percent in high-income countries. Although the tradability of services is far lower than goods nowadays, in 2018, the proportion of trade in goods in GDP was 46 percent and the proportion of services trade in GDP was only 13.3 percent. Yet since information technology has broken through the intangibility, perishability, and face-to-face instantaneity of services, it was predicted in the WTO's World Trade Report for 2019 that the proportion of services trade in trade will increase from 21 percent currently to 50 percent by 2040.[13]

The new development trend of international trade servicization in the upcoming 20 years will pose big challenges for China's policy of stabilizing foreign trade and its position as the world's largest trading country in goods. To stabilize foreign trade, industry must be stabilized first. At present, added value of the service industry only accounts for 53.9 percent of China's GDP, the tradability of services is lower than the world average (in 2018, the proportion of world services trade in GDP was 13.3 percent, and the proportion in China was only 5.6 percent), and the proportion of services trade in China's trade is only 14.6 percent, also lower than the world average (22 percent). The opening up of the manufacturing industry 40 years ago brought a great development in the manufacturing industry, casting China as a global manufacturing power and the largest trading country in goods. From the perspective of stabilizing foreign trade in the near and medium term, China's seizing of digital/intelligent opportunities in the service industry and timely launch of new opening up measures for the service industry during the pandemic are not only helpful for corner overtaking of the service industry, realizing leap-forward development, but also helpful for intelligent service transformation of the manufacturing industry in the contemporary GVC specialization system, so as to develop new advantages of China's high-end manufacturing and promote the integrated and coordinated development of the manufacturing industry and the service industry.

In order to prevent the pandemic spreading, some countries have posed restrictions on travel by air, which have influenced traditional services trade such as aviation, tourism, and logistics. But the latest data show that important changes have taken place in the structure of international services trade: the proportion of traditional services such as transport and tourism falls below 50 percent in the import/export of services trade, emerging services including computer and information services and royalties for intellectual property have grown at high speed, and their proportion in services trade increases steadily. China should seize the opportunity of more demand for information services, remote medical care, distance learning, etc. during the pandemic, grasp the general service trend of global trade structure and high-end tendency of services trade structure, launch a negative list of services trade, expand opening up of the service industry, promote concentration of the factors of production in high-end services, greatly increase the proportion of services trade in China's trade, and realize high-quality development of China's trade.

Third, we should seize the opportunity presented by the serious shortage of medical products during the global pandemic, accelerate transformation and upgrading of industry structure, expand the export of high-end medical equipment, traditional Chinese medicine products, and services, and foster new growth points of trade.

The impact of the pandemic on the global demand market has structural features. On one hand, due to supply chain disruption, intermediate goods trade and transport services decreased, and home quarantine led to decrease in services trade such as tourism and aviation; but on the other hand, to cope with the pandemic, demands for masks, protective clothing, and medical equipment rose suddenly and sharply, and home consumption, homeworking, and distance learning triggered an increase in demand for food, everyday consumer goods, and electronic products.

It is predicted in the Global Risks Report for 2020 published by the World Economic Forum that infectious disease would be one of the top ten global risks in the next decade.[14] This highlighted that global pandemic of infectious disease is a big challenge for human beings, and the huge demand in the international market for medical products, equipment, and services has just started. The population in China above 60 years old was 250 million in 2019, and related to this, more demand for medical and health products highlight the shortcomings of the supply-side structural reform in China. With the expansion of middle-income groups in developing countries, international market demand for medical products and services is promising.

China should seize the opportunities presented by the serious shortage of medical products in the international market, caused by the COVID-19 global pandemic, and the expanded international market demand for medical products and services in the future, meet international standards, improve product quality, and promote the export of medical equipment and relevant products, including low-end and high-end products. At the same time, China should make the most of the role of traditional Chinese medicine in fighting against the epidemic, increase national support for the traditional Chinese medicine industry, and construct a traditional Chinese medicine service export base. China should create an internationally known "Chinese service" brand to eliminate foreign technical barriers, establish a new network platform for traditional Chinese medicine services trade, utilize the high-quality traditional Chinese medicine service to promote the export of traditional Chinese medicine products, and foster new business forms of export in China's foreign trade and new growth points of services trade.

Fourth, we should seize the opportunity to regain investor confidence in China after the pandemic, take significant actions towards opening up in a timely way, create a good international business environment, and attend to the leading role of two-way investment on trade.

China is a manufacturing center for transnational corporations. The automobile supply chain was disrupted due to the outbreak of the COVID-19 pandemic in Wuhan in February, the automobile production of the United States, Europe, and Japan in China suffered losses. There was a call around the world to rethink the business model of "Made in the World," arguing for change to the high reliance of international production on China (China's exports accounted for 13 percent of total global exports) and high concentration in China (China accounted for 20 percent of intermediate product trade in the manufacturing industry, compared to only 4 percent in 2002), and for implementation of more diversified production and an open business model with a shorter value chain so as to avoid risks.

After the global COVID-19 pandemic, shutdown of automobile manufacturing in Europe and America has contrasted sharply with the resumed production of foreign-funded automobile factories in China. For this, China should remodel the GVC layout by means of two-way investment. We should seize the opportunity from regaining of investor confidence in China after the pandemic, launch significant measures for high-level and timely opening up, take advantage of the huge domestic consumption market, the good international business environment, and our image as an open and responsible big country to attract the investment of foreign merchants into Hainan Free Trade Port, Shanghai Pilot Free Trade Zone, etc. for high-end manufacturing and modern services, and promote high-quality development of China. Also, we should set up an overseas wholesale exhibition center, commodity market, specialty store, "overseas warehouse," and other international marketing networks, utilize overseas investment cooperation areas to push China's equipment, materials, products, standards, technologies, brands, and services to "go global," encourage a cross-border e-commerce platform to go global, and construct a regional value chain international production system in the Asian Pacific Region.

Fifth, we should seize the window of China's successful response to the pandemic, focus on the Belt and Road Initiative, optimize international market layout, and construct a community with a shared future for mankind.

The global pandemic epicenter is in the US and European developed economies. The United States, Italy, Spain, Germany, and Britain are severely afflicted by the global pandemic, this will exert an important influence on international market layout in which over one third of the trade with China in goods relies on the market of developed countries. After the US–China trade conflict in 2019, the order of precedence of the top four trade partners of China (the European Union, the United States, ASEAN, and Japan) has changed; ASEAN has surpassed the United States to become the second-largest trade partner of China, approaching the European Union in terms of total trade. In 2019, China's import and export trade with the European Union was RMB 4.86 trillion, an increase of 8 percent; trade with ASEAN was RMB 4.43 trillion, an increase of 14.1 percent; trade with the United States was RMB 3.73 trillion, a decrease of 10.7 percent; and trade with Japan was RMB 2.17 trillion, an increase of 0.49 percent.

Developed countries have led global market demand for a long time. But the latest data show that whether it be trade in goods or services trade, both emerging economies and developing countries are increasing the global consumption market. According to the forecasts, by 2025, emerging markets will consume two thirds of products in the world. By 2030, consumption of developing countries will account for more than half of global market consumption.[15]

The 65 countries along the Belt and Road Initiative have a total population of about 4.4 billion and an economic aggregate of about USD 21 trillion, accounting for 63 percent and 29 percent of global amounts, respectively; most of them are emerging economies and developing countries. In 2019, China's trade with the countries along the Belt and Road Initiative increased by 10.8 percent, import and export trade approached RMB 10 trillion, accounting for nearly 30 percent of China's trade, and the cumulative direct investment exceeded USD 100 billion. China should adapt to major changes in the international market environment and seize opportunities by urging enterprises to exploit the markets along the Belt and Road Initiative and neighboring countries while the United States and Europe are pandemic epicenters. China should release the economic and trade cooperation potential of the Belt and Road Initiative, develop new power in China's foreign trade, and together with developing countries, construct a community with a shared future.

Notes

1 The Global Value Chain Development Report 2019 jointly issued by the WTO, IDE-JETRO, the Organisation for Economic Co-operation and Development (OECD), the University of International Business and Economics, and the World Bank broke down production activities into three forms: pure domestic production, traditional trade, and value chain production (including a simple GVC network and a complex GVC network). According to the study, there are three

regional production networks in the world: "Factory in Europe," "Factory in North America," and "Factory in Asia." The United States and Germany are at the center of a complex GVC network, while China is at the center of a traditional trade and simple GVC network.

2 Customs: Exports and imports fell by 6.4 percent in the first quarter but the decline has narrowed, Sina Comprehensive Finance and Economics, April 14, 2020: https://finance.sina.com.cn/china/2020-04-14/doc-iircuyvh7676373.shtml

3 The head of the Service and Trade Department of the Ministry of Commerce introduced the development of China's service trade in January-February, Ministry of Commerce, March 31, 2020: www.mofcom.gov.cn/article/ae/sjjd/202003/20200302949932.shtml

4 Head of the Foreign Investment Department of the Ministry of Commerce talks about the attraction of foreign investment in the first quarter of 2020, Ministry of Commerce, April 15, 2020: www.mofcom.gov.cn/article/ae/sjjd/202004/20200402955393.shtml

5 AmCham China, COVID-19 Business Impact 60 Days in: Results from the March 2020 Flash Survey, March 25, 2020.

6 Ministry of Commerce, Fifty-four countries (regions) have signed commercial procurement contracts for medical supplies with Chinese enterprises, China News Net, April 7, 2020: www.mofcom.gov.cn/article/i/jyjl/e/202004/20200402952660.shtml

7 Overseas epidemic stimulated the demand for Western styple kitchen appliances, export orders of Galanz and other companies surged, Sina Finance and Economics, April 2, 2020: https://baijiahao.baidu.com/s?Id=1662846257123662810&wfr=spider&for=pc

8 Officials from the Ministry of Commerce talked about China's foreign trade operations from January to May 2020, Chinese Government Net, June 12, 2020: www.gov.cn/shuju/2020-06/12/content_5519128.htm

9 Officials from the Ministry of Commerce talked about China's foreign trade operations from January to May 2020.

10 The Ministry of Commerce held a regular online press conference, Ministry of Commerce, July 2, 2020: www.mofcom.gov.cn/xwfbh/20200702.shtml

11 The Ministry of Commerce held a regular online press conference, Ministry of Commerce, June 18, 2020: www.mofcom.gov.cn/xwfbh/20200618.shtml

12 Joint Prevention and Control Mechanism of the State Council, a press conference on March 13, 2020, on stabilizing foreign trade and foreign investment in response to the impact of the pandemic: www.mofcom.gov.cn/xwfbh/20200313.shtml

13 World Trade Organization, *World Trade Report 2019: The Future of Services Trade*, Geneva: WTO.

14 World Economic Forum, *Global Risks Report 2020*, Geneva: WEF.

15 McKinsey, *China and the World: Understanding the Changing Economic Nexus*, 2019.

10 Prevention and control of financial risks during the pandemic and the recovery process[1]

He Dexu

Based on the rapid spread of COVID-19 and its serious harm to human health, the World Health Organization (WHO) declared on March 11, 2020, that COVID-19 had the characteristics of a global pandemic. This chapter will discuss and analyze the relationship between the COVID-19 pandemic and financial risks, derivative financial risks under the impact of the pandemic, as well as the effective prevention and control of financial risks during the pandemic and recovery.

The pandemic and financial risks

With the globalization of finance, rapid development of financial industry, continual increase of financial efficiency, the enhanced financial effect, and the improvement of its status, finance is increasingly developing and promoting the development of the real economy. It is also experiencing or facing unprecedented uncertainties, instability, or drastic shock, which are manifested as financial risks. Finance is an industry that handles and manages risks. The existence of financial risks is inevitable, and financial risks are highly hazardous, can trigger crisis, and cause global negative externality on economy, society, and even national security. Under the impacts of the COVID-19 pandemic as a public health crisis, what kind of state will financial risks present?

The pandemic does not lead directly to financial risk

The unexpected global pandemic of COVID-19 has brought huge impacts and shocks on global politics, economy, and society.[2] Some risks that deserve attention also appear in the financial field. First, assets price in the financial market has fluctuated significantly and continuously. After mid and late February 2020, four "circuit breakers" occurred successively in the US stock market and created a new historical record as of March 23; decline of the stock index exceeded 30 percent (see Figure 10.1) in the United States, Europe, South Korea, and some emerging market economies; at the same time, crude oil price declined by more than 50 percent, and the price of copper, zinc, aluminum, and other metals declined by about 20 percent. Second, the long-end

DOI: 10.4324/9781003184447-11

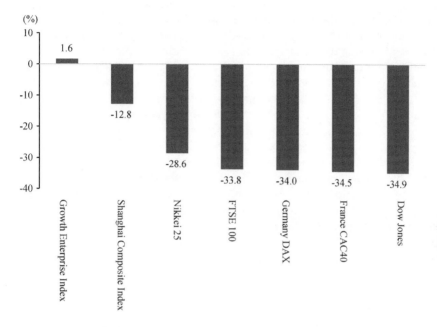

Figure 10.1 Stock index performance of the world's major economies (January 1–March 23, 2020).

interest rate has declined greatly, while credit spread has increased rapidly. On March 16, the Federal Reserve reduced interest by 100 base points on the basis of emergency reduction of interest by 50 base points at the beginning of the month. This reduced federal funds rate to 0–0.25 percent directly and drove the yield on the US 10-year treasury note down to 0.54 percent, and maximum decline during 2020 exceeded 130 base points. In contrast, the interest rate of US high-yield corporate bond increased, credit spread (the difference between the interest rate of high-yield corporate bonds and the yield of the 10-year treasury note) rose to 9.5 percent, almost equivalent to the level during crisis in the history. Third, the US Dollar Index has risen greatly. Affected by the COVID-19 pandemic, US economic downturn pressure increased continuously, but after mid-March, financial market turmoil triggered worry about dollar liquidity, investor demand for dollars increased significantly, and the US Dollar Index was pulled up strongly for about 8 percent, out of line with the fundamentals. Fourth, capital outflow pressure has been aggravated in emerging markets, and debt service pressure has increased greatly. Affected by the pandemic, huge capital flows out of emerging economies, and some debt-ridden countries find it very difficult to repay the capital and interest.

Does this mean that the pandemic will lead directly to financial risks? Theoretically, many factors may trigger financial risks, including drastic fluctuation of the macroeconomy, dramatic increase in debt, spillover effect of finance on the real economy, counterparty credit default, vulnerability of finance itself, financial market information disruption, lack of liquidity, and asset bubbles. In other words, financial risk is generated by numerous factors inside and outside the financial system, which influence each other, involving liquidity, leverage, and degree of association, they infect each other in the financial system and could lead to financial system collapse or loss of financial functions. In reality, on the one hand, the pandemic directly led to the Great Lockdown, disruption of personnel mobility and transportation, shutdown of shops, restaurants, and hotels, stoppage of public social activities, heavy losses in consumption and service industries, and further influenced aggregate demand. On the other hand, the pandemic directly led to the stagnation of enterprise production and operation, negative impacts on the global industry chain and supply chain,[3] impacts on all countries involved in the global supply chain, short-term "shock" of global economic activities, and further influenced aggregate supply. The stagnation of production and economic activities caused by the pandemic has influenced the labor market directly, causing a significant increase in unemployment. Finally, the pandemic influenced investor and consumer confidence directly, deteriorated market expectations. Therefore, the above-mentioned financial risks in the case of the pandemic are rooted in huge impacts of the pandemic on the real economy in terms of the market panic and emotions caused by insufficient preparations of investors and consumers for a sudden outbreak. In this sense, we can say that the pandemic does not lead directly to financial risks or necessarily cause financial risks, but clearly the pandemic will influence and exaggerate financial risks.

In the history of human development, various pandemics have injured human beings. Since the 20th century, several widespread, pernicious infectious diseases have emerged. Some viruses have spread all over the world, and some viruses have led to the deaths of tens of millions of people. According to historical statistics, of more than ten large-scale pandemics, from the 1918 Spanish flu to COVID-19, three caused a drop in the financial market in the same year. The financial market dropped the most in 1974, up to 27 percent.[4] Therefore, so far, there has been no financial risk or financial crisis simply or directly triggered by a pandemic (see Table 10.1).

The pandemic enhances the transmission mechanism of financial risks

Financial risks may be divided into different types, and based on different perspectives, different types of financial risks have different transmission mechanisms. Here we take an example of debt risk, a more typical financial risk, to describe and analyze its transmission mechanism. The pandemic hits both demand and supply, and the transmission mechanisms triggered by the pandemic that might increase debt risk include transmission in real sectors, mutual transmission between the real economy and financial system, and mutual transmission between developed economies and emerging

Table 10.1 Pandemic vs financial risk

Year	Disease	Affected countries	Infected/death toll	Performance of the MSCI global index in that year (data before 1990 refer to the performance of the US Dow Jones index)
1918	Spanish flu	First found in Camp Finston, Kansas, US, then in Spain	Approximate number of patients worldwide was more than 700 million; morbidity was about 20–40 percent, with a death toll up to 40–50 million	Increased by 10.51 percent
1926	Smallpox	India	Death toll of 500,000	Increased by 0.34 percent
1974	Smallpox	India	100,000 patients; death toll of 30,000	Decreased by 27.57 percent
2003	Severe acute respiratory syndrome	China, Southeast Asia, Canada, etc.	Over 8,000 infected patients; death toll above 700	Increased by 31.62 percent
2003	West Nile virus	US	9,862 cases, 264 of whom died	Increased by 31.62 percent
2009	A H1N1	214 countries	About 1.3 million infected persons; about 18,500 persons died	Increased by 31.52 percent
2013	Malaria	90 percent of the cases were in Africa	Globally, 207 million malaria cases, 627,000 of whom died	Increased by 20.25 percent
2014	Ebola	Several countries in West Africa	19,031 infected cases, 7,373 of whom died	Increased by 2.10 percent
2016	Malaria	90 percent of the cases were in Africa	Globally, 216 million malaria cases and 445,000 deaths	Increased by 5.63 percent
2016	Yellow fever virus	Angola, Congo, and Uganda	970 confirmed cases; 130 persons died	Increased by 5.63 percent
2016	Zika virus	24 countries, including Brazil	About 1.5 million cases	Increased by 5.63 percent

(*continued*)

Table 10.1 Cont.

Year	Disease	Affected countries	Infected/death toll	Performance of the MSCI global index in that year (data before 1990 refer to the performance of the US Dow Jones index)
2018	Cholera	11 countries in Africa	Nearly 1.2 million cases; more than 5,000 deaths	Decreased by 11.18 percent
2018	Yellow fever virus	Brazil	1,257 confirmed cases of yellow fever, 394 of whom died	Decreased by 11.18 percent
2019	Influenza B	Outbreak of a large-scale mixed influenza A and B occurred in the US in September 2019	Up to the present: at least 22 million cases in the United States, with 210,000 needing hospitalization and the death toll exceeding 12,000 persons	Increased by 24.05 percent
2019	Ebola virus	9 countries, including Congo (Kinshasa)	3,444 cases; 2,264 deaths	Increased by 24.05 percent
2020	COVID-19 virus	China, Italy, Spain, France, Iran, the US, and other countries	As of 9:00 on April14,2020:about 1.92 million global cumulative confirmed cases and cumulative death toll of nearly 120,000 persons	Decreased by 15.49 percent as of April 14

Source: Haisen et al.[12]

economies (see Figure 10.2). These transmission mechanisms are staggered and superimposed, and they aggravate the original debt risk.

Transmission in real sectors

Transmission of debt risk can be transmission in real sectors; that is, transmission between the non-financial business sector, the household sector, and the government sector.

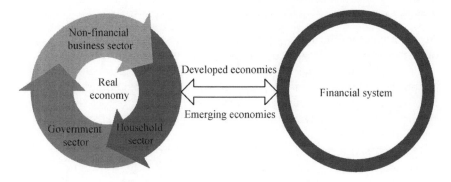

Figure 10.2 Financial risk transmission mechanism.

Debt risk is transmitted from the non-financial business sector to the household sector and the government sector. Amid a raging pandemic, shutdown first hits the non-financial business sector; that is, the supply side will be affected greatly. In case of limited production and even shutdown, income cannot cover debt burden, and the non-financial business sector will get trapped in a debt crisis. Here, the household sector cannot obtain wage income from the non-financial business sector as scheduled. After deducting necessary living expenses, even if the household sector has some savings, if the pandemic cannot be controlled in the short term, it cannot sustain debt with less income or even no income over a long period. The non-financial business sector will get stuck in business distress due to debt risk, so might decrease financial revenue of the government sector. Normally, the government sector assumes certain debt service pressure every year, but the decrease in financial revenue will increase such pressure, and the debt risk of government sector will aggravates.

Debt risk is transmitted from the household sector to the non-financial business sector and the government sector. On the demand side, the household sector's debt risk will decrease its consumption level; for the non-financial business sector, limited production means that circulation is not realized, and this adds insult to injury. At the same time, the household sector is also one of the important sources of financial revenue for the government sector; thus, the household sector debt risk might also decrease the financial revenue of the government sector and aggravate its debt risk.

Debt risk is transmitted from the government sector to the non-financial business sector and the household sector. The government sector creates a business environment for the non-financial business sector and provides public services for the household sector. If the government sector faces debt risk, the guarantee obtained by the non-financial business sector and the household sector might be reduced significantly, and debt sustainability will be affected in those sectors.

Mutual transmission between the real economy and the financial system

Active finance is the basis of active economy; stable finance is the basis of stable economy. Prosperous economy guarantees prosperous finance; and strong economy guarantees strong finance. Economy is the body and finance is the blood vessels; they co-existence and have common prosperity. Debt risk of the real economy will inevitably be transmitted to the financial system; in turn, the risk in the financial system will be transmitted to the real economy.[5]

Debt risk is transmitted from the real economy to the financial system. The non-financial business sector, the household sector, and the government sector are all related to the financial system. Debt of real economy sectors make up the assets of the financial system; while the assets of the real economy sectors are the debt of the financial system. This means that debt risk of any real sector will be transmitted directly to the financial system. If debt risk appears in several sectors of the real economy simultaneously, then the risk transmitted to the financial system is not a simple accumulation, but rather the trigger of a systematic debt crisis.

Debt risk is transmitted from the financial system to the real economy. The panic caused by pandemic is manifested as the correction in asset prices in the financial system. If the amplitude of correction in asset prices is too large, the assets value of real economy sectors will decrease relatively, but their debt will not be reduced correspondingly, so real economy sectors face the risk of debt default. After the outbreak of the pandemic, global asset prices declined significantly. In the stock market, the global stock market fell drastically due to the pandemic. Four circuit breakers occurred successively in the US stock market over ten trading days in mid-March, and the US stock market price fell faster than that during the periods of the 2008 subprime mortgage crisis and the 1929 Great Depression. Meanwhile, European stock markets, Japanese and South Korean stock markets, and the stock markets of emerging market countries (India, Vietnam, Brazil, etc.) also slumped. In the bond market, bond yield was "upside down"; that is, short-term yield was higher than long-term yield. At the end of January, the yield curve of US 3-month and 10-year treasury notes were upside down; the yields of 2-year and 5-year treasury notes were also upside down; the yield of the US 10-year treasury note, the most representative safe asset, dropped to below 1 percent, approaching zero interest rate. The upside down yield of US bonds is deemed an important signal of economic depression; it also means decline in long-term bond investment. In terms of bulk commodity, all prices dropped. Superimposing the collapse of the agreement by OPEC (the Organization of the Petroleum Exporting Countries) to cut output, international oil price dropped by about a third; as "hard currency," gold also declined rapidly by more than 10 percent after reaching a high point; the price of food commodities also declined somewhat.

Mutual transmission between developed economies and
emerging economies

Today, global economies are deeply integrated, and a "butterfly effect"[6] is inevitable. Like the undifferentiated spread of the COVID-19 virus, debt crisis in any country might be transmitted to other countries and even the world.[7]

The debt risk is transmitted from developed economies to emerging economies. The debt burden of developed economies is heavier than that of emerging economies. Thus, debt risk might first appear in developed economies, then be transmitted to emerging economies. The 2008 international financial crisis originated from US subprime loan defaults, then was transmitted from the United States to the rest of the world. The debt risk of developed economies is more common in the government sector and the household sector. The leverage of the government sector is 59.2 percent higher than that of emerging economies, and the leverage of the household sector is 30.7 percent higher than that of emerging economies, yet there is not much difference when it comes to the non-financial business sector.

The debt risk is transmitted from emerging economies to developed economies. Although the debt burden of emerging economies is lighter than that of developed economies, since the degree of economic development is lower than in developed economies, their economic and financial vulnerability is higher. If debt risk of an equivalent degree appears in developed economies, they can probably dissolve it by virtue of their powerful economic strength, developed financial system, and strict policy supervision; if this happens in emerging economies, there will likely be a weak response. Due to the supply of raw materials and organization of production in the global industry chain, emerging economies' debt crisis will spread to the consumption market of developed economies, thus leading to debt risk in developed economies.

Financial risks during the pandemic and recovery

Although the pandemic does not directly lead to financial risks, under the impact of the pandemic and even in the process of economic recovery after slowdown of the pandemic, strong vigilance should be maintained on transmission and aggravation of some financial risks.

Local government debt risk

Too large scale and too rapid growth of local government debt (including implicit debt) is one of the main factors that influenced China's economic transformation in the past few years, and this might trigger systematic financial risk. In fact, local government debt risk is also a direct manifestation of the financial imbalances that could not be compensated in a timely way and the aggravated fiscal vulnerability. Hit by the pandemic, local government debt risk tends to be aggravated, mainly in the following ways: the COVID-19 pandemic hit the financial revenue status of provincial and local governments in China obviously in the first quarter. With the exception of three provinces without published data (Anhui, Hebei, and Xinjiang), data shows that only Tibet had positive growth (5.7 percent) of revenue in the general public budgets; the remaining provinces had decreases to different degrees compared with the same period of 2019. The decline in 12 provinces exceeded 16 percent (more than the decline of national government revenue). In the first quarter, national revenue in the general public budgets decreased by 14.3 percent year on year, and expenditure decreased by 5.7 percent year on year. The fiscal revenue of Hubei Province was hardest hit by the pandemic, and revenue in the general public budgets declined by more than 47 percent, a drop of nearly half. The proactive fiscal policy of "vigorously improve quality and efficiency" decided at the Central Economic Work Conference at the end of 2019 has been fully upgraded to a proactive fiscal policy: "should be more active and productive." It is noteworthy that local governments have gradually recognized the signifi- cant impact of the COVID-19 pandemic on fiscal operations since March.[8] The Ministry of Finance rapidly arranged "triple-guarantee" related works, which supported basic-level government to guarantee the basic livelihoods of the people, guarantee wages, and guarantee operations.[9] Therefore, practical measures must be taken to prevent the pandemic risk from turning into local fiscal risk, especially local government debt risk.

The entry of local fiscal revenue into a negative growth zone

The decrease in local fiscal revenue is one of the major reasons for the increase in debt risk. Comprehensive reduction of taxes and fees and the impact of the pandemic will inevitably bring more difficulties for maintaining or increasing fiscal revenue. After 2015, year-on-year growth of China's fiscal revenue entered single-digit growth (8.4 percent in 2015 and 3.8 percent in 2019), and the fluctuations of local fiscal revenue increased. Previously, China's fiscal revenue maintained a double-digit year-on-year increase for 10 years, and the year-on- year growth of local fiscal revenue even exceeded 20 percent from 2009 to 2012. However, negative growth of local fiscal revenue appeared in some provinces (e.g. Heilongjiang, Jilin, Chongqing, Gansu, Ningxia, and Tibet) by 2019.

More seriously, 2019 is very likely the last year of positive growth of local fiscal revenue (3 percent), especially tax revenue. Figure 10.3 gives clear evi- dence of this. The underlying reason is that since the policy of comprehensive tax and fee cuts was implemented in 2018, government finance has alleviated the burdens on enterprises and society cumulatively by more than 3.6 trillion Yuan. Annual year-on-year growth of national tax revenue dropped below 5 percent directly, and was just 1 percent in 2019. The difficulties of local fiscal revenue are beyond imagination. The pressure to increase fiscal rev- enue in 2020 was considerably huge even though there was no impact by the pandemic. In order to cope with the impact of the pandemic, tax and fee cuts of 158.9 billion Yuan[10] were added into the preferential tax policy newly

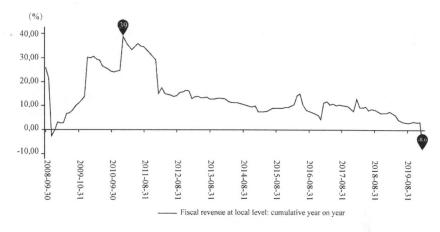

Figure 10.3 Growth trend of local fiscal revenue.

launched in 2020 to support epidemic prevention and control, and economic and social development. Plus the tax and fee cuts of 243.8 billion Yuan under a larger-scale tax and fee cut policy in 2019, that was further implemented in 2020, led to national cumulative tax and fee cuts of 402.7 billion Yuan in the first two months of 2020. In the first quarter of 2020, the national cumulative new tax cut was 341.1 billion Yuan. At this rate, total tax and fee cuts in 2020 might approach 3 trillion Yuan. According to a rough proportion (48.6 percent in 2019) of local finance in existing tax revenue, local finance should pay at least above 1.4 trillion Yuan for the tax and fee cuts.

The extraordinary growth of local fiscal expenditure

The growth of local fiscal expenditure increases debt pressure of local government. The growth of local fiscal expenditure has certain extraordinary characteristics: implementation of the new budget law relaxes the borrowing constraints of local government, and the gap of local financial resources increases continuously. The Budget Law of the People's Republic of China (Amendment) was implemented officially from 2015. With this law, the broad concerns of local government about deficit as well as self-initiated debt borrowing were deemed as "opening the front door, and closing the back door" to dissolve the debt risk of local government. From the perspective of results, nonstandard and nontransparent debts of China's local government were alleviated to a certain degree, and this led to the borrowing expansion of local government. Although the National People's Congress review the annual limit of the local government debt scale every year, the increasing debt limit year after year has become a main source of additional local financial investment expenditure since 2018, rather replacing outstanding debt and dissolving debt risk as in the past. Accordingly, the rapid increase of financial expenditure aggravates local financial imbalances. In the past 5 years, the average imbalance between revenue and expenditure of China's local government was 772.5 billion Yuan, while in the past 3 years, the average increased to 843.3 billion Yuan. The gap in local financial resources might not be converted to government debt completely; a part might be filled up by central transfer payments or other financial revenue forms. Yet the rigid growth of financial expenditure increases debt risk of local government, and this will surely increase further during or after the pandemic.

The increasing financial pressure of local anti-epidemic policies

In order to fight against the epidemic and resume work and production, both central and local governments have considered many approaches, but fiscal policy is at the top of the list. Take the example of affluent Guangdong: the provincial committee and provincial government proposed to attend to the fiscal function explicitly, adhere to "dual seizing, dual promoting" in the fight against the pandemic and the stabilizing of the economy, implement epidemic prevention and control funds totaling 12.673 billion Yuan at all fiscal levels throughout the province, provide powerful support for medical treatment, material support, and resumption of work and production, and alleviate the burdens on enterprises above 230 billion Yuan by means of tax reduction and exemption, deferred payment of taxes, and other measures. Although some provinces with fiscal difficulties did not publicize additional fiscal outlays, they have further improved subsidies and benefits of front-line medical and other workers for pandemic prevention and control, supported the supply of emergency materials for epidemic prevention and control, resumption of work and production, project construction commencement, bailout of micro, small, and medium-sized enterprises in the province, and planned and promoted epidemic prevention and control and resumption of work and production in a unified manner. These policies had key arrangements for pandemic expenditure, resumption of work and production, and stable employment; a part of relevant expenditure came from central allocation, but many local policies needed financial support at the corresponding levels. The current predicament is a huge fiscal pressure to ensure operations at all levels below provincial level, as the implementation and execution of anti-epidemic policies require a lot of financial funds. With the spread of the pandemic, local governments are in trouble. New finance debts will probably solve urgent needs, but will further aggravate debt burdens in the long run.[11]

Financial risks of real estate enterprises

Since 2017, a series of central and local policy arrangements for dissolving financial risks have functioned well and the leverage of industry sectors in national economy has showed certain downtrend; however, the work pattern of the real estate industry, especially real estate enterprises with a high leverage rate, has not improved significantly. Along with huge impact from the domestic and foreign COVID-19 pandemic on the supply and demand sides of the real estate market, financial risks of real estate enterprises have been exposed gradually, showing that measures tackling local spread need to be taken seriously.

Affected by the COVID-19 pandemic, from January to April 2020, the national sales amounts for residences, office buildings, and buildings for commercial use decreased by 16.5 percent, 37.5 percent, and 34.5 percent year on year, respectively. It can be seen from the sales performance of 22 real estate enterprises in the first quarter that the average sales target completion was only 12.7 percent of the annual target. Due to delayed sales collection and work resumption, turmoil of real estate stocks, and no obvious loosening at the policy level, the impact on real estate enterprises that rely on high debt ratio and high leverage rate for a long time becomes very evident, and the financial risks of real estate enterprises are being exposed gradually.

The increasing debt default and industry financial risks

Up to now, the assets/liabilities ratio of real estate enterprises is still at a high level. In 2019, the average assets/liabilities ratio of the top 100 real estate enterprises in China was 78.7 percent, and the average assets/liabilities ratio of 145 real estate enterprises listed in Shanghai and Shenzhen stock markets was 80.08 percent, far exceeding the reasonable range of assets/liabilities ratio, which is 40–60 percent. Among the top 50 domestic-funded real estate enterprises, nearly half had an assets/liabilities ratio above 80 percent, a relatively high financial leverage risk state. Data show that since the outbreak of the COVID-19 pandemic, new lawsuits, lack of credibility, illegal and abnormal operations, administrative penalties, serious offences, and other judicial and operational risk items of real estate enterprises have increased notably. In the first quarter of 2020, up to 74 real estate enterprises announced bankruptcy at the People's Court Network. It was estimated that real estate enterprises would face a centralized peak payment period for credit debt and other debts with interest in 2020; the industry debts due were about 1.46 trillion Yuan, and July 2020 was the peak month for debts due. Material breach of debts due has occurred in some large-scale real estate enterprises recently. In the downward market cycle of restricted financing channels and increasing debt ratio, debt recycling forms such as "return of old loan with new loan" and "borrowing short-term to repay long-term" are fairly common, and the financial turnover capacity of real estate enterprises is undergoing an ordeal.

The increasing risk pressure in local regions, upstream and downstream industries

Affected by the regional real estate market trend and regulation control policies, the assets/liabilities ratio of real estate enterprises shows great regional difference. Based on 74 real estate enterprises that suffered bankruptcy and liquidation in the first quarter of 2020, the ratio was high in central and western regions and third- and fourth-tier cities. Since local finance relies heavily on land grant and real estate market, the increasing assets/liabilities ratio of real estate enterprises might further increase local pressure for financial risk prevention and control. Meanwhile, the pandemic has also hit industries upstream and downstream of real estate hard, including construction work, building materials, home furnishing, hotels, conferences and exhibitions, and financing assurance. In the first 3 months of 2020, a higher and higher proportion of relevant enterprises announce bankruptcy proceedings. Textual analysis of keywords such as "building," "project," "building materials," and "hotel" carried out at the People's Court Announcement Network shows that up to 50, 113, 36, and 71 relevant industry enterprises in these four categories entered bankruptcy proceedings in the first quarter respectively. Also, up to 59 judgement documents, copies of bill of indictments and court summons referred to with "real estate guaranty." It can be seen that under the impact of the pandemic, the severe conditions in the mortgage guarantee industry involved with real estate require a high level of vigilance.

Overseas debt financing faces risk of turmoil in global financial markets

Affected by tight control of financing, many real estate enterprises actively seek overseas debt financing. In the first quarter of 2020, the size of overseas debt of real estate enterprises reached USD 27.7 billion, approaching the annual overseas debt in 2017, and all in US dollars. With worldwide spread of the pandemic, overseas stock markets remain volatile. Moreover, with the slump in oil price, liquidity squeeze, and the continuous strength of the US Dollar Index, the difficulties and risks of overseas debt financing to "return old loan with new loan" have increased gradually for real estate enterprises. Meanwhile, the mature size of overseas bonds of real estate enterprises will be up to US$ 45.3 billion in 2020. In case of strict control over overseas financing policy, appreciation of the US dollar, and continuous rise in the cost of overseas debt financing, the size of overseas debt of real estate enterprises is still growing quickly. This means that real estate enterprises have very strong financing needs for debt repayment peak. Along with the spread of pandemic and global financial market turmoil, foreign debt risk of real estate enterprises is also increasing gradually.

The aggravated risk differentiation in real estate industry

Against the background of strict financing supervision in 2019, market share of the top 100 real estate enterprises rose steadily to 61.5 percent, and their merger and acquisition amount accounted for 78 percent of total merger and acquisition of real estate enterprises, thus the industry concentration ratio increased quickly. Yet the declined profit margin, narrowed financing channels, increased financing cost, and unreasonable debt terms further pushed up the leverage and capital chain risks of small and medium-sized real estate enterprises in the centralized repayment period. In the first 3 months of 2020, there were 817 instances of bills of indictment and court summons involving the real estate field, most of which involved small and medium-sized real estate enterprises. During the continuous spread of the pandemic, special attention should be paid to the debt risk of small and medium-sized real estate enterprises and its diffusion to the local financial system. In addition, the impact of the pandemic on commercial property was also very great. The rent reduction for office buildings and shops all over China triggered by the pandemic worsened the conditions of commercial property enterprises that were already in a downward cycle, and many large-scale real estate enterprises with a higher proportion of commercial property faced very huge operation challenges during the pandemic.

Risk of small and medium-sized financial institutions

When hard-hit by the pandemic, active financial and fiscal policies should be implemented to support enterprises to pull through and prevent the deterioration of external demand, supply chain disruption, and getting into dilemma. Attention should also be paid to avoid the impact of massive enterprise defaults on the financial system, especially to prevent the impact on small and medium-sized financial institutions with relatively weak risk tolerance—mainly small and medium-sized commercial banks—and avoid a chain reaction that might trigger systematic financial risks. Small and medium-sized commercial banks should support epidemic prevention and control, real economy development, especially the development of small and medium-sized enterprises, further examine the pertinence, validity, and timeliness of their risk prevention and control, and plan and coordinate with the fight against the pandemic so as to boost growth and prevent risks as a whole.

Small and medium-sized commercial banks already faced
austere risks before the outbreak

Small and medium-sized commercial banks in China are mainly joint-stock commercial banks, local city commercial banks, rural commercial banks, rural banks, rural credit cooperatives, etc., and they mainly serve local economic development and small and medium-sized enterprises. Against a background of increasingly prominent structural conflicts between the domestic economy and finance, and the restrictions on talent, technology, capacity, internal management, etc., evident risk accumulation took place in some small and medium-sized commercial banks. Serious credit risk of Baoshang Bank and liquidity risk of the Bank of Jinzhou exposed in 2019 are typical examples.

From the perspective of risk category, small and medium-sized commercial banks in China faced more prominent credit risk, operational risk (including case risk), and liquidity risk before the outbreak.

From the perspective of credit risk, according to data publicized by the China Banking and Insurance Regulatory Commission, in the fourth quarter of 2019, the non-performing loan ratio of city commercial banks and rural commercial banks reached 2.32 percent and 3.9 percent, respectively, and the total non-performing loan balance of city commercial banks and rural commercial banks was 1 trillion Yuan, accounting for 42.3 percent of the amount of non-performing loans of banking financial institutions. That is, the overall amount of non-performing loans and the non-performing loan ratio of city commercial banks and rural commercial banks increased in 2018 and 2019, and their proportions in banking financial institutions also increased continuously. If bad debt write-off and the repackaged non-performing assets of city commercial banks and rural commercial banks in those two years are restored, the non-performing loan ratio will be even higher. Therefore, the small and medium-sized commercial banks represented by city commercial banks and rural commercial banks face very prominent credit risk.

In terms of operational risk and compliance risk, due to weak internal control management, the unenforceable triple-check of loans, and blind and radical business development, the China Banking Regulatory Commission has penalized small and medium-sized commercial banks for a large number of illegal operations, illegal guarantees, illegal bills, and false gold pledge cases since 2017. Illegal operations of small and medium-sized commercial banks were concentrated in credit services, bill services, asset management services, financial services, and payment settlement services. In recent years, the number of cases, especially in city commercial banks and rural commercial banks, increased notably. Some employees acted alone or colluded with external social outlaws to seize the funds of the banks or customers to provide illegal external guarantees, illegal sales of finance products, illegal lending, illegal issuance of bills, etc.

In terms of liquidity risk, although liquidity risk of the small and medium-sized commercial banks in China is controllable as a whole and no large-scale squeeze event has occurred, regional liquidity risk and liquidity risk of a single institution cannot be ignored. Small and medium-sized commercial banks have small fund transfer space, low proportion of highly liquid assets such as treasury notes and financial bonds, long loan maturities, low proportion of general deposits in debt funds, large inter-bank borrowing funds. They will face high liquidity risk in case of centralized maturities of deposits or finance products, default of key borrowers, sharp decline in asset quality, etc. City commercial banks and rural commercial banks are affected more directly by the regional economic environment, business benefits, and industry changes, and are more vulnerable to liquidity risk; this is worthy of great attention.

The risk of small and medium-sized commercial banks has increased significantly under the impact of the pandemic

Hit by the pandemic, the external operations environment of enterprises changed significantly. Enterprises, especially a large number of small and micro businesses and private enterprises, had to face disruption to production and operation order, upstream/downstream supply chain disruption, decrease in operating revenue and cash flow, sharp decline in benefits, and increased operation pressure. In fact, in recent years, China has been at a stage of economic downturn and structural adjustment, and financing problems have been prominent among private and micro and small businesses. Then the impact of the pandemic has further deteriorated the situation for enterprises, with many small and medium-sized enterprises suffering from tight or even broken capital chains and inability to repay loans even after loan extensions for a certain period. Industries such as catering, hotels, tourism, wholesale and retail, culture and sports, transportation, and low-end manufacturing were hit hardest. The global pandemic has exerted more and more impacts on business operations, including risk of disruption of industry chain and supply chain, blocked exports of some enterprises, chargebacks, and hindered imports in key parts of some enterprises. While most of these small and medium-sized enterprises are prime borrowers of small and medium-sized commercial banks, the income of small and medium-sized enterprises has decreased greatly. The decrease in profitability and repayment capacity will inevitably increase non-performing assets and decrease the asset quality of small and medium-sized commercial banks.

(1) Small and medium-sized commercial banks are facing pressure from a large increase in non-performing assets. After the pandemic outbreak, banking financial institutions conducted relevant pressure tests, and it can be seen from the results that the bad rate of the banking financial institutions with a good asset quality foundation, strong risk mitigation capability, and good borrower structure would generally increase by 0.2–1 percent, while the small and medium-sized commercial banks with a weak asset quality foundation and borrower structure hit hard by the pandemic face higher asset quality pressure. We should conduct careful and sufficient pressure tests, analysis, and evaluation to ascertain the base number and find a coping strategy as soon as possible. Small and medium-sized commercial banks originally under high pressure of exposure risk to non-performing assets found it more difficult to cope with systematic and regional risks and could not carry out prevention and control effectively after being hit by the pandemic.

(2) The liquidity risk of small and medium-sized commercial banks has been further magnified. On one hand, under the impact of the pandemic, small and medium-sized enterprises and individual businesses have to disrupt their production and operation activities, and general deposits of small

and medium-sized commercial banks, especially corporate deposits will inevitably decline, putting the liquidity regulatory index under pressure. On the other hand, hit by the pandemic, daily income of small and medium-sized enterprises in catering, transportation, wholesale and retail, and other industries has been significantly lower than expected, cash flow has decreased, short-term liquidity will inevitably decrease sharply, and relevant loans of such enterprises will be overdue or extended. This will weaken the fund return capacity of small and medium-sized commercial banks and inevitably hit the asset quality of small and medium-sized commercial banks; those employed in the industries hit by the pandemic will have less income or even temporarily lose their source of income. Their mortgage, credit card, and other personal credit repayment capacities have decreased, which will also influence the asset quality of consumer credit services of small and medium-sized commercial banks. From the perspective of the liquidity risk regulatory index, the impact of the pandemic on assets and liability services of small and medium-sized commercial banks will also be included gradually in the liquidity gap ratio, liquidity ratio, liquidity matching ratio, liquidity coverage ratio, net stable funding ratio (NSFR), and other indicators (see Table 10.2). It is especially noteworthy that for a long time, quite a few small and medium-sized commercial banks have sought extensive development, only laid stress on scale expansion, and put "profitability" first on the agenda, yet neglected "liquidity" and "security" and embedded major hazards for the generation of liquidity risk. Some small and medium-sized commercial banks have not established a perfect liquidity risk management system, lacked effective

Table 10.2 Impact of the pandemic on the liquidity risk regulatory index of small and medium-sized commercial banks

Service adjustment item		Liquidity gap ratio	Liquidity ratio	Liquidity matching ratio	Liquidity coverage ratio	NSFR
Asset side	Increase enterprise credit support	The short-term impact on the risk index should be evaluated in combination with the actual financing mode and maturity structure, etc. of small and medium-sized commercial banks; uncertainty exists in long-term cash flow.				
	Loan repayment extension	Large short-term cash flow gap	Down	Down	Down	Down
Debt side	Short-term deposit loss	Large short-term cash flow gap	Down	Down	Down	Down
	Extension of the deposit due	Mitigate short-term cash flow gap	Up	Up	Up	Up

liquidity risk identification, measurement, monitoring, control, and other technical means, cannot analyze borrower behavior and liquidity gap changes accurately at the first moment, and thus cannot realize dynamic and effective monitoring of liquidity risk in the whole process.

(3) The risk contagion between business operations and small and medium-sized commercial banks increases. The global pandemic has exerted direct impacts on enterprise production and operation and the stability of the global industry chain and supply chain. In recent years, the credit expansion, bill financing, and asset management products of banking and financial institutions relying on the industry chain and supply chain have increased substantially, with large stocks and increments. Once business operating conditions were hit significantly by the pandemic, relevant risks would become contagious, and centralized pressure of risk exposure on the banking and financial institutions, especially small and medium-sized commercial banks, would also trigger large scope systematic risks for small and medium-sized commercial banks if handled improperly.

Prevention and control of financial risks during the pandemic and recovery

Financial risks are extremely serious and should not be taken lightly at any time. In the process of economic recovery after the pandemic has slowed down, it is necessary to take more targeted prevention and control measures against different financial risks.

Prevention and control of local government debt risk under the impact of the pandemic

First, we should include income from government assets in financial income channels. An overall downtrend of local fiscal revenue has developed, and the pandemic has aggravated the rigid trend of local fiscal expenditure, which cannot be alleviated in the short term. Without considering the increase in local government borrowing, an alternative is to identify stable sources of fiscal income from abundant government assets. Large amounts of government assets, especially fixed assets, might be encashed in the forms of lease, securitization, or grant. To dissolve such systematic financial risks of local government debt at minimum cost, government should turn difficulties into opportunities, find ways to increase income, and stabilize financial revenue fluctuations in the future.

Second, central government should assume all financial expenditures for the fight against the pandemic and the economic recovery. Proactive fiscal policy may be more active and productive, and embodied in specific works. The pandemic impact and economic recovery have mostly achieved national goals and completed overall deployment, and central government may establish new emergency expenditure management methods for financial allocation of daily funds. If all epidemic prevention expenditures are assumed by central finance, the pressure on local epidemic prevention expenditures will be relieved greatly, helping normal and orderly system operations, avoiding shutdowns, and effectively relieving the borrowing impulse of local government.

Third, we should accurately evaluate local fiscal space. Through analysis of local fiscal revenue and expenditure and debt status, we should estimate the scale of disposable risk-free financial resources of local government in the future, carry out pre-controls to some degree, and identify the difference in fiscal affordability of districts with good financial resources and districts with poor financial resources. The actions under the constraints of fiscal space could give rise to proactive fiscal policy to effectively stimulate economic recovery and promote the debt financing function of local government, which is helpful to prevent debt risk and solve long-term unmatching problems between the financial resources and debts.

Prevention and dissolution of financial risks of real estate enterprises under the impact of the pandemic

For a long time, real estate enterprises in China have had too high proportion of indirect financing, especially bank credit, and have developed a financing structure that relies too much on banking and financial institutions, so their capacity to resist debt risk is relative weak. Against this background, wild fluctuation risk in the real estate market may be more easily converted to financial risks of banking and financial institutions, and then evolved to systematic financial risks. Therefore, we should make great efforts to prevent and dissolve the financial risks of real estate enterprises exposed to the global pandemic.

First, we should popularize pressure tests and a hierarchical evaluation system of real estate enterprises and further improve a risk early warning system in the real estate industry. Under the impact of the pandemic, a "monetary fund/(rigid expenses + short-term debts with interest)" index should be used to substitute the original generalized asset liability ratio index for the ultimate pressure test of existing real estate enterprises. We should carry out forecasting, troubleshooting, and scenario deduction for local liquidity risk and improve the hierarchical evaluation system for real estate enterprises. We should also, uncompromisingly and in a timely way, contain the financing behaviors of real estate enterprises with too long debt extension and the malicious practice of "return of old loan with new loan," classify real estate enterprises with debt defaults and unpaid due bonds to disclose default information, and normalize and restrain subsequent financing behavior. For real estate enterprises whose assets/liabilities ratio exceeds 90 percent, the ultimate pressure test result is less than 6 months, and in districts with average assets/liabilities ratio above 85 percent, a supervision department should keep an eye on their movement of funds and potential financial risks.

Second, we should classify and promote the debt replacement renewal of real estate enterprises and implement support policies. Fully considering the impact of the pandemic, with respect to projects with good expected comprehensive benefits and insufficient short-term cash flow, we should issue replacement bonds properly for debt replacement or renewal, and promote debt-for-equity swaps and other services of real estate enterprises. We should give appropriate extensions for short-term loans within 1 year without on-time repayment of capital and interest during the pandemic. And we should further relax pre-funding supervisory policy during the pandemic, postpone the payment term of some taxes and land transfer fees for real estate enterprises properly, and quickly implement enterprise house rental reduction and exemption, work resumption benefits and other policy measures.

Third, we should normalize overseas debt financing behavior of real estate enterprises and effectively prevent and control potential external financial risks. We should select foreign debt financing tools and financial products actively and securely, include the debt financing of overseas subsidiaries of domestic real estate enterprises into existing foreign debt statistics on the national treatment principle, and be wary of international speculators and hot money flowing into China's real estate market through overseas financing channels, which might trigger potential huge fluctuations in the stock market, currency market, and housing market. We should strictly normalize the foreign debt registration management system, only issue foreign debt for replacing medium- and long-term overseas debts due within the next year in principle, uncompromisingly eliminate excessive issuance of foreign debt, and raise foreign debt funds to repay domestic debt and other market irregularities of real estate enterprises. We should encourage real estate enterprises to redeem overseas dollar debt in advance according to international financial market changes during the pandemic and effectively prevent foreign debt costs from increasing risk brought by exchange rate fluctuations.

Fourth, we should comply with the uptrend of industry concentration ratio and promote financing structure optimization and transformation of real estate enterprises. We should also list the merger and acquisition loans of real estate enterprises during the pandemic separately from real estate development loans not in the strict supervisory scope of banking and financial institutions, and we should increase merger, acquisition and reorganization quality of real estate enterprises to effectively dissolve the financial risks of the real estate industry. We should encourage expansion of the direct financing proportion of real estate enterprises, quicken asset-backed security of real estate enterprises, and effectively promote normalized financing of the capital market, especially the stock market. We should actively expand diversified financing models, including real estate trust, bonds, funds, and real estate trust investment funds, gradually enhance assets liquidity of real estate enterprises, and effectively prevent and dissolve debt risk of real estate enterprises.

Prevention and dissolution of the risks of small and medium-sized commercial banks under the impact of the pandemic

Facing the impact of the pandemic, 2020 was a final year to prevent and dissolve major financial risks. In the preconditions of effective support for the real economy, we should prevent and dissolve the risks of small and medium-sized commercial banks according to the basic policy of "stabilizing overall situation, unified coordination, classified policy implementation and accurate bomb disposal."

First, we should carefully estimate and analyze the risks of small and medium-sized commercial banks. In particular, we should estimate non-performing assets that may be resisted under the provision coverage of small and medium-sized commercial banks and how long the resistance will last without liquidity crunch; we should estimate and assess the scale of risky assets that may be supported at the capital adequacy ratio level of small and medium-sized commercial banks and the capacity of capital to resist unexpected losses similar to the pandemic, and we should make quantitative analytical judgments. On the basis of risk estimates and pressure tests, we should conduct objective, accurate, scientific internal appraisal of control effectiveness for small and medium-sized commercial banks. Internal control appraisal is helpful for government at all levels and supervision departments to grasp the risk profile, management status, and risk controllability of small and medium-sized commercial banks in a timely and accurate way and further study and judge their capacity for sustainable development.

Second, on the basis of internal control appraisal, we should conduct accurate analysis of the internal control effectiveness of small and medium-sized commercial banks and perform classification and queuing. If the internal control system is basically effective, corporate governance is relatively perfect, and certain hidden risk only exists in single services, we should oblige the management of the institution to make profound corrections. If there is any major defect in internal control effectiveness, the regulatory authority should coordinate with local government management sector, organize deep verification. For high hidden risk, we should take decisive disposal measures to control risk exposure rapidly and decrease risk losses. In case of disordered internal management, serious control defects and moral risk and great potential risk contagion hazard, or if a chain reaction and mass disturbance might be triggered easily, or if through the internal control appraisal and risk investigation, there is major risk exposure which cannot be self-dissolved, government should rapidly organize takeover or custody. We should prevent and control the squeeze risk caused by insufficient liquidity, then verify risk exposure and management loopholes, and find risk handling measures item by item.

Third, on the basis of overall analysis and risk isolation, for specific risk categories of some small and medium-sized commercial banks, government should cut off mutual contagion of external borrower risk and bank risk according to the risk genesis to prevent mass disturbance. We should match the remedy to the problem and take specific stronger emergency response measures for classification and dismantling. If there is any greater risk due to excessive participation in local financing platforms, we should formulate unified planning to handle local debt risk and specifically define the handling responsibilities of local government. If controlled or implicitly controlled by major shareholders, industry borrowers are too centralized. We should combine industry and borrower risk dissolution, utilize assets reorganization, packaged for sale, equity transfer, bankruptcy reorganization, and other means, formulate a unified plan for borrower risk and bank risk, and take comprehensive measures to dissolve the risks. For illegal interbank business and asset management business that might easily create interbank risk contagion, we should introduce a transregional supervisory coordination and risk handling mechanism, carry out joint investigation and joint response, deal with large bonds one by one, and diversify risk properly. For internal and external collusion, internal malpractice, forming huge illegal guarantees together with online lending companies and guarantee companies, and illegally gaining bank credit, we should take necessary judicial means and compulsory measures against the violators and illegal enterprises, give recourse to funds and assets, compress exposure, and dissolve the risks quickly.

Fourth, in addition to necessary risk prevention and control measures, we should also improve associated mechanisms simultaneously. We should emphasize both incentives and constraints to stimulate the endogenous dynamics of small and medium-sized commercial banks and improve internal control system and risk management capability continuously. We should further improve and unblock capital supplement mechanisms of small and medium-sized commercial banks, broaden capital supplement channels and sources of small and medium-sized commercial banks, encourage local government, shareholder enterprises, and social capital to invest in small and medium-sized commercial banks, provide hierarchical support for small and medium-sized commercial banks to issue bonds and supplement capital, and develop stable capital supplement and capital constraint mechanisms. We should establish scientific, feasible, and effective talent transfer and exchange mechanisms, practically solve the problems of small and medium-sized commercial banks including severely insufficient talents, incomplete internal control systems, and weak risk management capability. We should establish a more rigorous supervisory penalty mechanism for small and medium-sized commercial banks with major internal control defects, weak management foundations, and even illegal operations. In addition to strict supervisory penalties, we should also restrict the scale of growth of their relevant services or all services, supervise and urge them to fundamentally break down the development model emphasizing scale in spite of quality, control existing risk, improve internal management, and lay a solid foundation for follow-up development. We should establish salary deferral and recourse mechanisms for management personnel and relevant posts in small and medium-sized commercial banks that trigger major risks, in addition to investigating relevant leader responsibility, management responsibility, we should also establish performance-evaluated salary recourse mechanism to retrieve the performance achieved at early stage, form strong personal interest constraints; We should establish a deferred salary payment system, link performance salary with credit asset quality and risk loss, tighten responsibility constraints, and restrict the blind business expansion impulse of small and medium-sized commercial banks. We should further improve the legal system and judicial procedures involving lawsuits and risk handling of banking and financial institutions, further revise relevant laws and regulations and judicial interpretation, strengthen law and discipline, intensify judicial punishment, maintain both vital interests of the people and the legal rights and interests of commercial banks, develop a good legal environment to stabilize finance and economy, and guarantee growth.

Construction of an all-round strategic system for financial risk prevention and control

Prevention and control of financial risk should start from the overall strategy of national security, follow basic financial rules, adhere to bottom line thinking, system thinking, and problem-orientated thinking based on national circumstances, construct a strategic system for financial risk prevention and control in compliance with actual situations in China; that is, establish and implement early recognition, assessment, monitoring, and control mechanisms against financial risks, an early warning and dissolution mechanism against systematic financial crisis, and a financial crisis rescue and handling mechanism, strengthen financial risk prevention and control infrastructure, and develop three-dimensional financial risk defense from structural risk to systematic risk, from internal to external, from local to central, from early warning and prevention to isolation and dissolution, and from rescue to gradual handling.

First, we should construct a strong financial risk early warning system. In terms of main influencing factors of financial risks, we should sort out and investigate the genesis, principles, contagion channels, and externalities of each risk point, further improve financial risk early warning system, and reduce the degree of information asymmetry in response to financial turbulence. One important aspect is to include the risk taking index, risk mispricing index, macroeconomic environment index, degree of association index, concentration risk index, etc. in the financial risk early warning index set, making efforts to fully cover all financial risks.

Second, we should develop a financial stress index that covers different subdivision sectors of the financial system, different areas, and different time frequencies so as to monitor financial stress status in real time. Specifically, we should integrate stress levels from different sources such as banking, the interbank market, the bond market, the stock market, and the foreign exchange market into a continuous statistical index to quantify the degree of financial system turmoil, and reflect the overall stress levels of different subdivision sectors, different areas, and the entire financial system caused by uncertainties and expectation changes. We should identify systemic stress periods of the financial system based on the degree of deviation of the financial stress index from its long-term trend, give early warning of financial turbulence, optimize the index system continuously, and increase early warning accuracy according to the deviations of the forecasts from actual situations.

Third, we should improve the currency policy framework, cognize new risk factors, select opportunities to promulgate monetary policy and reform measures, seek proper balance between the utilization of monetary policy rules and discretionary choice to draw on advantages and avoid disadvantages in the preconditions of further analysis of the domestic and international economic and financial market situations. On one hand, we should adhere to the multiple objectives of monetary policy; for example, stabilizing economic growth, the RMB exchange rate, and the financial market, supporting supply-side structural reform, and making efforts to smooth the transmission channel and mechanism of monetary policy. On the other hand, we should adhere to discretionary choice and ensure forward-looking, pertinent, and flexible currency policy responses.

Fourth, we should strengthen the infrastructure for financial risk prevention and control. Specifically, we should establish a unified framework of financial supervision, and with respect to the features of systematic financial risk in the new circumstances, such as wide coverage, strong correlation, and complicated spread, we should implement penetrating supervision and macro-prudential supervision. We should increase efficiency of financial services for the real economy, so as to deepen the supply-side structural reform, promote economic structural transformation and upgrading, coordinate international and domestic, central and local systematic financial risk supervision, continue to improve the accounting audit system, curb risk-taking propensity of enterprises, lay a solid foundation for the prevention and control of financial risks. We should quicken the construction of financial information, gradually alleviate reliance on foreign financial information and try to grasp rule-making power and the right to speak in important links of international investment banks, commercial banks, international liquidation and settlement systems, credit rating institutions, and public accounting firms. We should improve the legal framework for prevention and control of financial risk, quicken the legislation work to prevent financial risks, strengthen the construction of a corporate control mechanism in financial institutions, improve the legal system relating to capital allocation, and promote the reform of the foreign exchange reserve management system and investment structure and so on.

Notes

1 In the process of writing this chapter, Associate Researcher He Daixin, Associate researcher Li Chao, and Senior Economist Xu Zhenhui have provided relevant data and materials for help and support. We give special thanks to them.

2 M. A. Ruiz Estrada, *Economic waves: The effect of the Wuhan COVID-19 on the World Economy (2019–2020)*, available at SSRN 3545758, 2020.

3 Shen Guobing, The impact of COVID-19 pandemic on China's foreign trade and employment and the rescue measures, *Journal of Shanghai University of International Business and Economics*, 2nd issue, 2020.

4 The market drop may have more to do with the oil crisis, the fourth Middle East war, and the first oil crisis.

5 Zhang Xiaopu and Zhu Taihui, Reflections on the relationship between financial system and real economy, *Studies of International Finance*, 3rd issue, 2014.

6 The "butterfly effect" was proposed by American meteorologist Edward N. Lorenz in 1963. It refers to the fact that in a dynamic system, small changes in initial conditions can trigger a huge long-term chain reaction in the whole system.

7 Ye Yonggang, Yang Feiyu, and Zheng Xiaojuan, Research on the transmission and impact of national credit risk: A case study of the eurozone debt crisis, *Journal of Financial Research*, 2nd issue, 2016.

8 The Ministry of Finance of the People's Republic of China, Analysis and reflection on efforts to reduce the impact of COVID-19 on local financial operations, Ministry of Finance of the People's Republic of China March 31, 2020: http:// gs.Mof.Gov.cn/dcyj/202003/t20200319_3485034.htm

9 The Ministry of Finance of the People's Republic of China, Firmly hold the bottom line of "three guarantees" at the grassroots level–the Ministry of Finance elaborated policies to strengthen local governments' "three guarantees", Ministry of Finance of the People's Republic of China: www.Mof.Gov.cn/zhengwuxinxi/ caijingshidian/xinhuanet/202003/t20200306_3478814.htm

10 Among the four new policies released in 2020, the third set of policies focusing on reducing the burden on micro and small businesses and individual businesses and the fourth set of policies focusing on stabilizing foreign trade and foreign investment have been implemented since March, with the declaration period starting in April for statistical accounting. Among the first two sets, some are reported on a quarterly basis. With the coming of the big quarterly tax collection period in April, these policies will be included in the statistical accounting scope, and the statistical scale of tax reduction and fee reduction enjoyed by enterprises will be further expanded. Xinhua News Agency: www.Xinhuanet.com/2020-03/31/c_ 1125793133.htm

11 Wu Xiubo, Why have the Fed's efforts to return monetary policy to normal been frustrated? Analysis of the underlying reasons for the FED's interest rate cut, *Price: Theory & Practice*, 7th issue, 2019.

12 Z. Haisen et al., Will the pandemic trigger a financial crisis like that in 2008?: https:// new.qq.com/omn/20200326/20200326A04GG300.Html

11 Public health countermeasures

Short term and long term

Zhu Hengpeng and Pan Yuqing

The resource squeeze caused by the COVID-19 outbreak on the medical and public health system in China exerted huge pressure on patient admission and exposed the existing problems in the medical service system, public health system, and disease control system. With the gradual recovery of social and economic activities, normalized epidemic prevention and control puts forward higher requirements for risk prevention and dissolution capacities of the medical and public health system in China. How to join system mechanisms, move forward the prevention gateway, and "prevent minor disease from spreading into a pandemic,"[1] are important issues to be considered.

Practice shows that the effectiveness of public health management and disease prevention and control is affected by the promotion of resident health knowledge and early screening and, to a large extent, intervention capacity (including health management capacity of susceptible groups), while these are linked closely to the daily public health service and health management work of primary medical institutions. As "gatekeepers" of resident healthcare and outposts of epidemic prevention and control, if primary medical institutions closest to residents cannot function effectively, when patients flock to hospitals, the biggest drawback is that they find it "difficult to get medical treatment" and "expensive to seek medical care." Also decrease in disease screening and admission efficiency during the pandemic period will lead to cross-infection, thus weaken epidemic prevention and control situations.

Therefore, strengthening the service and epidemic prevention capacity of primary medical institutions should be the aim of development of the public health service system. We will analyze structural shortcomings of the medical and public health system, and discuss the exposed problems with institutional mechanisms in combination with the current status of China's health resource allocation. We will also put forward near-term and long-term policy suggestions for improving the public health service system.

DOI: 10.4324/9781003184447-12

Current status and problems of health resource allocation in China

Under the impact of the COVID-19 pandemic, medical and health resources in China have been in short supply. Some have suggested improving the allocation of beds, equipment, and staffing in public hospitals at all levels and increasing the supply of resources through government finance investment. But in fact, medical resources, especially hospital bed resources, are not in shortage in China; a surplus even exists. And high-speed expansion of public hospitals in recent years has reduced the capacity of primary medical institutions. The current dilemma is not the insufficient total amount of medical resources, but the lack of an effective cooperative system based on division of labor. Continuation of such a pattern will only weaken the service and epidemic prevention capacity of primary medical institutions and disorganize hierarchical diagnosis and treatment system and disease prevention and control systems, inconsistent with the requirements of General Secretary Xi Jinping to "strengthen prevention and control capacity building at rural, community levels, weave the first line of defense tightly."[2]

The contraction of serviceability and service scale of primary medical institutions caused by the expansion of public hospitals and its mechanisms are described below.

The imbalance of resource allocation structure, coexistence of excess and shortage

Through vigorous government investment over the past decade, China has eliminated shortage in medical resources. The number of doctors per thousand population of China was 2.77 persons in 2019, similar to the United States (2.6), Britain (2.8), Canada (2.7), and South Korea (2.3); the number of hospital beds per thousand population was 4.9, significantly above the median level of (Organisation for Economic Co-operation and Development (OECD) countries (3.9) and higher than 20 countries including Australia (3.8), Norway (3.6), the United States (2.8), and Britain (2.5).[3] As the anti-epidemic frontline, Wuhan's hospital resources are among the top listed in China, in 2018, the number of doctors per thousand population was 3.6 persons and the number of hospital beds per thousand population was 7.4—far higher than the national averages.

Expansion of high-grade public hospitals is the key driver of resource growth. From 2010 to 2018, the number of tertiary public hospitals in China increased from 1,258 to 2,263, and the number of beds and number of doctors increased at a higher speed: the number of beds per hospital increased from 830 to 1,008. In 9 years, the number of beds in China's public medical institutions increased to 2.19 million, of which about 56.5 percent were added due to expansion of tertiary public hospitals. The market share of tertiary public hospitals also increased rapidly by more than 10 percent in 9 years.[4]

During the expansion of public hospital resources, falsely high hospitalization rates are widespread, meaning excess of bed resources in China. Table 11.1 shows the number of hospitalizations per hundred employees with medical insurance in all municipalities directly under the central government, provincial capital cities, and sub-provincial cities in 2017, revealing the fact of excessive hospital beds in these cities. As is well known, medical resources are rich in Beijing: no employee needing hospital care has not been hospitalized in Beijing. Since tertiary grade A hospitals in Beijing receive many nonlocal severely ill patients, they will not arrange hospitalization of mildly ill patients who do not need to be hospitalized. Also the outpatient coverage level of employee medical insurance in Beijing is very high: the insured will not select hospitalization if they may be treated at a clinic. Therefore, the hospitalization rate in Beijing is at a reasonable level. With reference to this, the hospitalization rate of employees with medical insurance in all other cities is higher than that in Beijing, and the rate in most cities is even significantly higher than that in Beijing, showing excessive hospitalization in many districts. The widespread excessive hospitalization clearly shows the excess of beds in many districts.

The focus of the medical service system has continuously shifted to high-grade public hospitals. The most serious consequence is the collapse of hierarchical diagnosis and treatment system and the disease prevention and control system in China, so primary medical institutions cannot act as gatekeepers for resident healthcare and outposts of epidemic prevention and control. In December 2014, General Secretary Xi Jinping visited Shiye Town Health Center, Zhenjiang City, Jiangsu Province, with the aim of solving the problem of overcrowded large hospitals nearly always in a "wartime state." The reason for this problem was the siphoning of high-quality medical resources from the community level to high-grade public hospitals which expanded at high speed in the past dozen years, with the result being that serviceability and service scale at the community level declined day after day. In fact, the effectiveness of public health management and routine disease control work depends heavily on clinical serviceability of primary medical institutions as well as the community resident attraction and credibility based on this, so the decline in clinical serviceability at the community level has inevitably caused scarce capacity of public health and disease control, and routine work becomes formalistic and cannot achieve real effect.

In fact, high-speed expansion of tertiary public hospitals has been realized by siphoning high-quality doctor resources from secondary hospitals and primary medical institutions, and then siphoning patients and medical income. The reason is very simple: since the number of mature doctor resources in an area is relatively stable, rapid expansion of high-grade public hospitals generally will not increase doctor supply, but lead to competition for mature doctor resources in local low-grade health facilities or health facilities in underdeveloped areas. After scale expansion, tertiary hospitals commonly poach excellent doctors from local secondary hospitals or underdeveloped areas, and in

Table 11.1 Hospitalization rate of the employees insured by medical insurance in the municipalities directly under central government, provincial capital cities, and sub-provincial cities in 2017

City	Proportion of retirees (%)	Number of inpatients per hundred persons	Number of hospitalizations per hundred employees	Number of hospitalizations per hundred retirees	City	Proportion of retirees (%)	Number of inpatients per hundred persons	Number of hospitalizations per hundred employees	Number of hospitalizations per hundred retirees
Beijing	18.2	8.6	4.3	28.2	Qingdao	24.2	17.8	8.1	48.1
Haikou	17.9	9.8	3.6	38.1	Chengdu	24.5	18.2	8.5	48.4
Xiamen	7.3	10.4	9.2	26.2	Dalian	27.0	18.5	7.0	49.9
Fuzhou	21.8	10.8	5.3	30.5	Tianjin	36.3	19.1	7.2	40.1
Hefei	19.2	11.6	5.0	39.3	Shijiazhuang	31.7	20.2	11.4	39.2
Guangzhou	16.6	12.5	6.1	44.6	Zhengzhou	16.8	20.8	11.8	65.4
Nanchang	32.3	13.8	5.9	30.5	Changchun	33.2	21.3	12.1	40.0
Yinchuan	24.0	14.4	8.1	34.4	Kunming	27.9	21.6	8.6	55.1
Jinan	22.5	14.7	6.8	41.9	Xi'an	29.8	21.9	8.8	52.8
Shanghai	32.8	15.2	7.4	31.0	Tibet	22.8	22.7	19.1	34.9
Nanjing	24.2	15.4	8.4	37.3	Urumqi	21.9	24.3	18.2	46.4
Huhehaote	27.8	15.5	7.7	36.0	Wuhan	29.7	24.4	10.7	56.8
Taiyuan	33.4	16.0	7.8	32.3	Chongqing	28.9	25.5	11.7	59.4
Xining	34.8	16.4	10.0	28.5	Harbin	40.9	28.3	17.2	44.4
Nanning	23.7	17.1	8.1	46.0	Shenyang	40.9	29.3	14.3	51.0
Lanzhou	39.3	17.5	9.3	30.0	Ningbo	17.9	29.8	18.2	83.0
Hangzhou	19.0	17.6	12.7	38.5	Changsha	21.7	31.1	13.4	94.8

Source: Income, expenditure and supplementary information of employee medical insurance in the unified planning areas of China in 2017.

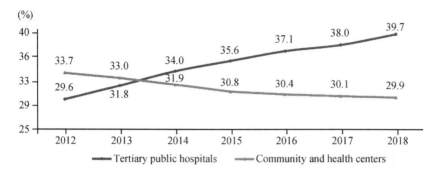

Figure 11.1 (Assistant) Doctor distribution in public tertiary hospitals and community medical institutions (%).

Source: China Health and Family Planning Statistical Yearbook (2013–2017), China Health Statistical Yearbook (2018–2019), Peking Union Medical College Press

turn secondary hospitals poach excellent doctors from the community level. In the distinct administrative hierarchy, mature doctors trained at the community level will be poached quickly by hospitals, and some community medical institutions cannot retain even university graduates.

With the expansion of high-grade public hospitals, the inverted pyramid structure of doctor allocation in public medical institutions becomes more significant, as shown in Figure 11.1. In 2012, only 29.6 percent of the doctors in the public medical system in China worked in tertiary hospitals, and in 2018, this proportion increased to 39.7 percent; in the same period, the proportion of the doctors who worked in primary medical institutions decreased from 33.7 percent to 29.9 percent. In addition, 37 percent of the doctors in public primary medical institutions are assistant doctors without the right to prescribe. While this proportion is only 1.3 percent in tertiary hospitals, the gap in actual serviceability of doctors is even larger.

Micro operating mechanism fails, public health service becomes formalistic

With the continued loss of doctors and patients in primary medical institutions, medical income declines, and primary medical institutions mainly rely on financial support. Since 2011, it has been common in China that the subsidies for basic fiscal expenditure obtained by primary medical institutions (excluding retirement funds) could cover the wages of all active staff and that about 40 percent of the subsidies may be used for other operational expenditures in these institutions. Urban community centers obtain the most abundant subsidies for basic fiscal expenditure; the current level of subsidies for basic fiscal expenditure is above twice the total wage income of the staff.

With the stable financial support for the institutions and staff, despite drought or waterlogging, primary medical institutions further lose enthusiasm to provide services. Take the example of the public health service. Basic public health service funding of public primary medical institutions is calculated according to the number of residents in the precinct. The standard per capita subsidy of basic public health service funding for residents was no less than 15 Yuan in 2009, and by 2020, this standard was adjusted to 74 Yuan and became an important income component of primary medical institutions. Regardless of whether services are actually provided, as long as they are filled up to the standard on the statement, primary medical institutions could obtain the fiscal subsidies for public health. Moreover, given the equalitarian distribution mechanism of getting an equal share regardless of the work done—no more gain for more work, no less gain for less work—naturally there is no incentive to work.

Under such a mechanism, the work completion status relies heavily on administrative assessment from top to bottom. In order to avoid work without effort or false report of workload, the assessment indexes are expanded continuously, raised without restriction; thus a lot of time has to be spent filling in assessment forms at the community level. "True fiscal money, false community work" was mentioned by the directors of some community health centers in our survey.

The universality of false, inflated data may be seen from official data. The Primary Health Department of the National Health Commission publicized basic public health service data at the end of 2015; according to this, the archiving rate of electronic health records of national residents was up to 76.4 percent, for managing 88.35 million and 21.64 million hypertension patients and diabetes patients, respectively, and managing the health of 118 million elderly people.[5] However, by 2017, the family doctor signing service items extended on the basis of the public health service at the community level had changed the coverage rate to "group coverage rate exceeded 35 percent, coverage rate of focus groups exceeded 65 percent"[6]—far lower than the coverage level archived 2 years ago.

Compared with the archiving rate of the public health service, the "shrunk" family doctor signing data still contains high moisture content. In 2017, according to data publicized by the National Health Commission, the family doctor signing service was available in more than 95 percent of Chinese cities, and more than 500 million people had their own family doctors.[7] The signing service fee was taken care of by medical insurance funds, basic public health service funds, and financial subsidies; this is an important source of the performance-evaluated salary of medical workers in public primary medical institutions. But the interesting thing is, in the survey interviews, even workers in departments paying for family doctor services, such as health departments, financial departments, and medical insurance departments, denied this signing rate. Although community health centers and health centers in some districts "signed" with residents successfully under public fund subsidies, in the second year, they asked that residents assume a small part of the signing service fee. However, this was rejected, and the motion for payment by private medical savings account did not pass either. This means that residents haven't actually enjoyed the signed service. After the outbreak of COVID-19, even the "health records" of key signing groups (also the population susceptible to COVID-19) failed to play a supporting role, so it can be seen that daily "health management" work is only formalistic.

Correspondingly, personal health records (PHRs) played a key role in epidemic prevention and control in China's Taiwan region. The PHR is core tool to search and track infected persons, close contacts, and susceptible populations. The health record has helped the Taiwan region to actively locate patients with severe respiratory symptoms for follow-up observation; previous health information and travel history records have also become important references for rapid identification of cases.[8] A national health information construction plan was set out in China's Taiwan region from 2004 and has been implemented since 2008. PHRs were prioritized (guided by the Family Medical Association). The plan centered on PHRs was promoted in 2013 for health information integration, and the development time was not notably earlier than on the mainland.[9] A key difference is the reliance to a large extent of PHRs on national health insurance information system, so it has stronger operability and usefulness. Compliance is also much higher than the practice with separate PHRs, disconnected from medical insurance system.

Transition of the service provision model in the medical and public health system

In recent years, government investment in medical care and public health increased significantly; meanwhile, financial investment has also increased notably for public primary medical institutions, but this cannot reverse the weak serviceability and trend of business shrinking at the community level. The service provision model should be reformed to strengthen work at community level.

The effect of ensuring and strengthening serviceability at the community level based on increased financial investment is not evident

National health financial statement data show that the financial investment obtained by primary medical institutions has grown rapidly. The proportion of investment at the community level in the fiscal "subsidy for supply side" increased from 29.2 percent in 2008 to 42.2 percent in 2018. Per capita financial investment in personnel on the regular payroll of primary medical institutions has changed from being lower than that of public hospitals in 2008 to currently being significantly higher. From 2008 to 2017, the ratio of the former to the latter increased from 0.88 to 1.67, of which urban community health centers obtained the highest financial subsidies, and basic subsidy levels even exceeded the per capita level of all financial subsidies in public hospitals. In the same period, the average basic subsidy per permanent employee in urban community health centers increased from 23,000 Yuan to 128,000 Yuan, an average annual increase of 21.2 percent; also the average basic subsidy per permanent employee in township hospitals increased from 9,000 Yuan to 90,000 Yuan, an average annual increase of 28.8 percent.

In terms of public health funding, in 2014, public primary medical institutions in China obtained financial subsidies for basic public health services of 30.09 billion Yuan, plus public health project subsidies of 4.82 billion Yuan—in total, 34.91 billion Yuan. In 2017, primary medical institutions obtained basic public health service subsidy income up to 49.23 billion Yuan and public health project subsidy income up to 8.11 billion Yuan—a total of 57.35 billion Yuan. Fiscal investment in public health funding of primary medical institutions increased on average 18 percent per year, far beyond the growth rate of fiscal investment in all public medical and health institutions in the same period (11.5 percent).

Financial security for primary medical institutions in poverty-stricken areas may also be received in a timely way. Take the example of Haiyuan County, Zhongwei City, Ningxia Hui Autonomous Region. Financial subsidy income per permanent employee of township hospitals already exceeded 100,000 Yuan in 2016, but if only considering permanent employees, the per capita financial subsidy exceeded 140,000 Yuan. Basic public health service (excluding personnel fund subsidy) and special subsidies for public health accounted for 40 percent, with no inadequate investment at all. Also there was idle equipment; for example, equipment was ready, but local health workers did not know how to use it.

However, the continued increase in fiscal investment has not changed the gradual shrinking of serviceability and service scale in public primary medical institutions. In fact, while fiscal investment increased year by year, the portion of medical visits in public primary medical institutions declined year by year. In 2010, 30.4 percent of clinic/emergency treatment services and 29.2 percent of inpatient service needs in China were taken care of in nearby public community centers or health centers; but in 2017, only 26.5 percent of clinic/emergency patients and 18.3 percent of inpatients visited public community centers and health centers—a decrease of 4 percent and 11 percent, respectively, in 8 years. This shows more and more deviation from the policy objectives for establishing a hierarchical diagnosis and treatment system.

This has been fully exposed in Wuhan City as an anti-epidemic frontline. From 2009 to 2018, the number of tertiary hospitals in Wuhan increased from 30 to 61, of which the number of tertiary grade A hospitals increased from 22 to 28 and the number of ministerial and provincial hospitals increased from 8 to 13. Siphoned by tertiary hospitals, primary medical institutions in Wuhan basically lost the serviceability to cover communities and towns/townships. In 2018, only 13.9 percent of the doctors worked in community institutions and health centers, and the proportion of their beds accounted for only

11.8 percent; only 17.8 percent of outpatients and 7 percent of inpatients visited community health centers in the whole year. This is why so many medical resources were unavailable in Wuhan after the outbreak.

The above-mentioned facts show no effect of building public hospitals and community health centers for hierarchical diagnosis and treatment systems by increasing financial investment and number of permanent employees to increase medical serviceability and disease control capacity at community level.

Transition of the public health service provision model

Due to institutional arrangements and corresponding financial investment mechanisms in the medical and health service system at community level, financial investment hasn't achieved the expected effect. Direct financial investment in the model of "feeding employees, feeding institutions" could not develop an effective public service provision system.

Compared with the effective experience of Singapore's community medical system in case screening and intervention during this pandemic,[10] the conclusion is more evident. Singapore's government has accumulated experience in the fight against SARS and H1N1. Among the more than 2,200 private clinics, government allocated funds to support more than 880 to act as Public Health Preparedness Clinics (PHPCs, similar to fever clinics in China), forming an integrated defense system that consists of public hospitals, community hospitals, and private clinics. In January 2020, Singapore received a COVID-19 pandemic alarm from Wuhan, China, and these more than 880 clinics started to prepare for pandemic sorting and referral. By contrast, in late January, Shanghai and Beijing started a Level 1 response and activated 110 and 101 fever clinics, respectively. The quantity was less than an eighth of that in Singapore, while the area of Singapore is only equivalent to Daxing District in Beijing City, and smaller than Pudong District in Shanghai City.

The scale of a PHPC in Singapore is similar to a private clinic in China. During epidemic prevention, the responsibility of PHPC clinics was to find suspected cases, carry out diagnosis, treatment, reporting, referral, and quarantine according to uniform standards, decrease missed diagnoses to the maximum extent possible, and avoid panic squeeze of public health resources as far as possible. The PHPC system shares medical information and could provide a reliable basis for tracing cases of infectious disease.

The reason why a private clinic network could play an effective role lies in its normal role as community health gatekeeper in Singapore. Family doctor clinics in Singapore must join the local Chronic Disease Management Programme (CDMP) and Community Health Assist Scheme (CHAS) before they can apply to join the PHPC system. The logic behind it is very simple: they could better realize risk monitoring and disease prevention and control functions in the case of a public health emergency only on the basis of daily health management for residents and by gaining the trust of residents. It is also worth mentioning that in addition to public health training, government financial support for PHPCs is mainly embodied in the supply of materials for response to public health events (e.g. personal protection materials, medicines, vaccines); in daily life, these clinics get service income mainly based on CDMP and CHAS, and sources of payment are medical insurance savings accounts and self-payments by patients.

According to international experience, whether in countries where public hospitals are dominant (e.g. the United Kingdom and Singapore) or in countries where private hospitals are dominant or public and private hospitals are mixed (e.g. the United States, Canada, Germany, and Japan), as medical and public health gatekeepers, about 90 percent of community medical institutions are private clinics, and most clinic/emergency needs of the nationals are met by them. Under dual action of the competitive mechanism and institutional design of medical insurance payments, these private clinics have the serviceability and enthusiasm to keep patients in the community, and they have obtained the full trust of community residents. After working in hospitals for many years, most medical graduates will leave hospitals and open their own clinics or work in both hospitals and clinics, strengthening their serviceability at the community level; thus a positive cycle has been developed.

Facts show that to fully activate resources and strengthen serviceability at the community level, primary medical institutions must have the ability to provide ordinary medical services trusted by community residents and have the enthusiasm to actively provide good health services. There is rarely any successful case in the world in which medical and health institutions at community level adopt the model of "feeding employees, feeding institutions" by government. Therefore, the way out is not to increase financial investment and staffing, but to adjust the financial investment system, change the "feeding employees, feeding institutions" service provision model, and recognize the role of competition and incentive mechanisms.

Policy suggestions for improving the public health service system

Where resources are not in shortage as a whole, further expansion of public hospitals, especially large-scale comprehensive public hospitals, is useless for increasing the of medical service provision; rather, it will enlarge the gap between hospitals and clinics, further squeeze survival and development space of small and medium health institutions, and bring more hidden hazards in public health management and disease prevention and control. We should carefully summarize the structural issues in the medical and health service system of China, find the drawbacks, and implement policies appropriately. The key to improving disease prevention and control capacity lies in solving the imbalance of medical resource allocation, vigorously developing small and medium health institutions, improving the medical and health service network at community level, and establishing a hierarchical diagnosis and treatment system.

On these grounds, we give near-term and long-term policy suggestions for improving the public health service system.

Near-term measures for improving the health service system

With respect to the urgent concerns around improving the medical and health service system, on one hand, we should consider how to increase effective service provision through structural adjustment and mechanism optimization given the fixed total amount of medical service resources in the short term, especially to make up current service drawbacks in primary medical institutions. On the other hand, we should continue epidemic prevention and control work, strengthen risk monitoring and prevention and control capacity of primary medical institutions, take effective measures to encourage the development of small and medium health institutions and the increase in service share, and avoid people gathering in large hospitals that might cause cross-infection.

First, we should acknowledge the role of Internet medical care to achieve timely and safe increase in medical care provision, convenience for people who need to see a doctor, and reduction of cross-infection risk. The effective measures that may be taken rapidly by government are to immediately release online first visits, release online sales of prescription drugs and guarantee their legitimacy, and explore inclusion of services in compliance with medical insurance compensation policy and prescription drugs sold online in medical insurance payments. To alleviate offline diagnosis and treatment pressures during the pandemic, remote diagnosis and treatment actions were taken in Wuhan, and medical insurance offices included part of online medical care in medical insurance payments. On the basis of such experience, we should improve policies concerning regulations and medical insurance payment methods for online first visits and online sales of prescription drugs as soon as possible to achieve large-scale, normalized provision of online medicine services, expand the number of doctors who could provide online services, mitigate offline hospitalizing pressure, reduce cross-infection in medical places to the maximum extent possible, and alleviate the psychological pressure on doctors caused by "illegal" online practices.

As supporting measures, with respect to online medical examinations, the government should encourage third-party social inspection agencies to examine patients according to diagnosis and treatment records and doctors' suggestions on online medical platforms, to ensure sufficient protection is provided and to alleviate medical resource shortage and avoid highly crowded public hospitals. We should allow online platforms capable of sales of drugs to connect with the online medical system platform as soon as possible for prescription information sharing, instant settlement, and real-time supervision. We should allow a network drug sales platforms within the health insurance directory, and we should provide an interface for connection with national medical insurance offices, ensuring that information on the whole chain is visible and checkable by medical insurance authorities, and enabling instant payment for the drugs in compliance with medical insurance compensation policy according to the medical insurance policy in the patients' district.

Second, we should construct a "medical and health integration (medical and prevention integration)" health service network at the community level. Medical and health integration is the development direction of the public health service system. Because health workers generally prefer more practical medical clinical services and lack enthusiasm for full-time public health work without clinical content, the integration of medical and health is helpful to attract and retain talent. And from the viewpoint of ordinary people, doctors who "may give medical advice" can be more easily trusted in public health work, including disease control work. Therefore, the combination of a medical service with a public health service is not only more acceptable to residents, but could also realize full coverage of the public health service. Previous practical experience shows that the effect of promoting knowledge of disease prevention and control and public health to ordinary residents, especially rural residents, is not ideal when there is no need for medical services, and it's very difficult to attract them to participate in health and hygiene knowledge promotion activities periodically. If the public health service is integrated when medical service is provided, this practice may achieve twice the result with half the effort. On the other hand, the combination of medical care and public health expands service content, offers more opportunities and larger growth space to local health personnel, lets doctors intervene earlier in the health management of residents, and meets the requirement of improving serviceability at the community level.

Therefore, public health institutions and medical institutions should not be established separately at the community level, and their works should not be arranged separately. Medical workers in primary institutions should assume public health and disease prevention and control work while meeting medical needs of the residents. While the center for disease control and prevention is arranged independently at national and provincial levels, disease control departments in prefecture-level cities and below, especially disease control departments and disease control services in counties (cities) and towns/townships, should be incorporated into corresponding medical institutions. At the same time, we should refer to the practice in Singapore, entrust public health and disease control services at the community level to corresponding primary medical institutions, and realize synergistic effects of integrating medical and public health services, including the disease control service.

In addition, an online medical platform network could be used to promote sinking of high-quality services, improve medical serviceability and disease prevention and control capacity at the community level, and realize coordination among medical and health institutions. In fact, some online medical institutions have realized connections between communities, health centers, village doctors, and clinics; some secondary public or private hospitals use online and other remote cooperation modes for service sinking to meet the needs of an expanding service radius. In this process, business cooperation, information, and technical exchange, may improve the quality of medical and health services obtained by residents at the community level, with effective training of health workers at the community level and increased medical care and public health service capacity.

Third, we should use medical insurance funds and public health service funds in a unified way. As stated in the Opinions of the Central Committee of the Communist Party of China and the State Council concerning Deepening of the Reform of Medical Insurance System, published on February 25, 2020: "Use medical insurance fund and public health service fund unifiedly, increase the payment proportion for primary medical institutions, realize effective connection of public health service and medical service." This means a change to the public health fund that was originally allocated directly to public primary medical institutions, instead providing unified payment for services of primary medical institutions. The key is to develop an incentive-compatible mechanism: if high-quality services attract more patients, more medical insurance payments will be obtained; the institutions or doctors who cannot obtain unified payments from medical insurance through effective services will naturally be eliminated. Under such a mechanism of more pay for more work, better pay for better work, survival of the fittest, workers have the enthusiasm to provide good medical services and public health services, and resources at the community level may be fully activated. More accurate incentive mechanisms may be realized by diversified design of medical insurance payment modes; for example, a capitation payment mechanism could motivate medical institutions and their medical workers to have sufficient enthusiasm to provide good public health services, reducing the need to obtain a maximum medical insurance payment balance.

Another advantage of a unified medical insurance payment is that, currently, public health tasks in rural areas are assumed by health center and village doctors, but the health center is responsible for evaluating village doctors and determines distribution of public health funds on this basis. In this pattern, the health center pushes the public health task down to village doctors very easily, but deducts money when evaluations identify unacceptable service provision. Thus, it's very difficult for village doctors to carry out public health work, and they lack the enthusiasm to do better work. If medical insurance departments are responsible for service payments and evaluation, this conflict of interest does not exist and we can take residents' choice as the basis of medical insurance payments, avoid the filling out of tedious evaluation forms by health center and village doctors, hand over the rights of supervision, evaluation, and choice to the people, and embody the goals of new social governance; that is, collaboration, participation, and common interest.

Another key measure is to include primary institutions run by the non-governmental sector, including clinics, into a unified payment network of medical insurance funds and public health funds. On one hand, medical insurance payments may be designed for integrated provision of medical services and public health services; on the other hand, primary medical institutions run by the nongovernmental sector participate in allocation of medical insurance funds, and they may compete with public institutions, promoting survival of the fittest, so as to improve overall efficiency of the health service system and allow residents to obtain more and better services. In addition, public primary medical institutions in rural areas hire many unofficial personnel. Most of these personnel are rural youths with medical college education; a substantial proportion of them have assistant doctor qualifications but could not become medical staff officially due to their registered permanent residence and quota restrictions. They are often responsible for filling out various reports, rather than participating in service provision directly. With the support of medical insurance payments, these talents may increase effective service provision, and improve resource utilization efficiency in underdeveloped areas through partnership practice or independent practice.

Fourth, we should increase financial investment to strengthen prevention and control capacity of local infectious disease hospitals and departments of infectious diseases in polyclinics in order to prevent further expansion of public hospitals from squeezing the survival and development space of primary medical institutions, medical institutions run by the nongovernmental sector, and new service forms, aggravating the resource allocation imbalance. We should further require implementation of the previous central document requirements, prohibit expansion of public hospitals in debt, and prevent the increase of local debt from forming a debt service burden of central finance in the future. Now that social forces have the enthusiasm to increase medical resources, it's unnecessary for government to borrow money for construction.

Fifth, considering the large surplus in individual accounts of medical insurance funds, deposited for a long time, we should grasp reform opportunities. We should turn the funds in individual accounts into unified medical insurance funds, establish unified planning for outpatients, alleviate people's payment burden, and share the payment pressure of medical insurance funds.

In 2019, income from private medical savings accounts of urban employees in China was 569.8 billion Yuan—a current surplus of 100.1 billion Yuan and a cumulative surplus of 827.7 billion Yuan. It was mentioned clearly in the Opinions concerning Deepening of the Reform of Medical Insurance System that: "We should include outpatient medical expenses in the payment scope of unified fund for basic medical insurance, reform basic private medical savings account of employees, establish and consummate outpatient mutual aid mechanism gradually." We could convert this individual account fund, that has a very large surplus, deposited for a long time, to a unified medical insurance fund in due time, and we should establish unified planning for outpatients to expand the unified medical insurance fund of employees significantly without increasing the burden of enterprises, individuals, and government so as to increase sustainability of the fund while increasing the security level notably, especially the level of outpatient coverage.

With this fund as support, we can establish unified planning of outpatient care for medical insurance of urban employees to compensate for outpatient treatment and as institutional compensation for cancellation of individual accounts. There are many problems with the operation of individual accounts, including high fund accumulation costs, interest rate of savings being lower than the growth rate of medical expenses, serious waste of funds, purchase of a large number of goods from drugstores outside the directory, lack of unified fund compensation for outpatient treatment, and heavy burden of groups with high outpatient expenditure, especially the elderly population. These influence the sense of gain people have from medical insurance. Cancellation of individual accounts and establishment of unified planning for outpatients might hurt young people that assume less medical expenses in the short term, but the elderly population with higher medical expenses benefit significantly. The latter is a high-risk group in this pandemic. Adjustment of the welfare system for this reason meets social expectations and could enhance people's sense of gain, which is the real policy intention.

The establishment of unified planning for outpatients increases security levels and improves the value-oriented strategic purchase effect of medical insurance. Guiding the diagnosis and treatment behavior of both doctors and patients may promote the development of small and medium health institutions, alleviate rushing of patients into large hospitals, boost capacity building of medical institutions at the community level, and promote the development of a hierarchical diagnosis and treatment system.

In the long run, this practice is also favorable to long-term sustainable development of medical insurance funds and increased risk tolerance of the whole society.

Improve the long-term plan for the public health service system

In the long term, this pandemic opens a window for reform of the medical and public health service system. In the long term, we should consider how to further activate human resources, integrate service systems, increase risk tolerance of public funds.

First, although medical resources in China have reached the median level of OECD countries from the perspective of beds and other hard facilities, the gap is still very large in terms of quality of medical workers and other soft capacity. The prevalence of community clinics, small and medium health institutions, and doctors is still severely insufficient, and medical resources should be increased significantly.

The key to increase provision is not to increase financial investment for further expansion of tertiary hospitals, but to solve the conflict between provision potential and medical system constraints. In fact, human resource supply is not in shortage in China. Less than 40 percent of medical and health graduates can enter the medical industry to do medical and public health work, as institutional constraints hinder human resource development. To solve the conflict, we should cancel the public institution staff identity system in the medical industry to realize free practice of doctors, eliminate human resource entry barriers and mobility barriers in the medical industry, and increase both quantity and quality of doctors on the basis of implementing ZBF (2011) No. 28 Opinions Concerning Further Deepening of the Reform of Human Resource System in Public Institutions, Personnel Management Regulations in Public Institutions, issued by the State Council in 2014, and Decision of the State Council on the Reform of Pension Insurance System for Workers in Government Organizations and Institutions in 2015.

Second, we should change the financial investment model from the fiscal investment model "giving consideration to both supply and demand" to a mainly fiscal subsidy model for the demand side. The subsidy for the demand side embodies "giving a better play to the role of government," while the supply side may establish a "competitive neutrality" principle, acknowledging the decisive role of the market in resource allocation. We should form a new pattern of social governance of collaboration, participation, and common interests in the medical services field and fully recognize the value-oriented strategic purchase function of medical insurance, letting it become a key policy brake to lead rational allocation of medical resources and construct an effective medical service and epidemic prevention and control system.

As long as direct financial subsidy for public service institutions still exists, a number of problems have to be considered; for example, establishing corresponding institutions for scientific assessment and evaluation, especially linkage with financial investment scale, structure, mechanism, etc. Management costs are very high in this respect, yet the effect of assessment and evaluation is fairly limited. Subsidy for the demand side is much simpler. For example, where only fiscal subsidy for medical insurance funds is available, only a per capita financial subsidy for residents' medical insurance needs to be considered. For medical insurance financing and corresponding financial subsidies of urban and rural residents, the State Council issues explicit instructional data at the beginning of each year; for example, the standard of financial subsidies from 2016 to 2020 was 420 Yuan, 450 Yuan, 490 Yuan, 520 Yuan, and 550 Yuan, respectively, and different districts may take this level as the bottom line for completion of tasks. It's simple and practical, popular and easy to understand: "act according to own ability, and do the best." Corresponding financial subsidies of government at all levels may be allocated in a timely way with little disagreement between departments and no criticism.

Third, we should fully mobilize social forces to participate in health governance, expand health teams at the community level, and increase health service efficiency: "not for all, but for usable." Primary medical institutions run by the nongovernmental sector, including private clinics, may survive in many districts including poverty-stricken areas without government financial support, and most of them have no medical insurance payments; this means that the payments have been accepted by residents. Data in the China Health Statistical Yearbook show that 60 percent of patients have selected institutions run by the nongovernment sector for diagnosis and treatment services at the community level. This aspect of social resources should not be neglected, but should be included in consideration of the public health system as a whole, so as to expand the medical and health service network at the community level and improve serviceability.

Therefore, we should make great effort to remove various implicit policy barriers, implement policies of the Party Central Committee and State Council encouraging social forces to run hospitals, and in particular implement the policy to cancel regional health planning of nonpublic medical institutions. Doctors may run clinics, day surgery centers, hospitals, inspection centers, and other small and medium health institutions without administrative approval; only business registration is required.

Fourth, we should take integration and sharing of information as a basis, promote service system integration and multiparty collaboration, enrich the health service network, improve serviceability, and promote industry development.

We should make reference to the experience in China's Taiwan region, take the current national unified medical insurance information system setup as an opportunity, start immediately to integrate personal health information scattered in departments and institutions, and construct electronic PHRs as a subsystem of the medical insurance information system. So as to remove the current separation of the two systems, we should eliminate the drawbacks of the very expensive yet useless health records. Since basically all people are insured at present, basic personal information and medical information of the insured has been automatically included in the medical insurance information system, and PHRs of all insured (i.e. all people based on this) have the features of low-cost, very high accuracy and practicability, and better compliance. Therefore, we could truly realize the goal of medical insurance card and PHR "record lifetime, serve lifetime, and guarantee lifetime."

Information integration also means resource sharing. We should take the medical insurance information platform as a carrier and make health information available to the residents and medical service institutions. Its greater significance is to assist the cooperation and service integration between different medical service institutions, and promote the development of the health service industry, especially the role of family doctors in the medical service system. Meanwhile, it increases communication efficiency between residents and medical and health institutions, helps residents to realize health management in a better way, and improves public service quality. In normal times, this measure may greatly ease residents' access to medical care and enhance the "sense of gain"; facing a public health emergency, health records may also serve as a basis for information management and realize effective risk identification, prevention, and control. This is also a specific reflection of improving national governance capacity.

Fifth, we should accelerate the process of citizenization of rural migrant workers, realize equal access to public services and full coverage, including for public health services, as soon as possible, eliminate any blind side in the prevention of major public health pandemic, and minimize risk.

We may draw a preliminary conclusion according to current international data. In terms of outbreak response at an early stage, the Singapore government performed in a timely and efficient way; however, due to neglecting the possible significant infection risk of foreign workers, large-scale outbreak occurred in the cluster regions of foreign workers in April 2020. This exposed the problems of the social and economic structure and the social governance system rather than the problems of the Singapore health service system. Even if the health system did everything right, rapidly and efficiently, structural issues in the society itself will also become crucial weak points in the virus attack.

The case of Singapore reminds us that in epidemic prevention and control, the epidemic prevention capacity of marginal groups determines the safety of the epidemic prevention system. The exposure probability of these groups to pandemic risk is higher: on one hand, they are often excluded from local social security systems; on the other hand, their residential and work environments are worse, and it's more difficult for them to obtain medical and health services and epidemic prevention supplies. Because these groups have been out of the visual field of mainstream society for a long time, their risks are more easily neglected. Thus, they become breakthrough points in the disease prevention and control system, allowing the virus to spread to other groups in society. This means that understanding how to improve the health status of these marginal groups and providing them with more medical and public health support, is critical to controlling the health risk of the whole society.

Mass population movements have been normalized in China. A large number of rural migrant workers also face crowded residential environments and poor medical and health conditions, lack means of personal protection, and cannot realize effective community quarantine. These are potential risk points for epidemic prevention and control.

Therefore, facing the pandemic crisis, our understanding of public health should not be "fragmented"; rather, we should regard it as an interconnected chain. In the long run, promoting the citizenization process of rural migrant workers, equal access to public services including medical and public health services and full coverage, and solving weak links in the chain are critical to improve overall risk prevention capacity of society. The medical and health service system should also adapt to the current status of large-scale and normalized population movement.

Notes

1 Remarks by Xi Jinping, General Secretary, at the 12th Meeting of the Commission for Deepening Overall Reform of the CPC Central Committee.
2 Remarks by Xi Jinping, General Secretary, at the 12th Meeting of the Commission for Deepening Overall Reform of the CPC Central Committee.
3 OECD country data is from the most recent year which is available on the OECD Stats website.
4 Source: National Health statistics Yearbooks.
5 Speech by Gao Guangming, Deputy Director General of the Grass-Roots Health Department of the National Health and Family Planning Commission at the Regular Press Conference on the Project of National Basic Public Health Service and Other Relevant Information: http://finance.sina.com.cn/roll/2017-07-10/doc-ifyhvyie0877020.shtml
6 2017 China Family Doctor Forum: www.Thepaper.cn/newsdetail_forward_1911376
7 2017 China Family Doctor Forum.
8 C. J. Wang, C. Y. Ng, and R. H. Brook, Response to COVID-19 in Taiwan: Big Data Analytics, New Technology, and Proactive Testing, *JAMA*, published online March 3, 2020.
9 Chen Hengshun, Liao Jingzhu, Hou Hongbin et al., Integration System of Health Care and Long Photo Information, *Taiwan Medicine*, 22nd issue, 2018.
10 Singapore has seen a surge in confirmed cases since April. The cumulative number of confirmed cases on April 22 had risen tenfold from the April 1 level, with more than 10,000 confirmed cases, and there were more than 43,000 confirmed cases in Singapore by the end of June. The outbreak in Singapore since April has resulted from the failure to effectively isolate infected foreign workers with mild or no symptoms, resulting in a large number of cluster infections. According to the *New York Times* (April 24, 2020, https://cn.Nytimes.com/asia-pacific/20200421/coronavirus-singapore/), "Singaporean authorities do not seem to fully recognize how contagious the virus is. According to the government, most of the new infections are mild or asymptomatic, and so far none has required intensive care, which may explain why outbreaks among migrant workers have not been detected earlier." Thus, on one hand, the government and the disease control system did not know enough about asymptomatic infected persons and ignored the protection of foreign workers. On the other hand, a large number of foreign workers lived in crowded and poor sanitary conditions, which made it impossible to conduct effective community isolation. There are deeper socioeconomic problems behind this. However, these problems do not negate the effectiveness of Singapore's community health service system. The conclusion that Singapore successfully delayed the outbreak in the initial phase of the epidemic prevention is still valid (by April, fewer than 1,000 cases were confirmed in Singapore). Of course, Singapore failed to control the outbreak in the end, indicating that the prevention and control of a major epidemic is a test of the governance system of the whole country and society, and it is far from enough to rely on an efficient medical and health service system. Relevant experience will be discussed below in "Improve the long-term plan for the public health service system."

12 Global spread of the pandemic and world economic outlook

Zhang Yuyan and Xu Xiujun

In recent years, due to the accumulation of various risks, the growth momentum of the world economy has been clearly insufficient, and sharp declines beyond market expectations occurred. Global spread of the COVID-19 pandemic became "the straw that broke the camel's back," triggering a new round of world economic recession. However, compared with the epidemic prevention and control and economic development situations of other major economies, China's economy has shown sufficient resilience and will play a more important role in the world economy.

World economic downturn beyond expectations before the epidemic outbreak

Before the outbreak of the COVID-19 pandemic, the world economy faced increasing downward pressure, and international trade and investment performance could not meet expectations. This brought hidden problems to the huge impact of the pandemic on the world economy. In this sense, the pandemic was a "blasting fuse" that accelerated the exposure of global economic risk.

Global economic growth declined beyond expectations

Before 2019, the world economy was widely expected to decline, but the scale of the slump was well ahead of market expectations. In 2019, the growth of the world economy was constantly declining. In contrast to the accelerated development of three quarters of the economies two years ago, nine tenths of the economies slowed down economic growth in 2019. According to the World Economic Outlook report issued by the International Monetary Fund (IMF) in April 2020, the global economic growth rate was 2.9 percent in 2019, a decrease of 0.7 percent compared with the previous year and a record low since 2010; it was 0.6 percent less than the value predicted by the IMF at the beginning of 2019.[1] The economic growth rate of developed economies was 1.7 percent, a decrease of 0.5 percent compared with the previous year; and the economic growth rate of emerging markets and developing countries

DOI: 10.4324/9781003184447-13

was 3.7 percent, a decrease of 0.8 percent compared with the previous year. The Tracking Indices for Global Economic Recovery—prepared jointly by the US Brookings Institution and the UK *Financial Times* to reflect global economy and actual economic activities, financial market and investor confidence in different countries—declined until October 2019 after its peak in January 2018.[2] Bloomberg's global gross domestic product (GDP) tracking index showed that from the beginning of 2018 to the third quarter of 2019, global economic growth slowed from 4.7 percent to 2.2 percent. From the perspective of major economies, in 2019, US economic growth decreased by 0.6 percent to 2.3 percent compared with the previous year, the eurozone economic growth decreased by 0.7 percent to 1.2 percent compared with the previous year, China's economic growth decreased by 0.6 percent to 6.1 percent compared with the previous year, and the growth in Latin America and the Caribbean dropped from 1.0 percent to 0.1 percent. As a special case, growth in Japan increased by 0.7 percent to 1.0 percent compared with the previous year. It's noteworthy that India's economic stall was severe: the growth rate was 4.2 percent in 2019, far lower than 6.1 percent in the previous year.

Meanwhile, international trade and investment growth was evidently sluggish. Data released by the World Trade Organization in April 2020 shows that in 2019, the growth of world trade in goods was −0.1 percent, 2.7 percent lower than the 2.6 percent predicted half a year before that.[3] Global trade growth lower than world economy growth appeared again in 2019, even though trade growth is faster than economic growth under normal conditions. According to data from Global Trade Alert, all countries launched 2,200 trade protection measures in 2018, an all-time high; only 676 of these were for promoting trade investment, 176 fewer measures than in the previous year.[4] International direct investment activities continued a downturn. According to the World Investment Report released by the United Nations Conference on Trade and Development in June 2020, inflows of global foreign direct investment (FDI) were USD 1.54 trillion in 2019, and growth was approaching merely 3 percent in case of a decline up to 12 percent in 2018. Within this, in 2019, FDI inflows of developed economies were USD 800.2 billion, a 5.1 percent increase over the preceding year; FDI inflows of developing economies were USD 699.3 billion, a decrease of about 0.2 percent compared with the previous year; and FDI inflows of transition economies were about USD 34.5 billion, a decrease of about 30.5 percent compared with the previous year.[5] Due to trade tensions and changes in investment policy, FDI inflows of South Korea in 2019 dropped to USD 10.57 billion, 13.3 percent lower than that in 2018; FDI inflows of Turkey dropped from USD 12.98 billion in 2018 to USD 8.43 billion in 2019, a drop of 35 percent. As a whole, the support of global trade and investment for global economic growth decreased. Positive data came from the trade balance field. The current account balance of three major economies—the United States, Europe, and China—did not exceed 3 percent of GDP. Overall fluctuation of exchange rate closely related to trade investment was not large. At the end of December, the euro depreciated by about 2.2 percent against the dollar compared with the previous year, RMB depreciated by 1.4 percent, and the yen appreciated by 0.8 percent.

Although the world economy slowed down in 2019 yet still increased by nearly 3 percent, and there was no recession, as predicted by some people, the most direct factor was the countermeasures taken by major economies in due time. The Federal Reserve reversed itself, decreased federal funds rate three times in a row in 2019 after raising the interest rate nine times in the past 3 years, and overnight, the call rate target decreased to a 1.5–1.75 percent range. Another sign of US monetary policy returning to easing was that the Federal Reserve stopped the unwind process and recovered debt purchase operation, purchased USD 60 billion short-term debt per month from mid-October 2019 to the second quarter of 2020. Europe moved in the same direction as the United States. The European Central Bank decreased the eurozone overnight deposit rate to −0.5 percent, maintained the eurozone prime rate as zero and left the overnight interest rate 0.25 percent unchanged, restarted European quantitative easing policy while keeping stable stock, and purchased debt of EUR 20 billion per month from November 2019. Many emerging economies and developing countries including BRICS (Brazil, Russia, India, China, and South Africa) lowered their interest rates and expanded government expenditure to different degrees. Deficit policy was one of the reasons for the ratio of gross government debt to GDP in emerging economies and middle-income economies rising from 50.8 percent to 53.8 percent in 2019. In other words, vigorous expansionary policy in the countries and growth inertia of major economies constituted the main support for world economic growth of nearly 3 percent in 2019.

Multiple factors lead to world economic downturn

As a whole, many reasons have led to world economic downturn in recent years, including short-, medium-, and long-term factors and deep institutional factors.

Short-term factors mainly originate from unilateralism and protectionism. The Trump administration observed unilateral and protectionist policies, which seriously suppressed global trade and investment and greatly influenced investor confidence. Kristalina Georgieva, Managing Director of the IMF, pointed out that cumulative economic loss caused by trade war might reach USD 700 billion, accounting for 0.7 percent of global GDP.[6] The immediate cause was insufficient global aggregate demand that comprised of investment demand and consumer demand. According to the estimate of the United Bank of Switzerland, in 2019, global consumer spending growth created a 10-year low. This was fully reflected in stable global prices with a slight decline and significant slowdown of economic growth. Data from the Federal Reserve Bank of Dallas showed that in the second and third quarters of 2019, the annualized growth rate of US nonresidential fixed investment dropped to 1.01 percent and 2.66 percent, respectively. Additionally, according to the estimate of the United Bank of Switzerland, in 2019, the growth of global consumer spending created a 10-year low; 40 percent of the global consumption slowdown came from India, and Turkey and China accounted for 25 percent each.[7] Unilateralism and protectionism hindered the international community from developing an effective resultant force to cope with global economic challenges, so negative effect of various risks expanded continuously.

Medium-term factors mainly originated from diminishing returns of monetary policy and fiscal policy. Diminishing returns of monetary policy and fiscal policy in all countries of the world, especially developed economies, is reflected in the fact that so-called Modern Monetary Theory became a focus of policy discussions. Sayuri Shirai, a former member of the Bank of Japan's Policy Board, pointed out the nature of this theory in "Modern Money Theory and Its Implementation and Challenges": the emphasis on expansionary fiscal policy reflected the disappointment with unconventional easing monetary policy performance, including lower than expected growth and inflation. The shrunk global manufacturing industry was a typical example.[8]

Long-term factors mainly originated from productivity slowdown. The population aging process is continually intensifying in the world's major economies, and the complicated influence of technological progress, especially the digital technological revolution, as well as the prioritizing of controlling and restraining economic systems and mechanisms over achieving healthy and sustainable economic development are main reasons for productivity slowdown. Productivity slowdown means profit-making and other expectations are unpromising in the long term; thus investment demand is inhibited. In addition, the growth of total factor productivity, that reflects overall efficiency of capital and labor, has also decreased gradually. According to IMF data, annual average growth of total factor productivity in developed economies in the period 2000–2007, before the international financial crisis, was 1 percent, and annual average growth dropped to 0.3 percent in the period 2011–2016 after the crisis; in the same period, growth in emerging markets and developing economies dropped from 2.8 percent before the crisis to 1.3 percent after the crisis.[9] Currently, the growth of total factor productivity is in a descending channel in both developed economies and emerging markets and developing economies.

The underlying reason for developed economies that accounted for more than a half of global GDP according to market exchange rate falling into a continued downturn period was described properly in "Why Rigged Capitalism is Damaging Liberal Democracy" by Martin Wolf, a *Financial Times* critic.[10] In the past 40 years, especially in the United States, people saw a dangerous triangle: growth of productivity slowed down, the gap between the rich and the poor grew, and financial shocks continued. This originated from rent-and-profit capitalism; that is, market and political power allowed privileged individuals and enterprises to extract huge rent value from all others. The capacity of the financial industry to create credit and funds provided a capital source for its activities, income, and profit. The explosive growth of financial activities since 1980 has not increased productivity growth, but raised the income of CEOs. Compared with 30 or 40 years ago, the concentration ratio of the US market has increased, the proportion of new enterprises entering the market has decreased, the gap in productivity and profit margin between leading enterprises and other enterprises has grown continuously, competition has been weakened, and monopoly rent has increased. Tax avoidance by big companies has been more shameful, because the companies and shareholders benefited from public goods provided by the state: safety, a legal system, infrastructure, a well-educated labor force, and a stable social and political environment. Companies also lobbied to support distorted and unfair tax loopholes and objected to necessary regulations on consolidation, anti-monopoly, financial misconduct, the environment and labor market, and rent value was also created. With western economies become more Latin-Americanized in terms of income distribution, their politics also became more Latin-Americanized. Populists became more xenophobic and promoted a rigged capitalism favorable to elites. These activities may even lead to the decline and fall of western liberal democracy itself.

Severe impact of the pandemic on the world economy

Due to long-term accumulation of various risks, the impact of the pandemic on the world economy amplified rapidly. If the pandemic continues to spread, the world economy might be sluggish for a long time.

Impact of the pandemic on the world economy

In recent years, a "three-lows three-highs" toxic combination has appeared in more and more countries; that is, low growth, low inflation, and low interest rates, and high debts, high income gaps, and high asset prices. Driven by the pandemic, various risks have continuously accumulated and been exposed, and the world economy has got stuck in recession gradually. For this, some international institutions slashed global economic growth expectations in succession. On March 23, 2020, David Malpass, President of the World Bank, said at the virtual meeting of G20 finance ministers that we should expect a major recession of the global economy. On the same day, the Institute of International Finance, headquartered in Washington, DC, issued a Global Macro Views report saying that affected by stagnation of economic activities, slump in oil prices, cumulative credit pressure, and other factors caused by the COVID-19 global pandemic, negative growth of world economy would appear in 2020 for the first time since 2009, and the economic growth rate would be −1.5 percent.[11] On April 14, the IMF released the World Economic Outlook report, stating that the worst economic consequence since the Great Depression of 1930 would appear in the world economy in 2020, and economic growth would drop to −3 percent.[12] Compared with the forecast in January 2020, this predicted value decreased by 6.3 percent. This was the most significant correction of world economy growth made by this organization in such a short time since its establishment. On June 24, the IMF published an updated World Economic Outlook and reduced the predicted world growth by 1.9 percent to −4.9 percent: economic growth of developed economies in 2020 was −8.0 percent, a decrease of 9.7 percent compared with the previous year; economic growth of emerging markets and developing economies was −3.0 percent, a decrease of 6.7 percent compared with the previous year.[13]

Rapid spread of the COVID-19 global pandemic has accelerated exposure to long-term cumulative risks in the United States and other major developed economies. Following the US subprime mortgage crisis in 2007, US economic recovery started after adjustment for one year, due to the implementation of unconventional monetary policy, and the stock market has maintained a mega bull market for up to 10 years and accumulated very thick asset bubbles. According to data in the WIND database, total market capitalization of US stock market at the end of 2019 was about USD 47.18 trillion, accounting for 220 percent of GDP, far beyond the level in 2007 prior to the international financial crisis. Besides an ultra-low interest rate environment, company buyback of shares was also an important reason for the rise of share prices. However, whether in the real economy or the financial market, the current situation is changing, and this will be expressed first in the stock market as an economic barometer in the future. On March 9, 2020, only four minutes after the market opened, the US stock market triggered a circuit breaker due to a decline of up to 7 percent; the closing price of US Dow Jones Industrial Average, the NASDAQ 100 Index and Standard & Poor's 500 Index fell by more than 7 percent. This was the second circuit breaker in the US stock market since October 27, 1997. On March 12, the US stock market triggered a circuit breaker again, creating a historic record of two in one week. The Federal Reserve released an emergency declaration to decrease the basic interest rate by 100 base points to 0–0.25 percent and launched a USD 700 billion large-scale quantitative easing plan on the day before March 16; then on March 16, the US stock market triggered a circuit breaker immediately after the market opened, and the closing price of the Dow Jones Industrial Average index fell by more than 12.9 percent, creating the highest drop in a single day since 1987. On March 18, the Dow Jones Industrial Average index triggered a circuit breaker again. Against the macro policy background, economic performance and asset prices separated from each other, and a 30 percent adjustment in the US stock market was perfectly normal. Therefore, it's not difficult to understand four circuit breakers being applied in less than 10 trading days in the US stock market, which was unique in the world stock history. The US stock market crash indicated unprecedented bubbles in the US stock market and other developed economies, and various economic risks reached unprecedented levels, so any disturbance might cause drastic shock in the market; the pandemic or other emergency events could be blasting fuses that ignite the cumulative risks. Although the US stock market rebounded thereafter, the signal released by significant fluctuations of the US stock market reflected a deep worry in the market about the future US economy.

Against this background, market forecasts of the US economy became increasingly pessimistic. On March 16, 2020, the Anderson School of Management at the University of California-Los Angeles released a report saying that the US economy was entering a recession, the predicted GDP in the second and third quarters of 2020 would decrease by 6.5 percent and 1.9 percent, respectively, and annual GDP would decrease by 4.0 percent compared with the previous year.[14] On March 21, the well-known Bridgewater Associates estimated that the COVID-19 pandemic might cause enterprise losses of USD 4 trillion in the United States, and the US economy would shrink by more than 6 percent in 2020 if powerful monetary and fiscal policy support was unavailable.[15] In June 2020, the IMF's World Economic Outlook predicted that US economic growth in 2020 would decrease by 10.3 percent to −8.0 percent compared with the previous year. Facing the upcoming economic depression, the United States could not launch effective response policy instruments. In terms of monetary policy, the lower limit of basic interest rate has been adjusted to zero, while the space of fiscal policy has also been very limited. After Trump took office, he launched large-scale tax cuts, so the fiscal deficit level increased somewhat. The debt problem was a centralized reflection of economic issues highlighted by the US government, and an important factor in pushing up US economic risk. Currently, the COVID-19 pandemic is leading to a drastic reaction by the US stock market, fully indicating US economic risk at such high levels that any disturbance might cause a drastic shock in the market. Meanwhile the COVID-19 pandemic is becoming a blasting fuse to ignite cumulative risks. Because the United States is the largest economy in the world, exposure of US economic risks will hit the US economy and will surely generate a powerful negative spillover effect on other countries, becoming an important influencing factor on the trend of the world economy in the future,.

In the medium and long run, major developed economies still face economic difficulties. Many European countries and Japan have set nominal interest rates to negative value. The United States is following them: the Federal Reserve has also adjusted the lower limit of the basic interest rate to 0 percent. Based on ultra-low interest rates and the different quantitative easing programs of central banks in different countries, some countries reluctantly held GDP growth to about 1 percent. It is noteworthy that the negative interest rate is abnormal: however, since policymakers in many countries cannot afford the political consequences of economic depression, normalization of monetary policy is merely rhetorical. So a drastic policy reaction by the US government and monetary authority to the stock market crash could only quench a thirst with poison and will continue the long-standing structural issues since the 2008 financial crisis, dragging the world economy into an era of negative interest rates. Monetary policy cannot substantially influence long-standing structural issues and will solidify the "three-lows three-highs" problems.

With the spread of the pandemic into more and more emerging markets and developing countries, the impact of the pandemic on the economy of these countries intensifies continuously. In emerging economies where the pandemic has spread quickly or the pandemic situation is serious, the short-term impact of the pandemic on economy has been revealed gradually: normal operation of tourism, air transport, hotels, catering, and other consumer services and industries related to foreign trade were hindered severely, residents' consumer spending was hit directly, and the investment willingness of enterprises decreased. In the medium and long run, stagnation of economic activities might lead to damage of industry chain, supply chain, and value chain reorganization and integrity. These impacts are expressed not only in severe loss in the real economy, but also in capital market turmoil, increase in capital flight and debt risk, etc. At the G20 Leaders' Summit, Kristalina Georgieva, also warned of the risks in emerging markets and developing countries, including the public health risk brought by the pandemic itself, sudden stagnation of world economy, capital flight, and other problems.

In other words, the pandemic hit the world economy hard, and negative growth of the world economy in 2020 was unavoidable. It will be more difficult for the international community to cope with compared to previous economic crises. The world economy might get stuck in a prolonged downturn. In March 2020, Anders Åslund, a senior researcher in the Atlantic Council of the United States, pointed out in his article Trump's Global Recession, published on Project Syndicate, that compared with the financial crisis period in 2008, the most significant difference in the current global recession lies in lack of US leadership brought by Trump in office; at the same time, there has been a rapid rise of debts in the world, and in particular the proportion of US public debt in GDP reached its highest level since World War II.[16] So it's difficult for all countries in the world to prevent and respond effectively to the global economic depression triggered by the COVID-19 pandemic.

World economy faces multiple challenges

Nowadays, the international community is increasingly "a community with a shared future" in which each has something of the other. Facing a complicated and severe global epidemic prevention and control situation and global economic challenges, no country cannot detach itself from the interconnected world; cooperation is the only correct choice for all countries to respond to global challenges and build a beautiful home for mankind. In particular, major economies in the world should strengthen unity, go forward hand in hand, assume responsibility to maintain a smooth global value chain, and recover the world economy jointly. Thankfully, G20 leaders have reached a consensus to revive confidence, maintain financial stability, and recover and realize more robust growth. Considering the world economy and the current development of the pandemic, the international community should further strengthen unity and form a combined force in the following aspects.

First, we should create drivers of economic growth. In the short run, countries should strengthen coordination in macroeconomic policies and collocate reasonable fiscal policy and monetary policy means to stimulate the economy. In this respect, at the special summit against COVID-19, G20 members decided to inject USD 5 trillion into the global economy. This released a powerful signal to the international community that the world's major economies would strengthen unity and cooperation. This is helpful to recover market confidence and boost morale for global economic recovery. This fund will provide support for the global economy hit by the pandemic and alleviate current downward pressure on the world economy to a great degree. Meanwhile, the positive effect of this measure will also lay a solid foundation for further capital investment and cooperation. In the long run, the key to economic growth lies in labor productivity growth. Currently, whether in developed economies or emerging markets and developing economies, labor productivity growth is in a descending channel. This needs the collaboration of all countries in the world in terms of technological innovation, international division of labor, human capital accumulation, and institutional mechanism reform to create sources of global economic growth jointly.

Second, we should keep the market open. In recent years, the world economy has been deeply hit by unilateralism and protectionism policies. What's more, unilateralism and protectionism have hurt confidence and determination of countries to promote an open-door policy and participate in global value chain specialization to a great degree, and more and more countries see reducing external dependency as one of the core contents of economic policy. After the pandemic outbreak, international economic and trading activities were severely disturbed, cross-border flow of important medical supplies, key agricultural products, and other commodities and services was hindered, and the global supply chain faced risk of disruption. Therefore, the international community should jointly create a free, fair, non-discriminative, transparent, predictable, and stable trade investment environment, and realize the goal of keeping the market open.

Third, we should control debt risk. With economic slowdown, major economies in the world implemented large-scale tax relief policies, and the government debt level repeatedly set new all-time highs. According to predictions by the IMF in October 2019, the proportion of gross government debt in GDP of developed economies was 103.1 percent in 2019, 32.2 percent higher than in 2007; the proportion of gross government debt in GDP of emerging markets and developing economies was 53.3 percent, 17.6 percent higher than in 2007. Among major developed economies, the proportion of gross government debt in GDP of the United States and Japan was 106.2 percent and 237.7 percent, respectively, in 2019, 41.6 percent and 62.3 percent higher than in 2007.[17] Meanwhile, private debt also increased significantly. In October 2019, the IMF released its Global Financial Stability Report, in which it studied eight major economies in the world—the United States, China, Japan, Germany, the United Kingdom, France, Italy, and Spain—and warned that, due to ultra-low interest rates, the total amount of junk bonds purchased by investors will probably reach USD 19 trillion in 2021, accounting for 40 percent of the corporate bond balance.[18] If there is any default, a "subprime mortgage crisis" for enterprises might occur. Vulnerability of shadow banking measured according to GDP aggravated in 80 percent of economies; this situation has only appeared in the most serious global financial crisis. In some emerging markets and developing countries, foreign debt pressure increased continuously. In the period 2007–2019, foreign debt dependency increased notably in 48 emerging economies. Under the impact of the pandemic, global economic growth slowed down significantly, and debt risk would be pushed up greatly by various large-scale stimulus policies.

Fourth, we should pay attention to the hazard of negative interest rate policy. At the level of policy rate, negative interest rate refers mainly to the negative interest rate on excess reserves implemented by the central bank for commercial banks. At the level of deposit/loan interest rate, it refers to the negative nominal interest rate of deposit/loan that is collected and issued by banks to depositors directly. At the level of market interest rate, negative interest rate previously referred to the gross interest paid in residual maturity of bonds being lower than the premium paid by investors to purchase bonds; for example, bonds of negative nominal yield appeared in Japan, Europe, and other countries and regions, and their scale has grown rapidly. To cope with the major impact of the pandemic on the capital market and real economy, the Federal Reserve made an urgent announcement on March 15 to adjust the lower limit of the basic interest rate to zero. It's widely believed that the Federal Reserve is not far from a negative interest rate. The appearance and spread of a negative interest rate influences the world economy in a complicated and extensive way, both directly and indirectly. Yet generally speaking, it will become a hotbed for gathering and accumulation of various risks and generate unmanageable negative effect; for example, it will squeeze the profit-making space of commercial banks, reduce enthusiasm of enterprises to increase efficiency and weaken the ability to fight against risks, disturb the basic function of market mechanisms to allocate resources, encourage speculators to borrow and invest in high-risk assets, aggravate currency mismatch risk in developing countries and emerging economies, etc. In addition, negative interest rate policy will further narrow the policy space for countries to cope with economic downturn.

Fifth, we should prevent sharpening of social conflicts. Since 2019, massive anti-government protests occurred in the United Kingdom, France, Italy, Spain, India, Iran, Iraq, Lebanon, Chile, Ecuador, Bolivia, Columbia, Guinea, and Ethiopia, among others, and escalated into riots, causing severe casualties and property losses. Frequent social riots are closely related to the continued downturn of economic growth, increased income differentiation, shrinking of the middle class, escalated ethnic and religious tensions, and prevailing populist thoughts. Intervention of external forces is also one of the main reasons for riots escalating in many countries. For deep reasons, incessant civil disturbances reflect the weak governing capacity of government in some countries, vulnerability to underemployment and employment brought by a rising proportion of the population with higher education, and awareness of public rights as a result of the popularization of information technology in new era. António Guterres, Secretary-General of the United Nations, has said that while the circumstances of the riots vary from country to country, it is clear that there is a growing lack of trust between people and political institutions and a growing threat to the social contract. These problems and trends are unlikely to change fundamentally in the short term, and under the impact of the pandemic, some new social problems and contradictions are constantly emerging. The international community is likely to enter a prolonged period of instability with far-reaching implications for the world economy.

China will play a more important role in the world economy

In the more than 70 years since the founding of the People's Republic of China, China's economy has shown great resilience and toughness in the face of various external shocks and internal challenges, and it has unleashed potential for sustained, high-speed growth. As with previous challenges to China's economy, the temporary negative impact of the COVID-19 pandemic will not change the long-term positive momentum, but rather will grant China a more important role in the world economy.

China has helped the international community to withstand the impact of the pandemic

To counter the impact of the pandemic on the world economy, China has provided necessary assistance to relevant countries in their fight against the pandemic and strengthened coordination and cooperation with other countries to jointly cope with the current threats and challenges in the world economy. China always maintains close communication with the World Health Organization, shares medical experience and epidemic prevention and control information and medical research in a timely manner with the international community, provides medical supplies and technical support for developing countries and other countries in need, takes practical action to promote cooperation of the parties in epidemic prevention and control and scientific research, and fully demonstrates the image of a responsible large country. Meanwhile, China has actively encouraged relevant parties to strengthen macroeconomic policy coordination under the frameworks of the United Nations and the G20, plays a constructive role in stabilizing markets, ensuring growth and people's livelihoods, and ensures openness, stability, and security of the global supply chain. Despite the impact of the pandemic on economic development, China has not slowed its pace of opening up to the outside world. To unblock the global industrial chain and boost world economic growth, China has also introduced a series of new measures to further improve the business environment and strengthen international trade, investment, and financial openness.

In terms of epidemic prevention and control, guided by the vision of a community with a shared future for mankind, China has actively provided necessary assistance to the international community. From the very beginning of the pandemic, China shared COVID-19 research information and the relatively mature diagnosis and treatment plan and technical route concluded with the international community, which provided important experience and technical support for relevant countries to control the pandemic. As early as February 19, 2020, WHO Director-General Tedros stated clearly at a briefing of the COVID-19 epidemic delegation that due to China's active efforts to control the epidemic disease, there was an opportunity to prevent the occurrence of a broader global crisis. At present, China's epidemic prevention and control efforts have achieved remarkable results. The number of confirmed cases has dropped significantly, and the pressure on the medical system to treat patients has been greatly relieved. With the resumption of work and production, the production capacity of medical products manufacturers has increased significantly, and the shortage of protective materials such as masks and disinfection products has been basically solved. As a country that has accumulated rich experience in fighting against the COVID-19 outbreak, China has close communication and coordination with the WHO and other international institutions and is taking positive action to help the international community to fight against the pandemic, providing aids within capacity for epidemic prevention and control and reducing impact of the pandemic in countries experiencing outbreaks, especially countries with severe outbreaks and developing countries with limited capacity to respond.

In terms of policy responses, China actively advocates for the role of the G20 and other international organizations and actively promotes new progress in international macroeconomic policy coordination and international development cooperation. As the primary platform for global economic governance, the G20 cooperation mechanism has achieved positive results in responding to the 2008 international financial crisis and promoting recovery in the post-crisis world economy. At a time when the world economy is again facing the risk of recession, the G20 will remain an important platform for macroeconomic policy coordination among countries and an important hub for policy coordination among international institutions. Compared with a decade ago, China can play a more important and constructive role in promoting global economic governance within the G20 framework, which was fully demonstrated at the Extraordinary G20 Leaders' Summit on COVID-19. In order to gather strong global forces to conquer the outbreak and to boost the morale of world economic recovery, President Xi Jinping proposed to resolutely fight a global war against the COVID-19 pandemic, carry out effective international defense against the virus spreading, support international organizations to play active roles, and strengthen international macroeconomic policy coordination at the Extraordinary G20 Leaders' Summit on COVID-19.[19] At the same time, under the impact of the pandemic, we need to fully tap into the huge momentum and potential of international cooperation under the Belt and Road Initiative. We will encourage more and more developed and developing countries to participate in the Belt and Road Initiative and promote regional and global economic integration, and we will continue to form an engine for international economic cooperation and world economic growth by expanding cooperation in third-party markets.

China will continue to lead global economic growth

As the world's second-largest economy, China's economy has maintained a high growth rate for a long time. Since the 18th National Congress of the Communist Party of China, China has actively pursued a new development philosophy focused on supply-side structural reform, deepened reform, and opening wider to the outside world, and it has created momentum for continuous high-quality economic development. In 2019, facing a complex and severe international environment and arduous tasks of reform, development, and stability, China's economy maintained steady performance on the whole, and its quality and efficiency were steadily improved, laying a solid foundation for securing a decisive victory in completing the building of a moderately prosperous society in all respects and combating poverty. According to the preliminary accounting results released by the National Bureau of Statistics on January 17, 2020, China's GDP in 2019 exceeded RMB 99 trillion, firmly ranking second in the world; the real growth rate was 6.1 percent, much higher than that of major developed economies such as the United States, Europe, and Japan.[20] China's economy has contributed about 1 percentage point to world economic growth, which shows how big a contribution China has made to world economic growth.

After the COVID-19 outbreak, China's economy has suffered a major shock. However, China's leading role in the world economy will not decline, but will be further highlighted. Benefiting from effective COVID-19 prevention and control and the policy measures to stabilize economic operation, China's economy has gradually moved in a stable and orderly direction and has shown strong resilience. Despite the increasing pressure on epidemic prevention and control in China, the situation of has continued to improve and the order of work and life has been restored at a faster pace. Under the guidance of national policies, we will coordinate epidemic prevention and control with the resumption of work and production to steer the world economy away from the impact of the pandemic. At present, we have made orderly progress in restoring and stabilizing employment, unimpeded transportation and ensured market supply, and made positive progress in the coordinated resumption of work and production in all links of the country-wide industrial chain. Benefiting from various targeted fiscal and monetary policies as well as adequate protection of masks, disinfection supplies, and other protective materials, by May 18, 2020, the average operating rate of industrial enterprises above designated size and the return rate of employees to work had reached 99.1 percent and 95.4 percent, respectively, basically returning to normal. Agricultural production has been effectively guaranteed by promoting the resumption of work and production of agricultural capital production enterprises and the opening and operation of wholesale stores of agricultural capital products such as seeds, fertilizers, and pesticides in rural areas.

In the short run, with respect to fiscal policy, China has appropriately raised its deficit ratio and increased support for the real economy. On the basis of implementing the policies of fiscal interest discount, large-scale fee reduction, and tax holdover introduced in recent years, we have also introduced special tax reduction and fee reduction policies during the epidemic control period. With respect to monetary policy, we have provided targeted credit support to industries, private companies, and micro and small businesses that have been heavily affected by the pandemic by lowering the required reserve ratio for commercial banks and deposit financial institutions. In the long run, China will increase support for innovative development, promote the upgrading of the industrial chain, make new breakthroughs in supply-side structural reform, and promote high-quality economic development. With a stable and healthy economy of China, the world economy will have the impetus to move forward. Despite the impact of the pandemic, China's economy will play a greater leading and driving role for the world economy. The Institute of International Finance predicted that China's economic growth would lead the world economy by 4.3 percent in 2020, an increase of 0.8 percent over 2019, 6.1 percent higher than the economic growth of developed economies and 1.6 percent more than that in 2019.[21] According to the IMF data, China would become the only major economy in the world to maintain positive growth in 2020, 5.9 percent ahead of the world economic growth rate, 2.7 percent higher than that in 2019 and 9.0 percent higher than the economic growth of developed economies, an increase of 4.6 percent over 2019.[22]

Looking ahead, China's economic development potential remains huge and it will remain the "locus" of the world economy. China has a huge market with a population of more than 1.4 billion. People's demand for a better life will create huge demand, and we can maintain steady economic growth by unlocking the potential of expanding domestic demand. China's industrialization, IT application, urbanization, and agricultural modernization are progressing steadily, and a new mode of economic development is taking shape at an accelerating pace, constantly promoting sustained and sound economic development. At the same time, the building of new institutions for an open economy has reached a higher level, and steady progress has been made in opening up the economy on a wider scale, in more areas, and at a deeper level. This will create new conditions for better utilization of resources in both domestic and international markets. This shows that China's economy remains a strong driving force and its leading role in the world economy will be further enhanced. China will continue to follow the principle of extensive consultation, joint contribution, and shared benefits and advocate the vision of a community with a shared future for mankind to make greater contribution to strong, sustainable, balanced, and inclusive growth of the world economy.

Notes

1 IMF, *World Economic Outlook April 2020: The Great Lockdown*, April 14, 2020: www.imf.org
2 Chris Giles, in London, 2019 Global Economy Enters Period of "Synchronised Stagnation," *Financial Times*, October 13, 2019: www.ft.com
3 World Trade Organization, Trade Set to Plunge as COVID-19 Pandemic Upends Global Economy, Press Release, April 8, 2020: www.wto.org
4 Global Trade Alert, Total Number of Implemented Interventions Since November 2008, March 28, 2020: www.globaltradealert.org
5 United Nations Conference on Trade and Development, *World Investment Report 2020: International Production beyond the Pandemic*, June 16, 2020: www.unctad.org
6 David Lawder and Andrea Shalal, US–China Tariffs Drag Global Growth to Lowest in a Decade, CNBC, October 15, 2019: www.cnbc.com/2019/10/15/reuters-america-update-1-u-s-china-tariffs-drag-global-growth-to-lowest-in-a-decade-imf.html
7 Caroline Grady, Emerging Markets Are Driving the Global Spending Slowdown, *Financial Times*, December 17, 2019.
8 Sayuri Shirai, Modern Money Theory and Its Implementation and Challenges: The Case of Japan, Voxeu, July 18, 2019: voxeu.org/article/modern-money-theory-and-its-challenges
9 IMF, *World Economic Outlook Update: A Firming Recovery*, July 24, 2017: www.imf.org
10 Martin Wolf, Why Rigged Capitalism is Damaging Liberal Democracy, *Financial Times*, September 18, 2019.
11 Robin Brooks and Jonathan Fortun, Global Macroeconomic View: Global Recession, Institute of International Finance, March 23, 2020: www.iif.com
12 IMF, *World Economic Outlook April 2020: The Great Lockdown*.
13 IMF, *World Economic Outlook Update: A Crisis Like No Other, An Uncertain Recovery*, June 2020: www.imf.org
14 David Shulman, U.S. Forecast: The Sum of All Fears, March 2020 Interim Forecast, March 12, 2020: www.anderson.ucla.edu/centers/ucla-anderson-forecast/2020-recession
15 Greg Jensen et al., The Coronavirus's $4 Trillion Hit to US Corporations, March 19, 2020: www.bridgewater.com
16 Anders Åslund, Trump's Global Recession, Project Syndicate, March 14, 2020: news.cgtn.com/news/2020-03-14/Trump-s-global-recession-OQyfnPEpMI/index.html
17 IMF, *World Economic Outlook: Global Manufacturing Downturn, Rising Trade Barriers,* October 2019: www.imf.org

18 IMF, *Global Financial Stability Report: Lower for Longer*, October 2019: www.imf. org

19 Xi Jinping: Working Together to Defeat COVID-19 in Times of Difficulty—Statement at the Extraordinary G20 Leaders' Summit, *People's Daily*, March 27, 2020, p 2.

20 National Bureau of Statistics of China, The Main Expected Targets for the Overall Stable Development of the National Economy in 2019 Are Well Achieved, January 17, 2020: www.stats.gov.cn

21 Robin Brooks and Jonathan Fortun, Global Macroeconomic View: Global Recession.

22 IMF, *World Economic Outlook Update: A Crisis Like No Other, An Uncertain Recovery*.

13 How to deal with the impact of the global economic recession

Li Xuesong, Wang Hongju, Feng Ming, Li Shuangshuang, and Zhang Binbin

Facing the deep recession of the world economy triggered by the pandemic, the world's major economies quickly adopted bailout and assistance policies. Strengthening international cooperation to fight the pandemic together and stabilizing and restoring the economy are the inevitable choices in response to the pandemic. The global crisis caused by the impact of the pandemic is essentially a crisis of people's livelihoods. It is suggested that we promptly launch and implement a bailout package to ensure security of jobs, basic living needs, operations of market entities, food and energy security, stable industrial and supply chains, and the normal functioning of primary-level governments, and firmly implement a strategy of expanding domestic demand and maintaining economic development and social stability. In extraordinary times, fiscal and monetary policies should increase countercyclical adjustments. Meanwhile, a package of supporting policies and effective reform measures must be introduced.

Response policies of the world's major economies

After the outbreak of the COVID-19 pandemic, many countries have adopted a package of policies including monetary and fiscal policies to support prevention and control of the pandemic, hoping to avoid a deep economic recession. Here, we give a brief summary of the response policies and measures of major developed economies such as the United States, Europe, and Japan.

Monetary policies

In terms of monetary policies, the response of the US Federal Reserve (the Fed) is most typical. After the spread of the COVID-19 pandemic in the United States aggravated, the Fed quickly adopted a series of policy measures to respond to it, mainly covering the following three aspects.

Cutting the policy interest rate drastically at an extremely fast pace. On March 3, 2020, the Fed temporarily announced its policy to lower the target range for the federal funds rate by 50 basis points before its next scheduled policy meeting. On March 15, the Fed once again cut the target range of

DOI: 10.4324/9781003184447-14

the federal funds rate by 100 basis points before its next scheduled policy meeting. After two consecutive interest rate cuts, the Fed's current target range for the federal funds rate has fallen to 0–0.25%, reaching the so-called "zero interest rate."

Implementing open-ended quantitative easing (QE) with ultra-conventional means. On March 15, the Fed launched a total of USD 700 billion of treasury and mortgage-backed securities asset purchase program funds, initiating a new round of QE. On March 23, the Fed upgraded its QE policy again. First, it removed the upper limit of purchase and switched to "purchase according to market conditions." In other words, limited QE was replaced by unlimited and open-ended QE. Second, the Fed expanded the scope of its asset purchases to include commercial mortgage-backed securities, exchange traded funds (ETF), and even individual corporate securities.

Restarting or newly creating a variety of credit support tools to allow more funds to flow to enterprises, residents, and financial institutions. First, we should restart the Term Asset-Backed Securities Loan Facility used during the 2008 financial crisis to promote the ultimate flow of funds to underlying assets such as student loans, auto loans, credit card loans, and small business bureau secured loans. Second, we should create two new credit support programs to provide targeted support to large employers: the Primary Market Corporate Credit Facility, which involves purchasing new bonds issued by investment-grade companies directly from the primary market; and the Secondary Market Corporate Credit Facility , which means purchasing stock investment-grade corporate bonds and related ETF products from the secondary market.

On the whole, the Fed has cut interest rates twice successively during two regular interest rate meetings in the two weeks after the pandemic in the United States, and it initiated open-ended QE with no upper limit. The Fed responded with a speed and intensity exceeding that during the 2008 subprime mortgage crisis, which is rare in its history. This is because, on one hand, it made passive adjustment after the financial market's violent turmoil since late February; on the other hand, it has fully realized that the pandemic may cause a large negative impact on the US economy and worried that the US economy will fall into a severe recession.

After the pandemic, the European Central Bank and the Central Bank of Japan adopted similar response measures. The only difference is that since the policy rates of the European Central Bank and the Central Bank of Japan were already low, there was no room for further rate cuts, so their monetary policy responses focus mainly on quantity. On one hand, the European Central Bank has increased the scale of asset purchases and proposed to implement an asset purchase program of EUR 750 billion by the end of 2020; on the other hand, it has expanded the scope of assets purchase under its QE program and reduced collateral standards for refinancing operations such as main refinancing operations, longer-term refinancing operations, and targeted longer-term refinancing operations. Meanwhile, the

European Central Bank's Banking Supervisory Committee also announced a temporary reduction in the capital regulatory requirements for banks to encourage banks to give more loans; and it required commercial banks not to issue dividends in the 2019 and 2020 fiscal years. During the COVID-19 pandemic, stocks will not be repurchased in the hope that the capital will be used to support the issuance of loans to households and businesses, as well elimination of non-performing loans.

After the spread of the pandemic, the Central Bank of Japan also launched a number of measures to ensure the stability of the financial market and encourage the issuance of loans. Specifically, it includes: increasing the size and frequency of treasury bonds purchase; providing loans to financial institutions through special capital supply operations to support the financing of the corporate sector; accelerating the pace of the Central Bank of Japan's purchase of ETFs and Japanese real estate investment trusts; and temporarily expanding the scale of targeted purchase of commercial paper and corporate bonds. In addition, Japan has also lowered its risk assessment requirements for commercial banks after the outbreak of the pandemic, allowing commercial banks to assign zero risk weight to publicly secured loans. This can also be seen as a specific way of coordinating fiscal policy and monetary and financial policy.

In short, after the outbreak of the COVID-19 pandemic, major economies such as the United States, Europe, and Japan have all rapidly implemented large-scale monetary policy operations. First, in terms of price, the Fed quickly cut the interest rates to zero and guided various market interest rates downward, thereby reducing the financing costs of the real economy. Second, in terms of quantity, the central banks of the United States, Europe, and Japan have increased the amount of assets purchase under their QE programs and meanwhile expanded the scope of assets purchases to inject ample liquidity into the market and avoid liquidity tightening. Third, they announced a phased reduction in the assessment requirements for banks and other financial institutions, encouraged financial institutions to give more loans to enterprises and residents, and allowed enterprises and residents to postpone the repayment of principal and interest.

Fiscal policies

If the monetary policies adopted by the major economies such as the United States, Europe, and Japan after the outbreak of the COVID-19 pandemic are similar to those after the 2008 global financial crisis, then vigorous fiscal policies will be a prominent feature of the major economies' response strategies. The governments of the United States, Europe, Japan, and other countries have all launched large-scale fiscal expenditure plans.

The US government adopted the Coronavirus Aid, Relief, and Economic Security Act, the Payroll Protection Program and Medical Consolidation Act, the Coronavirus Preparedness and Response Supplemental Appropriations

Act, and the Families First Coronavirus Response Act. In total, a fiscal policy package with a total value of approximately USD 2.4 trillion, 11.5% of the US gross domestic product (GDP) has been launched, covering USD 250 billion in tax refunds for individuals; USD 250 billion of unemployment benefits; USD 24 billion of food security programs for the most vulnerable groups; USD 510 billion of loans and guarantees to prevent corporate bankruptcy and support the Fed's programs; USD 359 billion in Small Business Administration loans and guarantee programs to help small businesses retain jobs; USD 100 billion of investments in hospitals; USD 50 billion of transfer payments to state and local governments; and about USD 49.9 billion of international relief funds.

At the European Union (EU) Finance Ministers' Meeting, it was agreed that member states can flexibly control their fiscal budgets in response to the impact of the pandemic and support the economy. They can temporarily disobey the EU's fiscal discipline requirements, and the fiscal deficits of member states are allowed to account for the traditional warning line of over 3% of GDP. As of April 9, 2020, the EU and its member states have proposed a fiscal policy package totaling approximately EUR 540 billion, equivalent to approximately 4% of the total GDP of the 27 EU countries. Specifically: (1) the European Stability Mechanism is allowed to provide the member states of the eurozone with funds not exceeding 2% of GDP (a total amount of EUR 240 billion) in 2019 for health-related expenditures; (2) EUR 25 billion of government guarantees will be provided to the European Investment Bank to provide capital support of up to EUR 200 billion to enterprises (especially small and medium-sized enterprises); (3) SURE, a temporary loan instrument of EUR 100 billion, will be set up to ensure that workers receive an income and businesses keep their staff. It is guaranteed by EU member states. On May 8, the European Commission further strengthened its support for the economies and debts of member states in the form of supplementary documents, and it extended the validity of the interim policy framework to the end of 2020 or June 2021.

At the EU level, the European Commission has proposed a fiscal policy plan of approximately EUR 37 billion (0.3% of the GDP of the 27 EU countries in 2019). Specifically, the Coronavirus Response Investment Plan will be established to support public investment in hospitals, small and medium-sized enterprises, and the job market; the public health crisis will be included in the scope of support of the EU Solidarity Fund, and a ceiling of EUR 800 million will be provided to member states severely affected by the pandemic in 2020; EUR 1 billion will be set aside in the EU budget to provide guarantees for the European Investment Fund, thereby incentivizing banks to provide financing for small and medium-sized enterprises; and deferred debt repayment will be allowed.

In addition to EU-level response measures, European countries have also launched more vigorous fiscal policy plans at the national level. The German federal government has proposed a supplementary budget worth

EUR 156 billion, equivalent to 4.9% of Germany's GDP. The French government announced a fiscal plan of EUR 100 billion, exceeding 4% of France's GDP, to deal with the pandemic, including liquidity support. The Italian government proposed an emergency fiscal plan totaling EUR 25 billion, equivalent to 1.4% of Italy's GDP.

The Japanese government has launched a fiscal policy package totaling JPY 117.1 trillion, roughly equivalent to 21.1% of Japan's GDP. The specific measures mainly include three aspects: cash distribution to households and enterprises affected by the pandemic, delay in tax and social security payments, and preferential loans. These measures aim to realize policy intents in four areas: support coronavirus prevention and control, and expand diagnosis and treatment capabilities; protect workers and enterprises; promote the recovery of economic activities after the pandemic; and enhance the flexibility of Japan's economic structure.

In short, after the outbreak of the COVID-19 pandemic, major economies such as the United States, Europe, and Japan have all launched large-scale fiscal policy plans. On one hand, these plans aim to enhance coronavirus detection and patient treatment capabilities, and support prevention and control of the pandemic; on the other hand, they will rescue and bail out residents and companies affected by the pandemic so as to preserve employment opportunities and maintain the basic operation of the economy.

Strengthening international cooperation to deal with the global economic recession

The COVID-19 pandemic has become the most serious global public security crisis in this century. It brings a new major change factor in the "great change unseen in a century," which will plunge the global economy into a downturn second only to the Great Depression. However, unlike the Great Depression, in which the economic downturn was related to overcapacity, this economic downturn stems from the unprecedented Great Lockdown in various countries; that is, economic downturn is an inevitable result of responding to the pandemic. Effective control of the pandemic is an important prerequisite for lifting the lockdowns and recovering the economy.

In the era of globalization, before effective therapeutic drugs and vaccines are developed and widely promoted and applied, as long as the pandemic cannot be controlled on a global scale, no country will be able to be absolutely safe. In this scenario, it is impossible to completely lift the lockdown measures, and the impact of lockdown on the economy cannot be eliminated. In particular, developing countries with relatively weak medical and health conditions are facing special difficulties in responding to the pandemic. This means that strengthening international cooperation to fight the pandemic and stabilizing and restoring the economy is the inevitable choice to deal with this pandemic.

International cooperation and special difficulties

International cooperation

At present, facing the negative impact of the COVID-19 pandemic on the global economy, groups of countries, international organizations, allied countries, and political parties of various countries have taken collective actions by issuing joint statements or jointly implementing bailout measures to overcome the difficulties.

The G20 was the first organization to react, and it advocated cooperation to fight against the pandemic and stabilize the economy. As early as February 23, 2020, at the first meeting in 2020 of central bank governors and finance ministers of the G20 nations, the ministers said in a joint statement: "We will enhance global risk monitoring, including of the recent outbreak of COVID-19. We stand ready to take further action to address these risks." Later, the G20 followed up the evolution of the epidemic in a timely manner, recognized the importance of taking joint actions to stabilize the economy, and formulated a joint action plan in a relatively short time.

First, on March 6, 2020, the central bank governors and finance ministers of the G20 nations issued a joint statement specifically on COVID-19, stating:

> We are closely monitoring the evolution of COVID-19 including its impact on markets and economic conditions. We welcome the measures and plans put forward by countries to support economic activity. We are ready to take further actions, including fiscal and monetary measures, as appropriate, to aid in the response to the virus, support the economy during this phase and maintain the resilience of the financial system.[1]

Then the G20 coordinators issued the Statement of the G20 Coordinators on COVID-19 on March 12, emphasizing that "this pandemic urgently requires an active response from the international community."[2]

The more important action occurred in late March. Suggested by G20 member South Korea and Spain as a permanent guest invitee, the G20 coordinated in a timely manner and held a special leaders' video summit on March 26, making a pledge "to inject over $5 trillion into the global economy to counteract the social, economic and financial impacts of the pandemic" and "to realize the goal of a free, fair, inclusive, non-discriminatory, transparent, predictable, and stable trade and investment environment, and to keep our markets open." The summit required the finance ministers to formulate a joint action plan as soon as possible.

On April 15, the G20 held a video conference of finance ministers and central bank governors to discuss the global economic situation under COVID-19 and implement three important results of the Extraordinary G20 Leaders' Summit.[3] First, it approved the G20 Action Plan-Supporting the Global Economy through COVID-19, which clarifies the guiding principles and next specific actions to fight the pandemic. Second, it adopted the Debt Service Suspension Initiative for the poorest countries to cope with the risk of debt vulnerability of low-income countries caused by the pandemic. Third, it urgently mobilized the resources of international organizations such as the World Bank and the International Monetary Fund (IMF) to support developing members in coping with challenges.[4]

The International Financial Institution and the G7 Group took action at almost the same time in early March to draft measures to stabilize the economy. On March 2, the President of the IMF and the President of the World Bank Group issued a joint statement expressing their readiness to help member countries deal with the life, health, and economic challenges brought about by COVID-19.[5] The next day, the World Bank Group announced it would provide USD 12 billion of financial support to help countries respond to the COVID-19 pandemic.[6] The IMF also announced on its website that the organization would support countries to respond the impact of COVID-19 on the economy through emergency financing, expansion of existing loan projects, subsidies for debt relief, and arrangements for new financing.[7]

On March 3, G7 central bank governors and finance ministers held a conference call and issued a joint statement, stating that they would use "all appropriate policy tools to achieve strong, sustainable growth and safeguard against downside risks from the fast-spreading coronavirus." On March 16, G7 leaders held a video conference and also issued a joint statement stating that "we are mobilizing the full range of instruments, including monetary and fiscal measures, as well as targeted actions, to support immediately and as much as necessary the workers, companies and sectors most affected," and they requested that central bank governors and finance ministers coordinate efforts to formulate and implement measures to stabilize and promote economic growth.[8]

Meanwhile, in order to cope with the pressure of the shortage of US dollars in the international financial market under the impact of COVID-19, the United States, based on the experience of the 2008 financial crisis, introduced US dollar swap arrangements to reduce the stress on US dollar financing in the international market. On March 19, the Fed announced a major expansion of the swap lines to the central banks of nine other countries, including providing US dollar liquidity in amounts up to USD 60 billion each for the central banks of Australia, Brazil, South Korea, Mexico, Singapore, and Sweden, and USD 30 billion each for the central banks of Denmark, Norway, and New Zealand. These US dollar liquidity arrangements will be in place for at least six months. The Fed stated that these loans, like the loans already established between the Fed and other central banks, were intended to help alleviate the pressure on the global US dollar financing market, thereby reducing the impact on domestic and foreign loan supply to households and enterprises.

As the pandemic was spreading, a wider range of cooperation initiatives were launched globally in April. On April 2, the Communist Party of China and more than 240 important political parties and international organizations in more than 110 countries issued a joint appeal, stating:

> We encourage all countries, while devoting efforts to epidemic control, to adopt an integrated approach to ensure economic and social development, take targeted measures to protect vulnerable groups and the SMEs, and honour their commitment to people's living standards and social progress. We call on all countries to step up the international coordination of macroeconomic policies to maintain stability of global financial market as well as that of industrial and supply chains, and to reduce or exempt tariffs for trade facilitation so as to prevent world economic recession. Countries are also encouraged to maintain an appropriate level of international exchanges, in particular to facilitate the cross-border transportation of urgently needed medical equipment and protective materials for the fight against COVID-19.[9]

Shortly after that, on April 3, the Group of 77 and China issued a joint statement

> calling on the international community to take coordinated and effective measures to maintain the stability of the global financial market and supply chain, including reducing tariffs and eliminating trade barriers, especially for pharmaceuticals and health care products, to promote unimpeded trade and promote global economic recovery.

The Group of 77 and China "called upon the international community to adopt urgent and effective measures to eliminate the use of unilateral coercive economic measures against developing countries."[10]

Special difficulties in international cooperation

Faced with the dual impact of COVID-19 and economic recession, the international community needs more than ever to unite to overcome the difficulties. However, we are facing unprecedented special difficulties in international cooperation.

The subjective dilemma. In recent years, trade protectionism is rising in some countries, and competition among major countries is increasingly fierce. The current international economic and trade order is facing the risk of disintegration. In this context, the willingness of major powers to cooperate internationally has declined. In the face of COVID-19, political prejudice has repeatedly appeared. To shirk responsibility instead of actively cooperating to fight COVID-19 has become a diplomatic priority of some countries. As a result, the world is faced with a situation in international cooperation quite different from that of the 2008 financial crisis.

The objective dilemma. On one hand, there are difficulties in cooperation to control COVID-19. Due to the shortage of anti-COVID-19 supplies, countries have fallen into a battle for medical supplies. On the other hand, there is a contradiction between controlling COVID-19 and stabilizing the economy. While controlling COVID-19, many countries objectively need to adopt strict border lockdown measures, which will inevitably lead to restrictions on international trade, investment, and movement of people. However, to stabilize the economy, countries need to adopt open foreign policies as much as possible and lift lockdowns.

Further strengthening international cooperation to cope with the global economic recession

Uniting and cooperating to fight the global pandemic

The prerequisite for economic recovery is that COVID-19 is effectively controlled, while the essential requirement for effectively controlling the COVID-19 is international solidarity and cooperation. Joshua Lederberg, winner of the Nobel Prize in Medicine in 1958, predicted that "The single biggest threat to man's continued dominance on the planet is the virus." At present, facing the coronavirus, a common enemy of mankind, as General Secretary Xi Jinping put it, "Only by cooperating and responding together can the international community overcome this pandemic."[11]

First of all, we should actively promote multilateral cooperation and strive to secure an early victory in the global battle against the pandemic. We should abandon political prejudice as soon as possible and fight the pandemic together by upholding the vision of a global community of shared future. We should promote international scientific and technological cooperation, jointly strengthen information exchanges in areas such as epidemic surveillance, disease diagnosis, and vaccine research and development, and work together in scientific and technological research to achieve breakthrough results as soon as possible. In addition, in the development and use of vaccines, we should adhere to the notion of putting human life first rather than putting profit first to ensure that the use of vaccines will benefit the greatest share of the population after vaccines are successfully developed. We should actively fill the funding gap of the World Health Organization (WHO). Faced with the situation where the United States is about to be cut off its funding to the WHO , other members of the WHO should actively take joint actions to fill the funding gap in a timely manner to ensure its normal operation.

Second, regional cooperation mechanisms should be actively applied to promote joint regional prevention and control to achieve positive results. President Xi Jinping advocated at the ExtraordinaryG20 Leaders' Summit on COVID-19 that "Discussions are also needed regarding the establishment of regional emergency liaison mechanisms to enable quicker response to public health emergencies." To fight COVID-19, regional cooperation is essential. Compared to global cooperation, countries in the same region have similar cultures and face relatively fewer obstacles in cooperation in fighting the pandemic. Presently, China and South Korea have established a joint epidemic prevention and control cooperation mechanism led by the two foreign ministries and run by multiple departments such as health and civil aviation; this has played a positive role in strengthening communication and coordination of epidemic prevention and control between the two sides. For China, regional cooperation can be extended to East Asia. Specifically, we can consider promoting the ASEAN (Association of Southeast Asian Nations)-China-Japan-Korea (10 + 3) platform to establish a regional joint prevention and control cooperation mechanism for East Asia, and provide fund support for fighting COVID-19 in the region through financial institutions such as the Asian Development Bank and the Asian Infrastructure Investment Bank.

Third, we should explore new models of bilateral cooperation and point-to-point assistance to fight COVID-19. Although Europe and the United States are the global epicenters of the pandemic, for the world, the worst situation would be that developing countries and least developed countries with relatively backward medical and health conditions have become new epicenters. Therefore, it is necessary to make preparations in advance. In addition to actively supporting these countries through multilateral and regional cooperation, we can also encourage developed countries or developing countries that have effectively controlled the COVID-19 to provide pairing assistance to developing countries and least developed countries with severe epidemic situations based on the model of assistance in Hubei. Assistance methods include sharing anti-COVID-19 experience and providing medical teams, anti-COVID-19 supplies, and financial support. Most importantly, we should ensure that citizens of these countries can get therapy drugs and vaccines at affordable prices in the future.

Coordinating and responding to the global economic recession

Stabilizing the economy is an essential part of the endeavors to fight the pandemic. As the pandemic subsides and the "major lockdowns" end, promoting economic recovery is the top priority of all countries. Global coordinated action is the first policy choice for improving the effectiveness of stabilizing and restoring the economy.

First of all, just as the G20 worked together to pull the global economy out of the 2008 financial crisis, stabilizing and recovering the global economy while fighting the pandemic requires strong multilateral cooperation. Multilateral cooperation needs to focus on the following aspects. First, reduce trade and non-trade barriers that impede cross-border trade and global supply chains, and repair international trade and global value chains as soon as possible. In view of the fact that some countries tended to adopt trade protectionism during economic downturns, the G20 needs to exert its role in coordinating global trade policies so as to reach cooperation agreements on reducing taxes and non-tariff barriers. Second, stabilize the global financial market and reduce substantial capital flows through coordination of monetary and financial policies. Third, provide more multilateral assistance to countries with financial difficulties, including providing preferential financing, grants, and debt relief.

Second, we should actively bring into play the economic and financial safety net function of regional cooperation mechanisms. As far as China is concerned, we can consider launching the Chiang Mai Initiative Multilateralization/the ASEAN + 3 Macroeconomic Research Office mechanism with ASEAN, China, Japan, and South Korea (10 + 3) to actively play its financial assistance function. Meanwhile, we should actively acknowledge the role of regional cooperation mechanisms such as the Belt and Road Initiative, the Shanghai Cooperation Organization, the BRICS (Brazil, Russia, India, China, and South Africa) members, the African Union, the League of Arab States, Central and Eastern Europe, and the Community of Latin American and Caribbean States. As far as the EU countries are concerned, appropriate assistance may be provided to members in financial difficulties and part of their debts may be reduced or exempted, especially for members of southern European countries that have been severely hit by the pandemic and whose financial situation is not very optimistic.

Third, we must explore new possibilities for bilateral cooperation and put aside differences to reverse the situation. On one hand, as the largest developing and developed countries—China and the United States, respectively—should temporarily put aside conflicts and continue to play the leading role in international cooperation to jointly cope with the crisis. On the other hand, in the face of turmoil in the international financial markets, various countries can consider stabilizing exchange rates through currency swap agreements to ensure liquidity in their financial markets based on actual needs.

Bailout and assistance policies

The global crisis caused by the impact of the pandemic is essentially a crisis of people's livelihoods. The impact of the pandemic disrupted the normal economic cycle and caused great difficulties, especially for micro, small, and medium enterprises and low-income groups. The pandemic is spreading around the world, and all countries have adopted active prevention and control measures. Restricted by key technical factors such as detection technology, therapeutic drugs, and vaccine research and development, the scope and timing of the spread of the pandemic at home and abroad are extremely uncertain. We should be keenly aware that epidemic prevention and control is an arduous and long-term task, fully promote the resumption of work and production in normalized epidemic prevention and control, and restore normal economic and social order. We should seize strategic opportunities, keep worst-case scenarios in mind, and turn crises into opportunities. It is suggested that we promptly launch and implement a bailout package to ensure security in jobs, basic living needs, operations of market entities, food and energy security, stable industrial and supply chains, and the normal functioning of primary-level governments, firmly implement the strategy of expanding domestic demand, and maintain economic development and social stability.

When formulating bailout and assistance policies, we should fully estimate the uncertain impact of the global economic recession on our country, and take targeted and powerful measures to expand domestic demand, effectively expand public investment, promote work relief, and vigorously promote industrial upgrading and sustained economic recovery.

To take targeted and powerful measures to expand domestic effective demand, we must strictly distinguish the impact of the pandemic from structural, institutional, and cyclical contradictions and problems, and distinguish the anti-COVID-19 goals and short-term countercyclical macro-control goals from medium- and long-term supply-side structural reform goals. we should pay attention to balancing the relationship between securing stable growth and preventing risks and take into account both current and long-term interests to minimize "aftereffects."

Timely launch and implementation of a package of bailout and assistance policies

Facing the impact of the pandemic, we must attach great importance to the issue regarding the survival of micro, small, and medium enterprises from the strategic perspective of maintaining national economic security and social stability. From the perspective of epidemic economics, before the pandemic is completely controlled, the limited bailout resources should be prioritized to people's livelihoods, supporting micro, small, and medium enterprises and residents that are facing income and cash flow rupture and strengthening the development of businesses related to epidemic prevention, control, and treatment. The bailout policies should maximize and efficiently send funds to micro, small, and medium enterprises and residents most in need. The government's package of bailout and assistance policies should give full play to the decisive role of the market in allocating resources and try to avoid structural distortions in the medium and long term.

Given that there is still great uncertainty in the evolution trend of the global pandemic and that may take a longer time for the economy to return to a normal state, the bailout package can be prepared for 2 years (2020–2021) and then flexibly adjusted when the situation changes. Specifically, the bailout policy package should include the following six aspects.

Bailing out micro, small, and medium enterprises temporarily in difficulties with a view to ensuring stability in employment

Micro, small, and medium enterprises that are temporarily in difficulties can file a bailout application to the banks. Bailout will be prioritized for enterprises that have not laid off employees and which provided data on corporate income tax and value-added tax, and bank account income and expenditure records in 2019, and enterprises with good tax records in the past. This part of bailout loan interest is borne by the central and local governments, and the specific ratio can be determined in accordance with the tax sharing ratio.

Bailing out low- and middle-income groups to expand consumption

Based on the actual situation of the pandemic evolution, governments should strike a balance between medium- and long-term interests, further increase the deficit rate in 2020, or issue special treasury bonds to guarantee people's subsistence and expand effective domestic demand. For the 600 million people with monthly household income per capita less than 1,000 yuan, given that some of them have insufficient savings deposits to withstand the impact of the second outbreak of the pandemic and another suspension of production/operations, the central and local governments together with the authorities of finance, tax, and social security should strengthen real-time monitoring. On one hand, central and local governments should continue to implement bailout policies such as suspending repayment of bank loans and reducing or exempting their housing rents; on the other hand, central and local governments should step up efforts in poverty alleviation. The central government may issue temporary living allowances through transfer payments based on local conditions, while local governments may appropriately increase the distribution of cash to go through the hard times together.

Increasing transfer payments to ensure basic operations

There are relatively acute contradictions between fiscal revenues and expenditures in areas severely hit by the pandemic and poverty-stricken areas, and these areas are facing difficulties in ensuring basic operations. This is mainly because there are not many sources of fiscal revenue in these areas, and some areas have heavy historical burdens. The impact of the pandemic has blocked their economic cycle to a certain extent, causing rupture of reduction of part of their fiscal revenues, so they are unable to meet rigid fiscal expenditures. To ensure basic operations, we should improve the national county-level fiscal treasury monitoring mechanism, strengthen the monitoring and supervision of the management of county-level treasury funds, identify risks in time, and resolve difficulties as soon as possible. We must also identify the "gap" in basic financial resources in areas with difficulties. The central government and provincial governments should determine the proportion of transfer payments based on the causes of shortage of funds in areas with difficulties and different situations, such as the impact of the pandemic or the causes of poverty, and give priority to ensuring pure public expenditures. In addition, according to changes in the population and economic development at the basic level, we should scientifically optimize the long-term mechanism of basic-level governance, optimize basic-level operations, reduce stress and endow people with power, make social resources and people's livelihood services more accessible, and delegate management authority to the basic level to guarantee that more manpower and material and financial resources are allocated to the basic level. Finally, we should speed up the reform of the budget performance management system, extend performance management to the basic-level units, and cover all funds to ensure that every yuan is paid for what it is worth.

Lifting restrictions on household registration to promote urbanization, metropolitan development, and urban–rural integration

We should break through the blockades of vested interests, completely lift restrictions on new household registration in cities with a population of less than 10 million, raise the level of equalization of basic public services, release the consumption and investment potential that can be stimulated by settlement of migrants and farmers in cities, and release the huge potential of urbanization and metropolitan development and inject vitality into China's economic development and domestic demand.

Implementing flexible real estate policies to meet the rigid and improvement needs of residents

We should uphold that "housing is for living in, not for speculation," truly implement "one policy for one city," and launch a nationwide population–land linkage policy. We should relax restrictions on local real estate sale and purchase based on factors such as real estate prices, housing vacancy rates, inventory levels, per capita housing area, and migrant population to meet residents' rigid demand and demand for more and better housing, attach importance to properly solving the financing difficulties of developers, and give local governments greater decision-making power. In the past 5 years, there has been a net influx of people into cities, and an appropriate amount of policy-based public rental housing should be built according to the influx of people. Public rental housing should be built at reasonably selected sites and integrated with the industrial layout to prevent policy-oriented interest arbitrage.

Improving the consumer environment to release potential consumer demand

We should improve the development environment of the metropolitan area, solve the difficulties in urban parking and traffic congestion, and lift restrictions on car purchases. We should support the development of the logistics industry, reduce logistics costs, improve cold chain logistics, and expand online and offline consumption. We should plan and guide healthy consumption, improve the medical and healthcare and disease prevention system, and increase investments in the construction of urban public sports facilities.

Increasing investment in old and new-type infrastructure to
accurately fuel future development

We should appropriately launch more special debt projects in the metropolitan areas, reduce the proportion of capital, increase the intensity of land remediation, promote the construction of public projects such as rail transit and underground pipeline networks in metropolitan areas, improve investment efficiency, and create work relief jobs. We should launch national public hospital renovation, expansion, and upgrading projects. From the perspective of transformation and upgrading, we should encourage enterprises to invest in new types of infrastructure, provide discount support for relevant investment loans of enterprises, promote the construction of new technologies such as 5G and related new-type infrastructure, encourage the consumption of 5G terminal products, and accelerate the formation of a 5G industry chain.

Fiscal and monetary policies in extraordinary periods need to strengthen countercyclical adjustments

In the face of the once-in-a-century global pandemic and the global livelihood crisis, in order to support the implementation of the above-mentioned bailout and assistance package, fiscal and monetary policies must set clear anti-crisis targets and strengthen countercyclical adjustments and policy implementation during extraordinary periods.

Increasing the deficit rate and the scale of special bond issuance,
and issuing special treasury bonds

According to the government work report, this year's deficit rate will be set at more than 3.6%. The three measures of raising the fiscal deficit ratio, issuing special Treasury bonds to counter the impact of COVID-19, and increasing local government special bonds can form a new expansion scale of 3.6 trillion yuan, bringing the total scale to 8.51 trillion yuan. After the pandemic outbreak, we should further speed up the implementation of fiscal policies. Local governments should speed up amendment of local budgets so that policies that directly reach the grassroots level and directly benefit enterprises and the people run ahead of the market entities that get into difficulties, increase the speed and intensity of the accurate implementation of bailout policies, give top priority to helping micro, small, and medium enterprises and low- and moderate-income citizens overcome difficulties, vigorously support tax and fee reduction and rent and interest reduction, and expand consumption and investment. In view of the shortage of investment project reserves in some regions, the central government should carry out top-level design and launch more bundled investment projects in the public sector across the country. For the newly unemployed group, we should ensure that subsistence allowances cover all families in difficulty while ensuring the current standards and speed up exploration of measures to provide living allowances and price subsidies for uninsured unemployed persons. At present, about 205 million people are covered by unemployment insurance in China, accounting for only 26.5% of all employed persons and about 46.5% of the total urban labor force. Unemployment insurance coverage is not high, so it is urgent to provide special livelihood support for uninsured unemployed persons.

Maintaining a prudent monetary policy in a more flexible and appropriate way to ensure reasonable and sufficient liquidity

In the second half of this year, we should ensure the appropriate growth of monetary credit and social financing and reduce the cost of social financing. However, we should prevent empty operation of funds for arbitrage, strictly prevent provision of funds to zombie enterprises, and prevent aftereffects of loan assistance. We should employ tools such as targeted re-lending and rediscount to increase support to key areas, key industries, and key enterprises to counter the pandemic. We should markedly increase medium- and long-term loans to manufacturers, increase the amount of financing in the growth enterprise market, and accelerate the return of Chinese companies listed on the US stock exchanges to Hong Kong or the Shanghai and Shenzhen stock exchanges. We should encourage banks to issue perpetual bonds to replenish capital and enhance their lending capabilities, increase the write-off of bad debts of financial institutions, and dispose non-performing assets to resolve potential risks in the financial system.

Introducing a package of supporting policies and effective reform measures

Paying close attention to the short-term impact and mid- to long-term impact of the pandemic on the global industrial chain and supply chain, and speeding up improvement of the weak links in supply chains

First, based on the fact that there is a close tie between the supply chains of China and many other countries, such as the United States, Germany, Japan, and South Korea, we should pay close attention to the evolution of COVID-19 overseas and do what we can to help other countries and regions to prevent and control the virus.

Second, we should accelerate the process of regional integration of China, Japan, and South Korea, and strengthen the integration and coordination of the supply chain and industrial chain of East Asia.

Third, we should investigate and get a clear picture of the supply guarantee for key imported products, such as machinery and equipment, automobile and ship manufacturing, power generation equipment, aerospace, precision instruments, medical equipment, pharmaceuticals, and chemicals, during the pandemic period, and make sure that we have alternates and spares in case the supply chains are disrupted.

Fourth, we should step up efforts to build a system for global supply chain risk early warning, improve supply chain flexibility in traditional industries and emerging industries of strategic importance through independent innovation and key suppliers' self-supply, and make plans for initiating the alternates of supply chains.

Fifth, from the medium and long-term perspective, we should maintain and consolidate the fundamentals of the manufacturing industry in China, improve the weak links in innovation capabilities, the *neck*-sticking links in supply chains, and the weak links in corporate cross-cultural management capabilities and international collaboration capabilities, and treat enterprises of different ownership equally to prevent enterprises from moving out to other countries too quickly.

Sixth, we should improve and strengthen the transnational exchange mechanism for high-end talents in aircraft manufacturing and other industries.

Striving to realize the goals of poverty alleviation and ensuring stability in employment and basic living needs

First, we should take extraordinary measures to effectively solve the problem of poverty in key groups such as the final "0.6%" population and the severely impoverished areas such as the "three regions and three prefectures." In the short term, strong government leadership is still needed.

Second, we should attach great importance to the issue that the population that have just gotten out of poverty and low-income groups above the poverty line may return to poverty due to their weak ability to resist risks, focusing on the population above the margin line, strengthening market-based poverty alleviation channels, and consolidating the achievements in poverty alleviation.

Third, we should optimize the working mechanism at the final stage. For the disadvantaged groups who are really unable to get out of poverty through developmental means, it is necessary to promptly realize the function of social policies in poverty alleviation by securing basic needs.

Fourth, we should encourage rural migrant workers who have returned seasonally and who have difficulty returning to work in the short term to make overall arrangements for employment expectations throughout the year, and we should participate in the construction of rural revitalization to reduce income losses and pressure on living expenses.

Fifth, we should optimize epidemic prevention and control measures and accelerate the full resumption of work and business operation in the life service industry, and promote the rapid recovery of micro, small, and medium service enterprises and individual industrial and commercial households to recoup employment-related losses through measures such as expanding consumption. We should optimize the urban management mode, guide vendors without fixed locations to resume businesses in an orderly manner, and support flexible employment.

Sixth, we should continue to implement targeted assistance measures for enterprises in difficulties, such as phased social insurance premiums relief and exemption, extension of discount loan periods, and rent reduction and exemption. We should continue to improve employment service guarantees for workers, simplify the application procedures for unemployment subsidies, expand the scope of unemployment insurance payments, and strengthen employment assistance and entrepreneurship support for people in need. Focusing on groups with employment difficulties, we should create new public welfare posts for guaranteeing people's livelihoods in areas such as urban management, public security joint defense, and ecological protection, and realize the labor reserve system and the "employer of last resort" function of the government.

In addition, the shrinking period of employment opportunities is also a window in which there will be low-cost human capital investment opportunities. We should increase the enrollment of junior college students and students in master's degree programs, encourage jobseekers to participate in more training and education courses, and increase social human capital reserves while delaying employment. It is also necessary to prevent secondary problems, such as shrinkage of employment opportunities and increase in the unemployed population, triggering social stability.

Deepening opening up and cooperation, and ensuring stability in foreign trade and foreign investment

First, we should actively urge export enterprises to resume work and production when the pandemic has been basically controlled domestically, and promote the export of medical supplies such as protective clothing, ventilators, and masks while meeting domestic demands, to help other countries and regions to prevent and control the pandemic.

Second, we should further implement the Foreign Investment Law, improve the business environment, and prevent rapid industrial transfer and relocation of enterprises to other countries and regions due to the pandemic. On the premise of strictly implementing COVID-19 control measures, we should ensure the efficiency of customs operations and the level of trade facilitation. The 2020 version of the negative list for foreign investment market access should be issued to further relax market access and encourage foreign investment in areas such as emerging industries, high-tech, energy conservation, and environmental protection.

Third, we should continue to cut tariffs, especially promoting temporary tax cuts on medical supplies together with other countries.

Fourth, we should continue to deepen opening up at home and accelerate the opening of power, telecommunications, railways, oil, natural gas, and other industries and fields to private enterprises.

Fifth, we should actively urge and steer the G20 to play its role in jointly countering the pandemic and recovering the economy, promote establishment of the G20 pandemic response and economic stability working group, and actively promote China's experience in response to the pandemic to play a greater role in international governance.

Promptly launching effective reform measures to improve institutional weak links

First, we should fully implement negative list management and lower the threshold for enterprise innovation, entrepreneurship, and mergers and acquisitions.

Second, we should introduce a cross-provincial human–land linkage policy, promote the transfer of land quota at the provincial level, and solve the problem of insufficient land quota in cities with population inflows.

Third, we should improve systems and mechanisms in the field of public health, expand the enrollment of students of medicine and nursing majors, and increase support for medical and nursing students. We should promote the income reform of the medical system, establish an effective and significant family doctor system, improve the level of medical services, and ease the contradiction between doctors and patients. We should continue to simplify the procedures for trans-regional settlement of medical insurance accounts and promote national overall planning for various types of social security.

Fourth, we should comprehensively strengthen the reforms to streamline the government, delegate power, and improve government services to improve the quality of government services. We should vigorously promote the construction of digital government, continue to optimize the government service environment, improve government service efficiency, and simplify the approval procedures.

Fifth, we should speed up the establishment of the bankruptcy system and credit system for natural persons and resolve the debt burden of natural persons. Residents and natural persons should be allowed to apply for bankruptcy, providing new opportunities for their lives and employment in the next economic cycle.

Sixth, we should speed up reform to transfer the equities of state-owned enterprises to social security funds and improve the efficiency of state-owned capital operations.

Keeping worst-case scenarios in mind and preventing various imported risks

Under the extraordinary situation of epidemic prevention and control, in the economic work in 2020, we must keep worst-case scenarios in mind and forestall systemic risks.

First, to strictly guard against imported COVID-19 cases, we should keep a close watch on the development of COVID-19 overseas, strengthen information exchange and policy communication with the WHO and key countries, strengthen efforts in information collection, analysis, and forecasting, and keep abreast of the spread of COVID-19 around the world and the progress of COVID-19 prevention work. We should strengthen the quarantine and epidemic prevention work at customs, with a focus on quarantine observations for people and goods originating from the regions where COVID-19 has broken out and surrounding areas. In accordance with international practices, entry restrictions should be adopted for people from the hard-hit countries and regions. We should strengthen information statistics for Chinese citizens in overseas affected regions, study and judge the necessity and feasibility of large-scale evacuation of Chinese nationals from affected regions, and formulate emergency plans.

Second, to prevent major financial risks, we should carry out stress tests for systemically important financial institutions under the pandemic outbreak to ensure the stability of the commercial banking system. We can add capital or adopt other means to hedge the pressure of bad debts caused by the pandemic. We should prevent the spread of panic in overseas capital markets to domestic and foreign countries, and prevent asset prices from skyrocketing and plunging. We should pay close attention to changes in the balance of international payments and stay especially alert to the derivative risks of excessive short-term hot money inflows. On the basis of maintaining the two-way volatility of the RMB exchange rate, we should prevent short-term periodic appreciation of the RMB exchange rate from exacerbating operating difficulties for foreign trade enterprises. We should study and judge the foreign debt crisis and local currency exchange rate crisis in some emerging market countries triggered by the shrinking dollar liquidity and deterioration of balance of international payments, and formulate emergency plans in advance to tackle the contingent situation of a large-scale economic crisis in emerging markets. While making good use of the opportunity of slump in international oil prices, increasing crude oil imports, and reforming and expanding petroleum strategic reserves and commercial reserve systems and mechanisms, we must also stay alert to the geopolitical secondary risks that may be triggered by the slump in oil prices, which may affect the security of China's petroleum supply chain.

Third, to prevent external factors from disturbing food security, we should seize the current "opportunities" in the rural and agricultural sector that is relatively less impacted, strengthen agricultural production, stay alert to the continued tendency for non-grain planting areas, and improve the incentive mechanism for grain planting to enhance the ability of high-level grain self-supply. We should ensure unimpeded flow of grain import channels, ensure a certain level of grain self-supply, increase investment in grain production through advanced technologies, optimize the structure, and greatly improve the quality of grain. Meanwhile, measures should be taken to secure the import of core grain products with a large gap to ensure the normal operation of some food manufacturing and breeding industries.

Notes

1 G20 Finance Ministers and Central Bank Governors, Statement on COVID-19, March 6, 2020: https://g20.org/en/media/Documents/G20%20Statement%20on%20COVID-19%20-%20English.pdf
2 Statement of the G20 Coordinators on COVID-19, Ministry of Foreign Affairs of China, March 13, 2020: www.fmprc.gov.cn/web/wjbxw_673019/t1755427.shtml
3 Relevant persons in charge of the Ministry of Finance answered the questions in interviews with reporters about the G20 Finance Ministers and Central Bank Governors Meeting, Ministry of Finance of China, April 17, 2020: www.mof.gov.cn/zhengwuxinxi/caizhengxinwen/202004/t20200417_3499844.htm
4 The meeting requested the World Bank and other multilateral development banks to provide emergency financing support to its developing members, with a total amount of USD 200 billion, and requested the IMF to be ready to mobilize its USD 1 trillion loan capacity and further mobilize resources, including studying the establishment of new financing support tools, etc., to provide more financial support and services to developing members.
5 IMF, Joint Statement from Managing Director, IMF and President, World Bank Group, March 2, 2020: www.imf.org/en/News/Articles/2020/03/02/pr2076-joint-statement-from-imf-managing-director-and-wb-president
6 World Bank, The World Bank Group Announced Immediate Provision of US$12 Billion in Financial Support to Help Countries to Counter the COVID-19 Pandemic, Chinese website of the World Bank, March 4, 2020: www.shihang.org/zh/news/press-release/2020/03/03/world-bank-group-announces-up-to-12-billion-immediate-support-for-covid-19-country-response
7 IMF, How the IMF Can Help Countries Address the Economic Impact of Coronavirus, March 9, 2020: www.imf.org/en/About/Factsheets/Sheets/2020/02/28/how-the-imf-can-help-countries-address-the-economic-impact-of-coronavirus
8 G7, G7 Leaders' Statement, March 16, 2020: https://china.usembassy-china.org.cn/g7-leaders-statement/
9 Joint Open Letter from World Political Parties Concerning Closer International Cooperation Against COVID-19 (full text), Xinhuanet, April 2, 2020: www.xinhuanet.com/world/2020-04/02/c_1125806860.htm
10 G77, Statement by the Group of 77 and China on the Covid-19 pandemic, New York, April 3, 2020: www.g77.org/statement/getstatement.phpf?id=200403
11 Telephone Conversation with President Tokayev of Kazakhstan on March 24, 2020, Xinhuanet, March 24, 2020: www.xinhuanet.com/politics/leaders/2020-03/24/c_1125762683.htm

References

UNCTAD, Global Investment Trend Monitor: Impact of the Covid-19 Pandemic on Global FDI and GVCs (Updated Analysis), March 27, 2020: https://unctad.org/en/PublicationsLibrary/diaeiainf2020d3_en.pdf.

IMF, Maintaining Banking System Safety amid the COVID-19 Crisis, March 31, 2020: https://blogs.imf.org/2020/03/31/maintaining-banking-system-safety-amid-the-covid-19-crisis/

IMF, Global Uncertainty Related to Coronavirus at Record High, April 4, 2020: https://blogs.imf.org/2020/04/04/global-uncertainty-related-to-coronavirus-at-record-high/

14 Humanist economics after the pandemic

Peng Wensheng

The novel coronavirus (COVID-19) has spread widely around the world, and its impact on the economy has been much greater than expected. It has even caused worries about a "great depression" of the economy in Europe and the United States. In China in 2020, an important controversy was whether, given the impact of the pandemic, economic growth targets should have been set. If yes, at what level and how much policy support would be needed to achieve these targets? The impact of the pandemic on the economy is key to thinking about the current and future economic operations and policy response.

What we want to emphasize is that the impact of the pandemic is different than the general economic periodic fluctuation; nor can it be compared with the Great Depression of the 1930s or the global financial crisis in 2008. The source of the pandemic is an exogenous impact that has nothing to do with the economy, whose transmission mechanism that affects the economy is not the same as the endogenous impact of the economy (such as the stock market crash or the financial crisis). The pandemic situation is related to human health and safety. The impact of the pandemic situation is not a purely economic problem. We should have a humanistic and economic perspective when thinking about macro policies.

Huge uncertainties in economic forecast

Many countries are implementing various forms of social distancing to slow down the spread of the virus. In the early days of the global pandemic, many European and American countries were reluctant to take these measures, and some European countries even hoped to sacrifice some "beloved people" to achieve a "herd immunity" effect. With the spread of the pandemic, European and American countries finally took action and began to promote social distancing and cessation of economic activities. China was the first to be hit by the pandemic and also the first to adopt strict quarantine measures. Thanks to these measures, China has controlled the domestic pandemic in only a short period of time, but its economy has also suffered a huge blow.

Our economic forecast is based on our understanding of the recent economic operation mechanism, which is basically linear extrapolation. The

DOI: 10.4324/9781003184447-15

assumption behind it is that the model remains unchanged. However, this assumption sounds unreasonable when the economy encounters huge exogenous shocks. China's economic data from January to February, including industrial added value, social retail sales, and investment, were significantly lower than expected, and the recent number of initial jobless claims in the United States was significantly higher than expected,[1] indicating the errors brought about by the mechanism changes. At present, when we look at future development, we still face transnormal uncertainties.

First of all, there is great uncertainty about the source and future evolution of the pandemic. We can consider the following three scenarios.

Scenario 1: The global pandemic will be effectively controlled in the next 2–3 months. According to the estimation model of the quantitative analysis group of Everbright Securities Research Institute, if all continents adopt quarantine measures similar to those after Italy's lockdown, major European and American countries will have reached a new peak of new confirmed cases in mid-April, while South America and Africa, where the virus developed later, will see the peak in early or mid-May. If the quarantine measures are not so strict (similar to the situation in the United States in early April), then major European and American countries will reach a peak of new confirmed cases in late April, while South America and Africa will see it in late May and early June.

Scenario 2: The pandemic develops in a wave-like manner in developing countries and its spread time is prolonged. As of mid-April, the novel coronavirus has spread to more than 180 countries and regions. Under the assumption of trans-regional migration of infected persons, the global pandemic may show a wave-like development trend and significantly delay the end of the pandemic. The so-called wave-like development refers to the migration of the population in areas with serious pandemic to low-risk areas based on safety considerations, resulting in the first or multiple outbreaks of the pandemic in low-risk areas. This, in turn, will prompt the migration of population in the region to other low-risk areas, causing the first or multiple outbreaks or even recurrence of the pandemic in low-risk areas. From a global perspective, due to weak prevention and control capabilities in developing countries, South Asia, South America, and Africa are highly vulnerable to future wave-like development of the pandemic, which may delay the end of the global pandemic to the second half of 2020 or even longer. Under such circumstances, global governments need to work together to assist developing countries in identification, quarantine, and rescue of infected persons. At the same time, it also means that other countries must extend their measures to curb "importation of the novel coronavirus," which will have a greater drag on the global economic growth than in the first case.

Scenario 3: The novel coronavirus prevails as the virus and will coexist with human beings for a long time.[2] Worse still, the novel coronavirus spreads in the form of "guerrilla warfare" in various regions and of the world and in different seasons, and often mutates into new subtypes. From 2010 to 2015, the global average number of respiratory cases and deaths caused by influenza was 88,000.[3] The fatality rate of the novel coronavirus is higher than that of influenza virus, so the annual death toll may also be higher than this figure. This not only has a longer-term impact on economic activities, but also brings more challenges to the global medical system. Judging from the current situation, the research and development of effective treatment methods and vaccines requires a long time, and governments need to allocate social resources to deal with the pandemic within a longer time span.

Second, there is transnormal uncertainty about the impact of the pandemic on the economy. Until vaccines and specific drugs are successfully developed, the control of the pandemic must rely on quarantine measures. The impact of quarantine on economic activities is not the impact of supply and demand as we generally understand it. It is embodied as a physical restriction that prevents people from going out to work and consume. One important influencing factor of a general economic periodic fluctuation is price flexibility. The more flexible the price is, the stronger the mechanism of economic self-stability will be. For example, lower demand may increase the unemployment rate and lower the workers' wage level. The latter improves the profitability of enterprises, prompting them to increase their demand for labor and increase employment. However, under the pandemic situation, we are facing physical restrictions, price adjustment failure, and the pandemic impact falling entirely on quantity, thus greatly affecting the real economy, including employment and economic growth. General economic analysis and prediction are based on our understanding and control of price elasticity. Under extreme circumstances when prices cannot play a role, there will be greater uncertainty of economic forecasts.

Transnormal uncertainty means high possibility of making mistakes in the economic forecasts. There exists too optimistic and too pessimistic prediction of the pandemic spread, but the cost of making mistakes is different. Assuming we are looking back in 6 months, if we are too optimistic about the evolution of the pandemic and relax the quarantine measures too early or by too much, the result will be recurrent outbreaks of the pandemic but rapid recovery of the economy. However, if we are too pessimistic about the evolution of the pandemic and do not relax the quarantine measures fully and in time, the result will be that the pandemic is effectively controlled, but the employment and economic growth will suffer great losses due to slow economic recovery.

Which of these two misjudgments does more harm to the economy and society? The latter has a great impact on economic activities, but the economic losses may be covered later. The former leads to recurrences of the pandemic and irreversible loss of life, but there will be greater economic cost to be paid in order to finally contain the pandemic. Obviously, the cost of making the second mistake (too pessimistic judgment on the evolution of the pandemic) is smaller. The difficult problem facing the policy is how to balance the protection of human life safety and health while maintaining normal economic activities, which involves how to view the benefits and costs of quarantine measures.

How to reckon the economic cost of quarantine measures?

Facing the pandemic, we need to answer a fundamental question: which is more important, the lives saved or economic losses caused by quarantine measures? This is an easy and a difficult question to answer. With regard to saving the lives of our relatives or other individuals, the answer is clear: life is priceless. However, as far as the whole society is concerned, it is impossible for us to invest resources indefinitely to save lives. For example, we will not stop developing expressways just because we want to avoid traffic accidents; nor will we ban all chemical plants just because we want to avoid air pollution. In other words, as far as the whole society is concerned and as far as public policies are concerned, every life has a price.

Under the impact of the pandemic, compared with the losses caused by the economic shutdown, whether it is "worthwhile" to contain the pandemic through social distancing to save lives, or how to measure social efforts in this regard, has become a public concern. How, then, can we strike a balance between so many lives saved and the economic losses caused by the quarantine measures?

In the economics literature, there is a concept called value of statistical life (VSL). Economist Thomas Schelling proposed in his 1968 chapter "The Life You Save May Be Your Own" that the VSL be used to estimate the monetary value of life and calculate, from a statistical point of view, how much money society is willing to pay to reduce the risk of unit death.[4] For example, if a society is willing to pay UDS 10,000 to reduce the risk of death by 0.1%, then the value of this life estimated by society is equal to USD 10 million. As for society, the VSL method gives a certain social price to every life. Despite the incessant voices of ethical disputes, the VSL has gradually become a relatively accepted method to calculate the value of life in the field of public policy. According to calculations by the US Environmental Protection Agency, the average VSL for people aged 18 and above in the United States in 2020 is USD 11.5 million.[5] The VSL, as an indicator to measure people's willingness to pay to reduce risks and an indicator of marginal cost to improve safety, has been widely used in the evaluation of public policies such as medicine, environment, and transportation safety.

As far as this pandemic is concerned, the VSL can be used to calculate the life value saved by social distancing, which can be compared with the economic losses caused by quarantine measures. Greenstone and Nigam wrote a paper in March 2020 (*Does Social Distancing Matter?*) in which the economic benefits of "social distancing" are estimated by the probability of mortality reduction at different ages caused by quarantine measures (see the left half of Table 14.1).[6] Greenstone and Nigam believe that if social distancing in the United States helps reduce the mortality rate of people of different ages during the COVID-19 pandemic, a total of 1.76 million lives of different ages can be saved by October 2020, and a total of USD 7.9 trillion in social losses can be avoided.

Using Greenstone and Nigam's method, we assume that by virtue of social quarantine measures, the mortality rate of the COVID-19 pandemic in China decreases by a similar extent to that in the United States at different ages, while the unit VSL in China and the United States is directly proportional to per capita GDPs in the two countries. In this way, we can roughly calculate that China's quarantine can save about 5.9 million lives of different ages, and the social income calculated by VSL is about CNY 34 trillion.

According to Table 14.1, the social losses avoided by quarantine measures in the United States during the COVID-19 pandemic are close to USD 8 trillion. On the other hand, in terms of the economic losses caused by quarantine, if the daily economic activities in the United States are reduced by 20–40% due to quarantine, 90-day lockdown and quarantine may reduce the annual GDP of the United States by 5–10% as compared with the expectation, and the corresponding economic losses are about USD 1 trillion to USD 2 trillion. For the United States, the quarantine measures may produce far more social benefits than economic losses.

Similarly, from the perspective of VSL, China has avoided a loss of about CNY 34 trillion or about 35% of China's GDP in 2019 as a result of lockdown measures. We also assume that China's daily economic activity falls by about 20–40% due to quarantine, then the 90-day national quarantine measures may lead to a decrease of CNY 5 trillion to CNY 10 trillion in its GDP this year, which is about 5–10% of annual GDP. For China also, the social benefits of quarantine measures have far outweighed the possible economic losses.

In fact, the social benefits of quarantine measures may be greater than the estimates in Table 14.1. Not only can quarantine measures reduce the mortality rate caused by the pandemic, but they can also increase social benefits in other ways. First, quarantine can reduce uncertainty brought about by the pandemic and help people plan for the future. Second, quarantine measures not only help to control the spread of the pandemic, but also reduce the spread of other infectious diseases and reduce the probability of accidental deaths such as traffic accidents. Third, quarantine measures also reduce runs on medical resources and improve the survival probability of patients suffering other diseases.

There are different opinions on how to measure the value of life. Of course, the above estimation is also controversial. These figures are listed mainly to emphasize the particularity of the impact of the pandemic.

When we think about the downward pressure on China's economy in 2020, we cannot simply compare it with the original growth target in 2020,

Table 14.1 Revenue from quarantine measures in China and the United States by value of a statistical life

Age	Mortality reduced by quarantine (%)	Population of the United States (000,000 persons)	Percentage of total population (%)	Deaths reduced by quarantine in the United States (persons)	Unit VSL in the United States (USD 000)	VSL revenue from quarantine in the United States (USD trillion)	Population in China (000,000 persons)	Percentage of total population (%)	Deaths reduced by quarantine in China (persons)	Unit VSL in China (CNY 00)	VSL revenue from quarantine in China (CNY trillion)
		United States					*China*				
0–9	0.001	39.8	12.4	398	1,470	0.01	159.3	11.4	1,593	1,598	0.03
10–19	0.003	41.4	12.9	1,242	1,530	0.02	146.9	10.5	4,407	1,663	0.07
20–29	0.015	45.0	14.0	6,750	1,610	0.11	196.3	14.1	29,445	1,750	0.52
30–39	0.041	42.7	13.3	17,507	1,580	0.28	213.4	15.3	87,510	1,717	1.50
40–49	0.078	40.2	12.5	31,356	1,380	0.43	226.7	16.2	176,820	1,500	2.65
50–59	0.311	42.9	13.3	133,419	1,030	1.37	203.2	14.6	631,978	1,120	7.08
60–69	1.137	36.4	11.3	413,868	670	2.77	149.7	10.7	1,702,262	728	12.40
70–79	2.632	21.3	6.6	560,616	370	2.07	70.2	5.0	1,848,408	402	7.43
80+	4.818	12.4	3.8	597,432	150	0.90	29.5	2.1	1,423,474	163	2.32
Total				1,762,588		7.96			5,905,898		34.00

Source: US Environmental Protection Agency; National Bureau of Statistics, China.

Note: VSL is the price in 2020.

or compare it with the economic growth in 2019 to assess the extent of the losses; nor can we simply compare it with the Great Depression or the global financial crisis in history. The pandemic itself is a disaster from nature. Knowing that quarantine measures have a great impact on economic activities, governments of various countries intend to take quarantine measures in order to reduce the loss of people's lives and health. Economic growth promotes people's well-being, and quarantine measures ensure the safety of life and also promote people's well-being. The two should be viewed in a comprehensive way.

Bailout policy is also a social insurance

Affirming the value and necessity of quarantine measures does not mean that macro policies have not responded to the economic problems caused by quarantine measures. In fact, all governments are taking countermeasures against the pandemic. The scope and scale of macro policy measures are beyond our conventional understanding, but the general direction is to rescue but not stimulate the economy. Physical quarantine causes production and consumption to stall and makes enterprises and individuals encounter sharp drop in income and tight cash flow. The policy response is to increase subsidies to individuals and enterprises, especially to small and medium-sized enterprises. Fiscal policies (tax cuts, transfer payments) and structured lending (or policy-based finance) are implemented as the main measures. The central bank of course can increase liquidity supply to calm panic in the financial market.

The reason why quarantine measures are said to be a bailout rather than a stimulus for economic growth is that they restrict people's production and consumption activities and play little role as monetary stimulus. The bailout policy is intended to help the affected enterprises and individuals get over the difficulties and avoid large-scale corporate bankruptcy and long-term unemployment so that economic activity can rebound quickly and return to normal after the pandemic fades away. That is to say, the pandemic seems to be pressing the pause button of the machine, while the bailout acts in terms of maintaining the machine; therefore, as long as the machine is still there, the economy will return to normal quickly after the pause button is cancelled.

An important perspective of the bailout policy is structural relief, which is linked to income distribution. The non-contact economy during the pandemic highlights the new structural nature of income distribution. In the past, our attention was on the gap between a very small number of rich people (1%) and the vast majority of residents (99%). During the pandemic, the widening income gap is more reflected in the differentiation between non-contact economy practitioners (about 20%–30%) and contact economy practitioners (about 70%–80%). During the COVID-19 pandemic, practitioners in finance, education, science and technology, high-end services, and other industries have not been affected too much, because they can work online or remotely, but the low- and medium-income groups, including manufacturing workers and low-end service industry employees, have been hit heavily by the pandemic.

How should we understand the impact of the pandemic on contact economy practitioners and the policy relief? In addition to the perspective of relief, there is also the perspective of social insurance when discussing the bailout policy. Quarantine measures to contain the pandemic have the nature of externality: that is, they require all people's cooperation. If some people do not cooperate, the quarantine effect will be greatly reduced. For contact economy practitioners, the benefits of cooperating with quarantine measures are social, but should the cost (loss of not working) be entirely borne by themselves? Obviously, from the perspective of the overall interests of society, this kind of personal loss should be socialized; that is, shared by the whole society. In the end, this kind of social insurance can only be borne by the state government.

This is why fiscal policy has played a major role in all countries during the pandemic. However, it reflects the differences in social governance mechanism, development stage, and historical path, and there are differences during implementation of the social insurance mechanism in different countries. An important feature of Europe is that the wage burden (70%–80%) of enterprises is directly transferred to government finance (including self-employed households) for an initial period of 3 months, while the United States mainly relies on the existing unemployment relief system plus one-time cash payment. Policy difference has resulted in a significant increase of unemployed persons in the United States, but it is a different case in Europe. While cash distribution in the United States attracts attention, social security in Europe actually plays a better role.

The US cash distribution policy is a bit like a helicopter drop in that it is effective in dealing with demand shocks, but less useful in dealing with supply shocks. In fact, large-scale unemployment itself will aggravate the impact of the pandemic on the supply side of the US economy, or it will be an important carrier of the supply impact. Although such a high probability of unemployment is short-lived and the jobless persons concerned have also received government relief, unemployment after all means the separation of employees from their employers, which is not conducive to the preservation and accumulation of human capital. Compared with Europe, the US model does little good for the recovery of economic activities after the pandemic.

China's policies and measures to contain the pandemic are also obviously different from previous policies in response to the downward pressure of the economy. They are more linked to rescuing enterprises and individuals, including targeted exemption of value-added tax and tax refunds, phased relief of social insurance premiums for enterprises, financial discounts on loans, deferred payments of housing provident funds by enterprises, deferred tax declarations, etc. However, compared with developed countries, especially Europe, China's social security system is still in a developmental stage where it seems difficult to implement relief measures. Because of this, for China, the key to combating the pandemic is to protect employment from the supply side; that is, combining rescue of enterprises with requirement for no layoffs, which is conducive to sustainable economic growth.

Supply-demand balance and growth targets

There is a controversy over the nature of the impact of the pandemic: is supply or demand hit more by the pandemic? During the outbreak period, quarantine measures restrict people from going out to work and consuming, so they impose an impact on both supply and demand. After the pandemic fades away, demand and supply will recover at the same time. This is the biggest difference from the general economic fluctuation. During the downward period of the economic cycle or the financial crisis, the economy faces insufficient demand, which is reflected in the downward trend of growth and employment, accompanied by deflationary pressure. Under the impact of the pandemic, the economic growth and demand for employment declined, but there was no deflationary pressure. One meaning of this difference is that macro policies oriented by demand stimulus may increase the pressure of rising prices, and macroeconomic operation is characterized by stagflation.

According to this logical reasoning, China's future economy will face two challenges.

First, from a dynamic point of view, the problems of supply and demand can be transformed into each other. As far as China is concerned, the large-scale spread of the pandemic in local areas has been basically blocked. The shortage of labor supply in the first quarter brought about a drop in people's incomes, which means that the total demand in the second quarter will be affected. Therefore, certain demand management is reasonable. This perspective may not be applicable to the current situation in the United States, and especially not to Europe, because the spillover effect of supply on demand is not as large as that in China, which indicates the effect of social insurance measures by European and American governments.

Then, for a globalized economy, due to the different time points when the pandemic spreads in different countries, the supply shock of one country may spill over into the demand shock of another country. In the second quarter, with the steady progress of China's resumption of work and production, the shortage of external demand (export orders) has become an important obstacle, and the stimulation of internal demand has certain rationality.

So how do we understand the supply–demand balance in a dynamic and open economic environment? Is insufficient aggregate demand the main contradiction at this stage? Globally, there is no mismatch between demand and supply. In the first quarter, China faced shocks on both supply and demand. From March to May, such double shocks began to appear in Europe and the United States, followed by other countries and regions. For example, on March 19, Tesla announced that two US factories were temporarily shut down. On March 21, Italy announced that all production activities in nonessential industries across the country would be suspended. China's external demand orders declined in the second quarter, as did its external supply (import supply).

Under normal circumstances, one channel that can be used to ease inflationary pressures is imports. However, the spread of the pandemic may inhibit overseas supply. Against the background that the global pandemic situation has not been significantly alleviated, the supply-side constraints cannot be underestimated. The large-scale demand stimulus may be more reflected in the upward pressure of inflation than just the trade deficit (China's large-scale stimulus after the 2008 global financial crisis led to a sharp drop in the trade surplus).

A fundamental question is: which is more important, the supply shock or the demand shock? First of all, the pandemic shock is a real variable shock, not a nominal variable one (such as monetary policy tightening), and the hedging effect of monetary policy is limited. At a deeper level, the physical restrictions brought about by the quarantine measures reduce the role of money, and Saye's law, which is generally not applicable under monetary economic conditions, is now applicable instead; that is, supply creates demand, or supply is the most essential. The policy risks oriented by demand stimulus are stagflation and rising asset prices, especially the real estate bubble.

The judgment that supply is more important than demand also has implications for the goal of economic growth. Generally speaking, macro policies have established a relatively mature mechanism in aggregate demand management, but they have a limited effect on easing supply constraints. In other words, when supply becomes the main contradiction, the constraints on economic growth are relatively rigid. The key is that there is great uncertainty about the impact of such rigid constraints on economic growth, which is a problem that needs attention when we reset economic growth targets for 2020.

An objective and rational approach is to regard the first half of 2020 as a special period and treat COVID-19 as a disaster that happens once in a century and which cannot be hedged by policies. Macro policies are oriented to promote economic growth to come back to its potential level in the second half of the year; for example, a year-on-year growth rate of 5–6%. Doing so can help us "forget" the special impact that has already occurred and is not subject to man's will, focus on sustainable growth in the future, and boost people's confidence. In fact, as mentioned above, the value of quarantine measures to ensure the safety of people's lives far exceeds the GDP loss caused by these measures. GDP only shows the side of losses caused by pandemic prevention and control measures but cannot reflect the side of ensuring the safety of people's lives. Given the particularity of the pandemic, we need to take a comprehensive view of this year's economic and social development.

Supply-side structural reform after the pandemic

To formulate policies for getting out of the pandemic, we will focus on improving the supply capacity. During the global pandemic of COVID-19, people from all walks of life have great disputes over the policy orientation, especially after the United States introduced a USD 2 trillion relief bill and intends to launch another USD 2 trillion infrastructure plan. There are more disputes over whether China should also launch relief or infrastructure stimulus plans. Based on the above analysis, the key to getting out of the pandemic is to attach importance to the supply side. The current policy should be such that effective measures are taken to promote the resumption of work and employment while containing the pandemic.

A safe and orderly withdrawal from social distancing is the key to the policy of resuming normal production and life in the next few months. The premise of withdrawing from social distancing is that the spread of the pandemic is strictly controlled within a small range and there are few runs on short-term relatively limited medical and medical resources. Before COVID-19 vaccines are successfully developed and distributed, we need to make sustained efforts in at least two aspects: setting up a large-scale coronavirus testing and quarantine system, and carrying out effective epidemiological investigation. This not only requires the whole society to invest more manpower and material resources, but also depends on an efficient social organization and management system.

At present, China's pandemic containment is facing an arduous task of "preventing the coronavirus from re-entering the country to cause a new wide spread of the pandemic." In order to harness the spread of the pandemic in a small range, it is necessary not only to test and quarantine symptomatic patients imported internally and externally, but also to test and quarantine asymptomatic infected persons and to track and test these infected persons and their contacts. The larger the testing range, the shorter the testing cycle time; and the more accurate the location of contact infection, the more controllable the spread range of the pandemic. "Identifying and quarantining potential infected persons in a timely manner" is the key to strictly harnessing the spread of the pandemic within a small range and gradually withdrawing from social distancing. This is a social system project that requires close cooperation among medical treatment, community, public security, customs, scientific research, and other sectors.

As far as macro policies are concerned, from either a domestic or an international perspective, the current discussions have paid little attention to COVID-19's impact on the supply side, because they overemphasized the asymmetric demand stimulus. This may cause greater derivative damage to the economy and sow the seeds of stagflation.

Therefore, macro policies should focus on restoring and enhancing the supply capacity while making more efforts in implementing social insurance compensation in the first quarter so as to avoid implementing pure demand stimulus measures without improving supply capacity. There are two aspects worth discussing: how to combine increasing demand with promoting new supply, and how to maintain the existing supply capacity.

Specifically, one possibility is that the government will increase its investment to create a number of temporary or general-purpose jobs in such fields as quarantine and inspection, production of pandemic prevention materials, and agriculture and logistics where a supply gap exists due to the pandemic shock; that is, having jobless persons employed instead of just giving unemployment benefit. Second, we will vigorously loosen municipal management measures and allow or subsidize people to increase their employment and supply capacity; for example, encouraging jobless persons to be street vendors. Third, efforts should be made to increase tax cuts or provide targeted rescue funds to improve the survival probability of enterprises and prevent sharp contraction of production capacity, including increasing and providing financial support for financing guarantees for small and medium-sized enterprises. Finally, the public and private sectors should be guided to invest more in infrastructure and technology of the digital economy so as to improve the efficiency of the service industry and increase employment opportunities in the non-contact economy.

In response to the once-in-a-century disaster, the intensity of fiscal expansion should break through inertial thinking constraints. For instance, it is necessary and reasonable to increase the one-time government debt of about 10% of GDP in response to COVID-19's impact on the economy. The key therein is how to make good use of this transfer of resources to promote sustainable economic development.

The above are just a few concrete and possible examples. What matters is the paradigm of thought. The pandemic has brought about shocks on both demand and supply. This is more than an economic problem, so macro policies should not be oriented to traditional demand stimulus. Initiating large-scale infrastructure construction is not advisable, and it is absolutely inappropriate to stimulate demand by building more houses. Policy response needs a perspective of humanistic economy.

Notes

1 National Bureau of Statistics, The National Economy Has Withstood the Impact of the COVID-19 Pandemic from January to February, National Bureau of Statistics, March 16, 2020: www.stats.gov.cn/tjsj/zxfb/202003/t20200316_1732232. Html
2 Stephen M. Kissler et al., Projecting the Transmission Dynamics of SARS-CoV-2 through the Post-Pandemic Period, *MedRxiv,* March 6, 2020.
3 Chinese Center for Disease Control and Prevention, *Technical Guide for Influenza Vaccination in China (2019–2020)*, October 15, 2019.
4 Thomas C. Schelling, The Life You Save May Be Your Own, In S. B. Chase (ed.) *Problems in Public Expenditure Analysis*, Brookings Institute, pp. 127–161, 1968,

5 In 2015, the US Environmental Protection Agency estimated that the VSL in 2020 would reach USD 9.9 million (denominated in 2011 US dollars). After we have adjusted it for inflation and denominated it in 2020 US dollars, the VSL in China is about USD 11.5 million.

6 Michael Greenstone and Vishan Nigam, *Does Social Distancing Matter?* Becker Friedman Institute for Economics Working Paper No. 2020-26, 2020.

Index